LETTER WR
LANGUAGI

MW00778470

Letter Writing and Language Change outlines the historical sociolinguistic value of letter analysis, in both theory and practice. The chapters in this volume make use of insights from all three 'Waves of Variation Studies', and many of them, either implicitly or explicitly, look at specific aspects of the language of the letter writers in an effort to discover how those writers position themselves and how they attempt, consciously or unconsciously, to construct social identities. The letters are largely from people in the lower strata of social structure, either to addressees of the same social status or of a higher status. In this sense, the question of the use of 'standard' and/or 'non-standard' varieties of English is in the forefront of the contributors' interest. Ultimately, the studies challenge the assumption that there is only one 'legitimate' and homogeneous form of English or of any other language.

ANITA AUER is Full Professor of English Linguistics at the University of Lausanne.

DANIEL SCHREIER is Full Professor of English Linguistics at the University of Zurich.

RICHARD J. WATTS is a former Full Professor of English Linguistics at the University of Bern, now retired.

STUDIES IN ENGLISH LANGUAGE

LETTER WRITING AND LANGUAGE CHANGE

General editor: Merja Kytö (Uppsala University)

Editorial Board
Bas Aarts (University College London), John Algeo (University of Georgia),
Susan Fitzmaurice (University of Sheffield), Christian Mair (University of Freiburg),
Charles F. Meyer (University of Massachusetts)

The aim of this series is to provide a framework for original studies of English, both present-day and past. All books are based securely on empirical research, and represent theoretical and descriptive contributions to our knowledge of national and international varieties of English, both written and spoken. The series covers a broad range of topics and approaches, including syntax, phonology, grammar, vocabulary, discourse, pragmatics and sociolinguistics, and is aimed at an international readership.

LETTER WRITING
AND
LANGUAGE CHANGE

EDITED BY

ANITA AUER
University of Lausanne

DANIEL SCHREIER
University of Zurich

RICHARD J. WATTS
University of Bern

CAMBRIDGE
UNIVERSITY PRESS

CAMBRIDGE
UNIVERSITY PRESS

University Printing House, Cambridge CB2 8BS, United Kingdom

One Liberty Plaza, 20th Floor, New York, NY 10006, USA

477 Williamstown Road, Port Melbourne, VIC 3207, Australia

314-321, 3rd Floor, Plot 3, Splendor Forum, Jasola District Centre, New Delhi - 110025, India

79 Anson Road, #06-04/06, Singapore 079906

Cambridge University Press is part of the University of Cambridge.

It furthers the University's mission by disseminating knowledge in the pursuit of
education, learning and research at the highest international levels of excellence.

www.cambridge.org
Information on this title: www.cambridge.org/9781108713160

First published 2015
First paperback edition 2019

A catalogue record for this publication is available from the British Library

Library of Congress Cataloging in Publication data
Letter writing and language change / edited by Anita Auer, University of Lausanne;
Daniel Schreier, University of Zurich; Richard J. Watts, University of Bern.
pages   cm – (Studies in English language)
Includes bibliographical references and index.
ISBN 978-1-107-01864-8 (hardback)
1. Letter writing – Social aspects – English-speaking countries.   2. Written communication – Social
aspects – English-speaking countries.   3. English language – Variation.   4. English letters – History
and criticism.   I. Auer, Anita, 1975– editor of compilation.   II. Schreier, Daniel, 1971– editor of
compilation.   III. Watts, Richard J., editor of compilation.
PE1483.L46   2014
808.6 – dc23   2014007607

ISBN 978-1-107-01864-8 Hardback
ISBN 978-1-108-71316-0 Paperback

Every effort has been made to secure necessary permissions to reproduce copyright material in this
work, though in some cases it has proved impossible to trace or contact copyright holders. If any
omissions are brought to our notice, we will be happy to include appropriate
acknowledgements on reprinting, and/or in any subsequent edition.

Contents

Figures

Tables

Contributors

BARBARA ALLEN Lecturer in English Linguistics (now retired), University of Sussex and University of Gothenburg at the University of Sussex, United Kingdom

ANITA AUER Full Professor of English Linguistics, University of Lausanne, Switzerland

ALEXANDER BERGS Professor and Chair of English Language and Linguistics, University of Osnabrück, Germany

JUAN CAMILO CONDE-SILVESTRE Professor of English Historical Linguistics, University of Murcia, Spain

STEFAN DOLLINGER Assistant Professor of English Linguistics, University of British Columbia, Canada

STEPHAN ELSPAß Professor of German Linguistics, University of Salzburg, Austria

TONY FAIRMAN Independent Researcher, Maidstone, United Kingdom

SUSAN M. FITZMAURICE Professor and Chair of English Language, University of Sheffield, United Kingdom

JUAN MANUEL HERNÁNDEZ-CAMPOY Professor of English Sociolinguistics, University of Murcia, Spain

MARIANNE HUNDT Professor of English Linguistics, University of Zurich, Switzerland

MIKKO LAITINEN Professor of English Linguistics, Linnaeus University, Sweden

LUKAS PIETSCH Reader in English Linguistics, University of Hamburg, Germany

DANIEL SCHREIER Professor of English Linguistics, University of Zurich, Switzerland

LUCIA SIEBERS Assistant Professor of English Linguistics, University of Regensburg, Germany

RICHARD J. WATTS Emeritus Professor of English Linguistics, University of Bern, Switzerland

Preface and acknowledgements

The present volume originated in a colloquium entitled 'Heterogeneity versus homogeneity in language: Searching for a "standard" in letters', which was held at Utrecht University, 12–14 November 2009 and organised by the editors of this volume. As the title of the colloquium indicates, it was our aim to bring together (socio)historical linguists who have worked with (manuscript) letters and/or compiled letter corpora of geographical, social and stylistic varieties of English. On invitation, papers were presented by the following (socio)historical linguists (in alphabetical order): Barbara Allen, Anita Auer, Stefan Dollinger, Stephan Elspaß, Tony Fairman, Susan Fitzmaurice, Marianne Hundt, Mikko Laitinen, Terttu Nevalainen, Lukas Pietsch, Daniel Schreier, Lucia Siebers, Richard Watts and Laura Wright. The expertise of these scholars covers not only the history of letter writing in English, i.e. different varieties of English, but also different methodological and theoretical approaches to the topic.

Unfortunately, not all the presenters were able to contribute a chapter to this volume. Hence, in order to cover the earlier letter-writing periods in the history of English, some additional scholars, notably Alexander Bergs, Juan Manuel Hernández-Campoy and Juan Camilo Conde-Silvestre, were invited to contribute chapters to the present volume. For this reason, the present volume should not merely be seen as the proceedings of a colloquium but as a volume that sheds light on the state of the art of letter writing and language change.

As the editors of this volume, we would like to thank the contributors to the colloquium and all the contributors to this volume for their great work and for their patience with the volume editors. We would also like to express our thanks to Merja Kytö, the series editor, and to Helen Barton, the commissioning editor, for their support throughout the editing and publication process of this volume.

CHAPTER I

Setting the scene: letters, standards and historical sociolinguistics

Richard J. Watts

1. Fishing for the 'standard' language?

I open this introductory chapter with a well-worn simile, one used frequently, but in most cases without the user thinking of its more tangible implications: Deciding to focus on letter corpora as data sources for plotting the history of a language is *like opening up a can of worms*. We are confronted with a squirming mass of problems. An angler, of course, is used to this, and s/he simply chooses one fat worm for her/his hook to catch the plump fish lurking in the shallows.

The simile of the can of worms can easily be converted into a cognitive metaphor that projects the field of angling onto the field of historical linguists plotting the history of language A. In this case, the worms take on a dual function. On the one hand, just one worm can be used to catch the plump fish of the history of language A, but on the other hand, there are so many other worms that they could potentially catch a whole shoal of histories, thus presenting problems for the historical linguist. Linguists who are only interested in catching one fish might be well advised to push all the worms back into the can except for the one chosen and then be satisfied with the fish thrashing at the end of the line. Metaphorically speaking, this is what has happened in plotting the histories of most languages; the plump fish lurking in the shallows a moment ago is in effect the standard variety of the language concerned. As Mattheier (2010: 353–4) non-metaphorically maintains,

> [t]he concept of a 'national language history' has dominated the view of what historical linguistics should be concerned with in relation to virtually all European languages, and continues to do so today. The theoretical starting point of this view – which at the very least needs to be seriously questioned – is that the 'standard' language is the genuine teleological goal of any historical language development. And the path trodden by a speech community in developing a standard language, a unifying language, a literary language, at the same time represents the central content of language history. Most German language histories, but also the histories of other languages, are constructed along these lines.

So it might be easier and much less of a mess to close the lid on the can and ignore all the other worms squirming inside, since those worms potentially attract other fish, or, in terms of the metaphor, other alternative histories of language A.

However, the metaphor falters at precisely this point. Typical anglers are not satisfied with just one fish, but seem perfectly happy to sit by the bank of a river or a reservoir or a disused canal to see how many fish they can bag in a day's angling. They might release some of the fish into the water and carry the rest back home, or they might even release them all. The can of worms will be reopened several times, and other worms will be extracted from the squirming mass and put onto the hook. The contributors to the present volume, for which the editors have chosen the title *Letter Writing and Language Change*, are not simply historical linguists; they are also sociolinguists, and as such they resemble typical anglers in that they are prepared to reopen the can again and again to take a closer look at the 'problems' and to avoid 'the catastrophic implications for the following period of history of such formulae as "one people, hence one language" or even "one language, hence one state"' (Mattheier 2010: 354).

The particular can of worms with which we are concerned in this book is letter corpora illuminating 'language history from below and from above', terms that will need some explanation in Section 3. And although the collection is devoted to English letter corpora, in the spirit of Klaus Mattheier, we have included a chapter that justifies his allusion to the fact that 'the histories of other languages' – in this instance German – consist of the same very restrictive use of the can of worms.

2. Sorting out the worms: three fundamental problems

Before we open the sluice-gates into the weir for our historical sociolinguists to fish for other histories of English (or, in the case of Chapter 3, German), we need to discuss the nature of the worms in their cans. To do this I will temporarily leave the extended metaphor, while asking the reader to bear it in mind when reading. Three major problems confront historical sociolinguists: (1) the tendency to transfer their attention from the nature of human language in general to the linguistic constructions and sociolinguistic functions of individual languages; (2) the implication underlying the assumption that 'the "standard" language is the genuine teleological goal of any historical language development' (an assumption rejected by Mattheier), i.e. that a language can be looked at as a homogeneous system; and (3) the nature of the sparse data available to all historical linguists, whether sociolinguistically inclined or not. I shall look briefly in the remainder of this section at each of these large 'worms' in turn before looking at other smaller but no less significant worms waiting in the epistological data corpora to be examined.

2.1 Human language vs. a language

The first problem (or worm) that historical sociolinguists need to grapple with is the perennial one of defining the countable term 'language' itself, since it is only when we have an adequate way of conceptualising *a* language rather than human language in general that we can even begin to talk about 'a history' or 'histories' of

English (or, in Chapter 3, of German). In Watts (2011: 119–20) I attempt to provide a socio-cognitive account of why linguists prefer to talk about 'languages' rather than human language. Human language as such can be understood as a cognitive ability 'to acquire, store and . . . use a set of abstract constructions' (p. 118) in social interaction with others. The set is systematic and human beings can 'manipulate [it] as and when the need arises'. I equate this ability with what Weinreich, Labov and Herzog (1968) refer to as 'orderly differentiation'. The ability is social as well as cognitive because it 'enables us to use the variety of language we have acquired to mediate our physical, social and mental worlds, and the worlds of others', and 'to enlarge and expand our own individual mental worlds in infinite ways' (Watts 2011: 118). For the purposes to which we put our own individual varieties of human language, i.e. dealing with the everyday contingencies of social life with others, we do not need to give a name to the variety that each of us shares within a community. Why, then, do we still do this?

From a cognitive point of view, the shift from human language to *a* language is a perfectly natural move to make, and again it is a social move. This shift is defined in Watts (2011: 120) as follows:

> It is clear that we all need to function as 'ratified' members of a social group, and to be ratified we are constrained to acquire the linguistic constructions that others use. In point of fact, we cannot do otherwise. The step from language to *a* language involves the projection of a blend from one mental space to another, in which the constructions we use are mapped onto a cognitive frame that then becomes embedded in our long-term memory (see chap. 1 and Fauconnier and Turner 2002). The frame is then projected as 'the property' of the group: its 'language'. So the shift from human language to *a* language is essentially the construction of a metaphorical blend in the minds of the members participating in the group's activities.

If individuals refuse to make this blend, they will find it hard to become members. So it is hardly surprising that we accept the validity of the existence of 'English' or 'German' or 'Tzeltal' or whatever. The problem enters when the social group or groups begin to develop communal stories (or what I call 'myths') to 'explain, justify and ratify' the existence of those languages.

2.2 *The myth of the homogeneous language*

This brings us to the second general problem (or worm): the homogeneity myth. Having socio-cognitively constructed *a* language, the next move is an effort to define the variety of language that is legitimate for a community as large as, say, the nation-state, i.e. to construct *the* language. As we are by now well aware (see, e.g., Milroy and Milroy 2012; Joseph 1987; Grillo 1989; Crowley [1989] 2003; Bex and Watts 1999), this step is the ideological construction of a discourse archive in which the variability, changeability and creativity of a language – its heterogeneity – is not only challenged but even openly denied.

When people complain that dialect X is no longer spoken *purely*, or when they excuse themselves for not being able to speak language Y *perfectly*, or when they bemoan the fact that younger speakers are constantly introducing strange words and constructions into language Z, they are driven by a belief in the homogeneity myth. The belief is in 'a language of total uniformity in both written and oral form, a language of stasis', 'the cultural carrier of history, education, religion, politics, law and literature' (Watts 2011: 116). It is a universal myth, not one that is just applicable to English (see Mattheier 2010), and it has a very long history indeed. But despite its long history, it only came truly into its own in Europe from the early eighteenth century on, and flourished throughout the long nineteenth century as one of the major driving forces in discursively constructing the concept of the nation-state. Its effects are still with us today, and one of the aims of historical sociolinguistics has been to deconstruct that myth and the ideologies that it has spawned.

Foremost among those ideologies is that of the 'standard language', which discursively constructs a specific variety of a language as the sole acceptable, legitimate and, above all, written form of language for the nation-state. The nineteenth-century use of the term 'standard language' is interchangeable with terms such as 'the national language', 'the language of the educated', 'the language of refinement', the *Kultursprache*, and so on (cf. Crowley 2003; Grillo 1989; Mugglestone 1995; Watts 2011; Hackert 2012). For the purposes of social interaction, it was meant to be a *horizontal* unifying factor in the state across geographical regions and a *vertical* unifying factor through social strata. As such, it was conceptualised as unchanging (even though it was perfectly clear to nineteenth-century linguists that language did change through time) and invariable (even though it became clear throughout the twentieth century that there were wide variations in style, register and contextual use).

The idea of the standard language acting as a unifying factor across social classes, however, was no more than a cynical justification for promoting the standard and delegitimising dialectal varieties and reducing their use (if not actually stamping them out). It thus became a perfect means for socially discriminating between the 'refined' or 'polite' sector of society and the 'vulgar' rest (see Chapter 4 by Fairman). In addition, it was used as a perfect argument to support the conviction that all other varieties of English were not English at all, but merely 'debased', 'corrupt' versions of English, or not even exemplars of human language. 'The English language' is best conceptualised as a set of linguistic varieties clustered around a number of prototypical linguistic constructions that could, for want of a better term, be labelled 'English', some more closely than others, such that there is considerable doubt in linguists' minds as to where the boundaries lie. In fact, the boundaries turn out to be very fuzzy. For example, is Tok Pisin a variety of English? Is Old English really English? When does a variety of English become 'not-English'?

As sociolinguists, the contributors to this collection of chapters on letter corpora agree with the need to consider heterogeneity and variability seriously and to resist the temptations of the homogeneity myth and the ideology of the standard. But caution is needed at this point! This does not mean that standard English, however we define it and to whichever region of the world in which English is acquired as a first language we assign it, is not also a bona fide variety of English. Of course it is, and as such it has its own kinds of heterogeneity and variability (see Trudgill 1999). From the point of view of historical linguists, and in particular historical sociolinguists, the contributors also agree, as Trudgill and Watts (2002) argue, that it is time to consider alternative histories of 'English', to vary our perspectives in order to avoid the danger of the 'funnel view' of the history of English in which the end point is the standard (see Watts 2011: ch. 12).[1]

2.3 The problem of the data

Problem number 3 is a major stumbling block for both historical linguists and historical sociolinguists. Before the end of the last decade of the nineteenth century, our only source of data was written, either in the form of manuscripts, handwritten notes, protocols and memos, glosses inserted into longer manuscripts, and so on, or from the end of the fifteenth century on in the form of printed texts. Data sources providing evidence of how people used language in everyday social interaction are thus scarce to non-existent (see Schreier, Chapter 14; Schneider 2002). If we are interested in unearthing written material from which we can piece together alternative histories of English, i.e. histories of non-standard varieties of English and ways in which the vast majority of the population, rather than a small 'educated' and socially privileged elite, used those varieties, our sources are very restricted indeed. Speakers of non-standard varieties of English were almost inevitably to be found among the social classes below the gentry, and even though a considerable number of the gentry and a few among the aristocracy are known to have used non-standard varieties in everyday social interaction, their written communication from the middle of the eighteenth century on was almost invariably modelled on the emerging standard variety.

We therefore need to gain access to written sources which can be shown to emanate from the lower sectors of the social spectrum. Two such sources are diaries and letter collections, genres which one might reasonably expect to yield traces of non-standard varieties of English or, before the beginnings of the standardisation process at the end of the sixteenth century, at least some indication of how other sectors of society than the privileged gentry and aristocracy used their own varieties of English. We are fortunate in having a number of excellent corpora of personal correspondence to work from (see the reference section), so we are not short of letters to examine. What we discover, however, is not always what we expected to find, as I shall discuss in Section 4. Before opening that specific can of worms,

---

[1] In Watts and Trudgill (2002) we use the term 'tunnel view' rather than 'funnel view'. The differences are minimal, but I now prefer the term 'funnel view', which can be used much more easily as a metaphor to illustrate the wrongheadedness of focusing the history of English (and by extension of other languages) uniquely on the standard language (see Watts 2011, 2012b, 2012c).

however, I need to outline some of the general principles on which this collection of chapters on letter writing has been compiled.

3. Sociolinguistics and historical linguistics

Sociolinguistic approaches to the historical study of languages appear to offer a natural extension of two early forms of sociolinguistics, *interactional sociolinguistics* and *variationist sociolinguistics*, both of which date back to the 1960s. It is thus all the more surprising that, apart from Romaine's pioneering work (Romaine 1982; cf. the discussion in Chapter 2 by Hernández-Campoy and Conde-Silvestre), historical sociolinguistics only really began in earnest in the 1990s, heralded in by Jim Milroy's *Linguistic Variation and Change: On the Historical Sociolinguistics of English* (1992).

The principal focus of *interactional sociolinguistics*, initiated by the work of Gumperz and Hymes (see, e.g., Gumperz and Hymes 1964, 1972; Gumperz 1982; Hymes 1964, 1974), was the nature of the language used by individuals in their social interactions with others, i.e. in their attempts to become ratified members of social and cultural groups. The genesis of interest here was located, on the one hand, in new forms of sociological theorising that emerged from around the end of the 1950s on inspired by Garfinkel (1967) and Goffman (1959) as a reaction to the top-down theorising of Talcott-Parsons, and on the other hand, in a revival of anthropological interest in the significance of language in cultural systems (Hymes 1974). Major foci of interactional sociolinguistics were the various ways in which individuals negotiated meanings through contextualising language in interaction, cross-cultural differences in language use and the conceptualisation of language use in social interactions as a form of performance.[2]

Variationist sociolinguistics positions itself as the study of language use in variable forms of social structure. It stresses the fact that variation in the use of linguistic constructions can be correlated with social factors such as social class, gender, age, religion, ethnicity, life-style, demographic development, etc., and it looks for a set of objective methodologies to make statements about language variability within different speech communities. Like interactional sociolinguistics, it can also be seen as a reaction against the generative linguistic focus on the nature of linguistic competence and the exclusion of social factors from the study of language constructions. Since variationist sociolinguistics has also concerned itself with plotting ongoing changes in the linguistic behaviour of speech communities, one would have expected a much greater involvement by sociolinguists in the issues of language history at an earlier stage in its development, particularly since one of the seminal texts in present-day historical linguistics, 'Empirical foundations for a theory of language change' by Uriel Weinreich, William Labov and Marvin Herzog

[2] The term 'performance', which is currently enjoying a revival of interest in present-day sociolinguistic research, should not be understood in a Chomskyan sense, i.e. as the realisation of linguistic competence in the actual use of language, but rather as a presentation of the self and a construction of community identity using language and other semiotic systems.

(1968), specifically maps out possible new approaches to the historical study of language based on notions such as variation, heterogeneity and change.

There are significant possible reasons why sociolinguistic approaches to language histories took so long to catch on. In variationist sociolinguistics, sophisticated quantitative methods have been developed to test the significance of the results of wide-scale research projects, the interconnections between the variations noted and the reliability and representativity of the data themselves. To apply quantitative methods, it is necessary to have a large enough database, which only controlled research methodologies have so far been able to provide. It is difficult, though not impossible, to apply such methodologies to the relative paucity of data available from earlier periods in the history of a language, particularly since earlier than the last decade of the nineteenth century only written data were available. However, even here new corpora,[3] painstakingly assembled and tagged, have begun to open up opportunities for using the familiar methods of variationist sociolinguistics. The difficulty in using interactional sociolinguistics on historical data is that the sociolinguist needs to observe performance and social interaction as it emerges,[4] which is clearly not possible with written data from the past. However, close observation of ethnographic material in the recent past and the present offers possibilities for projecting this knowledge back into the past in interpreting the data available.

By the 1990s it had become clear that language varieties change for a complex network of reasons, some internal, i.e. as a result of the possibilities for variation in social practice offered by all linguistic systems (Labov 1994), some external, i.e. as a result of changing interconnections between forms of speaking and social and cultural factors (Labov 2001), and some cognitive, i.e. as a result of the individual and small group needs to use language to perform acts of identity and to exercise influence over others in emergent ongoing social interaction (see Labov 2010).

In 1992 Jim Milroy used the insights of extensive research carried out with Lesley Milroy on language variation in and around Belfast to argue for the significance of social network theory in tracing out what had become known as the *actuation problem*, i.e. the problem of how innovative variation is taken up and diffused within and between speech communities. Since Milroy's ground-breaking book, it has become abundantly clear that both interactional sociolinguistics and variationist sociolinguistics have exerted an influence on the use of sociolinguistic theory and methodology in investigations into the histories of languages and language varieties.

---

[3] For a list of data corpora in English which includes the major significant corpora in English historical linguistics, see the VARIENG homepage at the University of Helsinki (www.helsinki.fi/varieng/CoRD/corpora/corpusfinder/index.html). Of particular significance here are the *Corpus of Early English Correspondence (CEEC)* from 1403 to 1681 and the *Corpus of Early English Correspondence Extension (CEECE)* from 1653 to 1800.

[4] This, of course, is hardly ever possible in dealing with modern data, since the database is almost always a recording of what occurred, thus presenting further difficulties of transcription, interpretation and the ever-present observer's paradox (see Labov 1972: 209; 'The aim of linguistic research in the community must be to find out how people talk when they are not being systematically observed; yet we can only obtain these data by systematic observation').

Eckert's work (Eckert 1989, 2000; Eckert and Rickford 2001; Eckert and McConnell-Ginet 2003) introduces the important concept of *communities of practice* into both variationist and interactional sociolinguistics, thus paving the way for a possible convergence of these two approaches. For example, Eckert now uses the term 'Third Wave Variation Studies', which she defines on her website (www. stanford.edu/~eckert/thirdwave.html) as a 'focus on the social meaning of variables'. She goes on to state the following:

> [The Third Wave of Variation Studies] views styles, rather than variables, as directly associated with identity categories, and explores the contributions of variables to styles. In so doing, it departs from the dialect-based approach of the first two waves, and views variables as located in layered communities. Since it takes social meaning as primary, it examines not just variables that are of prior interest to linguists (e.g. changes in progress) but any linguistic material that serves a social/stylistic purpose. And in shifting the focus from dialects to styles, it shifts the focus from speaker categories to the construction of personae.

'Styles', as a means of constructing identities, are determined by sociolinguistic variables in the construction of personae and identities. As Eckert points out, this shifts the focus in sociolinguistics away from dialects (or linguistic varieties) to the means used by individual speakers in emergent interaction (and performance) to stylise themselves in different ways. In addition, the comment that 'variables [are] located in layered communities' makes another focus-shift from speech communities to communities of practice.

The chapters in this volume make use of insights from all three 'Waves of Variation Studies', and many of them, either implicitly or explicitly, look at specific aspects of the language of the letter writers in an effort to discover how those writers position themselves and how they attempt, consciously or unconsciously, to construct social identities. The letters are largely from people in the lower strata of social structure, either to addressees of the same social status or of a higher status. In this sense the question of the use of 'standard' and/or 'non-standard' varieties of English is in the forefront of our interest. I also wish to make it clear that, while some chapters make use of Labov's categories of 'change from above' and 'change from below', others refer to 'language histories from below'. Labov meant his terms to be understood as change that occurs in a speech community unconsciously ('from below' the level of consciousness) or consciously ('from above' the level of consciousness). The term 'language histories from below' emanates from the work associated with the Historical Sociolinguistics Network (HiSoN), first formed in 2005. The guiding principle behind the concept is incorporated in Mattheier's words of caution that the 'standard' language should not be 'the genuine teleological goal of any historical language development', and that a focus on the language varieties of the underprivileged sections of society, which for centuries has constituted the vast mass of the overall population in virtually all European states, would lead to 'other' potential histories. Independent of HiSoN, this was also the guiding principle behind the collection of essays published in Watts and Trudgill (2002), as it is the guiding principle behind the present collection.

Looking at 'letters from below', however, does not preclude looking at letters written before the movement to standardise English got really underway in the eighteenth century, and two of the chapters (Chapter 2 by Hernandez-Campoy and Conde-Silvestre and Chapter 7 by Bergs) deal with what is probably the most well-known letter collection of all in English, the Paston letters (1422–1509). Similarly, it does not preclude a quick look at 'language history from above', which is the focus of Chapter 9 by Fitzmaurice, who focuses her attention on letters written by aristocratic members of the Kit-Cat Club in the early eighteenth century. But looking at letters from below and above the social surface of what was termed 'refined' society at the turn of the nineteenth century, or letters that preceded the movement toward standard English, reveals rather more worms in the can than might have been anticipated, and it is those worms which form the focus of the following section.

4. Unanticipated worms

The first problematic worm in the can concerns the need to make a distinction between text and manuscript. As Fairman (Chapter 4) rightly points out, there is a world of difference between studying the original handwritten letter (or a facsimile thereof) and studying a printed version of it, even given the attempt in the printed version to represent false starts, unusual spellings, idiosyncratic use of punctuation, and so on.[5] This is not because handwriting reveals character traits. Who knows, perhaps it does? What the original handwriting reveals is whether the letter writer, given the fact that s/he did not make use of an amanuensis, had received some schooling in the art of writing. In some of the chapters, the handwriting gives strong evidence that this may indeed have been the case. In addition, as Fairman (Chapter 4) notes, 'minutiae can be sites of special linguistic interest', which in itself justifies the use of original handwriting. The problem, of course, is that it is less time-consuming and thus less expensive to base corpora on printed materials. As Fairman argues, we need to focus our attention as sociolinguists on manuscript material in addition to – perhaps rather than – print material, particularly in view of the fact that the basis for electronic corpora is often print material, i.e. on grammatically schooled data.

Some of the handwriting in the letters analysed in Barbara Allen's chapter (Chapter 11) indicates a type of schooling that stressed the visual aesthetic quality of the writing itself, whether or not the writer introduces into the letter different spelling variants, influences from her/his dialect and a lack of appreciation for the conventions of letter writing as a genre. In individual cases we have almost no way

---

[5] A classic example of the kind of interpretative mistakes that can be made by focusing on the text rather than on the manuscript is provided by researchers of *Beowulf* (Kiernan 1997; Watts 2011: ch. 2).

of knowing what amount of schooling any of the letter writers may have acquired, but we do seem to have evidence that schooling of some sort or another may have been more widespread than is generally thought. At the very least – and assuming the lack of an amanuensis, of course – those who were taught to write were also taught to produce writing of an aesthetically high standard.[6]

In like manner, it is also striking how some of the pauper letters display evidence of an awareness of letter-writing conventions, e.g. how to address the addressee appropriately, how to finish off the letter, how to format the address at the top of the letter, and so on. Letter-writing appears to have been a self-reflexive activity, a form of performance in which the writer had an opportunity to present her/himself in a particular way. In performing a positive 'self', writers who were able to present themselves effectively may have increased their chances of receiving monetary relief and avoiding the dismal fate of internment in a workhouse, and there is evidence that letter writers, for this very reason, often enlisted the help of others to write for them (see Chapter 4 by Fairman and Chapter 10 by Laitinen). Certain linguistic constructions can thus be taken to index forms of stylisation in which specific social roles are enacted. One such type of stylisation involves the production of linguistic constructions that lie outside the everyday linguistic competence of the letter writer, in particular constructions that may have represented the writer's conceptualisation of the 'standard' language. Frequently, such attempts to perform the standard miss the mark, but are, for this very reason, important indications for ways in which non-standard speakers perceived the social significance of a variety of English that was regularly projected by those in power in the first half of the nineteenth century as the only 'legitimate' form of language.

There is a difficulty here, however. If we expect letters to social institutions and persons of 'authority' from socially discriminated writers to contain rich evidence for non-standard varieties of the language, we are likely to be disappointed. Although non-standard constructions are relatively common in 'letters from below', they only give us hints with respect to those varieties and are not likely to present us with extensive examples of how people wrote in their own dialect. This is even the case in personal family letters (see Chapter 14 by Daniel Schreier) or letters by immigrants writing home to family and friends (see Chapter 12 by Lukas Pietsch and Chapter 3 by Stephan Elspaß). The constraints imposed on letter writers to use the standard are far more revealing of what non-standard speakers imagine to be the standard than of their own dialects. In post-colonial communities of English speakers, notably in North America, efforts towards homogenising 'new standards' may not correspond at all with what speakers write in communication with others via letters, as we can see in Stefan Dollinger's contribution to this collection in Chapter 6. As Schreier shows (Chapter 14), even in personal letters,

---

[6] My own memories of primary school education in the England of the early 1950s confirms the significance of the 'handwriting-must-be-conventionally-and-classically-elegant' school of thought. Children were regularly given gold stars to stick into their exercise books if they met the strict 'calligraphic' levels set up by their teachers. I also remember how disappointed I was that I never received any gold stars for writing.

we find frequent examples of hypercorrection in a situation in which correctness is or can be assumed to be a secondary issue. In such cases we are again confronted by fascinating cases of stylisation in attempts to construct and perform specific identities within the community of practice of the family.

Letters from both below and above contain important evidence of linguistic insecurity. Susan Fitzmaurice's contribution (Chapter 9) shows how members of the Kit Kat Club, who might generally be assumed to have a steady control of the standard 'legitimate' language, still display variation and insecurity. In this case, however, we need to ask what differences there might be between the manuscript originals of the letters and the form in which they are committed to the print medium. As Fairman points out, this is and remains a crucial question in letters first committed to the page in the form of handwriting and then presented in print 'after the event'. There is highly likely to have been a significant degree of editing in this transition, and the differences between manuscript and printed version can also be shown to reveal instantiations of stylisation, this time, however, on the part of the editors rather than the letter writers themselves.

Marianne Hundt's chapter (Chapter 5) is particularly interesting in this respect, since the corpus is a printed one containing letters written from New Zealand to individuals and institutions in Britain extolling the virtues of New Zealand as a goal of emigration, the idea being to use the letters to attract more emigrants. In this case, we are unfortunate not to have the original handwritten letters, but we can still locate remnants of the letter writers' non-standard varieties. At this point, it becomes interesting to consider why these features were not also 'corrected'. What were the social purposes of the editors of the letters? Was it to stylise the emigrants to New Zealand as being of working-class origin, or at least as not being formally educated, in an effort to attract more members of the lower social orders to emigrate? Was it to present New Zealand as being the appropriate goal of emigration for honest hard-working people? And was this second stylisation also aimed at inducing a larger percentage of the lower social orders to be prepared to leave Britain?

Hundt's chapter raises another issue that is dealt with explicitly in Chapter 10 by Mikko Laitinen and, more indirectly, in Chapter 13 by Lucia Siebers, viz. the effects of mobility/migration within vertical and horizontal spaces on the heterogeneity of the language of letter writers 'from below'. Laitinen uses another area of modern sociolinguistics – Blommaert and Rampton's theory of globalisation and mobility – to show that the authors of pauper letters requesting relief from their home parishes were well aware of the need to use forms of stylisation to achieve those ends when they were geographically distant from the addressee – even though they produced neither standard English nor their own dialectal vernaculars. In addition, they also had an awareness of social as well as of geographical distance. Sievers uses language contact theory to show that even in situations where there was in all probability no contact with speakers of Scotch-Irish varieties of English, African American vernacular letter writers display a surprising propensity to display precisely those linguistic features that would be associated with that form of contact. We are left with the feeling that ordered heterogeneity in the sense of Weinreich, Labov and Herzog's seminal article is somehow at play here.

The opportunities here and elsewhere in the contributions to this volume are rich and exciting in their combination of approaches to sociolinguistics. Juan Manuel Hernandez-Campoy and Juan Camilo Conde-Silvestre in Chapter 2 make a broad sweep and outline the differences between First Wave Variation Studies and Third Wave Variation Studies, but at the same time they are concerned to combine the merits of both approaches in providing new insights to the analysis of the Paston letters. Similarly, in Chapter 7 Alexander Bergs takes a new look at those same letters, focusing more on tracing out signs of the scribes themselves, thus involving us in a more Third Wave-oriented kind of analysis. In Chapter 8 Auer takes on the job of showing that stylistic variation in Late Modern English letters – at different social levels – is largely determined by the written linguistic repertoire an individual was able to accumulate by way of formal and informal instruction, self-improvement and practice. Auer does this by combining a discussion of educational opportunities and the levels of literacy attained through various forms of education at different social levels. She also gives an outline of existing letter-writing norms, with a qualitative analysis of letters written by women from different places in the social hierarchy, notably the elite, the middling sort and the labouring poor.

Letters, therefore, both 'from above and below', present us with a large number of worms, many of them unanticipated. The fat worm to catch the 'standard' has been passed by in favour of a large selection of alternative worms that successfully challenge the hegemony of histories of English aiming only at the 'legitimate' form of language in the eighteenth and nineteenth centuries. Sociolinguistic studies are now broad enough to explore other alternatives and to help in the complex reconstruction of histories from below. In particular, the individual writer is at the centre of all these contributions – as a person who needed, through letter writing, to construct social identities in the complex and frequently frightening new world of industrial nineteenth-century Britain, or as a member of new colonial (and by now postcolonial) communities in which the standard language was a newly emerging form of English, or as a member of newly constructed communities of practice beyond the family dealing with the workplace, with emigration, with the need to stay alive somehow, and the need to challenge the dominance of the 'educated' with their unchallenged assumption that there is only one 'legitimate' and homogeneous form of English.

I deliberately used the present tense in the very last clause of the long sentence closing the previous paragraph precisely because the problem of standard vs. non-standard, although not nearly as virulent as it was throughout the nineteenth century and well into the twentieth, is still with us today and periodically raises its head in the areas of education and the workplace. If that is the fish that has been caught by our sociolinguist anglers, then it should be taken home and eaten. Others can be set free to produce more fish for future fishing expeditions. The sluice-gate to the weir has now been opened, the anglers are ready below the weir along the sides of the river waiting to make their catch, and the can of worms remains open for each of them to dip into at their will.

CHAPTER 2

Assessing variability and change in early English letters

Juan Manuel Hernández-Campoy and Juan Camilo Conde-Silvestre

1. **Approaches to 'variation' and 'change' in sociolinguistic research**

This chapter looks at variability and change from two different points of view – First Order Variation Theory and Third Order Variation Theory – through the study of early English correspondence. The indexical nature of the social meaning of inter- (social) and intra- (stylistic) speaker variation in the sociolinguistic behaviour of speakers, as Eckert (2012) points out, has been chronologically approached from three analytic perspectives, waves or generations. In this epistemological evolution since the beginning of sociolinguistics, there has clearly been a shift from deterministic and system-oriented approaches (language as a collective system: *langue*) to more social constructivist and speaker-oriented ones (language as individual performance: *parole*) (see Hernández-Campoy and Cutillas-Espinosa 2012: 7). During the 1960s, the mechanistically based paradigm of the First Generation assumed that speech and the stylistic repertoire are 'determined' by the major macro-sociological categories of socioeconomic class, gender, age and ethnicity, providing us with general patterns in their aggregate data. In the 1980s, the ethnographic-based paradigm of the Second Generation set out that speech and the stylistic repertoire are 'determined' by social configurations – rather than categories – of multiplex relationships within the social networks of speakers and their mobility, providing us with a more concrete local (or locally defined) perspective on the dynamics of variation and sociolinguistic behaviour at large.

Some common assumptions in this respect are the following: (i) variables carry complex indexical meanings in the macro-sociological matrix after the correlation of linguistic (dependent) and extralinguistic (independent) elements, where significance is understood as the causality relationship between linguistic and extralinguistic data in some kind of speech community; (ii) dialect differentiation is determined by the relative frequency with which particular variants are used in relation to their potential occurrence under the influence of prestige (overt/covert); and (iii) standardness is a function of those extralinguistic factors, with the vernacular having some special relevance. In this way, the use of non-standard variants correlates inversely with speakers' socioeconomic status, gender, age, ethnicity, social networks, mobility or level of speech formality. If the speech community was a significant element in the First Wave sociolinguistic scenario, in the Third the community of practice is crucial.

More recently, at the beginning of the twenty-first century, a Third Generation of sociolinguists have stressed the individuality of speakers by making use of a constructivist approach based on speaker's agency (individual action), stance and performativity to more accurately account for the nature of the indexical relations between linguistic and extralinguistic variables. This new approach is acutely aware of the fact that language acts *are* acts of identity. Therefore, the uses of variation are now understood not simply as reflecting, but also as constructing social meaning, and the focus has shifted from speaker categories and configurations to the construction of personae. Not only does variation reflect the multifaceted shaping of human relationships for the transmission of social meaning, but it is also a resource for identity construction and representation, and even social positioning; and accents, dialects and their styling are markers of this social meaning (see Podesva 2006; Auer 2007). Like any other social stereotypes, these different ways of speaking constitute prototype categories within a wider frame that comprises not only ideological components, but also markers from a wide variety of dimensions, such as speech, physical appearance, dress, dance, music, etc. (Kristiansen 2008: 72–3).

Linguistic variation is then the instrument, or resource, for linguistic performance, rhetorical stance and identity projection, where individuals (rather than groups) and the individual voice are actively responsible for the transmission of sociolinguistic meaning in terms of a speaker's personal and interpersonal social identity and authenticity (see Giddens 1991: 82–5; Johnstone 2000: 417). This is a proactive model that accounts for variation as a resource for creating as well as projecting one's persona, in terms of the speaker's agency, to construct identity and positioning in society, where the individual voice is seen 'as a potential agent of choice rather than a passive, socially constructed vehicle for circulating discourses' (Johnstone 2000: 417). Repeated patterns of stance-taking can come together as a style associated with a particular individual, which becomes ethnographically and interactionally relevant. Additionally, for this purpose, as Johnstone (2000: 419) states, the individual voice plays a crucial role in our understanding of the linguistics of language in its social context (see also Englebretson 2007; Jaffe 2009). In this way, identity is dynamic and all speech is performance – with speakers projecting different roles in different circumstances – since we are always displaying some particular type of identity, and this, in turn, would contradict the idea that the vernacular is the most 'natural' form of speech and does not require speakers to put on roles (see Schilling-Estes 2002: 388–9). As such, this stance implies a focus on 'the vagaries and unpredictability of the individual's language variation and performance' (Bell 2007: 92), i.e. how individuals position themselves in society through their linguistic usage.

2. Letters and sociolinguistic research in the history of languages

Historical sociolinguistics appeared in the 1980s as an interdisciplinary field that 'focuses on trajectories of changes completed at early stages of the language and employs variationist methods to investigate these changes' (Milroy and Gordon 2003: 176). Assuming (i) that the evolution of linguistic and social systems always occurs in relation to the sociohistorical situations of their speakers, (ii) that the past should be studied in order to understand and explain the present (and vice versa) and (iii) Labov's (1994) *uniformitarian principle*, Romaine (1982, 1988) developed this multidisciplinary discipline through the integration of historical linguistics and sociolinguistics. Theoretically, its main objective is 'to investigate and provide an account of the forms and uses in which variation may manifest itself in a given speech community over time, and of how particular functions, uses and kinds of variation develop within particular languages, speech communities, social groups, networks and individuals'; while methodologically, 'the main task of sociohistorical linguistics is to develop a set of procedures for the reconstruction of language in its social context, and to use the findings of sociolinguistics as controls on the process of reconstruction and as a means of informing theories of change' (Romaine 1988: 1453).

The development of historical sociolinguistics has had a crucial impact on historical linguistics, both theoretical and methodological. Firstly, it has triggered a new interest in tracing heterogeneity in the history of languages, in contrast to the search for homogeneity that guided research over the last 200 years. Secondly, historical sociolinguistics has provided methodological principles and tenets that allow researchers to trace new dimensions of historically attested changes along the social and linguistic dimensions. With the assistance of ancillary disciplines like corpus linguistics and social history, research in the field is now scientifically well grounded, enjoying both empirical validity and historical confidence. Thirdly, this discipline has also triggered an interest in the non-standard perspective, promoting research on the history of non-standard varieties. Finally, the discipline of historical sociolinguistics has highlighted the role of new genres and text-types as materials worth studying to shed light on language variation and change: diaries, travel accounts, court records, recipes and especially letters (both private and official) have now become indispensable documents for historical sociolinguistic research (see Jucker 1995; Nevalainen and Raumolin-Brunberg 1996, 1998, 2003).

Now, once maturity has been reached, the analytical practices developed by historical sociolinguistics must be expanded to join the Third Generation of early twenty-first-century sociolinguists, by accounting for the meaning of variation with constructivist approaches based on speaker's agency, stance, authenticity and performativity. Admittedly, historical sociolinguistics has come of age, but it still relies heavily on what we can observe today in instantiations of emergent social practice for the simple reason that we are in a difficult position to observe social practice in the past.

This chapter deals with letters as a source for the study of variability and change in the history of English and, as such, it is fully integrated within historical sociolinguistic research. Letters have been most suitable material for historical sociolinguistic research (Nevalainen and Raumolin-Brunberg 1996: 39–54; Conde-Silvestre

2007: 51–2; Palander-Collin, Nevala and Nurmi 2009), since they have allowed us to trace change through a speech community as conceived by the First Wave approach. Unlike many surviving documents from the past – especially from the earliest stages – letters are non-anonymous texts, signed by an author and addressed to one (or more than one) known reader. The identification of both communicative characteristics implies that 'psycho-biographical' data about them can, with a certain amount of luck, be traced, either because the author and the recipients were of the 'better sort' and, as a result, information about them survives, or, if it does not, because the letters themselves may provide the context to reconstruct it. The possibility of retrieving personal information has facilitated the analysis of some of the sociolinguistic variables traditionally correlated with linguistic production, e.g. age, gender, education, professional background, social status, social network, social and geographical mobility – if the surviving letters are autographed documents and their written words were the proper 'utterance' of their authors, with no mediation of scribes or secretaries.[1] What the First Wave of sociolinguists has so far ignored is the individual (or individuals if there was an amanuensis) and how each of them performs a role through the act of letter writing itself. This is an important fact which may allow us to draw our attention to the emergent individual act of letter writing and the language needed to address an issue appropriately, i.e. in a socially commensurate way.

This new dimension can be substantiated in the fact that, to a certain extent, letters are intended as dialogic exchanges, reflecting the personal communicative style of an author who maintains and negotiates a particular social relationship with his/her addressees in the situation and purpose of the letter: whether the relationship is closer (e.g. kinship, friendship) or more distant (professional, business-like). Correspondence, therefore, has been understood as better suited than other genres for research on the variety of styles that could have affected changes in the history of languages, if only because, typologically, letters may contain as many styles of writing as the relationship between their participants permits: '[F]amily correspondence . . . tends to be more informal and involved than letters written to more distant acquaintances, which often concern business, administrative or legal matters' (Palander-Collin, Nevala and Nurmi 2009: 12). Yet, with the new constructivist approaches to style, according to the goal of the letter writer and the person to whom it is addressed (plus also the social context of the activity of letter writing itself), these documents can reveal sociolinguistic styles which may lead to interesting interpretations of social meaning. But to what extent these may be used to plot change is then debatable.

[1] The possibility of establishing a one-to-one relationship between the linguistic output of each letter and the personal profile of its producer is crucial for historical sociolinguistic research and involves the following dimensions, which should be carefully considered when planning research in the field: (a) authorship of the original, i.e. whether the text was actually written by the person in whose name it was composed or by a secretary; (b) the prospects of identifying as many details as possible of the writer's social background at large; and (c) editorial intrusion in the original with respect to mainly grammar and spelling (Nevalainen and Raumolin-Brunberg 1996: 43).

3. Letters as evidence for the study of variation and change at the individual and community levels

The preservation of letters written by the same individual over different periods of his/her lifetime and, more often, the existence of collections of correspondence written by members of several generations from the same family or circle adds an interesting dimension to historical linguistic research based on correspondence. In addition to the attested validity in detecting the provenance (change from above/below)[2] and direction of long-term changes, as practised by First Wave socio-linguists, they are also useful to analyse the linguistic behaviour of individual speakers over more or less prolonged periods of time – ideally a complete life span – and thus to trace how a change in progress diffuses longitudinally in real time along a group of homogeneous speakers. In this sense, 'generational change' and 'communal change' are well-established terms in synchronic sociolinguistics. The former refers to a situation in which individual idiolects remain reasonably stable while a given change evolves in the community; the latter, however, envisages speakers who may alter their production during the course of their lifetimes, so that 'diffusion' (Labov 2007) is a function of the accumulated alteration of individual language habits in the same direction, to the point that, in situations of communal change, lack of stability characterises both the individual and the community. Labov posits that 'individual speakers enter the community with a characteristic frequency for a particular variable, maintained throughout their lifetimes; but regular increase in the values adopted by individuals often incremented by generation, lead to linguistic change for the community' (Labov 1994: 84).[3] 'Generational' and 'communal' changes are

---

[2] First Wave research based on these corpora has confirmed the relevance of letters in the reconstruction of the sociolinguistic contexts of language changes in the past and has consolidated the historical validity of some 'sociolinguistic universals', e.g. the curvilinear hypothesis, the distinctions between 'overt' and 'covert' prestige, 'changes from above' and 'changes from below'. Moreover, the analysis of epistolary documents has allowed linguists to trace the diffusion of historically attested changes over social, geographical and temporal spaces, and to establish their correlations with age, social status, occupation, gender and mobility (see Nevalainen and Raumolin-Brunberg 1996, 2003; Conde-Silvestre 2007; Hernández-Campoy and Conde-Silvestre 2012). The Labovian distinction between 'changes from above' and 'changes from below' has traditionally been, in this respect, a heuristically useful one, whose historical validity has also been confirmed by the analysis of correspondence from the past. With respect to changes from above, from the Renaissance on, the role of official correspondence in establishing written language norms worthy of imitation should be highlighted (see Benskin 1992 for English; Deumert and Vandenbussche 2003 for an overview of standardisation in other Germanic languages). Regarding 'changes from below', the availability of private correspondence written by people without full access to formal education makes the genre a most useful locus to trace their diffusion, historically elusive. Thus, aspects of non-standard pronunciation, morphology and even syntax have been reconstructed at a time when standard norms in Europe were already well established; in the same way, these materials have allowed researchers to trace the diffusion of changes initiated in the vernacular along the lower echelons of society. But, at this point, a clear distinction has to be made between this traditional 'change from above/change from below' perspective and the recent 'language history from below' (see Watts' discussion of these terms in Chapter 1).

[3] Some scholars (Labov 1994: 83–4; Sankoff 2005: 1011; see also Eckert 1997; Raumolin-Brunberg 2009: 170–1) have used the label 'lifespan change' to designate the individual counterpart of long-term 'communal changes': cases in which 'individual speakers change over their life-spans in the direction of a change in progress in the rest of the community' (Labov 1994: 84). Age-grading is another commonly recognised situation related to the

Table 2.1 *Percentage of -(e)s in three successive apparent time analyses of materials in the* CEEC *(1530–1629) (Raumolin-Brunberg 2005: 43; Nevalainen and Raumolin-Brunberg 2003: 88)*

	Time of writing	1580–99 %	1600–19 %	1620–39 %	Generation %	Total
Year of birth	Before 1530	2	–	–	2	50
	1530–49	17	7	–	15	366
	1550–69	28	59	85	52	591
	1570–89	–	67	61	63	488
	1590–1609	–	79	82	82	373
	1610–29	–	–	77	77	75
	Total %	20	57	74	–	–
	Total occurrences	572	576	795	–	1943

not mutually exclusive, although Labov initially proposed that different changes in different subsystems are more likely to follow one pattern or the other: phonology and morphology tend to follow the generational model, while syntax and the lexicon adopt a communal-like patterning. The application of historical sociolinguistic methodology has permitted scholars like Helena Raumolin-Brunberg (2005, 2009; see also Nevalainen and Raumolin-Brunberg 2003: 86–92) to show that Labov's view does not hold categorically for all morphological changes in the history of English – especially in the Early Modern period – by proving that some changes may follow both patterns at the same time. We also believe that generational and, especially, communal changes, on account of their life-span quality, could function as an interesting locus where First Wave and Third Wave approaches to change and variation can be conflated.

In a pilot study, Raumolin-Brunberg traced the shift from *-(e)th* to *-(e)s* as the third person singular present indicative ending in the *Corpus of Early English Correspondence* (*CEEC*) for the period 1530–1629. The author correlates the distribution of *-(e)s*, in a kind of apparent time study,[4] grouping the date of birth of the correspondents into six cohorts of twenty years (see the rows in Table 2.1), together with three generational ranks based on the time of letter writing (see the columns in Table 2.1). In this way she manages to detect a generational change in progress: the first two columns, 1580–99 and 1600–19, show the greater use of *-(e)s* when younger writers are considered, while the global percentage by generation offered

patterning of variation and change in the community, whereby the use of one variant recurs in certain cohorts in successive generations to decline again once speakers are over the critical age. Due to its fading nature, it is very difficult to detect this situation in historical data. It goes without saying that 'stability', at both community and individual levels (Milroy 1992: 2–4, 32–3) is by far the commonest situation, obviously not excluding the presence of lectal variability inherent to speakers and languages.

4 In apparent-time (or cross-sectional) studies, the speech of older informants is compared with that of younger informants, whereas in real-time (or longitudinal) research the speech of a given population group is compared from at least two different points in time. See Eckert (1997) and Hua and David (2008) for more details.

in column 4 shows an increasing pattern progressing from the older down to the younger informants (Raumolin-Brunberg 2005: 44). This generational patterning does not exclude the possibility that the percentages of -(e)s increased as people grew older, i.e. during their life spans, as typical 'communal changes'. For instance, the informants born in the period 1550–69 clearly altered their preferences for -(e)s over time. In the period 1580–99 they chose the incoming form in 28% of the cases, which was raised to 59% in the period 1600–19 and reached 85% in the time span 1620–39 (2005: 44).

In a recent paper, Raumolin-Brunberg (2009) has considered the same issue concentrating on the letters by three correspondents, Sir Walter Ralegh (1554–1618), Philip Gawdy (1562–1617) and John Chamberlain (1553–1628), between the years 1579 and 1625, when they were 27–64, 17–54 and 44–72 years old respectively. In addition to the rate of -(e)s replacing -(e)th in the third person singular present indicative, the author traces other changes in progress: the increasing use of affirmative periphrastic do, the rate of use of the same pro-form in negative statements and the spread of who in restrictive relative clauses to the detriment of which. Raumolin-Brunberg finds a significant cline from more to less idiolectal stability in the three writers: only John Chamberlain altered his linguistic behaviour by increasing the use of the relative connector who and, accordingly, shows the most stable idiolect. He is followed in the cline by Philip Gawdy, who increased the percentages of who systematically during his lifetime and shows a rise–fall pattern with regard to both the third person singular ending and the affirmative periphrastic do. The most innovative speaker was Sir Walter Ralegh, whose changing practices affected the use of all four variables throughout his life span (Raumolin-Brunberg 2009: 175–89). One overt explanation lies in age differences: the letters by Chamberlain were produced at an older age (44–72 years) while those written by both Gawdy and Ralegh correspond to middle age: 17–54 and 27–64 respectively. Another likely explanation has to do with the fact that they were both immigrants to London, where the incoming variants were rapidly diffusing. This would mean that Gawdy (a native of Norfolk) and Ralegh (a Devonshire man) accommodated their linguistic practices to incorporate the forms that were common in their new domicile, possibly in connection with upward social mobility (Raumolin-Brunberg 2009: 190–2). In any case, the tendency for both authors to increase the proportion of the incoming variants at middle age supports the possibility that generational and communal changes are not mutually exclusive categories and shows that apparent-time studies can be useful methods to detect life-span changes in the history of languages.

Following a Third Wave sociolinguistic theory, letters may also be useful to analyse and account for the motivation(s) for variability in individuals and their stylistic choices for the construction of identity, as seen above. In this way, we may understand Ralegh's behaviour in Raumolin-Brunberg (2009) as that of an adult with a far less constrained relation to language, who, accordingly, could use it more creatively. The problem here is the extent to which all three subjects settled down to the constructions involved through their life span by becoming more used to the linguistic conventions prevalent in the genre of letter writing, i.e. that with age, the constructions they used were adopted as the appropriate 'style' of letter writing. After all, we have no way of knowing how much variation they displayed in oral communication, and Ralegh's creativity would indicate that variation may very well have been a feature in the oral styles of Chamberlain and Gawdy.

In the following sections our own analysis based on historical correspondence will be carried out in order to test the relevance of some of these categories in the past. With this aim, one change in progress in the transition from Late Middle English to Early Modern English – the diffusion of <th> to the detriment of <þ> and <ð> – will be analysed in a corpus of fifteenth-century English correspondence, namely the Paston letters, as available in digital format from the University of Virginia Electronic Text Center (http://etext.virginia.edu; see also Davis 1971). Special attention will be given to some sociolinguistic constraints in this historically attested change – and its characterisation as a 'change from above' or 'from below' – as well as to the possibility of reconstructing the linguistic behaviour of individuals and, as a result, its patterning as a 'generational' or a 'communal' change. Therefore, this will be a First Wave analysis, though with the aim of highlighting some of the problems with that kind of analysis when a focus is placed on the social meanings that we can interpret from the uses of the individual letter writers.

4. The Paston letters as sources of variability and change in fifteenth-century English

4.1 Informants: the Paston family and their correspondence

The Paston letters is a collection of 422 authored documents (letters and notes) written by fifteen members belonging to different generations of this Norfolk family mainly during the fifteenth century (from 1425 to 1496), with roughly 246,353 words. The historical and philological interest of these documents is outstanding, not only because they offer data on the political and domestic history of England, but also because they were composed at a crucial period in the development of the English language.[5]

In fact, ever since Richard Blume undertook his analysis of the language of the Paston letters in 1882, the corpus has been subject to a variety of studies from different linguistic and stylistic stances (see, among others, Davis 1954; Escribano 1982, 1985; Schäfer 1996; Gómez-Soliño 1997; Tanabe 1999; Wood 2007). More akin to the sociolinguistic approach are Norman Davis' comparison of some idiolectal traits peculiar to the brothers John Paston II and John Paston III, from the third generation of the family (1983), Alexander Bergs' (2005) analysis of the deployment of several morphosyntactic features – including personal pronouns, relative

---

[5] Further information on the Paston Family can be found in Davis (1971), Bennett (1990/1995), Richmond (1990/2002, 1996), Barber (1986), Gies and Gies (1998) and Castor (2004), among others.

Table 2.2 *Informants*

Informant	Born–died	Date of letters	Age when letter writing	Geographical location and mobility	Profession	Social networks
William Paston I	1378–44	1425–44	47–66	Norwich London	Steward of the Duke of Norfolk, J.P. Norfolk, Serjeant-at-Law	weaker ties loose-knit
John Paston I	1421–66	1444–65	23–44	Norwich Cambridge Yarmouth London	J.P. Norfolk, M.P. Norfolk	weaker ties loose-knit
Edmond Paston I	1425–9	1447–9	22–4	Norwich London	n.d.	stronger ties close-knit
William Paston II	1436–96	1452–96	16–60	Norwich Cambridge London	M.P. Newcastle under Lyme and Bedwyn	weaker ties loose-knit?
Clement Paston II	1442–79?	1461–6	19–24	Norwich Cambridge London	n.d.	weaker ties loose-knit
John Paston II	1442–79	1462–79	20–37	Norwich London Bruges Barnet Calais Neuss Yarmouth	Knight, M.P Norfolk, J.P. Norfolk, M.P. Yarmouth	weaker ties loose-knit
Edmond Paston II	1443?–1504?	1471–92	28–49	Norwich Cambridge Calais London	n.d.	weaker ties loose-knit
John Paston III	1444–1504	1461–85	17–41	Norwich Barnet Calais Bruges Framlingham	In command of Caister, J.P. Norfolk, M.P. Norwich, Sheriff Norfolk-Suffolk, Knight	weaker ties loose-knit
Walter Paston	1456–79	1479	23	Norwich Oxford	n.d	stronger ties close-knit?
William Paston III	1459–1504?	1478–92	19–33	Norwich Eaton London	n.d.	stronger ties close-knit?
William Paston IV	1479–1554	1495	16	Norwich Cambridge	n.d.	stronger ties close-knit?

connectors and constructions with a 'light' verb of the type V + NP – in connection with external variables and, especially, with the social networks established by some of the correspondents – and, finally, Hernández-Campoy and Conde-Silvestre's study of the adoption of incipient standard written norms by different members of the family, also in connection with such factors as gender, age and mobility (social and/or geographical) (1999; see also Conde-Silvestre and Hernández-Campoy 2004; Hernández-Campoy 2008, 2012).

The analysis undertaken in this chapter belongs to this well-established tradition of linguistic approaches to the Paston letters and concentrates on the autographed documents issued by the male members from four generations of the family covering a time span of seventy-eight years from 1425 to 1503 (see Table 2.2).[6] Chronologically, our first informant is William Paston I (1378–1444), the only son of Clement Paston, the founder of the dynasty, who is described in a document from the 1450s as 'a good plain husbandman [who] lived on the land that he had in Paston, on which he kept a plough at all times of the year' (Barber 1986: 11). William was trained as a lawyer in the Inns of Court in London, acted as counsel for the city of Norwich from 1412 and even became steward to the Duke of Norfolk in 1415 as well as Justice of the Common Bench in 1429. Although evidence of his personal contacts is scant, upward progress in the social scale is obvious and, through his different positions and jobs, some degree of geographical mobility between, at least, London and his manors near Norfolk should also be assumed. The letters analysed range from 1425 to 1444, when he was in his late 40s to mid 60s.

John Paston I (1421–66) was educated at Trinity Hall and Peterhouse, Cambridge, and the Inner Temple in London. As the eldest son of William (and his wife Agnes Berry), he took over the family estates and wealth. In 1440 he married Margaret Mautby. As far as his career is concerned, he tried to follow in his father's footsteps, becoming Justice of Peace for Norfolk (1447, 1456–7 and 1460–1466), Knight of the shire (1455), and MP for Norfolk (1460–2). His letters range from 1444 to 1465, when he was a middle-aged man (23–44 years old).

Edmond Paston I (1425–9) was William I's second eldest son; very little is known about him, apart from the fact that he studied in London, at Clifford's Inn. Few letters by him survive, and they all belong to the years 1447–9 when he was still a young man of 22–4.

William Paston II (1436–96), the third son, also studied at Cambridge. He married Lady Anne Beaufort, daughter of the Duke of Somerset. From 1450 onwards

---

[6] The analysis of handwriting in the Paston correspondence has led some scholars to conclude that a number of female members of the family were illiterate or, if they were not, they did not write their letters themselves. For instance, the letters attributed to Margaret Paston (*c.* 1422–1484) appear in as many as twenty-nine different hands, which, together with the absence of even a signature by her, suggest that 'she could not write and called on whichever literate person was available at the time' (Wood 2007: 51). The possibility that, despite the absence of her own handwriting in the documents, she dictated the letters herself has been contemplated by Bergs (2005: 79–80) provided that the profile of the same scribe has been shown to differ when writing for different family members. Nevertheless, to avoid the problem of female authorship and the risk of gender distortion, we have decided to focus only on the eleven male members.

he frequently travelled to London, where he acted as MP for various constituencies (Newcastle under Lyme and Bedwyn, in Wiltshire). He quarrelled with his brother John I over inheritance of their parents' lands. A whole range of letters by him survives, covering most of his life span (from 1452 to 1496, from the age of 16 to 60).

Clement Paston II (1442–79?) was William's youngest son. As with Edmond I, very little is known about him, apart from the fact that he studied at Cambridge and later lived in London, where he wrote most of his letters to his brother John I between 1461 and 1466 when he was in his early 20s.

The male members of the third generation of the family – direct descendants of John Paston I – were the following: John Paston II (1442–79), the eldest son of John I. From the internal evidence of his correspondence, he has often been described as a 'gentleman of leisure', or *bon vivant*, interested in books, tournaments and love affairs (Barber 1986: 20; Bergs 2005: 66). Sometimes he failed to defend the family interests adequately and is often accused in his mother's letters of overspending. His political career indicates that he was a highly social and geographically mobile character. In 1461 he had joined King Edward IV's court and was knighted two years later. He was also MP for Norfolk between 1467 and 1468, when he remained in London, and later accompanied Princess Margaret to Bruges on the occasion of her marriage. In the 1470s he became a soldier and participated in different battles in the Wars of the Roses, both in Britain (Barnet in 1471), and on the Continent (Calais, Bruges and Neuss, 1472, 1473). He died in 1479, at 37 years of age, and his letters range from 1462, when he was 20, to that date.

Edmond Paston II (1443?–1504?) was educated at Cambridge and later at the Staple Inn in London. He spent some time in Calais with his brother John II. He was indentured to the Duke of Gloucester for service with the king in 1475. After a stay in London, he returned to Norwich, where he married Catherine, daughter of John Spelman. After her death in 1491, Edmond married Margaret, daughter of Thomas Monceaux. The letters analysed correspond to the years 1471–92 when he was 28–49.

John Paston III's (1444–1504) career ran parallel to that of his brother John II. He often travelled throughout the country (Wales, Newcastle) and abroad in the service of the Duke of Norfolk: in fact, he was also in Bruges accompanying Princess Margaret in 1468, and at the Battle of Barnet (1471), where he was wounded. An interesting difference from his brother John II is that in the 1470s and 1480s he remained in the manors that the family owned in Norfolk, although he occasionally visited London and Calais: as MP for Norwich (1485–6), Sheriff of Norfolk and Suffolk or 'councilor' to the Lord High Admiral, the Earl of Oxford. In 1487, after his participation at the Battle of Stoke, he was knighted and in the 1490s performed several duties as deputy of the earl. He married Margery Brews and had two sons: Christopher and William IV. After Margery's death in 1495, he married Agnes, daughter of Nicholas Morley of Glynde (Sussex). His letters range from 1461 to 1485, when he was 17 to 41.

Very little is known about Walter Paston (1456–79) apart from the facts that he studied at Oxford and that he fell ill after his graduation in 1479 and spent the rest of his days in Norwich. Just one letter is included in the collection (from 1479, when he was 23).

William Paston III (1459–1504?) was the youngest son of John I. Little is known about him apart from the fact that he studied at Eton and was not able to go to Calais because of some illness, which discharged him from the earl's service. The letters by him date from 1478 to 1492, when he was 19–33 years old.

Finally, William Paston IV (1479–1554) was the second son of John III and therefore belongs to the fourth generation. He studied at Cambridge and was a knight. He married Bridget, daughter of Sir Henry Heydon of Baconsthorpe (Norfolk). Just one letter is included in the collection, from 1495 when he was 16.

Regarding social status, it is obvious that the members of this family evolved from the middle-high position of the professional lawyer William Paston I, to the higher position attained by John Paston II and John Paston III, who became members of the court nobility when they were knighted in the 1460s and 1490s respectively. This could be taken as an indication of the upward social mobility of a family that certainly prospered in the course of three generations; in fact, Castor (2004: 7) describes them as 'an ambitious nouveau riche family striving to leave their humble origins behind as the Wars of Roses unfold around them'. Within the family, as Bergs (2005: 69–71) shows, John I, John II and John III were the central members towards whom the rest gravitated (they wrote 74.4% of the documents preserved), whereas Walter, William I, William III and William IV certainly occupied rather marginal roles.

4.2 Variable (th)

The progressive adoption of the spelling variant <th> to the detriment of the old runic <þ> will be analysed. It is well known that the spellings <þ> and <ð>, which were used interchangeably in OE for the voiced and voiceless dental fricative consonants [θ] and [ð], began to be replaced in ME by the digraph <th>, which was taken from the Roman alphabet. The progress of this change also involves the disappearance of <ð>, which, according to Lass (1992: 36), 'began to yield to <þ> in the thirteenth century, though it remains sporadically through the fourteenth'. Despite having been adopted later than the Irish form <ð>, the growth in popularity and the longer survival of <þ> is explained by Scragg (1974: 10) 'by the fact that confusion with similarly shaped graphs was less likely' (see also Hogg 1992: 76). The use of the modern digraph <th> had already been attested in the Anglo-Saxon period, particularly in the spelling of vernacular names in Latin texts (Benskin 1982: 19), but it was reintroduced through Latin influence on Anglo-Norman scribes in the twelfth century (Benskin 1977: 506–7, 1982: 18; Hogg 1992: 77; Lass 1992: 36; Stenroos 2006). It is worth quoting the explanation given by Benskin:

> In the aftermath of the Norman Conquest, English as a written language was displaced for nearly all administrative purposes by Latin and, to a lesser extent, by French. Immigrant Norman scribes, given the frequent task of spelling in their Latin and

French texts English vernacular names having [θ], did merely what any number of English scribes from *before* the Conquest would have done: they wrote <th>. For some of these continental writers, <th> may perhaps already have been a familiar combination: those who had read or written much about Biblical texts would certainly have been aware of it. Be that as it may, in adopting the Anglo-Latin <th> as the written correspondent of a sound which was not part of their own language, the imaginations of the Norman scribes were hardly being taxed: the separate elements of the combination, <t> and <h>, were thoroughly familiar symbols. (Benskin 1982: 19)

Both Latin and Biblical influence point to the presence of external prestigious norms which certainly triggered the *actuation* of this spelling change, whose diffusion in writing is unquestionable. Thus, the spread of <th> can be classified as a historical change from above. As such, the Roman-based spelling became popular during the fourteenth century (Blake 1992: 10). The digraph <th> began to affect [θ]-segments first (as in *think* or *myth*), medial [ð]-segments later (as in *brother*), and then initial [ð]-segments, as in *they* or *than* (see Benskin 1982: 18).[7]

4.3 Results

The distribution of variable (th) in the documents analysed – 280 letters by eleven male informants from the Paston family, covering a span of seventy-eight years, from 1425 (date of the first letter available by William Paston I) to 1503 (the last letter by John Paston III) – is reflected in Table 2.3, with a total result of 20,786 tokens, 4,343 corresponding to variant <þ> and 16,443 to <th>.

In order to carry out the sociolinguistic study from a time-depth generational perspective, all documents available were organised into sixteen five-year cohorts, as displayed in Table 2.4.

In the aggregate, the different members of the Paston family, generation after generation, clearly illustrate the gradual adoption of the new form <th> and the subsequent extinction of the old <þ> throughout the fifteenth century. For this, the patterns of 'orderly' and 'structured' heterogeneity found in the variable (th) throughout these seventy-eight years may be understood as a symptom of the encroachment of <th> into the expected <þ> contexts. The transition from the

---

[7] Our interest in this particular change has been activated by Alexander Bergs' analysis of <th>, < þ> and <ð> in *The Peterborough Chronicle*, as an ideal locus to reconstruct a historical pattern of structured heterogeneity by concentrating on the sociolinguistic behaviour of a single 'speaker' – the scribe – rather than on a group (2007b). As such, he detected an incipient situation of orderly heterogeneity where <þ> and <ð> were preferred for grammatical words, while <th> was used for lexical items; the coexistence of all three spellings and the presence of <th> in such highly constrained environments is a clue that by 1155 it had not influenced the linguistic system, to the point of being a 'non-successful speaker innovation'. This hinders the reconstruction of its actuation as a change in progress, unless its diffusion over successive centuries – our current concern in this chapter – is also considered: 'It is only when we have compared this with the successful innovation processes in about 1450 that we can get some more clues about the fundamental problem of actuation, that is the question, how, when, and why an innovation enters into the system and is implemented in an orderly fashion' (Bergs 2007b: 54).

Table 2.3 *Variable (th), distribution per informant and letters*

Informants	Abbreviation	Letters/ documents	Words	\<th\> tokens	\<þ\> tokens	Total (th) variable
William Paston I	WP1	10	6,035	221	620	841
John Paston I	JP1	44	33,490	3,551	815	4,366
Edmond Paston I	EdP1	1	326	23	20	43
William Paston II	WP2	33	15,554	1,408	500	1,908
Clement Paston II	CP2	7	3,314	244	212	456
John Paston II	JP2	85	48,996	5,076	1,420	6,496
John Paston III	JP3	78	44,222	367	97	464
Edmond Paston II	EdP2	8	3,865	4,869	556	5,425
Walter Paston	WaP	4	1,327	102	17	119
William Paston III	WP3	9	4,579	572	83	655
William Paston IV	WP4	1	137	10	3	13
TOTALS		280	161,845	16,443	4,343	20,786

Table 2.4 *Age and period of letter writing*

Period	Age of informants at the time of available correspondence										
	WP1	JP1	EdP1	WP2	CP2	JP2	EdP2	JP3	WaP	WP3	WP4
P1: 1425–9	47										
P2: 1430–4	52										
P3: 1435–9	57										
P4: 1440–4	62	19									
P5: 1445–9		24	20								
P6: 1450–4		29		14							
P7: 1455–9		34		19							
P8: 1460–4		39		24	18	18		16			
P9: 1465–9		44		29	23	23		21			
P10: 1470–4				34		28	27	26			
P11: 1475–9				39		33	32	31	19	16	
P12: 1480–4				44			37	36		21	
P13: 1485–9				49			42	41		26	
P14: 1490–4				54				46		31	
P15: 1495–9				59				51			16
P16: 1500–4								56			

categorical use of the conservative form to the categorical use of the innovating one takes place through a stage of variability where both variants live together, with documents in which there was vacillation between the two forms.

Longitudinally, as reflected in Figures 2.1 and 2.2, the incoming \<th\> spreads according to a positive linear pattern, so that if by 1425 there was a historical change at an early stage (only 23.6% of attested usage), seventy-eight years later, in the very

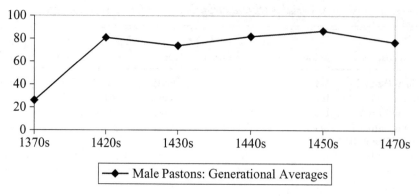

Figure 2.1 Average usage of the innovating form <th> per birth date of the male members of the Paston family (1370s: WP1; 1420s: JP1, EdP1; 1430s: WP2; 1440s: CP2, JP2, EdP2, and JP3; 1450s: WaP, WP3; and 1470s: WP4)

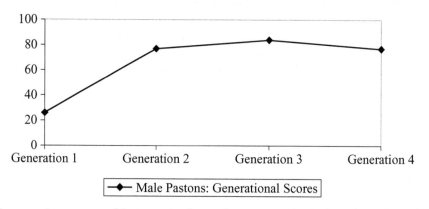

Figure 2.2 Average usage of the innovating form <th> per generation in the male members of the Paston family (Generation 1: WP1; Generation 2: JP1, EdP1, WP2 and CP2; Generation 3: JP2, EdP2, JP3, WaP and WP3; and Generation 4: WP4)

early 1500s, the change was already in the last stages of introduction into the system, showing, for instance, 100% usage in the correspondence by John Paston III. This looks like a clear example of a generational rather than a communal change, since it proceeds gradually, cumulatively and successively from generation to generation. The oldest informants show lower scores for the incoming <th> than the younger ones, so that the accumulated slope of the lines in both individual and generational terms shows the unarrested advance of the change in progress.

The individual linguistic behaviour (Figure 2.3) yields different levels of adoption of the innovating <th>, both synchronically and diachronically: John Paston I (81.3%), John Paston II (78.1%), John Paston III (89.7%), Walter Paston (85.7%), William Paston III (87.3%) and William Paston IV (76.9%) are the most advanced users, while William Paston I (26.2%), Edmund Paston I (53%), and Clement

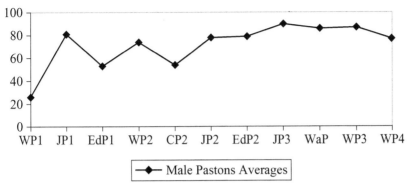

Figure 2.3 Average usage of the innovating form <th> among the male members
of the Paston family

Paston II (53.5%) appear to be the most conservative informants. The chronological patterning of the change in connection to each informant's age is obviously associated with the results. However, the possible contribution of sociolinguistically distinctive factors, such as geographical and social mobility, yielding different chances for each of the informants to establish weaker or stronger ties in loose-knit or close-knit networks, cannot be discarded. Special mention should be made here of Clement Paston II and his nephew John Paston II. They show a generationally divergent behaviour with regard to the use of <th>. The generational distance in their kin relationship (uncle–nephew), which is absent as regards their age and date of letter writing – both were born in 1442 and their first available letters were written at the age of 19/20 – is, however, linguistically manifested in the radically different percentages of the innovating <th>: 56.8% (Clement Paston) and 81% (John Paston) in period 8 (1460–4) as well as in their average behaviour (53.5% and 78.14% respectively). Obviously, given that age was not a determinant influence here, some other extralinguistic factor(s) must have played a role. From the point of view of First Wave sociolinguistic theory, social networks and mobility could have affected them. As seen above, John Paston II belongs to the third generation of the family. His political career as a high courtier and soldier made him a highly social and geographically mobile person who could have established weak ties in loose-knit networks (in places as different as Norwich, London, Bruges, Barnet, Calais, Neuss and Yarmouth). In contrast, Clement Paston II belongs to the second generation of the family and was a much less mobile informant than his nephew John II (Norwich, Cambridge and London). Social mobility and the type of personal relationships they were involved in might have determined their different linguistic practices, in connection with an enhanced capacity to adopt innovations. Finally, the possibility that linguistic changes in progress correlate with socially mobile speakers, who are aware of the overt prestige that certain linguistic variants obtained, confirms that the spread of <th> can be considered a change from above.

Table 2.5 *Informants and letters*

Informants	Letters/ documents	Words	% letters written	\<th\> tokens	\<þ\> tokens	Total (th) variable
William Paston I	10	6,035	3.6%	221	620	841
John Paston I	44	33,490	16%	3,551	815	4,366
Edmond Paston I	1	326	0.4%	23	20	43
William Paston II	33	15,554	12%	1,408	500	1,908
Clement Paston II	7	3,314	2.5%	244	212	456
John Paston II	85	48,996	30%	5,076	1,420	6,496
John Paston III	78	44,222	28%	367	97	464
Edmond Paston II	8	3,865	2.9%	4,869	556	5,425
Walter Paston	4	1,327	1.4%	102	17	119
William Paston III	9	4,579	3.2%	572	83	655
William Paston IV	1	137	0.4%	10	3	13
TOTALS	280	131,704	100%	16,443	4,343	20,786

However, from the perspective of Second and, especially, Third Wave socio-linguistic theories, if we get to the heart of the 'community of practice', a geo-graphically mobile person would have the ability to shift style appropriately, i.e. to construct and play out new identities, since human identity and social organisa-tion are after all flexible. Particular individuals do not permanently and invariably belong to the same groups, but rather adopt different identities and different social activities at different times. New constructions might then have been a feature of communities of practice at a higher social level, whereas those at a lower social level would not have had the ability to shift from one variant to the other. Both John Paston II and Clement Paston II could therefore be orienting themselves to different identities in order to transmit a particular social meaning, which could inevitably be reflected diagnostically in the different personal use of \<þ\> and \<th\> in their letters. In fact, in terms of the impact and social meaning of their respective corre-spondence, at least at a family level, as Table 2.5 shows, their presence and relevance (peripheral vs. nuclear role) within the family corpus is clearly different: 30% vs. 2.5%.

The fact that John II is anchored to a supra-local practice in his body of letters, despite addressing 65 (76%) out of his 85 documents to his family members (John I, John III and Margaret), suggests that he is being performative and overtly embracing authenticity – rather than shifting to a more casual style. There are both personal and ideological factors underlying his choice in performativity. It is undeniable that there is a true attempt to be faithful to his identity. Thus, he provides a perfect illustration of the view now commonly held in sociolinguistic studies that all linguistic usages and all identity displays, even the most 'authentic', are in reality performances, since we are always shaping our speech – and ourselves – to fit who we want to be and how we wish to be viewed in every individual situation, and across the course of our careers and lives.

A close scrutiny of the correspondence by some of these informants, particularly William Paston I, John Paston I, William Paston II and John Paston III, suggests a distinctive and often changing pattern of linguistic behaviour over their lifetimes, which opens the possibility for this change in progress to share the characteristics of both generational and communal changes (Figure 2.4) under the influence of performativity. It may even be determined by a wider variation of the communities of practice in which they were expected to perform, as a closer study would probably allow us to detect in the letters. For instance, William Paston II and John Paston III individually typify a proper life-span change, showing the increasing adoption of <th> over the course of their lifetimes – between the ages of 16–60 and 17–41 respectively – in the direction of a change already in progress in the community. John Paston I, on the other hand, does not exhibit this positive progression, but preserves a consistent (and very high) percentage of <th> for variable (th) throughout his lifetime, between 23 and 44. Incidentally, William Paston I shows a radical move in the direction of the incoming variant late in his life: his production of <th> is within the limit 24%–34% in the first three five-year cohorts, but soars to 89% in the period 1435–40, when he was in his late 50s. Similar changes in late adulthood are attested in the language use of William Paston II, who reaches a categorical use of <th> in the 1480s, when he was in his mid-40s, and John Paston III with a similar behaviour in the 1470s, when he was a mature man in his early 30s.

Alexander Bergs (2007b), in his own analysis of fifteenth-century English correspondence, has detected similar changes in adulthood, which he explains as a result of the lack of either standard norms or of a rooted standard ideology at the time: 'Speakers before 1500 may have had fewer problems in adjusting or changing their personal language use, as there was no or hardly any prestigious "standard" or ideology of a standard' (2007b: 42). Raumolin-Brunberg claims, in the studies mentioned above, that the possibilities of a life-span change, like those attested here, increase when (i) the features affected have been acquired as variable ones and (ii) parallel to the harmony of competing variants: 'The more equal the proportion of rivalling variants are, the more likely it is that one of the variants will increase . . . and gain dominance during the speaker's life' (2005: 48). While it is true that our informants from the Paston family must have acquired <th> when it was still in competition with <þ>, i.e. as a variable in the community, and that the existence of only two competing forms must have facilitated their ability to change their behaviour in adulthood, we also believe that aspects of their biography, pointing to social status and mobility as well as, within a Third Wave approach, to identity construction, could nicely fit into the pattern. This would especially be the case in a typical 'change from above', which would, to a certain extent, qualify Bergs' assumption concerning the lack of normative pressures at the time.

Biographical information, reconstructed from the internal evidence afforded by the letters themselves, could help us to speculate on possible reasons why these members of the family radically changed their written practices so late in their lifetimes. In the case of William Paston I, for instance, he had been trained as

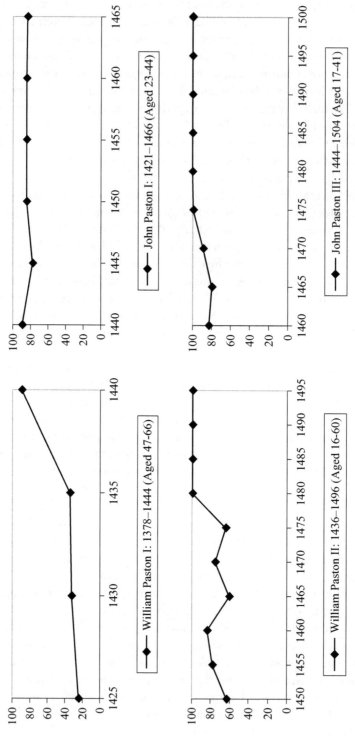

Figure 2.4 Progression of the adoption of the new form <th> in William Paston I, John Paston I, William Paston II and John Paston III

a lawyer in London and developed an important professional career both in the capital and in Norfolk (he became Justice of the Peace in 1418, Sergeant at Law in the 1420s and Justice of the Court of Common Pleas in 1426). In the 1430s and 1440s he tried to promote his transition from a wealthy professional to a landed gentleman by buying manors and land (Castor 2004: 13–24). He seems, therefore, to have involved himself in a campaign of upward social mobility, which could have found a counterpart in his linguistic repertoire when he adopted those well-advanced innovations which had started to enjoy prestige (changes from above), such as the spelling <th> as opposed to the already archaic and rural <þ>. While no evidence is available to confirm William Paston II's reasons for adopting the new spelling in his mid-40s, the biography of John Paston III is full of details which also point to intense mobility in the period when the definite adoption of <th> took place, which might have allowed him to diversify the number and types of communities of practice in which he had to function. In the 1470s he participated in several battles on the Continent (Calais, Neuss) as part of King Edward's renewed campaigns in France; the death of James Gloys, who was the family chaplain and trustee of John's mother, Margaret Paston, in the management of the family estates, offered him a chance to gain a position of greater responsibility in the family affairs and in his mother's household. At that time he also met Margery Brews, the daughter of a Norfolk knight, with whom marriage would certainly ensure promotion on the social ladder for him (Castor 2004: 270–5, 281–2). Although this is speculative, the definite adoption of the prestigious innovation <th> when he was already in his 30s might somehow be connected to the prospects of thriving in the permeable society of late fifteenth-century England.

Consideration of these patterns reveals that the use of the incoming innovation <th> to the detriment of <þ> was not exclusively a generational or communal change in aggregate data, as the First Wave theory would suggest, but also, and crucially, part of style, stylisation, performance and identity construction at the individual level, as Third Wave approaches would diagnose. As a well-advanced historical change in progress, the incoming variant <th> was in the process of becoming part of the community norm, not excluding individuals in their maturity from changing their linguistic behaviour, increasing their production of the innovation and, as a result, incorporating a typical 'change from above' into their repertoire performatively in order to transmit a specific social meaning and social positioning as part of identity construction.

5. Conclusion

A First Order approach can demonstrate the progress through a speech community of an ongoing change, as we have been able to demonstrate with the example of <th> taking over from <þ/ð>. But the use of these variants for individual writers must have represented a stylistic choice, and attempted construction of identity, which also underlines the role of performativity in language change, as advocated by Third Order approaches.

Despite some expected difficulties concerning representativeness and statistical validity, the preservation of collections of fifteenth-century private correspondence, involving writers of different sex, age, social class, personal circumstances and geographical location, offers a very useful corpus on which to carry out quantitative sociolinguistic analyses. The historical and philological interest of these documents is outstanding, especially, as in the case of the Paston letters, because they were composed at a crucial period in the development of the English language, when a range of 'changes from above' and 'from below' were in progress. This collection of letters may also be seen as marking an early stage in the normative formation of a letter-writing tradition. As such, the value of these epistolary documents is twofold: on the one hand, they show the evolution of the incipient standard language, and, on the other, they provide us with an idea of the vernacular reality present in both their writers and the period. They are also a useful locus to test and sometimes qualify the concepts that First Wave sociolinguists have developed in connection with contemporary changes in progress, such as the distinction between 'generational' and 'communal' changes. Additionally, Third Wave sociolinguistic approaches can also help us account for the social meaning of these patterns of variability and change from a 'language history from below' qualitative – rather than quantitative – perspective, and the grouping of historically attested changes into some of these patterns offers an interesting ground to test this proposal. As such, this study demonstrates that the traditional quantitatively based conceptualisations are not sufficient to account for all the linguistic choices. More recent conceptualisations of variation as creative and strategic, focusing on performativity, and as essential to identity projection and creation and the furthering of one's specific situational goals, can also be used to explain people's linguistic choices.

CHAPTER 3

Private letters as a source for an alternative history of Middle New High German

Stephan Elspaß

1. Alternative language histories

In the introduction to their book *Alternative Histories of English*, editors Watts and Trudgill ponder about the following idea: What if we were 'historical linguists of the "English" language in the year 2525 looking back at the year 2000'? They continue as follows:

> It is likely that what we would see would be a richness in terms of dialects . . . on a par with the richness that Old English and Middle English present to us now, and possibly more so. Unfortunately, however, histories of English as they are typically written most often ignore this richness. (Watts and Trudgill 2002: 1)

The general approach of the book is very different from traditional language historiography. The blurb on the back cover reads:

> Most histories of English in use at undergraduate and graduate levels in universities tell the same story. Many of these books are sociolinguistically inadequate, anglocentric and focus on standard English. This leads to a tunnel vision version of the history of the standard dialect after the Middle English period. (Watts and Trudgill 2002: back cover)

Like Watts, Trudgill and also Milroy (1992), who have started to call traditional views of language historiography into question and have presented different perspectives on the history of English, I am interested in an alternative approach to historical linguistics and language historiography. In this chapter, I will present a view of the history of Middle New High German (*c.* 1650 to *c.* 1950, see Elspaß 2008) which differs considerably from common textbook knowledge of German historical linguistics and particularly disagrees with its presentation of the standardisation history of German. In Elspaß (2005) I proposed and elaborated on a German language history from below, based on an analysis of nineteenth-century German letters. The theoretical framework of a 'language history from below' (which goes beyond Labov's notion of a 'language change from below', see Section 2) follows other grassroots histories which have been developed in the last forty years or so – military, religious, political and other histories 'from below'. In the second section of the chapter, I will briefly outline this concept and attempt to answer the question as to why it took linguists so long to come up with an alternative language historiography and something equivalent to a 'history from below'. In Sections 3 and 4, I will present aspects and features of a nineteenth-century German language history from below and its implications for an alternative view of standard languages and the history of standardisation.

2. What is a 'language history from below', and why did this concept emerge so late?

Traditional histories of modern standard languages – not only German – have primarily concentrated on unification and standardisation processes. Their approach was deeply rooted in nineteenth- and early twentieth-century nation-state ideologies and politics. In effect, authors of language histories collaborated with politicians, historians and writers in constructing images of unified nations with autonomous cultural traditions that were sometimes projected backwards to the Middle Ages and beyond. Language and literature were considered crucial factors in the creation of national unity, particularly when there was no political unity (see Durrell 2000). Jacob Grimm's rhetorical question in the foreword of the colossal German Dictionary encapsulates this widespread view among nineteenth-century intellectuals: 'Was haben wir denn gemeinsames als unsere Sprache und Literatur?' ('What else do we have that does unite us – apart from our language and literature?') (Grimm and Grimm 1854: III).

Thus, for a long time, language history was presented as the one long road toward a uniform standard language, marked by certain milestones, and only prominent figures (like Martin Luther for Germany) and only carefully selected texts written by elite writers qualified as such milestones. From the nineteenth to the end of the twentieth century, textbooks on national language histories of the modern period were dominated by this teleological view. Generations of scholars and teachers have used such textbooks and thus joined the march on this imaginative road to standard languages. As such, language history was largely reduced to the study of the language employed by only a tiny minority of the population, concentrating on printed language and portraying 'classical' authors (like Schiller, Goethe or Thomas Mann in Germany) as role models for language norms and style. 'Non-standard' variation – let alone hand-written language use from the *non-elite* – was usually regarded as 'bad language' (see Davies and Langer 2006) and not considered as suitable data for linguistic research. In an act of what James Milroy identified as 'sanitary purism' in the historiography of English (Milroy 2005: 324–6), such data were simply ignored in textbooks. The inevitable consequence of these practices are *incomplete* language histories full of *witte vlekken* 'blank areas', as van der Wal (2006) put it. If we were to characterise this long philological era, we might aptly call it the 'language historiography in a view from *above*'.

An alternative or rather radically different approach to the history of language which I termed a 'language history from *below*' was inspired by several questions that were not addressed – usually not even raised – in traditional language historiography, such as:

- Who counts as a speaker/writer in language historiography?
- Which texts are used in language historiography?

Such questions led to further issues:

- Which speakers/writers have been neglected so far?
- Which texts have been neglected or even ignored so far?
- What would our language histories look like if we took such speakers/writers and such texts seriously and complemented our textbooks with chapters on the language use of lower and lower middle classes and/or on letter writing?

And finally:

- What would textbooks look like if we took, say, informal texts by members of the majority of the population as a starting point of the (hi)story of modern languages?
- What would historical grammars look like if we considered the grammatical forms used in such texts as unmarked default forms and grammatical forms in printed texts as marked forms? Would, say, the grammar of Standard German look a bit more like the grammar of Yiddish today, if the standardisation process had started later (see Timm 1986)?

The 'language history from below' approach has been encouraged by the adoption and adaptation of pragmatic and sociolinguistic theory to the study of historical linguistics in the last thirty years or so. This has not only led to different methodological approaches, but also to a search for text sources beyond the textbook canon. Scholars working within the framework of historical sociolinguistics and/or historical pragmatics started to unearth a wealth of documents belonging to various text types, particularly to so-called 'ego-documents', such as private letters, chronicles and personal diaries written by farmers, soldiers, artisans or housemaids (see Elspaß 2012a). The next important step forward to obtain a wider picture of language history was to recognise such documents as historical text sources in their own right. Until the 1970s, such sources had remained virtually unnoticed by the linguistic profession (with a few notable exceptions, e.g. Spitzer 1921).[1]

In a 'view from below', texts such as letters or diaries often constitute the only authentic trace of people who have not yet formed part of our cultural memory. Up until the nineteenth century, people from this strand of society were a 'silent majority', insofar as even if they were not able to read and write, their texts constituted only a minority of texts that were actually written. With the mass literacy drives of the nineteenth century and mass migration, however, this situation changed rapidly. Members of the lower and lower middle classes produced a volume of letters, diaries and other handwritten texts which is unprecedented in the history of writing (see Section 3 for the case of German). Such ego-documents provide not only a 'worm's eye view' on everyday life, but also give a valuable insight into

---

[1] It is noteworthy that earlier scholars like Wyld (1920: 361) and Rydén (1979: 23) have also advocated the use of such material in their works.

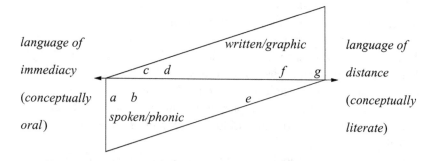

Exemplary text types: a = private talk (face to face), b = private talk (telephone), c = informal
chatroom talk, d = private letter, e = academic talk (monologue), f = academic paper, g =
legislative text

Figure 3.1 The model of 'language of immediacy vs. language of distance' following Koch and
Oesterreicher (1985: 18, 23; 1994: 588)

variants and varieties of the written language of their time – and these language
users are sometimes at the very centre of linguistic change.

However, a language history from below not only aims at a long overdue emancipation of roughly more than 95% of the population in language historiography,
more importantly, the concept of 'from below' also pleads for a different starting
point in the description and explanation of language history. In linguistic terms, the
shift of perspectives to texts from the private domain and to handwritten material
demands an acknowledgement of informal language registers which is fundamental
to human interaction. Prototypically, such registers are represented by speech in oral
face-to-face-interaction. For the time before the introduction of audio-recording
technology at the end of the nineteenth century, language historians do not have
data from spoken language at their disposal. But this does not mean that an analysis
of conceptually oral language in history is impossible. To explain the notion of
'conceptual orality', I refer to Koch and Oesterreicher's (1985, 1994) model of the
'language of immediacy vs. language of distance' (*Nähesprache vs. Distanzsprache*,
cf. Figure 3.1).

In this model, Koch and Oesterreicher have clarified the crucial difference
between the medium (spoken and written language) and the 'mode' or linguistic conception (conceptually oral and conceptually literate language) of texts and
discourses. In contrast to the clear dichotomy between the 'written' and the 'spoken' medium, the linguistic conception of a text can be established only relative to prototypical texts of 'immediacy' and prototypical texts of 'distance'. In
fact, Koch and Oesterreicher's model tries to overcome the linguistically naïve
distinction between spoken and written language by placing a given text of a
particular text type on a continuum between oral and literate, according to a specific combination of communicative parameters, such as the degree of familiarity

Prototypical communicative parameters of "language of immediacy"	Prototypical communicative parameters of "language of distance"
• dialogue • familiarity of the partners • face-to-face interaction • free development of topics • private setting • spontaneity • involvement • maximum cooperation of partners • subjectivity • …	• monologue • unfamiliarity of the partners • space–time separation • fixed topics • public setting • reflection • detachment • minimum cooperation of partners • objectivity • …

Figure 3.2 Prototypical communicative parameters of 'language of immediacy' and 'language of distance' according to Koch and Oesterreicher (1985: 23) and Oesterreicher (1997: 194)

and cooperation of the communication partners, the fixedness of topics, etc. (see Figure 3.2).

For text types in the written medium (see the upper triangle in Figure 3.1), which language historians usually deal with, let us consider two extremes. Texts of what can be termed 'written orality' such as personal letters (exemplary text type d in Figure 3.1) are not only functionally, but also linguistically similar to the grammar of a spoken dialogue in a 'language of immediacy' setting, whereas a literate text such as the one that you are reading right now (exemplary text type f in Figure 3.1) is prototypical of the 'language of distance'.

The attempt to approach the language of immediacy in language history through the written medium is impeded by the fact that there are no texts which would represent the prototypical language of immediacy (or prototypically 'oral' texts) in history. In pre-twentieth-century Germany and most other Western European countries, the normal everyday language – which, as argued above, constitutes the basis of human interaction – was a local dialect. Hardly anybody, however, wrote a letter in a local dialect, because if people had learnt to read and write, they would use a 'schooled' variety in writing. Nonetheless, private letters represent dialogic and informal private communication between partners who are familiar with each other. Thus, not only in terms of corpus size and regional as well as social distribution, but also their degree of 'immediacy', private letters (and emigrant letters, in particular) are probably the most suitable texts for a language history from below approach and form an ideal testing ground for the study of language variation and change in historical linguistics – considering that such texts should be 'as close to speech, and especially vernacular style as possible … stem from several authors from different social classes, possibly also age groups, and both sexes, and … represent varying stylistic levels … display variability … [and] provide reasonably large token frequencies of individual variants' (see Schneider 2002: 71). Moreover, a historical grammar of the (Early) Modern period 'from below', i.e. from the beginning of standardisation efforts, would most certainly not start from the language of print, but from the language represented in such private letters, be they written by paupers or by members of the nobility.[2]

As noted above, the 'language history from below' approach has to be distinguished from Labov's concept of 'language change from below' which primarily refers to changes 'below the level of social awareness' (Labov 1994: 78; see also Watts, Chapter 1, this volume, and Hernández-Campoy and Conde-Silvestre, Chapter 2, this volume). With respect to progressive norms of usage such as those illustrated in Section 4.3 below, however, a connection between both concepts can be easily drawn. Labov's assertion that language change from below 'may be introduced by any social class, although no cases have been recorded in which the highest-status social group acts as the innovating group' (*ibid.*) supports our emphasis on considering the 'voice' of lower-status groups, and his notion of changes from below as 'systematic changes that appear first in the vernacular' (*ibid.*) encourages our focus on the language of immediacy in a language history from below.

3. A nineteenth-century 'language history from below' of German

In my research on 'language history from below' in nineteenth-century German, I focused on texts from conceptually oral written language, viz. private letters. In the German-speaking countries of that time, even people from the lowest ranks of society learnt to read and write. In their everyday life at home in some German, Austrian or Swiss village, town or city, such people rarely had any reason or opportunity to write. Migration, however, constituted one of the few occasions when letter writing became a necessity as it facilitated the continuation of personal communication after a disruption of face-to-face interaction. In the context of mass emigration in the long nineteenth century, up to 100 million private letters were sent from German immigrants to the United States (Helbich, Kamphoefner and Sommer 1988: 31–2). From an overall corpus of some 9,000 to 10,000 letters of emigrant correspondence which are accessible in public archives, I analysed 648 letters by writers from all German-speaking countries and regions with a total of 700,000 words (or rather graphic units). Sixty of the 648 letters were written by 25 people (mostly men) with secondary or higher education, and 588 letters by 248 writers – men and women – with primary education only. Most letters were written by people who were in the process of emigrating or who had just emigrated (mainly to the US). Several letters were written by relatives or friends of the emigrants at home. To my knowledge, this is the largest and most representative corpus of nineteenth-century informal writing in German which has been analysed linguistically so far.

One aim of my corpus study was the *reconstruction of grammatical norms of usage in nineteenth-century lower-class writing*. I tried to demonstrate that the analysis of

---

[2] To take texts from an ego-document displaying a certain degree of 'language of immediacy' as a starting-point is exactly what Ágel and Hennig (2006) have in mind for their project on a new historical grammar of New High German.

such texts can not only supply missing evidence in the study of grammatical change, but also contribute significantly to explanations of language change. Out of thirty-two grammatical phenomena which were analysed (see Elspaß 2005: 196–374), I will only give a selection of nine examples of norms of usage, i.e. variants which were not accepted in nineteenth-century prescriptive grammars. From the grammarians' point of view, these variants were considered 'bad language' in nineteenth-century literate language. They can be divided into three groups:

- variants representing older, i.e. seventeenth and eighteenth-century norms of usage of written literate German;
- variants which used to be acceptable in seventeenth- and eighteenth-century German written (even printed) 'language of distance' but have been stigmatised and become 'non-standard' features in German;
- variants which are widespread (and as such standard norms of usage) in colloquial German, but considered 'non-standard' in the nineteenth century as well as today.

4. Grammatical standards of nineteenth-century German

4.1 Old norms of usage of written literate German

I will start with a group of variants which were commonly used in seventeenth- and eighteenth-century written and printed language, but were considered outdated and no longer acceptable in nineteenth-century literate German. They are noteworthy as they are clearly features of a 'language of distance' adopted in texts representing a 'language of immediacy'.

4.1.1 Non-finite subordinate clauses

(1) *daß ihr in Angst und Sorgen sind wegen mir, weil   ihr   so   lange   keinen*
                                                       . . . because you so-long   no

   Brief bekommen
   letter *got [have]*
   'that you must be afraid and worried because of me, because you haven't
   had a letter from me for such a long time'

        (Anna Maria Schano from Korb-Steinrainach, Swabia, letter from 18 March 1849)

A particular type of non-finite clause in German is characterised by the omission of the auxiliary verbs *have* or *be* in subordinate clauses with the perfect predicate. These constructions were very prominent in seventeenth- and early eighteenth-century chancery style. Eighteenth-century prescriptive grammarians like Johann Christoph Gottsched (1700–1766) branded the use of such clauses as a 'bad habit' (*Unart*), which did not stop him employing them in his own writings (see Härd

1981: 127). Härd (*ibid.*) suspected that the subsequent decline of such non-finite subordinate clauses was not primarily due to the influence of the grammarians and their judgements, but due to the ongoing consolidation of the verbal frame construction in German, which requires a finite verb at the end of the subordinate clause. In spite of (or rather in ignorance of) the verdicts of nineteenth-century grammarians, writers (even people with elementary school education) continued to use the non-finite clause constructions in nineteenth- and early twentieth-century literary and epistolary style (von Polenz 1999: 351). In the letter corpus it is noticeable, however, that the use of such clauses was limited to formulaic language at the beginning or at the end of the letter. Formulaic language tends to preserve conservative grammatical constructions (see Elspaß 2012b).

4.1.2 -gen-*diminutives*

(2)   *es sind hier in der Willischtz das heißt klein* Städtgen *oder Dorf es sind hier auf 250 Personnen Deutsche . . . was macht mein Petters Georg u. seyn* Christingen *hat er eine Stelle und sein Sie verheirathet*

      in this 'Willischtz' which means '*little town*-{DIM}' or village, there are about 250 German people . . . what's happened to my (friend) Georg Peters and his *Christine*-{DIM}, does he have a job, and are they married?

                                                       (Martin Weitz from Schotten, Hessia, letter from 29 July 1855)

Eighteenth-century written German saw three competing variants of the diminutive form, *-gen*, *-chen* and *-lein*. In the spoken German dialects, several other variants were in use, such as *-l*, *-le*, *-la*, *-li*, *-el*, *-ken*, *-ke*, *-che*, *-cher*. In the first half of the eighteenth century, the old West Central German diminutive form *-gen*, which was in fact pronounced like the form *-chen* (Wegera 2000: 46), spread out, in writing, over other German regions. It eventually became the leading variant south of the Benrath line. It was not until the second half of the eighteenth century that it gave way to the *-chen* diminutive, which has remained dominant until today. The diminutive variant *-lein* always played only a minor role and was/is mostly employed for euphonic reasons, particularly after <g> and <ch> (e.g. *Bächlein* 'little creek'). Even eminent authors from the West Central German dialect areas, however, like the young Goethe (1749–1832), continued to use *-gen* in their writings until Johann Christoph Adelung (1732–1806) in his *Deutsche Sprachlehre* (1781), which is considered to have been the leading German school grammar until the mid-nineteenth century, prescribed '*chen* (not *gen*)' (1781: 102). The *-chen* diminutive is clearly the dominant variant in the nineteenth-century letter corpus. Apart from the odd use of *-lein* and some dialect forms like *-le*, *-li*, *-l* and *-el* in letters from Swabian, Swiss, Austrian and Silesian writers, the use of *-gen* by fourteen writers from the West German region is most noteworthy. An interference of spoken dialect can be ruled out. Most probably, the writers in the West employed a variant that had 'officially' disappeared by the end of the eighteenth century. The fact that some grammarians at the beginning of the nineteenth century took the trouble to label the *-gen* variant as incorrect is a reliable indicator that it was still in use. From the regional distribution in the West, it can be concluded that it still had the status of a norm of written usage there. It seems to have been passed on to new generations of writers who considered it as 'correct'.

4.1.3 *First and third person singular -e in strong verbs*

(3)   *ich habe mich sehr Gefreut, da ich Löcke* Sahe
        I was very happy when I *saw*-{e} Löcke.

(Christine Elderinck, from Schüttorf, Westphalia, letter from 10 January 1870)

Another feature of Early Modern 'literate' German is the use of an *-e*-morpheme in the first and third person singular preterite of 'strong' irregular verbs, which would otherwise have no ending at all, e.g. *ich sah* 'I saw'. It was probably developed analogous to the *-e*-preterite of regular verbs, e.g. *ich baut-e* 'I built', and was still very common in eighteenth-century texts. When textbook authors decided that these forms had disappeared at the end of the eighteenth century, they probably looked at the printed works of classical authors like Goethe. In his early works, Goethe used such forms and only allowed a 'correction' in the 1786/87 revision of his works, in accordance with the prescriptive norms of Adelung's grammars (Habermann 1997: 462). Gottsched and Adelung had rejected the use of this *-e*-variant, arguing that it would obscure a clear distinction between the preterite and the imperfective subjunctive, while Southern German grammarians denied that this would cause a problem to readers and thus still regarded it as correct (von Polenz 1994: 261). According to Paul (1917: 198–9), the *-e*-preterite in 'strong' verbs occurred only in isolated instances in early nineteenth-century texts. In my private letters, however, writers kept using it until the end of the nineteenth century. It is noteworthy again that a feature representing an old norm of usage in literate written German surfaces in passages which are characterised by formal (and formulaic) writing, as in Example 3. Another indicator of the formal style of this phrase is the use of the temporal-causal conjunction *da*.

4.2 *Former norms of usage in written (and spoken) German – 'non-standard' in nineteenth-century and present-day German*

Secondly, I will present three examples of old norms of written and spoken usage, which have undergone increasing stigmatisation and are considered non-standard features in nineteenth-century and present-day German.

4.2.1 Past participle without the ge-prefix

(4)

wen ich das gewußt häte häte ich eich den Acker nicht geben ['gegeben'] *jezt hatt*
                        . . . had I   you the field   not   {Ø-}*given*   now has
sich   der Arme Franz so fiel   blagt ['geplagt'] *damit. . .*
{REFL PRO} the poor Franz so much {Ø-}*slogged*   with it . . .
'If I had only known, I wouldn't have given the field to you. Poor Franz has had so much work with it . . . '

                                    (Theresia Mandl from Burgenland, letter from 06 February 1923)

The *ge*-prefix as a marker of past particle forms (also still productive in Old English) became a compulsory conjugation morpheme in written German no earlier than the eighteenth century (von Polenz 1994: 261). It appears both with irregular verbs, like *geben* 'to give', and regular verbs, e.g. *plagen* 'to work hard, to slog'. Only the auxiliary verb *werden* in passive constructions (e.g *ich bin bestohlen worden* 'I was robbed'), prefix-verbs (e.g. *bestehlen* 'rob' – *ich habe bestohlen* 'I have robbed') and verbs ending in *-ieren* in German do not take a *ge*-prefix. Up to the late eighteenth century, participles without the *ge*-prefix of frequently used verbs like *kommen* 'come', *finden* 'find', *gehen* 'go', *essen* 'eat', *bringen* 'bring' appear even in printed texts. Hoffmann (1988: 179) has shown that until the mid-eighteenth century, grammarians merely proposed using the *ge*-prefix uniformly for indigenous verbs. Adelung (1781: 274), however, labelled forms without *ge*-prefix as *pöbelhaft* and *widerwärtig* ('vulgar' and 'disgusting'). In line with Adelung's view, nineteenth-century grammars treated these forms as incorrect. In nineteenth-century letters, writers from the North of Germany and writers from the South, including Austria (cf. Example 4), use forms without the *ge*-prefix quite frequently (and more often than writers from central German dialect areas). Forms without a prefix in the North can be directly attributed to interference from West Low German dialects which do not have past participle prefixes at all. Writers from Upper German dialect areas, however, dropped the *ge*-prefix only in the group of frequently used verbs mentioned above. It appears that people in the North abandoned participles without *ge*-prefix altogether because the colloquial language in the North gradually moved closer to the standard, and non-prefix forms were increasingly regarded as 'dialect markers'. In the South of Germany and in Austria, however, where there is no such clear-cut division between standard varieties, regiolects and dialects, these forms are perfectly acceptable in colloquial German today (see Eichhoff 2000: 4–74: map *(ge-)kauft* 'bought').

4.2.2 Double negation

(5) es sind nur Euchen   und Pabele   kein *Fichten oder Dannen Baum*
     it are only oak+{PL} and poplar+{PL} *no*   spruce or   pine   tree

     ist hier nicht
     is here *not*
     'There are only oak trees and poplars. No spruce or pine tree is/can be
     found here.'

(Matthias Gamsjäger from Goisern, Upper Austria, letter from 9 December 1896)

Double negation is stigmatised in many Germanic languages today and considered
as non-standard (see Cheshire 1998 for English). In early German grammars, double
negation was presented as a 'legitimate, sometimes even positive . . . rule of German'
(Langer 2001: 167). The stigmatisation of poly-negation as a typical feature of
lower-class language started in the second half of the eighteenth century (Davies
and Langer 2006: 258–9). Grammarians such as Schötensack (1856: 557) claimed
that New High German had adopted the 'law' from Latin grammar that a double
negative makes a positive, i.e. an affirmative statement. According to textbook
knowledge (e.g. Admoni 1990: 187), double negation had virtually disappeared
from written German by the beginning of the eighteenth century. This is already
refuted by evidence from Schiller, Goethe and some nineteenth-century writers who
employed double negatives repeatedly in their works to create particular stylistic
nuances (see Paul 1920: 334). Out of 248 writers in my emigrant letter corpus
who had received primary education, only 32 (12.9%) could be identified as using
double negatives in their letters. Twenty-eight of them grew up in Central or Upper
German dialect regions. It can be concluded, then, that double negation had not
disappeared from written German and that it had basically become a regional
variant in Southern German – which it still is in this area in colloquial German (see
www.atlas-alltagssprache.de/runde_3/f07f_f08a/, 29 January 2012).

4.2.3 tun-*construction*

(6) sie brauchten den Doctor der that   *mehrere Tage 2 mal den Tag*
     they needed the doctor; he *do*+[PRET SG] several days twice the day

     ihn besuchen
     him *visit* [INF]
     'they needed a doctor; he came to see him twice a day for several days'

(Bernd Farwick from Neerlage, Westphalia, letter from March 1867)

(7) jezt tun   *wir* Treschen *aber ganz anders wie dort*
     now *do*+[PRES PL] we *thresh* [INF] . . . '
     'Now we are threshing the grain, but we do it in a different manner
     than there'

(Josef Schabl, from Burgenland, letter from 13 August 1922)

In German, as in English, the verb *tun* 'do' can be employed as a full lexical verb as well as an auxiliary. Phrases with auxiliary *tun*, which can mark habitual (6) or progressive aspect (7), are usually considered as non-standard German. Such *tun*-constructions gradually disappeared from written German in the seventeenth and eighteenth centuries due to an almost systematic stigmatisation of the construction by grammarians of that time (see Langer 2001). Gottsched called it 'old-fashioned' and 'ridiculous' (*altväterlich, lächerlich*) and ascribed it to the lower classes (Langer 2001: 206). In his authoritative *Language History of German*, von Polenz (1994: 263) writes that constructions with auxiliary *tun* had disappeared by the end of the eighteenth century, except for some vernacular texts from the Upper German region. In the letter corpus, however, more than 28.2% (70 out of 248) of letter writers with primary education from all over the German-speaking countries used auxiliary *tun* at least once in their letters (Elspaß 2005: 258–9). Again, as with past participles without the *ge*-prefix and double negation, this feature, which is mostly considered non-standard today, is widely used in colloquial standard German, particularly in the South (von Polenz 1994: 263; Schwitalla 2006: 127–8; www.atlas-alltagssprache.de/runde_3/f08b-c/ 29 January 2012), and auxiliary *tun* is clearly accepted in colloquial standard German.

4.3 Norms of usage in colloquial German – 'non-standard' in nineteenth-century and present-day German

The final group consists of grammatical variants which clearly constitute norms of usage in colloquial German in the nineteenth century as well as today, although some of them have gradually emerged in standard German contexts in the last few decades. In general, however, they have been declared 'incorrect' and thus 'non-standard' in the prescriptive grammaticography of the last two hundred years.

4.3.1 Particles wie *and* als wie *after the comparative*

(8)

Es ist beteudtend besser als wie   *in Deutschland. Aber man muß auch*
         . . . better [COMP PART {als wie}] in Germany

    strenger Arbeiten   als wie
. . . stronger work [COMP PART {als wie}]

in Deutschland . . . Und ist auch mit unsern Geschäft
in Germany

    nicht   so   *gut*   als   *hier*
. . . not [EQUAT PART {so}] good [EQUAT PART {als}] here . . .
'It is considerably better than in Germany. But you also have to work harder than in Germany . . . And our business is not as good as here'

(Christoph Barthel from Kirchhagen, Hessia, letter from 15 August 1847)

Table 3.1 *Use of comparison particles after the comparative*

Writers with	*denn*		*als*		*wie*		*als wie*	
Secondary education	0	0.0%	39	90.7%	4	9.3%	0	0.0%
Primary education	4	0.7%	347	59.6%	182	31.3%	49	8.4%

In the prescriptive tradition of grammar writing in German, the use of *wie* or *als wie* instead of *als* after the comparative is frequently marked as non-standard. Since the publication of Adelung's grammar (1781: 479), the prescriptivists' rule is as follows: to mark difference, an adjective in the comparative form plus the particle *als* 'than' is to be used (in formal language also *denn*), to mark agreement, the adjective is in the positive form, preceded by *so* and followed by the particle *wie* 'as . . . as' (in formal language also *so . . . als*). The grammarians of the nineteenth century aimed at a clear iconic distribution, i.e. one conjunction was to stand for one grammatical form, thus *als* after comparative and *wie* as the standard unmarked form after positive (although *als* was permitted in certain stylistic contexts). In nineteenth-century letters, only educated and experienced writers complied with this norm, whereas in nearly 40% of the instances in which writers with primary education use a particle after a comparative, the 'incorrect' forms *wie* and *als wie* appeared (Table 3.1).

The use of *wie* and, to a less widespread extent, *als wie* after the comparative is a well-known characteristic of colloquial German today (see www.atlas-alltagssprache.de/runde_0/karten/groesser-als-wie-als_wie.jpg, 29 January 2012). From a functional point of view, a clear distinction between *als* and *wie* is redundant, because the positive is already marked by *so* preceding the adjective, e.g. *so stark wie* (like *as strong as* in English), and the comparative by the suffix *-er*, e.g. *stärk-er wie/als* (like *strong-er than*). Thus, some researchers consider the use of *wie* as the future default particle to mark agreement (after positive) or difference (after comparative) with adjectives (e.g. Thurmair 2001: 97).

4.3.2 wegen *and other prepositions with the dative (or accusative)*

(9) *ich bin* wegen dem Geld *nicht Soldat geworden*
    'I haven't become a soldier *because of* the money-[DAT]'

(Carl Niedenhofen from Siegburg, Rhineland, letter from 28 September 1862)

From a prescriptive perspective, 'old' prepositions, like *dank* 'thanks to', *statt/anstatt* 'instead of', *trotz* 'in spite of', *während* 'during', *wegen* 'because of' and 'new' prepositions, like *hinsichtlich* 'with regard to', *jenseits* 'on the other side of', *oberhalb* 'above', *ungeachtet* 'despite', are to be used with the genitive case. In nineteenth-century letters, the 230 contexts in which such prepositions were used render only 104 instances in which the grammatical case can be clearly identified. Again, educated and experienced writers predominantly comply with the school

Table 3.2 *Use of grammatical case after 'prepositions governing the genitive'*

Writers with		Genitive		Dative or accusative	Case not clear or preposition followed by *von*
Secondary education	13	81.3%	3	18.7%	(28)
Primary education	14	16.1%	74	83.9%	(98)

grammar norms, whereas semi-educated writers use the 'incorrect' dative or even the accusative in 83.9% of all documented instances (Table 3.2).

The most prominent and most frequently used preposition with the genitive is *wegen*. In the nineteenth-century letters, it accounts for more than two thirds (71 = 68.3%) of all instances. In 60 out of 64 instances in which the grammatical case after *wegen* can be identified, writers with primary education use the 'non-genitive' case (see Elspaß 2005: 322–3 for details). *Wegen* is a particularly blatant example of the discrepancy between a prescriptive standard and the standard of usage. From Adelung (1781: 349) to the modern Duden (2007: 985), grammars have insisted on the use of the genitive case after *wegen*, although the widespread use of the dative is well known (*ibid.*; cf. www.atlas-alltagssprache.de/runde_o/karten/karten/wegen_des-dem.jpg, 29 January 2012).

4.3.3 *Modal* nicht brauchen *without* zu

(10) *das Geld* brauch *ich* nicht *auf einmahl* zahlen
the money *need* [PRES SG] I *not* at once *pay* [INF]
'I don't have to pay back the money at once.'

(Fritz Koy from Kadlub, Silesia, letter from 10 March 1853)

The verb *brauchen* with the negation particle *nicht* and a full verb in the infinitive has two variants in German, one with the infinitive particle *zu*, and the other without *zu*. Generations of school children had to learn the mnemonic phrase 'Wer *brauchen* ohne *zu* gebraucht, braucht *brauchen* gar nicht zu gebrauchen' ('If you use the verb *brauchen* without *zu*, you shouldn't use *brauchen* at all'). The prescriptive norm in the school grammar standard is that the verb *nicht brauchen* 'not need to' is to be used with the infinitive particle *zu*. As with all mnemonic phrases which try to

Table 3.3 *Use of* nicht brauchen *with or without particle* zu *and the infinitive*

Writers with	*nicht brauchen* + V without *zu*		*nicht brauchen* + V with *zu*	
Secondary education	1	16.7%	5	83.3%
Primary education	24	24.2%	75	75.8%

pronounce a ban on particular grammatical features, they reflect the fact that these variants are in frequent use. In this particular case, first instances of *nicht brauchen* without *zu* have been found in early nineteenth-century texts (von Polenz 1999: 351). Modern grammars see a progressive grammaticalisation of *nicht brauchen*, some consider it already as a modal verb, which would explain the loss of the infinitive particle *zu* and also the increasing loss of the *-t*-suffix in the third person singular (see Eisenberg 2004: 464). In the nineteenth-century letter corpus, in almost a quarter of the relevant instances (25 of 105), writers use *nicht brauchen* without *zu*, writers with primary education in almost a quarter of all instances. Whereas the grammaticalisation process of *nicht brauchen* in present-day German seems to be most advanced in the South of Germany and Austria (see www.atlas-alltagssprache. de/runde_7/f06a/, 29 January 2012), the twenty-five instances of *nicht brauchen* without *zu* can be attributed to writers from both the North and the South.

4. Conclusions

The data from the nineteenth-century corpus of emigrants' private letters anal-ysed in this chapter throw light on an alternative history of New High German which is very different from the picture that traditional language historiography has presented. From a nineteenth-century prescriptive point of view, the forms presented and investigated here were seen as outdated, incorrect, ungrammatical, not acceptable – in short, 'bad language'. Moreover, in a nineteenth-century lan-guage historiography 'from above', they are non-existent. From a purely descriptive perspective, however, they clearly constituted norms of usage, in one case (*wegen* with dative instead of genitive) even the clearly dominant variant in private letters written by people with only primary school education. Moreover, if we take the viewpoint of such writers, the language which they used in their letters was what they were able to use in the written medium after some years of primary schooling. They certainly cared for linguistic adequateness, particularly in their use of formu-laic language, and they had a certain self-perception of the stylistic limitations and the calligraphic quality of their own writing (see examples (11) and (12)):

(11)　*Ich habe mich in der Eile oft schlecht ausgedrück und schlecht geschreiben; aber ich denke das macht unter Brüder nichts aus.*
　　　'In my hurry I have not expressed myself well and have written badly, but I think that does not matter between brothers.'

　　　　　　　(Johannes Hambloch from Littfeld, Siegerland, letter from 02 December 1853)

(12)　*Muß mein schlechtes Schreiben entschuldigen, die Kinder stoßen einem so oft an.*
　　　'[You] Must excuse my bad writing. The children keep bumping me.'

　　　　　　　(Pauline Greving from Holthausen, Westphalia, letter from 30 December 1888)

There is, however, no clear indication in the letter corpus as to whether the writers considered the words and forms they used as grammatically 'wrong'. It may be the wrong question to ask what they considered as 'correct' or not, because it is doubtful that grammatical correctness was an issue that mattered outside grammar school and grammar book contexts very much. Writers with primary education had not attended grammar schools, and it is very unlikely that they used grammar books. We even have evidence that they used exactly the grammatical forms that they had learned in primary school, see Examples (13) and (14) from private texts of writers who are known to have worked as primary school teachers:

(13)
Das hier auf der Nebenseite . . . ist das letzte so er diesem Büchelgen *einverleibt hat.*
                                                    book-[DIM]
Er ware   *seit anfangs July kräncklich . . . Das Brod, welches im Herbst* wegen dem
    was-{e}   because of the
bevorstehenden Kriege   *nicht wohlfeil war fängt im Januar 1833 an abzuschlagen.*
impending war [DAT-{e}]
'This here on the left side . . . is the last (thing) he has incorporated in this book. He had been ill since the beginning of July . . . Bread, which was dear last autumn because of the impending war, has become cheaper since January 1833.'

(Johannes Huppertz, farmer, sexton and primary school teacher from Konzen, Eifel region,
diary entrance from 21 December 1807 and from 5 January 1833)

(14)   *. . . daß doch des Vaters Auge weiter   sieth, gewöhnlich,*
                                        further sees
    als wie   *das des*
    [COMP PART {als wie}] that of the
    Sohnes . . . er würde vielleicht beßer ausmachen denn
    son   better fare   [COMP PART {denn}]
    ich . . . er wird ein
    I

    guter americaner abgeben, beßer wie *ich . . .*
    ' . . . that a father's eye sees further than that of the son . . . he would maybe fare better than me . . . he will be a good American, better than me . . . '

(Friedrich Martens, farmer, painter and schoolteacher from
Delve, Dithmarschen, letter from 18 April 1858)

We have no reason to doubt that these two teachers taught norms of usage in school which they thought to be adequate in their own writing, notwithstanding the fact that some of the variants they used were unacceptable from a school grammarian's point of view because they were considered 'outdated' (*-gen* diminutive, third person singular *-e* in the strong verb, see Example (13)) or 'colloquial non-standard' (*wegen* + dative in Example (13), *wie* and *als wie* after the comparative in Example (14)).

There are two conclusions to draw from the analysis of letters and other ego-documents in this chapter. Firstly, these written texts and their non-random display of variation cast doubt on the traditional historiographies' presentation of a more or less diglossic language situation in nineteenth-century German, with dialects in the spoken medium and a uniform standard German in the written medium. A more realistic picture is that written as well as spoken German consisted of a wide range of text and discourse types between the two extreme poles 'language of distance' and 'language of immediacy' – and a wide range of what may most aptly be conceptualised as 'varieties in the minds of the writers'. In written German, a small minority of schooled writers made use of what they considered a uniform variety of written German and which they employed in registers conforming to a 'language of distance', particularly in print. This is the variety behind traditional textbooks' presentation of a 'nineteenth-century standard German' as the final stage in the history of German. On the other end of the continuum, constituting 'language of immediacy' in the graphic medium, we find a kind of *Schriftdeutsch* ('written German') or *Hochdeutsch* ('high German') which, from the perspective of even barely schooled writers, was – and still is for many speakers today – different from their 'normal' spoken language (i.e. their everyday dialect), but also fit for use in private correspondence. Using these varieties and these registers, this multitude of writers in effect drew on a wide range of different norms of usage. These varieties and registers were available to the vast majority of people who knew how to read and write in the nineteenth century.

Secondly, the study has demonstrated that historical 'language of immediacy' is not only an excellent, but probably the most adequate starting point for the analysis of the dynamics of language variation and change. In displaying the simultaneous existence of regional and social variants and the overlapping developments of old and new variants, it describes language change more satisfactorily than models which present, say, a clear-cut diachronic sequence of consecutive variants (i.e. 'eighteenth-century German', 'nineteenth-century German'). Moreover, the analysis of historical 'language of immediacy' is actually the only way to trace back and explain *current* language change. When people continue to use grammatical forms in spoken language which have been declared as 'non-standard' (e.g. past participles without the *ge*-prefix, double negation, *tun*-construction), there must be a good reason for that, in particular when it turns out that these forms used to be perfectly acceptable not only in nineteenth-century informal writing, but also in the formal written language of earlier times. There must be an even better reason for the fact that some forms, which were already stigmatised in the early days of the prescriptive tradition (e.g. in school grammars), have spread out to become 'normal' in non-regional spoken German (e.g. *(als) wie* after the comparative, use of 'prepositions governing the genitive' with the dative, *(nicht) brauchen* without *zu*). The analyses have shown, for instance, that contrary to popular belief the use of the preposition *wegen* with the dative (instead of the genitive) is not a symptom of a present-day loss of the genitive in German (or, even in the opinion of many academics, a symptom of the decay of the German language), but that this was already the default case in the nineteenth century. Moreover, this result is perfectly in line with the observation that the genitive basically died out in spoken 'language of immediacy' (in this case: the dialects) at the beginning of the New High German period and that it could only survive in the *Schriftsprache*, i.e. the written 'language of distance' (Behaghel 1900: 219).

The cases of the genitive and the comparative particle raise the last and more fundamental issue to be addressed here. In a view 'from below' that I have focused on in this chapter on an alternative history of Middle New High German, it is not the 'loss of the genitive', the 'neglect of the distinction between *als* and *wie*', the 'decline of dative-*e*' that linguists have to explain, but the survival or even revival of such grammatically redundant forms and distinctions in written literate language and their persistence in the prescriptive tradition. Such explanations go far beyond the scope of this chapter, and it appears that they need to be of a sociolinguistic, not of a systemic nature.

CHAPTER 4

Language in print and handwriting

Tony Fairman

1. Introduction

Since about 1450, when Johannes Gutenberg built the first European printing press, European languages have been written in two modes: handwritten manuscripts and printed texts. Until 1867, when the first commercially successful typewriters were sold, all written language – bills, notices, laws, letters, poems, sermons, plays, stories, novels and so on – originated as manuscript. To convert manuscript into print, authors collaborated with editors, readers and printers to ensure that what the author had written by hand conformed with the printworthy variety of the language (English, German, etc.). Of all the manuscripts ever written, few, and, in particular, almost none written by the lower classes have been printed (see appendix for illustrations of lower-class letters).

In my research I focus on the English written by English artisans and the labouring poor from *c.* 1750 to 1835, near the start of the linguistic era commonly called Late Modern English (LME, 1700–2000). Most of those writers were schooled only in 'the mechanical parts of reading and writing' (Hansard 1816: 425), which included copying but not self-expression. Today we call them 'the lower classes', but during that socially more stable period they were called 'the lower ranks of people' (Smith 1776: I.viii.36[1]). Such schooling continued in the UK until universal schooling was introduced in 1870. Even though there has been some interest in lower-rank manuscript letters and other related documents in recent years (see, for instance, Vandenbussche 2006 for Germany (a research summary), Nordlund 2007 for Finland, Yokoyama 2008 for Russia, Fairman 2008b, 2012 for England, van der Wal *et al.* 2012 for the Netherlands and Dossena and Del Lungo Camiciotti 2012 for other European countries), many linguists still base their research and their claims about language on printed material, most of which has been edited from manuscript material. Therefore, they research the standardised language of the higher ranks only. At this point in time I do not see any agreed methodology/standards with regard to the editing practices of Late Modern English manuscript material, nor an agreed

---

[1] In the reference section at the end of this book, I list the edition of Adam Smith I consulted. There are many editions, each with a different pagination, but the same chapter and section numbers. To enable readers to find the quotation in any edition, I give the section not the page number, as I do for Quintilian (Section 4).

theory that combines manuscript data and printed data. In that vacuum the print-based Standard ideology distorts manuscript data.

In this chapter I shall therefore discuss ideas, categories and methodology which must be agreed on before manuscript data are entered into corpora and/or data collections that are considered representative of the people living in a certain period, i.e. the Late Modern English period in this case. The ultimate aim is that manuscript data should be added comprehensively and without distortion to the printed data that largely make up 'representative' corpora today, to become part of mainstream linguistic research.

The organisation of this chapter is as follows: in Section 2 I sketch the state of affairs with regard to the 'Standard' ideology. Section 3 illustrates how editors and scholars have dealt with handwritten and printed modes over time. Section 4 discusses literacy, schooling and related factors during the Late Modern English period, as factors that are needed in order to contextualise transcribed and digitised data. The concluding section (5) brings my observations together and argues for a sociolinguistic model that combines handwritten and printed literacies.

2. The 'Standard' ideology

Since the 1980s scholars (Lass 1987; Greenbaum 1988; Fairman 1989, 2012; Milroy 2001; Elspaß 2007; Watts 2011) have pointed out that what is understood as a theory of a whole language is, in fact, an ideology (see the *OED* definitions below), because it is based on only a part of the language.

Linguists use the terms 'theory' and 'ideology' with different meanings. For example, Hodge and Kress subsume 'theory' under 'ideology' (1993: 6):

> Ideology is . . . a systematic body of ideas, organised from a particular point of view. Ideology is thus a subsuming category which includes sciences and metaphysics, as well as political ideologies of various kinds, without implying anything about their status and reliability as guides to reality.

For Barton all schemes of ideas are theories (1994: 15–17):

> The main differences between everyday and professional theories are that the latter are often more articulated and explicit; often they aim to be more general, they can be checked in more systematic ways . . .

In this chapter I use 'theory' and 'ideology' as defined in the *OED*:

> THEORY: a hypothesis that has been confirmed or established by observation or experiment and accepted as accounting for known facts.

> IDEOLOGY: a systematic scheme of ideas, usually relating to politics or society, or the conduct of a class or group, regarded as justifying actions, esp. one that is held implicitly or adopted as a whole and maintained regardless of the course of events.

A theory becomes an ideology if attested observation contradicts its hypothesis. For example, Greenbaum (1988: 36) identified an ideology as follows: 'A grammar of present-day English is a grammar of the standard dialect of English, which is implicitly identified with the language as a whole'. But eight years later in *The Oxford English Grammar* (1996), he followed the Standard ideology and explicitly identified the Standard with the language.

James Milroy, too, identified and conformed to the ideology by collocating 'Standard(ize/ization)' almost as often with 'variety/ies' (20 instances) as with 'language(s)' (28 instances, 2001: passim). Elsewhere, the phrase 'Standard language' is also shape-shifted semantically between 'a language with a Standard' and 'a Standard which is the language'.

The ideology of Standardisation includes four facts:
1. Writing is the only source of historical data.
2. Only the Standardised variety is printed.
3. After 'non-standard' varieties were first recorded outside the UK – in the USA, India and Australia, for example – one variety in each country was eventually reclassified as the national Standard.
4. If written language is noticed outside the Standards, it is classified as 'non-Standard'.

The ideology also includes three assumptions:
1. The only mode of writing is print.
2. 'The only legitimate language was written standard English displaying the features of classical syntax and a classical lexicon' (Watts 2011: 214).
3. Language is autonomous.

With regard to autonomy, Lass writes (1980: 120) the following:

> Linguists have . . . normally treated language as if it were an autonomous natural object (or an autonomous formal system): 'language changes' – it is not (necessarily) speakers that change it.

Street, too, argues that literacies and languages are not 'autonomous . . . independent of social context' (1995: 161). But, because Standard ideology includes autonomy, languages are analysed on a single dimension, which is simultaneously the Standard and a standard, as Allen does with 'nineteenth-century vernacular' elsewhere in this volume (Chapter 11). She wants 'to posit a continuum, from a variety close to but recognisably different from the educated standard at one end, to extreme non-standard at the other, from acrolect to basilect' (p. 204).

These facts and assumptions have guided the study of LME since the grammarian Robert Lowth (1710–87). Milroy (2001: 534) wrote that 'the Standard/non-Standard dichotomy is itself driven by an ideology – it depends on the prior acceptance of the ideology of standardization and on the centrality of the standard variety'. He continues later as follows (2001: 547):

> [T]he establishment of the idea of a standard variety, the diffusion of knowledge of this variety, its codification in widely used grammar books and dictionaries, and

its promotion in a wide range of functions – all lead to the devaluing of other varieties.

Elspaß looks at the ideology of Standardisation in historical sociolinguistics as follows (2007: 3):

> Up until the late 20th century, language historians were primarily concerned with unification and standardization processes and fostered what could be called a 'language history from (and of) above'. Variation and other linguistic 'digressions' from a pre-supposed 'standard' have often been shrugged off as 'bad' language . . . and disqualified as invalid or simply 'wrong' data for linguistic research.

Two reasons can be advanced for why linguists persist, 'regardless of the course of events', with an ideology, after its schematic flaw has been pointed out:

1. Linguists look only at print and, therefore, see only 'Standard' German, English, Dutch, etc.
2. Ideological inertia in a theoretical vacuum. No other scheme exists, powerful enough to counteract the Standard ideology.

To read, understand and analyse 'non-Standard' data with an ideology that devalues them and even implies they are not part of the respective languages – that is the problem. Manuscripts produced by all levels of society provide data with which the Standard ideology can be challenged.

3. Dealing with printed and handwritten modes

Handwriting is not so easy to digitise as print, which generations of linguists have studied. And in those cases where printed material was/is based on manuscript data, editors and scholars in various fields, whether history, literature or linguistics, did and do not have an agreed practice for transcribing the material. In this section, I provide four examples of differences between printed text and original manuscript, illustrating Late Modern English as well as present-day practices:

1. Samuel Johnson (1709–84) based his *Dictionary of the English Language* (1755) on printed texts. For him, therefore, '[t]he normative situation is that of the literary man' (Horgan 1994: 1), and he assumed Lords Bolingbroke and Shaftesbury and other men wrote every word printed in their names. But whereas Lord Chester-field's published letters to his son are in an impeccable English of the time when they were printed (Stanhope 1774), the spelling and some other features of his manuscripts (Kent History and Library Centre [Maidstone] [KHLC(M)]: Stan-hope, U1590/C6/1) conform with practices common in the period during which he wrote them, 1739–1753. His Lordship's use of the apostrophe, however, did not conform with any printworthy practice during the LME period (see Table 4.1).

2. Frank Baker edited John Wesley's works (1703–91) and 'had for-saken . . . antiquarian minutiae, modernized' Wesley's punctuation and spellings, expanded most of his abbreviations and changed initial upper to lower case graphs,

Table 4.1 *A Chesterfield letter (Bath, 26 October 1739) and the printed version*

Chesterfield (1739)	Dent, pp. 2–4 (Stanhope 1774)
Poeticall beautys (etc.) – touches 'em (etc.) – cruell (etc.) – Musick (etc.) – gett, sett (etc.) – touch'd, play'd (etc.)	poetical beauties – touches them – cruel – music – get – set – touched, played (etc.)
incorrectly and unelegantly	incorrectly or inelegantly
It is not enough to speak the Language he speaks in, in it's utmost purity	It is not enough to speak the language he speaks in, in its utmost purity
tell him what it was that you wanted	tell him what it was you wanted
you understand what is mean't by Oratory	you understand what is meant by oratory

'for smoother reading' (1980: XXV, 127–8, 'On Editing Wesley's Letters'). Baker too ignored line- and page-breaks.

But antiquarian minutiae can be sites of special linguistic interest. To hyphenate or capitalise consistently, writers had to understand why they performed those operations. Grammatically schooled writers used hyphens and capitals as grammatical and syntactic labels, which mechanically schooled writers (see Fairman 2007c) could not do because they had not been taught grammar. In *HERMES: OR, A Philofophical Inquiry Concerning LANGUAGE AND UNIVERSAL GRAMMAR* James Harris outlined what became the grammatical ideology till well into the nineteenth century (1751: 1.11):

> GRAMMAR UNIVERSAL; *that Grammar*, which without regarding the feveral Idioms of particular Languages, *only refpects thofe Principles, that are effential to them all.*

Harris illustrated 'grammar univerfal' with examples from Latin and Latin-in-English: thus 'the Stile of *Cicero*' and 'the *Ciceronian* Stile', both being literal translations from Latin, but not 'the *Cicero* Stile', a noun cluster, no noun having an affix or particle to show its relationship to the others. Latin grammar does not permit nouns to 'perform the part of Attributes' (Harris 1751: 1.189). But it is 'an Idiom which our language is ftrongly inclined to' – Lowth's joke and comment about another Idiom: 'feparat[ing a Prepofition] from the Relative which it governs' (1762: 127).

Consequently, grammatically schooled writers did not know what to do when they could not avoid clusters. I illustrate the point with three examples:

i. Street Names: 'market-Street', 'Market-street', 'Market-Street', or 'Market Street'? The two nouns act as a single noun, which names a place. So, to hyphenate or not? To capitalise or not? My preliminary study of scripts and texts, including two Canterbury newspapers, one with a progressive English, the other with a Latinate title, *The Kent Herald* and *The Kentish Gazette*, suggests that between 1750 and 1850 writers changed from 'market-Street', 'Market-street' and 'Market-Street' to the modern 'Market Street';

ii. Place Names: Grammatically schooled tourists to the Lake District encountered '*Carf-close-reeds*. I chuse to set down these barbarous names, that any body may enquire on the place, & easily find the particular station that I mean' (Thomas Gray. Toynbee and Whibley. 1769/1971: III, 1080, Letter 506).

iii. When William Wordsworth wrote his popular guide to the Lake District (at least five editions, 1820 to 1835), his famous choice to use 'the real language of men' in *Lyrical Ballads* (1800: 'Preface') conflicted with his schooling in Latin grammar in English. For example,

    1. he and his publisher named the book *A Guide through the District of the Lakes*, thereby avoiding a cluster in the title, which would have compelled other gentlemen, and ladies, to perpetrate a grammatical impropriety;

    2. the local meanings of 'water' 'mere' and 'dale' compounded the cluster problem, as this selection from many instances of three avoidance strategies shows: (a) Of: 'lake of Hawswater, vale of Wensley, hill of Dunmallet', (b) Hyphen: 'Deep-dale, Castle-hill, Saddle-back, water-falls'; (c) One word: 'Borrowdale, Saddleback, waterfalls'.

3. With regard to letters by mechanically schooled writers, people transcribe them with varying accuracy and for their own purposes. They therefore produce printed editions that differ more or less from the original manuscripts. For example, the historian Thomas Sokoll (2001) did not record line- or page-breaks but transcribed close to the manuscript originals and thereby produced a printed edition of pauper letters that can be used by both historians and linguists. The historians Alysa Levene *et al.* also transcribed letters as run-on text (2006: Vol. II) but their transcriptions are further from the originals, as, for example, in Levene *et al.* 2006: II, 11, Letter 5:

> Gentellmen I beg pardon for writing to you but my husband as ad the misfortune to fall from a barge *on* on tuesday weeke 27 of may and hurt his hip that he have not been able to follow his imployment sins [. . .]

But if I enter my transcription with line breaks,

> Gentellmen I beg pardon for writing to you but my
> Husband as ad the misfortune to fall from a
> Barge ~~on~~ on tuesday weeke 27 of may and hurt
> His hip that he have not bene able to fallow his
> Imployment sins [. . .]

we see that the writer, Frances Soundy (June 7 1828. Berkshire Record Office: Pangbourne, D/P/91/18/10) followed a rule: capitalise the first graph on each line. Levene *et al.* made only a small change by not recording original line-breaks. But that small change can lead to different interpretations of a linguistic feature and of the writer.

4. Failure to transcribe line-breaks erases another significant detail. John Murray writes of his transcription of Thomas Gray's account of his visit to the Lake District in 1769 (2012: 32): '[T]he text has been lightly edited to make it easier to read. A

capital letter has replaced Gray's small letter at the beginning of each sentence' and three other 'light' editings. Murray, too, ignores line-breaks. But Gray drew lines, as others did, to fill spaces he left at the ends of lines, which makes it impossible to decide whether or not he hyphenated a phrasal verb as some writers schooled in Latin grammar in English did. For example, Murray transcribes (2012: 41):

> W^d. [Wind] E; & afterwards N: E:. About 2m: [miles] from the town [Keswick] mounted an eminence called Castle-rig, & the sun breaking out discover'd the most beautiful view . . .

But in his facsimile of the same passage we see (Murray 2012: 155):

> W^d. E; & afterwards N: E:. about 2m:
> from the Town mounted an eminence
> call'd Castle-rig, & the sun breaking –
> out discover'd the most beautiful –
> view . . .

Therefore, diachronic changes in the minutiae by which grammatically schooled, higher-rank writers solved their grammatical-syntactic problems can signal slow changes in the ideology which privileges schooled English – the diminishing Latin-influenced selection of features and the increasing selection of features which had been characteristic of lower-rank writing.

But, to see those signs of change, linguists must use source data from printed and manuscript material. If linguists use only printed material as the source for electronic corpora, they see only the collaborated, final (printed) version of higher-class, grammatically schooled data which then serve as the sources for linguistic research and statements about 'the English language' overall (for example, Stubbs 1996; Biber *et al.* 1998).

An unacknowledged quote in Michael Toolan (2007: 272, italics added) suggests that eighteenth-century factors might generate an 'abhorrence among modern linguists' of the labour involved in working with manuscripts (see Barton on ecology in Section 4):

> We did not have, in the past, easy access to and inspectability of the kinds of evidence that facilitate the identification of collocations, multi-word prosodies, and similar statements about quasi-idiomatic lexical patterning. But the evidence was always there, and if one had had enough *harmless drudges* to help one pore over texts, record and count instances . . . By the same token there was in the past sufficient material to enable (indeed, to make seem natural) other kinds of linguistic analysis (of a non-collocation-oriented variety), for good or ill, including the writing of grammars and dictionaries.

Samuel Johnson was not the only eighteenth-century gentleman who associated 'drudge' with unskilled, repetitive manual labour. The anonymous writer of 'A Little Learning is a Dangerous Thing' (*Gentleman's Magazine* 1798: 820) wrote the following:

> No one will be willing to undertake the moſt ſervile employment, or the meaneſt
> drudgery, if his mind is opened, and his abilities increaſed, by any tolerable ſhare of
> ſcholaſtic improvement: yet theſe employments and this drudgery muſt be neceſſarily
> performed. Society cannot poſſibly ſubſiſt without them;

Biber *et al.* claim that doing 'historical and stylistic analyses by hand...
would...have ruled out the investigation of complex co-occurrence patterns'
(1998: 228). But in pre-electronic times, the classical scholar Adam Parry (1935/1971)
analysed complex co-occurrence patterns in Homer's *Iliad* and *Odyssey* (about
28,000 lines, almost 200,000 words) and revolutionised the understanding of epic
poetry. Manuscripts have to be transcribed manually (Bowers 1976), but linguists
cannot rely on transcriptions scholars make for their disciplines. If, therefore,
linguists are to enter manuscript language accurately into corpora, they have to
overcome a linguist's abhorrence of manual labour and, like Dr Johnson, learn
about language by drudgery. They will thereby learn about the language they are
transcribing, a necessary preparation for digitising and researching the digitised
data without distortion.

4. Literacies and schooling 1750–1870

Several linguists (L. Milroy 1980; Street 1995; Mühlhäusler 1996; J. Milroy 2001;
Fairman 2012) argue that language does not exist in a vacuum; it is a social construct.
Gillian Tett, an economist, who, like Street, was trained first in social anthropology,
also argues against taking a social construct 'in itself' (2009: 298) and relates the
vacuum to power:

> [w]hat social anthropology teaches us is that nothing in society ever exists in a vacuum
> or in isolation...Social 'silence' serves to maintain power structures.

Street makes literacy a basic concept in his anthropological work, and warns that
'one [must] be more wary of grand generalizations and cherished assumptions
about literacy "in itself"' (1995: 29). For Barton literacy is 'ecological' – '[an] activity
[which] influences and is influenced by the environment'. Restricting his analysis
'mainly to print literacy' (1994: 23), Barton specifies three levels and 'eight headings'
(1994: 33–5):
- Social: different literacy and speech practices; different cultures or historical
  periods; social settings; systems of information exchange;
- Psychological: technology of thought; awareness, attitudes and values towards
  literacy;
- Historical: individual; social.

Historical sociolinguists cannot investigate under all those headings easily –
individual histories, for example. Moreover, although much religious and secular
material was printed for the lower ranks to read (Vicinus 1974: 7–9), it is almost
impossible to find out what lower-rank individuals actually read (Spufford 1982:

48). Nevertheless, Barton's eight headings for analysing print can provide a frame within which to analyse manuscripts.

Adapting Barton (1994: 37–8) for investigating written language in history, I take 'literacy' as a basic concept, understanding literacies as patterns of activity identifiable in what people wrote in particular contexts and times.

There are three points to note: first, no one learns to write as children learn to speak: by just being around when it is done. Literacy must be schooled, that is, imparted by purposed activities in schools, in one-to-one relationships: a tutor at home, a master teaching his apprentice to write bills and business letters, or an adult teaching the Vai script to a Liberian teenager (Scribner and Cole 1981: 64–8), or self-tutoring. Schooling involves the use of books and methods, which do not originate and are not used in a vacuum either. The applied linguistic contributors to *The Social Construction of Literacy* (Cook-Gumperz 1986) also know that literacy does not exist in a vacuum.

Secondly, in Europe literacy was taught according to more or less the same ideology from Marcus Fabius Quintilian's *Institutio Oratoria* (publication date unknown, AD 35 to *c.* 100) till the late nineteenth century (Fairman 2005):

> [1.1.19] the elements of literary training are solely a question of memory, which not only exists even in small children, but is specially retentive at that age. [1.1.27] As soon as the child has begun to know the shapes of the various letters, it will be no bad thing to have them cut as accurately as possible upon a board, so that the pen may be guided along the grooves. [1.1.30] As regards syllables, no short cut is possible: they must all be learnt, and there is no good in putting off learning the most difficult; this is the general practice, but the sole result is bad spelling. [1.1.31] The syllables once learnt, let him begin to construct words with them and sentences with the words. [1.1.35–6] I would urge that the lines, which he is set to copy, should . . . convey some sound moral lesson. At the tender age of which we are now speaking, when originality is impossible, memory is almost the only faculty which can be developed by the teacher.

If children of any social rank were taught to write during the Late Modern English period, they all began, whether in schools or home tutoring, by forming each graph 'in all its various hands' (Caffyn 1998: 132, boys' boarding school, Henfield, 1786).

Thirdly, intelligence and aspiration were psychological influences then as now. If 'a quick child [during] the firſt Stage of Life' (Nelson 1753: 296) skipped an ideologically determined stage, observers noticed the anomaly but still believed the pedagogical ideology, because they had no alternative. For example, Jane Aikin remembered in a letter (8 February 1784) to her forty-year-old daughter, Anna Letitia Barbauld (McCarthy 2009: 21):

> I once . . . knew a little girl who . . . at two years old could read sentences and little stories in her *wise book* roundly without spelling, and in half a year more read as well as most women.

Aikin was impressed because her daughter's quickness confounded the ideology.

4.1 Lower-rank schooling

The British higher and middle ranks disagreed about schooling the lower ranks at all. Among those who opposed it was Samuel Parr (1786: 48):

> Others have told us, that knowledge lifts the minds of the poor above their fituation, and agitates them with fantaftic defires, which never can be realized. By employing them in the eftablifhed bufinefs of the place, or in fomething clofely allied to it, you prevent their minds from wandering, even, *if*, under other circumftances, they were difpofed to wander, into ideal fchemes of greatnefs. You fix their attention to the ftation in which they are certainly to act, and you prepare them for acting in it with propriety and fuccefs.

Adam Smith was among the most influential supporters of schooling the lower ranks (1776/1976: V.i.f. 52):

> But though the common people cannot, in any civilized fociety, be fo well inftructed as people of fome rank and fortune, the moft effential parts of education, however, to read, write, and account, can be required at fo early a period of life, that the greater part even of thofe who are to be bred to the loweft occupations, have time to acquire them before they can be employed in thofe occupations.

The few records of schooling the lower ranks that survive show that parishes varied in their provision of schools, for example:

1. After checking all records in the two Sussex archives, John Caffyn (1998) noted that between 1700 and 1799 only 112 out of 293 Sussex parishes provided free schooling for children of the poor. More parishes probably did school their poor, but the records have not survived;
2. The London Diocese Book (London, Guildhall Library: Ms 9557) contains records of school inspections from 1787 to 1814. These records are unreliable in some respects because different clergymen inspected the schools using different criteria. But none of the nine Archdeaconries is recorded as having schools for the poor in more than 30% of its parishes.

Parents who taught their own children probably taught as they themselves had been taught in childhood.

In Britain, the Industrial Revolution facilitated social mobility. This scary novelty coalesced in higher-rank minds with fears of democracy generated by the French Revolution and spurred them to use schooling to maintain the social order. '[W]e cannot enforce it too earnestly or repeat it too often' wrote the poet Robert Southey in 1812 (printed in 1832: 146–9, one repetition suffices. No 'f'):

> [n]ational education is the first thing necessary. Lay but this foundation, and the superstructure of prosperity and happiness which may be erected will rest upon a rock.

To prepare the lower ranks to be 'good servants in agriculture, and other laborious employments' (Giddy, *Parliamentary Debates*, Vol. IX, col 798, debate on Samuel Whitbread's Parochial Schools Bill. 13 July 1807. No 'f'.) and give them 'a fufficient portion [of inftruction] to give their minds a right bias' (Colquhoun 1806: 141; also see 'Curricula' below), the higher ranks founded and managed Sunday Schools and two nationwide systems, and drew up their curricula:

- Institutions:
  1. The Society for Promoting Christian Knowledge (1698). Robert Raikes (1786), Sarah Trimmer (1787) and Hannah More (1789) also established Sunday school movements.
  2. The National Society for the Education of the Poor in the Principles of the Established Church (Rev. Andrew Bell and the Madras system, 1811).
  3. The British and Foreign Schools Society (Joseph Lancaster and non-conformist schooling, 1814).
- Management: those who donated money sat on the charity-school committees. For example:
  1. in 1762 the committee of trustees of Romford Charity School, Essex, consisted of two reverends, one captain and six misters; in 1766 it consisted of three reverends, three esquires and three misters (Essex Record Office: Romford, D/Q 24/2: Committee Minutes and Accounts Book);
  2. on July 27 1820 the committee of the charity school in Stanhope St Thomas, County Durham, consisted of one reverend, one esquire and thirteen misters (Durham Record Office: Stanhope St Thomas, EP/St 11/1/1, Committee Minute Book).
- Curricula: James Nelson stated the case: 'nice grammatical Rules are not ftrictly the Province of Boys in common Life' (1753: 390). Therefore, the schools used spelling- not grammar-books, nor epistolary manuals (see Francis Place below) and taught only:
  1. spelling, which included confusing divisions of words into syllables;
  2. forming the graphs 'in the various hands now in use' (Caffyn 1998: 166, boarding school, Lewes, 1769);
  3. copying, usually from religious books (Fairman 2008b: 62–3) and
  4. reading the Bible.

Charity schools taught the Church of England catechism from *The Book of Common Prayer* (1549), which is 'part of the statute law of the land' (Wilson 2005: 227). Below is the part of the catechism, which contains 'ftate of life', a phrase which upper-rank writers tended to use about the lower ranks but not about themselves:

> *Queftion.* What is thy duty towards thy Neighbour?
> *Anfwer.* . . . To honour and obey the King, and all that are put in authority under him: To fubmit myfelf to all my governors, teachers, fpiritual paftors and mafters: To order myfelf lowly and reverently to all my betters: . . . Not to covet nor defire other men's goods; but to learn and to labour truly to get mine own living, and to do my duty in that ftate of life, unto which it fhall pleafe God to call me.

After learning the mechanical parts of literacy, lower-rank children began to work and forgot much or all of their mechanical literacy if they did not use it; or they became apprentices and were trained in other literacies, suited to their future 'ſtates of life', such as writing bills and keeping accounts. If the higher ranks noticed any ability among the lower ranks to reflect (exhibit 'straw'. See Joseph Priestley, Section 4.2), they thought it, as Aikin did, anomalous to the prevailing ideology and potentially socially dangerous.

Nevertheless, a few lower-rank scholars, like Thomas Paine (1737–1809), William Cobbett (1763–1835), Francis Place (1771–1854), John Clare (1793–1864) and others with determination, intelligence and aspiration, developed their mechanically schooled literacy in two directions: (1) a literacy unfit for print, because many could not and others, like John Clare (Storey 1985: 12, letter, mid 1819), would not write 'Standard': 'Putting the Correct Language of the Gentleman into the mouth of a Simple Shepherd or Vulgar Ploughman is far from Natural'; (2) the printable schooled literacy to 'inform or entertain the public' (Lowth 1762: ix) – Francis Place (1771–1854), a tailor and political activist, took this direction and wrote of his lower-rank schooling (Thrale 1972: 41):

> The only book I ever saw in the school for teaching Arithmetic was Dilworth's School Masters Assistant, the reading book the Bible . . . The mode of teaching was this. Each of the boys had a column or half a column of spelling to learn by heart every morning. He also wrote a copy every morning. In the afternoon he read in the bible and did a sum, on thursdays and saturdays he was catechised . . . It must be evident that as far as schooling went, very little could be obtained at this school.

4.2 Higher-rank schooling

On the other hand, higher- and some middle-rank children, after short mechanical schooling, were grammatically-schooled in 'GRAMMAR . . . the Art of rightly expreſſing our thoughts by Words' (Lowth 1762: 1). John Lyons clarifies how 'grammar' was understood then (1968: 133):

> The noun 'grammar' goes back (through French and Latin) to a Greek word which may be translated as 'the art of writing'. But quite early in the history of Greek scholarship this word acquired a much wider sense and came to embrace the whole study of language, so far as this was undertaken by the Greeks and their successors. The history of western linguistic theory until recent times is very largely the history of what scholars at different times held to fall within the scope of 'grammar' taken in this wider sense.

The ideology did not allow writers to 'inform or entertain the public' (Lowth 1762: ix) unless they had learnt grammar. Priestley (1733–1804) discussed Quintilian's views on 'originality' (1761, 1826 edition: ix):

> We muſt introduce into our ſchools *Engliſh grammar*, *Engliſh compoſition*, and frequent *Engliſh tranſlation* from authors in other languages. The common objection to

Englifh compofition, that it is like requiring brick to be made without ftraw (boys being fuppofed to be not capable of fo much reflection, as is neceffary to treat any fubject with propriety,) is a very frivolous one.

By 'our fchools' Priestley meant the schools that prepared higher- and middle-rank children for their 'ftates of life'.

4.3 Literacies and schooling – a summary

Within different social, psychological and pedagogical contexts writers practise literacies in two modes: print, which only grammatically schooled writers can produce, and manuscripts, which almost any writer can produce. Gillian Sutherland summarises nineteenth-century schooling (1971: 3):

> Elementary education in nineteenth-century England and Wales was not simply education for all those of a particular age group: it was not synonymous with 'first-stage' or primary education. It was education for a class, for the 'labouring poor' . . .

Learner writers of all ranks began with Quintilian's 'literary training', which, in Tett's words (2009: 298), 'serve[d] to maintain power structures'. It did not train the lower-rank majority in grammatically schooled literacy, which prevented them from (among other indexical activities) 'writing Letters with Propriety' (Dodsley 1754: xvii).

Nevertheless, literacy without Propriety was not illegal. The lower ranks would not have written thousands of requests for parish assistance in their mechanically schooled literacies, if their higher-rank readers had refused them against the law ('An Act to prevent the Removal of Poor Persons until they shall become actually chargeable'. 1795. 35 GeoIII, c.101) because they were written without 'Propriety'.

My aim in explaining literacies, particularly lesser-known lower-rank literacies, is to highlight some of the processes concealed in abstract words like 'context', 'ideology' and 'hegemony' (Gramsci 1971), and try to counter well-established beliefs that the 'Standard' is the only literacy and, therefore, most writers 200–300 years ago were 'semi-literate' (Romaine 1998: 18) or 'unusually illiterate' (Willan 1970: 23).

'Texts may travel easily, but the system of use, value and functions in which they were produced usually do not travel with them' (Blommaert 2008: 6). Jan Blommaert's point about cross-cultural geo-travel applies also to intracultural time travel (see Toolan in Section 3). Without a change of values, linguistics will stay stuck with the values of Johnson's time and with the language of the grammatically-schooled minority.

4.4 Literacy – the statistical perspective

So far in this section I have tried to illustrate the differences in schooling and writing practice that people from different social ranks received and what other factors could have had an influence on their literacy. In the remainder of this section I shall be concerned with the statistical perspective on calculating literacy in Late Modern England.

4.4.1 Marriage registers

The Hardwicke Marriage Act (1753) required all brides, grooms, witnesses and clergymen to mark or sign a marriage register. Many registers are now in Record Offices and historians have used them to calculate rates of 'literacy'.

There are two main problems with their calculations: first, calculation 'has revealed an astonishingly varied picture of parishes with different combinations of high and low male and female illiteracy, and of improvement and deterioration in illiteracy rates' (Schofield 1981: 208; see also Fairman 2005). Schofield's range of 'literacies' can be linked to unequal provision of schooling and teachers' competence.

The second problem is: What do historians mean by 'literacy'? By counting the marks and signatures in marriage registers, historians estimate that 60–70% of the population of England and Wales c. 1800 were 'literate' (Laslett 1971: 232; Lawson and Silver 1973: 192–3). But among them were writers who
1. could write only their own names (up to 10%, Fairman 2006: 56–61);
2. practised 'non-Standard', mechanically schooled literacy;
3. practised 'Standard', grammatically schooled literacy.
Therefore, we can reliably claim only that about 60% could write letters.

4.4.2 Censuses

Patrick Colquhoun (1745–1820) calculated the population of England and Wales in 1803 as 9,343,561, and he listed it by status, income and occupation (Colquhoun 1806: 23). He derived his figures from 'information provided by the recent census, the income-tax returns, and the 1802–3 survey of paupers, [which] modern historians have seen little reason to challenge' (Hilton 2006: 126). Boyd Hilton (2006: 127–8) groups Colquhoun's ranks into three social orders by annual income:
1. Upper order (+£800 p. a.): royalty, temporal and spiritual lords, baronets, knights, eminent businessmen, esquires.
2. Middle order (£120–799 p. a.): civil servants, lesser businessmen, ladies and gentlemen, clergy, legal profession, people in arts and sciences, wealthier freeholders, shopkeepers and tradesmen, military and naval officers, farmers, wholesalers, manufacturers, shipbuilders, pedagogues, shipowners, managers of lunatic asylums, engineers and builders, actors and musicians, tailors and dressmakers.
3. Lower order (less than £120 p. a.): innkeepers, shop assistants and clerks, military and naval half-pay officers, pedlars, lunatics, prisoners, pensioners, lesser freeholders, artisans, merchant seamen, fishermen, canal workers, miners, seamen, labourers, common soldiers, paupers, vagrants (prostitutes, gipsies).

The totals for Hilton's three orders are:

Upper order	99,215	1.1%
Middle order	2,569,200	27.5%
Lower order	6,675,146	71.4%
TOTAL	9,343,561	100%

But grouping occupations by income creates problems when estimating literacy memberships; for example, Hilton put shopkeepers into the middle order. Many shopkeepers who supplied the higher ranks did write grammatically schooled English. For example, most bills which shopkeepers presented to General Lord George Harris of Belmont House near Faversham, Kent are in grammatically schooled English.[2] More shopkeepers, however, supplied the lower ranks and parishes, and their bills are often in mechanically schooled English.[3] The same distinction in literacy can be made among the artisans in Hilton's lower order (Fairman 2006: 73–4).[4]

We can think of Hilton's orders as three 'pools'. Writers of 'Standard' and 'non-Standard' varieties are likely to be in the higher and lower pools respectively. We need to learn more about writers in the middle pool before we can describe their literacies accurately.

However, if we assume that all members of Hilton's upper and middle orders had been grammatically schooled, then 2,668,415 (47.6%) of the literate 60% (5,606,137) of Colquhoun's total population wrote 'Standard'. That leaves a majority, 2,937,722 (52.4%), who wrote 'non-Standard'.

These calculations favour the higher orders, so it is probable that 'non-Standard' exceed 'Standard' writers by more than 4.8%. In either case, grammars and histories 'of the English language' based on print omit the writings of that majority.

5. Conclusion

In the eighteenth century, as Caffyn (1998) documented in Sussex, entrepreneurs supplied schooling for middle-rank demand, which generated a pool of literacies. The higher ranks established two types of schooling, aimed to generate two literacies:

1. grammatical schooling and literacy for themselves to take part in public life and perhaps become authors;

---

[2] KHLC(M): *Harris*, U624/A1–123 (hundreds of bills, dated 1810–1825).

[3] For example ('|' represents a line break in the manuscript), 'A Bill of Cloas | for 5 yards of stuft for a goun 8[d] pr yard | for an aporn | for a homade Coat | W[m] Pott | March 1794' (Canterbury Cathedral Archives: *Chilham*, U191/12/17).

[4] For example, 'Stephen had not a shoes to his | foot that he could go out in atall' (letter, dated 'Sep[r] 11 1822 from M[r] Jn[o] Vaughan, a watch- and clock-maker, 'to the Gentlemen & Overseers of the parish of New Romney' about Stephen Wiles, an apprentice he had taken from the parish (KHLC(M): *New Romney*, P309/18/17).

2. mechanical schooling and literacies for the lower ranks as copyists and 'to teach people their place [rather] than to give them opportunities to advance' (Cannadine 1998: 48; see Sutherland in Section 4.3).

But some copyists became authors. If they aspired to a higher rank, they developed the literacy in which they had been schooled as far as they could towards their understanding of the prestigious, grammatically schooled, print literacy. But if they identified with the lower ranks, they had to construct their own literacies. Clare, for example, concluded that grammar 'pays nothing for the study' (Robinson and Powell 1984: 481; see also Clare in Section 4.1). Nevertheless, Robert McColl Millar (2012b: 91) reproduces one of Clare's finest sonnets, 'Emmonsails Heath in Winter', in Standardised dialect and punctuation, which I set beside Eric Robinson and David Powell's transcription from Clare's manuscript (1984: 212):

Standardised Clare (Millar)	Clare (Robinson)
I love to see the old heath's withered brake	I love to see the old heaths withered brake
Mingle its crimpled leaves with furze and ling	Mingle its crimpled leaves with furze and ling
While the old heron from the lonely lake	While the old Heron from the lonely lake
Starts slow and flaps his melancholy wing,	Starts slow and flaps his melancholly wing
And oddling crow in idle motion swing	And oddling crow in idle motions swing
On the half-rotten ash tree's topmost twig,	On the half rotten ash trees topmost twig
Besides whose trunk the gipsy makes his bed.	Beside whose trunk the gipsey makes his bed
Up flies the bouncing woodcock from the brig	Up flies the bouncing wood cock from the brig
Where a black quagmire quakes beneath the tread	Where a black quagmire quakes beneath the tread
The fieldfare chatter in the whistling thorn	The field fare chatters in the whistling thorn
And for the haw round fields and closen rove,	And for the awe round fields and closen rove
And coy bumbarrels twenty in a drove	And coy bumbarrels twenty in a drove
Flit down the hedgerows in the frozen plain	Flit down the hedge rows in the frozen plain
And hang on little twigs and start again.	And hang on little twigs and start again

Glossary (from Robinson and Powell 1984)
ODDLING: solitary
BUMBARREL: long-tailed tit, *Aegithalos caudatus*.

Millar's probably unwitting replacement of what Clare wrote with a Standardised version exemplifies the Standard ideology in two ways: (1) the ideology is silent about 'non-Standard' varieties, so it fills the vacuum by classifying features common throughout a language as features 'of the Standard' (see 'inertia/vacuum' in Section 2); (2) that reclassification appears to validate Millar's claims: (a) 'semi-literacy was essentially associated with Standard English' (2012a: 176); therefore, (b) 'the standard is the central point around which . . . Clare's usage orbits' (2012b: 96; see Milroy in Section 2), and (c) '[semi-literate writers] had a developed sense of what was 'correct' or 'proper'' (2012a: 176).

The written Standard certainly was present 'in the lives of dialect speakers' (Millar 2012b: 89), but not in their early nineteenth-century writings to the extent nor in the manner for which Millar argues. Their linguistic centre, after schooling for their 'ſtates of life' and without exposure to mass media, was their own speech. But, as Millar discovered when researching 'semi-literate' letters (2012a: 164), they did not write dialect. The Standard ideology recognises no other relevant categories, therefore he suggests: 'features which interest us in their writing are likely to be accidental' (2012a: 176).

If linguists and others (see Willan in Section 4.3) work with the 'Standard' ideology and an almost total 'denial of its own politics [...and] broader social and political concerns' (Pennycook 2010: 33), they can (1) model Standard literacy as 'the language', (2) classify what remains as 'dialect, vernacular, colloquial, semi-literate', or (3) discard it as 'non-Standard', '"wrong" data' (see Elspaß in Section 2) or 'accidental', which (4) implies it is the concern of historical applied linguists and not of linguists.

However, it has to be noted that (1) all ranks, upper, middle and lower, wrote as they did because they were brought up and schooled in particular ways, places and times; (2) grammars and histories of languages before 1877, when Thomas Edison invented the phonograph, have to be based on writing; (3) the ideology of the autonomous Standard hinders and/or distorts research into the writing of all ranks. Therefore, this chapter argues for a sociolinguistic model of pools of handwritten and printed literacies. As sources of data that the whole language community wrote, representative corpora ought in due course to contain (1) handwritten language of individuals of all social ranks and (2) print, which only collaborating writers in the minority middle and upper ranks could produce. After individual styles, hapax legomena and writos (slips of writers' pens, as typos are accidental but patterned slips of typists' fingers) have been identified and isolated, the structures of the language of all writers can be researched.

John Sinclair quotes Randolph Quirk on the prospect offered by corpora of researching larger chunks of text more easily than before: '[T]he implications are daunting' (Sinclair 1994: 12). Quirk and Sinclair worked with print and a 300-year-old autonomous model. I propose transcription by linguists and a social model with which to research handwritten and printed writing. The implications of that are daunting indeed – daunting and exciting or scary for anyone interested in language, as the idea of democracy was in the nineteenth century.

Appendix[5]

To illustrate the range of varieties in manuscripts, I present two letters in facsimile. To enable readers to experience the same drudgery (see Section 3) and learning curve *in terra nova* as I and others face when we begin researching manuscript writing, I present no transcriptions.

The Englishes in these manuscripts differ from the English in print on all linguistic levels, orthographic, lexical, grammatical and syntactic. And there is

---

[5] I thank the following for permissions to publish: the Somerset Heritage Centre for D/P/Ax/13/3/6 and the Herefordshire Record Office for Lyonshall AB55/82.

graphetics, a new level for handwriting to balance phonetics for speech (see Fairman 2012). The second 'her' in line 7 of Letter 1 is a rare example of dialect. The writers must have spoken dialect, but they did not write dialect (see Millar in Section 5).

   Letter 1 Somerset Heritage Centre. Axbridge, D/P/Ax/13/3/6. No date, about 1830.

Letter 2 Herefordshire Record Office. Lyonshall AB55/82. June 3 1830. When I set this letter as a transcription exercise, the fourth orthographic unit on line 2 has been transcribed: 'surprised [commonest], supprised, suppoved, approached, ?, unprobbed'. Manuscript data are not just there (section 1). Researchers need new reading skills.

CHAPTER 5

Heterogeneity vs. homogeneity

Marianne Hundt

1. Introduction

The development of post-colonial Englishes has been the focus of various studies. New Zealand English (NZE), in particular, has received a great deal of attention, with a detailed study on the emergence of the characteristic New Zealand accent based on recordings made in the mid-1940s, which included the first generation of New Zealand-born speakers (Gordon *et al.* 2004). Contemporary comments on the language during the early colonial period often remark on the *homogeneity* of the new variety that might (or might not) be the result of koïnéisation (see Schneider 2007: 18). The letters that form the object of study for this chapter, however, were written so soon after the arrival of the first settlers that koïnéisation cannot possibly have taken place. Furthermore, accommodation as an important driving factor for the koïnéisation process is more likely to have affected spoken interaction in the early colonial days, and evidence of dialect levelling and focusing are more likely to be evidenced in letters of later generations. This chapter therefore aims at describing some of the stylistic, social and regional heterogeneity of the *grammatical* input that is likely to have formed part of the base for the development of (written) New Zealand English grammar. The focus is on grammar because the letter collection was published in 1843, and the editing process is likely to have reduced possible spelling variants that might indicate regional pronunciations. In other words, the fine-grained analysis at all levels of linguistic structure that Fairman (2007a, 2008a) applies to his autograph letters is impossible to achieve with the edited material used in this study. However, the same editorial influence is much less likely to have had substantial influence on grammatical patterns, as we will see.

In Section 2 of this chapter, I will briefly describe the letter collections on which my study is based. In Section 3, I will survey some aspects of social, stylistic, regional and diachronic variability in the data. Section 4 focuses on relative constructions, mostly because the range of variation found with this syntactic

I dedicate this article to my former teacher and Freiburg colleague, Teresa Woods, who nurtured my latent interest in New Zealand as a post-graduate and kept sharing her views on the country's history, language, literature and culture over the years. I would like to thank Nicole Studer, who downloaded the letters from the Web and did the initial categorisation. For comments on earlier versions of this paper, thanks go to David Denison, Gerold Schneider, the participants of the Utrecht symposium, in particular Susan Fitzmaurice, and the editors of this volume.

pattern fits into several categories (social, stylistic, etc.). Section 5 will compare the New Zealand letters with an edition of roughly contemporaneous letters from America of emigrants from Lancashire, UK. The methodological focus will thus be on the degree of 'authenticity' of the edited letter collection and the question as to how reliable such data are as witnesses of language variation and change.

2. The letter collections

The main evidence for this study comes from a digitised version[1] of a collection of letters that was published in 1843 in London – i.e. it is a contemporary publication of letters that were mostly written in 1842. They are from settlers and labourers who had come to Wellington, Nelson and New Plymouth, the so-called Wakefield settlements of the New Zealand Company which had been established in 1840, the year that the Treaty of Waitangi was signed in which Britain gained sovereignty over New Zealand.[2] One of the probable reasons why the letters were published so soon after the establishment of the colony was that the systematic settlement through the New Zealand Company was not an instant success, so the favourable reports given in the letters can be seen as a form of advertisement for the Company's efforts.[3] The selection of the letters is likely to have been made primarily on the basis of content, i.e. favourable reports about the settlement at the expense of critical narratives; apart from the repeated 'complaint' that Wellington did not have a harbour, the letters paint a positive picture of life in the new colony.

The New Zealand letter collection includes both private and official letters as well as letters to the editor of a New Zealand journal or newspaper; the addressees are family and friends at home, people with an official function in the New Zealand Company or land proprietors back 'Home' in England; in the case of the letters to the editor, the audience was the general public.

The composition of this letter collection is obviously very unbalanced, and this is the main reason why I will not refer to it as a 'corpus', which should be a principled and (ideally) representative collection of texts. The letter collection is heavily skewed towards male authors. Furthermore, of the three letters by female authors, two are by the same writer. When the gender of the author is impossible to reconstruct (in the case of anonymous letters), it is more likely that they were written by men rather than by women.

---

[1] The letters were digitised by the Early New Zealand Books project at the University of Auckland, New Zealand. They can be found at www.enzb.auckland.ac.nz/document//1843_-_Letters_from_Settlers_and_Labouring_Emigrants (last accessed 17 January 2011).

[2] See http://history-nz.org/colonisation1.html (last accessed 17 January 2011).

[3] That New Zealand, for various reasons, was in need of promotion as a colony is described in more detail in www.teara.govt.nz/en/history-of-immigration/3 (last accessed 17 January 2011). 'To combat negative notions about New Zealand, the company used books, pamphlets and broadsheets to promote the country as "a Britain of the South", a fertile land with a benign climate, free of starvation, class war and teeming cities' (*ibid.*).

Table 5.1 *Composition of the New Zealand letter collection*

Genre	Gender	No. of letters	Total no. of words
Letters to the editor	male – n/a	9	6,729
Official letters	male – n/a	18	12,867
Private letters	anonymous	7	3,909
Private letters	female	3	1,180
Private letters	male	33	25,418
Private letters	female&male	4	2,448
Unclear[a]	male – n/a	12	10,866
Total		86	63,417

[a] The genre of some letters is unclear because not all the letters are quoted in full and the relevant information (usually gleaned from the opening of the letter) is thus missing.

Table 5.2 *Social background of male authors*

	Middle class		Craftsmen		Unavailable	
	letters	words	letters	words	letters	words
Official letter	7	4,985	1	593	6	6,204
Private letter	5	4,142	10	7,326	19	13,950
Total	12	9,127	11	7,919	25	20,154

The idea behind the Wakefield settlements was for the settlers to represent the social stratification found in Britain, albeit without the top and bottom layers (see Gordon *et al.* 2004: 40). However, for the letters by the settlers and labouring emigrants there is no explicit information on their social background: in some cases, the profession of the male authors can be inferred (mostly from the contents of the letter, less often from the heading), but there are others that do not allow us to assign the writer to a particular social grouping. Table 5.2 lists the available information for the official and the private letters that were written by male emigrants.

More often than not, information on the social background of the writers is not available. Where we do have the information, it will be interesting to see whether the social rank of the writer correlates with the degree of grammatical 'standardness' in their writing.

With respect to the regional background of the early immigrants, Gordon *et al.* (2004: 46) provide the following background information for the English settlers arriving through the New Zealand Company in the years from 1839 to 1850: 25.9% were from London, 20.8% from the south-east, 26.4% from the south-west and only 3.4% from Lancashire.[4] Settlers from Scotland only started arriving from

[4] See also www.teara.govt.nz/en/history-of-immigration/4 (last accessed 17 January 2011).

the late 1840s onwards (and mainly settled in the south of the South Island), so substantial admixture from Scottish dialects in the early settlements at Wellington, Nelson and New Plymouth can be practically ruled out.[5] Irish settlers during the early settlement period mainly arrived via Australia as free migrants (i.e. not through the Company); as they mostly settled in the Auckland region, their dialect, too, is unlikely to have played a significant role in the Wakefield settlements from which the letter collection stems (see Gordon *et al.* 2004: 40–1). But, as with information on social background, the evidence in the letters on the writers' regional origins is very patchy and only available for some of the private letters whenever the whereabouts of the recipients are revealed. In other cases, where the author of the letter is a well-known personality, we have more detailed background knowledge of their regional origin (e.g. with Captain Arthur Wakefield, whose brother Edward founded the New Zealand Company and who was born in Essex but grew up in London; at the age of eleven, he joined the navy and is therefore likely to have been extremely mobile regionally). For individual features in some letters, even the patchy information that is available may provide helpful clues.

While the letter collection is thus not a representative corpus of emigrant writing in the early days of colonisation in New Zealand, it serves as a valid starting point for a pilot study into variability in early New Zealand (letter) writing. The letter collection is also of a fairly limited size. Due to its skewed composition and limited size, the following analyses will mainly be of a qualitative nature. Evidence on non-standard usage was collected by closely reading through the letters and annotating potentially interesting patterns. In a second step, recurring structures were systematically studied against the background of available syntactic descriptions of nineteenth-century English (especially the detailed grammar provided by Denison in volume IV of the *Cambridge History of the English Language* (1998)). In order to assess the editorial influence as a homogenising factor in the New Zealand letters, they are compared with approximately contemporary letters from America of emigrants from Lancashire, the so-called *Cherry Valley Chronicles* (Dennett 1991). These are letters that were mostly written by Thomas Buckley (1794–1875), some by other family members, to Thomas' son Ralph between 1845 and 1875 (Dennett 1991: 5).[6] Thomas Buckley, a woollen weaver, had emigrated from a village near Manchester to America (Cherry Valley, a suburb of Leicester in Massachusetts) where he worked in a mill. The letters to Ralph and his family, who had stayed in England, narrate 'the family saga of births, marriages, deaths and daily living' against the background of 'national events such as the Civil War, in which five of the family served in the Northern Army' (Dennett 1991: 5). The earliest letters in the Cherry Valley collection are close in time to the New Zealand emigrant letters;

---

[5] There is one letter (613 words) by a Scottish settler (Alexander Perry, Esq.) in the collection.
[6] The collection contains two later letters, one from 1889, the other from 1895, that were written by members of the second and third generation of emigrants.

it is more diachronic than the New Zealand letters but more homogeneous in terms of genre and the social background of the writers. As a collection that was compiled with the aim of historical documentation rather than advertising a new colony, it provides a more faithful transliteration of the originals than the New Zealand letters. It is for this reason that the Cherry Valley letters were chosen: they allow us to assess the degree of homogenisation that is likely to have resulted from the editing of the New Zealand letters.

3. Heterogeneity

3.1 Social variability

Before I proceed to illustrate social variability of individual grammatical patterns, I will quote a couple of typical specimens from my collection. The first example is an official letter from a Devonshire farmer to one of the Directors of the New Zealand Company (29 December 1842):

(1)   SIR,

You were kind enough, in London, to express a wish to hear from me on my arrival here, giving you my opinion of the land. I deferred writing until I could judge fairly of its qualities, which I think I can do now. There is no doubt about it being good, *very good*; and much superior to any land at home. We can produce two good crops in one year, which *can't* be done in England: wheat, averaging sixty bushels an acre, and potatoes sixteen tons ditto.

There is no doubt about a working man doing well; thirty shillings a week being the general pay, and provisions only very little dearer than in the old country. I consider him better off than a farmer in England, who pays £100. rent. I intend going farther into the bush very soon, on a section of land I have taken of Mr. Molesworth.

I am, Sir,

Your most obedient Servant,

C. M.

This official letter is very close to the standard end of the cline; it features elements of a speech-like style such as *very good* and a contracted negation in the first paragraph, but it does not contain any obvious vernacular or other colloquial features. The second example is an extract from a private letter by a carpenter from Surrey (William Dew) to his brother James Dew (25 December 1842):

(2)   MY DEAR BROTHER,

I have *wrote* this second letter to you since I received yours, hoping that you, your wife and family, are all well, and my dear mother and all my brothers and sisters are all well. I am happy to say that *myself*, wife and family are all well, and we are all enjoying this day, together in a homely way, as Christmas is in the middle of summer. *We have for dinner* the roast beef of Old England, new potatoes, cauliflowers, plum puddings, elderberries; – we have none to make wine. *Sugar, we have plenty*, and very cheap. Beef is as low as 9d. per lb., mutton the same – flour is very cheap, at two pounds per 100. Our wheat is now in bloom; there is about 100 acres of wheat in the colony this year, *which is most of it among the poor people.* [...] I have a good crop of cauliflowers, *which I have had the praise of the colony for second beauty*: they have *sold well* at 6d. 4d. 3d. each, according to size. [...] We have had a dreadful fire, which has burnt about sixty of the best houses down to the ground, which is a great pull back to the colony. Thank God! we lost very little flour; the wind was *dreadful violent* from the north-west that night, which swept the whole of the beach, which looked awful. They are building ø up again more substantially with brick. Money is very scarce in the colony. *Give my duty* to Mr. A——, I want to ask one favour of him, that is, if he will let me some ground on these terms [...] if Mr. T—— will grant me that favour, I *would* return him many thanks, as I think it *would* be a good start for me. I have sent this letter by the Clydeside, that has been under repair at Wellington, which *is come direct to* England. She has brought with her a handsome present for the Queen, a sideboard, which is a specimen of our New Zealand woods: *me* and my partner sawed the stuff for it. I should like Mr. T—— to see it, as it is worth *any one*'s while to see it, as there is no wood in England to equal it; it surpasses *every thing*. We have the *most choice* wood of any island in the world. They are going on dressing the flax, which, if it answers, will be a great interest to the colony; it makes employment for the children, *which at present there is none for them.* My dear brother, if you come, mind and bring all the money you can with you, as tools can be *bought* here as *cheap* as at home, and other things reasonable. Pit-saw files ø very dear – at 1s. and 6d. each, ø would be a very good speculation to bring-some. If you *should have* an opportunity, send me a few dozen, as they would *pack* in a very small compass. [...] Give my duty to all inquiring friends: give my love to all my sisters, and tell Benjamin to be steady and industrious, and he will prosper. Ann *wishes her love* to her mother and father, and would be happy to have a letter from them.

I remain, yours *for ever*,

WILLIAM DEW, and family.

The letter contains a number of potentially interesting features (participle forms such as *wrote*, marking on adverbs, reflexive and oblique pronouns in subject position, relative clauses) that are variable. Some of these will be discussed in more detail below. Elliptical constructions (e.g. *Pit-saw files ø very dear – at 1s. and 6d. each, ø would be a very good speculation to bring-some*) are a feature that is typical of letter writing as a genre and will not be investigated systematically.[7] The letter also contains collocations (e.g. *give my duty to sb.* or *wish sb. love*) that are archaic or at least rare.[8] On the whole, it is remarkable that the letter contains conspicuously little non-standard material, such as multiple negation. The syntax, too, is relatively elaborate and contains numerous complex sentences, and a high incidence of relative clauses introduced by the formal relativiser *which*. At the same time, there are also more speech-like patterns, such as *Sugar, we have plenty, and very cheap.*[9] The following is a private letter that is much closer to a speech-like style:

(3)   DEAR FATHER, BROTHER, AND SISTERS,

I *write* you these few lines hoping it will find you all well. I have been expecting to hear from you before now, as there have been *three ships ø come here from England* since I left. I suppose it is cold enough now at home; here it is harvest. This is the finest wheat and barley country *that* ever *was seen, and that you would say if you were to see it.* We have a small harvest, as we had no time, when we came, to sow much, and no cattle to plough the ground. We *have got* plenty of potatoes, fine crops, and fine cabbages, – all vegetables grow well here. I wish you were all here; – this is a fine place for tailors and sawyers. I can get more money here than you can get at home. I have everything as good as at home – we bought a featherbed quite new for £6 the other day. I am about to buy a town section for £40. I am certain I should never have saved that sum at home, – many hundreds have gone through my hands since I have been here. I have bought great quantities of pigs, so you *must expect* I am doing something and saving money. As yet *I we have got* no bullocks or sheep to kill, but we shall have plenty soon. It is a fine country, the only thing we want is a harbour. The trees are always green and very large, from 80 to 100 feet in height without a branch. I have seen

---

[7] Ellipsis is probably simply a marker of familiarity. In a letter from Sir William Hamilton to his niece Lady Mary Hamilton (written on 14 August 1783), he omits the subject pronoun in 'but beg you will not put yourself to inconveniences'. Anita Auer (p.c.) points out that Lindley Murray (1795: 203) accepts the elliptical style 'in conversation and epistolary writing, yet, in all writings of a serious and dignified kind, it ought to be avoided'.

[8] The *OED* only yields one further instance of *give my duty to* in a letter from 1740 (adv. *wherever*); the expression *wish sb. one's love* might simply be an idiosyncratic variant of the formula *send sb. one's love*.

[9] One of the editors of this volume took these clauses as examples of a non-standard pattern as *which* was used in much the same way as that *and* would be used in narrative, i.e. as a conjunction linking coordinate clauses rather than a subordinator. My main point here is that *which* as a relativiser is the more formal option than *that*.

trees from six to eight feet through and through. The red pine is splendid timber for furniture, it is like mahogany. I *have three houses building*, some stone, some cob. If *we had only a harbour* this would be the finest place in the world. Flour is 5d. per pound, beef 7d., pork, fresh and salt, 7d. and 7 1/4d. per pound; potatoes from the English 1d. per pound, from the natives 3d. per pound; tea 6s., sugar 10d. men's shoes £1. 4s. per pair; fustian *trowsers* 9s., well made and lined; jackets £1. 4d.; spirits, as in England; beer and porter 1s. 6d. per pint. I have not kept an account of the number of pigs I have killed since I have been here – many hundreds, I should guess. Love to all friends, from your affectionate children,

SAMUEL AND F. CURTIS.

Some syntactic patterns are even close to being ungrammatical from the point of view of written syntax: the relative clause *that ever was seen* may have prompted the writer to continue with a *that*-construction, which is not a relative clause, but used in the sense of *and you would say so, too*. The juxtaposition of *I* and *we* (a planning error?) indicates that the letters were not heavily edited with respect to the grammatical features they contain. Other letters contain syntactic patterns that are similarly close to spoken syntax:

(4) As to the hills, *why they are the greatest blessing that we can have*, as the scenery is most beautiful, as the hills are mostly covered with trees.

> (From G. FELLINGHAM, journeyman printer, to his parents; March 12th, 1842)

(5) *I forget* the old fellow's name, but he is a great chief.

> (From Mr. H. S. TIFFEN, to his father at Hythe; April 2nd, 1842)

(6) *Now* a little about Port Nelson.

> (From JAMES HARPER, a settler at Nelson, to his friends at Wootton Bassett;
> April 17th, 1842)

(7) *Now, I think,* about six or eight weeks we shall have our land ready for choice;

> (From Mr. WILLIAM BAYLY, Yeoman, late of Clawton, in Devonshire, to his
> Parents; Feb. 29th, 1842)

There is evidence of some syntactic patterns that are non-standard at the time, for instance multiple negation. But the following two examples are the only instances in the whole collection:

(8) [. . .] of this island the great parts were mountains, which could *not* be cultivated by *no* means.

> (From Mr. WILLIAM BAYLY, Yeoman, late of Clawton, in Devonshire, to his
> Parents; Feb. 29th, 1842)

(9)   [. . .] I know I could not do so well in England as I can here, *nor no*
       labouring man besides;

(From JOHN and ANN FRENCH, working emigrants, to their parents,
near Ashburton, in Devonshire; 28th February, 1842)

Significantly, they are both from writers at the lower end of the social scale.
The fact that multiple negation is so rare in my data indicates that the letters
are, on the whole, very close to the standard end of the non-standard–standard
continuum. Negation is a pattern that is also of some interest in the context of
recessive grammatical patterns that I will turn to below (Section 3.4).

3.1.1 Adjectives as adverbs

Adverbs without overt adverb marking are a relatively frequently attested pattern
in my letter collection. The first kinds of unmarked adverb that we might think of
these days would be those in premodifying function in NPs (as in a *real bad day at
the office*) or AdjPs (as in *I feel real bad about this*). This kind of unmarked adverb
is occasionally attested in my data:

(10)   a.   [. . .] the wind was *dreadful violent* from the north-west violent from the
             north-west that night, which swept the whole of the beach, which looked
             awful [. . .]

(From WILLIAM DEW, to his brother, MR. JAMES DEW, Ham, Surrey,
25 December 1842; contents suggest that he is a carpenter)

       b.   [. . .] my choice [of land] is unfortunately beyond the 'thousand,' and
             consequently *desperate bad*;

(From MR. FRANCIS JOLLIE, to WILLIAM BLAMIRE, Esq., London,
20 December 1842 – official letter! – author employs other people
to manage his land, so must be of a higher rank)

However, the unmarked adverbs in my data mostly modify VPs, as for instance:

(11)   The natives here are wide awake to their own interests, and will not sell their
       pigs and potatoes for anything else than money or the utu, as they call it,
       and *charge very high* besides.

(From ROBERT ROSS, a Baker at Nelson, to a Gentleman in London,
30 November 1842)

The question is (a) whether such patterns should be considered non-standard at
the time of writing, and, if they were non-standard, (b) whether they occur mainly
in the writing of the lower social ranks in my letter collection. It could be argued
that the construction in (11) is elliptical and thus does not count as an example of
an unmarked adverb. However, the same author also provides us with the use of
unmarked *safe* in (12):

(12)   On the 15th October, 1841, the good ship Arab *arrived safe* in Port Nicholson Harbour.

> (From ROBERT ROSS, a Baker at Nelson, to a Gentleman in London,
> 30 November 1842)

We might argue that a verb like *arrive* gets a copula-like reading in such a context, which may have motivated the unmarked use of the adverb (see Nevalainen 1997 and Gisborne 2000 on the gradability of adjective and adverb function with verbs of appearance since Middle English). Similar semantic effects can be observed in the following examples:[10]

(13)   a.   We *arrived* here quite *safe* on February 26th [...].

> (From SIMON and JANE ANDREWS, labouring emigrants, to their parents,
> 8 March 1842)

       b.   The ship Timandra [...] arrived here last Wednesday, with all emigrants *landed safe*.

> (From Mr. WILLIAM BAYLY, Yeoman, late of Clawton, in Devonshire, to his
> Parents, 29 February 1842)

       c.   I was ordered to go on board of her by Captain King, and see all the things *taken out safe*, &c.

> (From A. and E. HOSKIN, to their Parents, 19 February 1842)

       d.   Dear friends, I am happy to say, that the people *behaved very kind* to all the passengers that came out in our ship;

> (From A. and E. HOSKIN, to their Parents, 19 February 1842; the contents
> indicate that one of the senders is a butcher)

Similarly, the process of purchasing goods is not *cheap*, but the low price of the products is a property of the goods in (14) and may thus have licensed the use of an unmarked adjective:[11]

(14)   a.   My dear brother, if you come, mind and bring all the money you can with you, as tools can be *bought* here as *cheap* as at home, [...].

> (From WILLIAM DEW, to his brother, MR. JAMES DEW, Ham, Surrey,
> 25 December 1842)

       b.   I have sixteen acres of perhaps as good land as any in the colony, [...]; it was *bought* very *cheap*, it cost about £2. the acre;

> (From JOSEPH WHITE, to his mother, 24 December 1842; a comment on
> labourers' wages indicates that the author is a labourer)

In other contexts, however, the copula-like reading is unlikely, especially if the focus is on an ongoing process rather than a resulting state:

---

[10]   The use of unmarked *safe* in the examples above is probably less problematic, from the point of standardness, than unmarked *kind* in example (13d).

[11]   Comments in Dew's letter suggest that he was a carpenter; the contents of the letter by Joseph White indicate that he was a labourer.

(15)   a. [. . .] I will *proceed slow*, but *sure*.

> (From MR. WILLIAM CULLEN, formerly of Huish Episcopi, near Langport,
> Somerset, 3 July 1842; farmer)

b. Cultivation *goes on very spare*: the reason is, that most of the landholders
    are gentlemen's sons, and know nothing about farming;

> (From JOSEPH WHITE, to his mother, 24 December 1842)

c. When we arrived in the Colony, many of the settlers were in doubt as to
    whether the Colony would ever go a-head, as the survey *had been going
    on* so miserably *slow*, [. . .].

> (From Mr. S. GILLINGHAM, to his Brother, Mr. ROBERT GILLINGHAM, of
> Camfield House, Shaftesbury, Dorset, 1 October 1842)

The first example in (15) is by a farmer (but occurs in a fixed phrase); comments on
labourers' wages in the context of the second example suggest that the writer, too,
was a labourer. The third example in (15), however, is from a letter addressed to a
person 'of Camfield House' and, since the addressee is a relative of the author, this
suggests that the author is of a higher social rank. In other words, unmarked adverbs
are not exclusively used by the lower social orders in my data. The combination of
a motion verb with an unmarked adjective strongly suggests an adverb reading as
well:

(16)   a. Our Governor *went direct* to Governor Hobson, [. . .];

> (From Mr. WILLIAM BAYLY, Yeoman, late of Clawton, in Devonshire, to his
> Parents, 29 February 1842)

b. I have sent this letter by the Clydeside [. . .] which *is come direct* to
    England.

> (From WILLIAM DEW, to his brother, MR. JAMES DEW, Ham, Surrey,
> 25 December 1842)

Instead of assessing the acceptability of the unmarked adverbs with certain verbs,
another approach might be to see how early they are attested as unmarked forms in
the *OED*. This approach will include the use of *quick* in (17), as well:

(17)   a. Please give my love to brothers and sisters, and tell them I should be
           happy *to see* them here as *quick* as possible.

> (From SIMON and JANE ANDREWS, labouring emigrants, to their parents,
> 8 March 1842)

b. They take us out in their canoes to learn to swim – they can swim,
    themselves, seven or eight miles at a time, and *do* it very *quick*, [. . .]

> (From GEORGE BEAVAN, of Wellington, to H. HENSHALL, of Whitchurch,
> Salop., 30 June 1842; contents of letter suggest that author is a tradesman)

Table 3 gives an overview of the adverbs that are attested as bare forms in my
data alongside their earliest attestation in the *OED*. Years in brackets indicate that

Table 5.3 *Adjectives as adverbs in the New Zealand letter collection*

Adjective/adverb	First attestation as unmarked adverb from *OED*	Stylistic comment
dreadful	(1682)	'now vulgar'
desperate	(1636)	'colloquial and dialectal'
safe	—	
kind	—	
cheap	1592	
slow	1500	
sure	(1400)	
spare	[1813]	['rare']
direct	1450	
quick	1300	

the adverbial use of the adjective is only attested in prenominal or pre-adjectival position. Additional stylistic comments are given in a separate column.

Table 5.3 nicely illustrates that a lot of the bare adverbs are attested from a relatively early stage, some adjectives even going back as far as Middle English in their function as adverbs (see Nevalainen 1997 and Gisborne 2000). With the exception of *slow*, the adverb function of the adjectives is subsumed under the entry that describes the adjectival use first. The information from the *OED* also fits in with my findings, i.e. that *dreadful* and *desperate* are attested in the pre-adjectival function rather than as modifiers of a VP (and that they are non-standard). The *OED* data further confirm that variability between the adjectival and adverbial function of adjective forms has a long pedigree in English and is not necessarily non-standard (and partly licensed in contexts where the verb has a resultative rather than process reading).

3.1.2 *Modals and mood in hypothetical* if-clauses[12]
In the protasis of conditional sentences, standard English requires either a subjunctive or indicative verb form. In the letter collection from New Zealand we also find modal verbs in this slot, as in (18):[13]

(18) a. [. . .] if Mr. T—— *will* grant me that favour, I would return him many thanks, as I *think* it *would* be a good start for me.

> (From WILLIAM DEW, to his brother, MR. JAMES DEW, Ham, Surrey, 25 December 1842)

  b. If I *should* be so fortunate for five years more as I have since I came here, and it *should* please the Almighty to spare me, I *think* I *shall* return.

> (From JOSEPH WHITE, to his mother, 24 December 1842)

---

[12] Inverted protases are also found (two instances), but this is a recessive pattern (see Denison 1998: 300).

[13] Note that (18a) has a sense of the lexical use of *will* about it rather than the modal meaning.

c. If you *should* come out, I *hope* we *shall* have the pleasure of building you
one.

(From CHARLES BROWN, Bricklayer, to the HON. A. TOLLEMACHE,
Ham, Surrey, 10 October 1842)

What all three examples have in common is that they seem to hover between a
conditional and a non-conditional reading because the expected order of tenses
in the protasis and the apodosis is not used, i.e. they combine a present with a
past tense and vice versa. This apparent violation of tense agreement seems to be
facilitated by the parentheticals with a verb of cognition (*I think*, *I hope*) that brings
these sentences somewhat closer to the spoken medium.

There is also some use of indicatives in hypothetical *if*-clauses:

(19) a. If her father *was* to see her he would not know her.

(From JANE CROCKER to her Father, MR. SAMUEL CROCKER, Revelstoke,
7 February 1842)

  b. Dear father, when we get together Jane is sure to say. 'now John, if poor
father *was* but here, and Samuel, how happy we should be;' and John's
answer is, 'I wish he *was*, my dear, he would be quite happy here, to see
our gardens and land, and to walk over them.'

(To MR. SAMUEL CROCKER, Revelstoke, from his Daughter-in-law;
10 February 1842)

This is not really surprising, though, since the indicative was the dominant variant
by the time the settlers migrated to New Zealand. In the ARCHER data that Auer
(2006) investigated, the relative frequency of the past subjunctive to the indicative
had declined to only 20.8% for the period 1750–99, but increased again towards
the end of the nineteenth-century to 27.4%.

3.2 Stylistic variability

The letter collection studied in this chapter has some inherent stylistic variability in that it samples different types of letters, namely private ones and official
letters, as well as a form that we might refer to as public letters (namely those
to the editor of a journal or magazine). In the introduction to Section 3.1, some
examples were quoted at length of the two different types of letters, illustrating
some of the variability, also with regard to the question of written vs. spoken
syntax. The letter collection provides both examples of spoken-like (see examples (4–7) above) as well as typically written syntax. The following instance is an
example of a syntactically complex sentence (with high register vocabulary) that,
however, contains quite a few examples of preposition stranding, a pattern that had
been under attack from prescriptivists since the eighteenth century (see Beal 2004:

84–5).[14] Denison (2007: 123–4), who investigates preposition stranding in a corpus of eighteenth-century letters, points out that preposition stranding is actually the older variant. The question is whether it is therefore not only an informal but also the more 'natural' option when compared with the 'written' alternative (pied-piping). We should thus not be surprised to find it used frequently in letter writing:

(20)　He has shewn that we are not so hemmed in as most of us fancied; that, after all, we have an immediate and easy communication with the neighbouring interior; that the settlement may still be formed in one *contiguous*, and comparatively speaking, compact block; and that our country lands may yet, in the great bulk, be *looked* forward *to* as of some tangible value; not mere *refuse*, impracticable swamp, hill or forest, but land, for the greater part, that we shall be able to *get upon*, and at once make *contributory*, in the shape of *pasturage*, if of nothing else, to the permanent prosperity of the settlement.

(From MR. FRANCIS JOLLIE, to WILLIAM BLAMIRE, Esq., London; 20 December 1842)

Examples of pied-piping can also be found in the letters, but, as in Denison's data, they are relatively rare. Examples in (21) are from a private letter and a letter to the editor, respectively. Pied-piping in the private letter is quite likely to be the result of editing.

(21)　a.　The houses *in which* we now live are built by the natives, [...]

(From JAMES THOMAS SHAW, formerly Shipwright in the Dockyard at Devonport, to a Friend in Plymouth; 16 February 16 1842)

　　　b.　Coralines exist on the rocks *from which* lime might be made in small quantities.

(Mineral Riches of New Zealand, From HENRY WEEKES, Esq., to the Editor of the *New Zealand Journal*; 10 April 1842)

Some letters combine high register vocabulary and elaborate syntax (22a) with, at times, somewhat colloquial constructions (22b and 22c):

(22)　a.　Porirua river, which begun to wind its way like a small stream, gradually getting larger, until at Porirua it became navigable, lay many feet below our path, the trees tall and gigantic, of all shades of green, towering one above the other with flax growing in tufts on every branch; flowers of every *hue* scattered about, and parrots, and numberless other birds adding a charm to the scene by their melody. The walk to Porirua, twelve miles from Port Nicholson, where we halted to dine, became,

[14] Beal (2004: 84–5) also notes that not all grammarians condemned the use of stranded prepositions in relative clauses; Lowth, for instance, merely viewed it as an informal variant that ought to be avoided in an 'elevated' style.

nevertheless, *fatiguing*, as it was all up and down hill, and the roots of
trees which lay across the path rendered walking both difficult and
irksome.

b. After staying four days, the winds being against the vessel going out, we
    tramped it home; [. . .]

c. Kaiwarra hill took us about an hour to get to the top, [. . .].

(From W. FERGUSON, to a Friend in England, 1 November 1842)

(22b) is an example of indefinite *it* with a denominal transitive verb, a colloquial
pattern that is on the increase in the Late Modern English period (see Denison
1998: 225–8); (22c) is an example of a syntactic blend in which *Kaiwarra hill* is a
locative that appears in the slot where we might expect a dummy-*it* subject (i.e. *It
took us about an hour to get to the top of Kaiwarra hill*). Thus, examples (21) and (22)
nicely show that letters are an often stylistically mixed genre.

3.3 Regionalisms

As pointed out in Section 2, background information on the regional origin of the
New Zealand emigrants is rather patchy. One way of getting at regional variation
in my data is by looking for grammatical regionalisms. Irregular verb forms are thus
an obvious choice for investigation. The letters contain only two instances of what
Anderwald (2007, 2009, 2011) refers to as so-called 'Bybee verbs', i.e. a strong verb
paradigm that is still relatively productive and can attract new members as evidenced
by Web data (historically, the 'Bybee verbs' are members of the verb class IIIa):

(23) a. In the morning, [. . .] we started off, and walked four miles farther,
          when we came to the rocky settlement Pa, and had our usual meal,
          potatoes and tea, which we *drunk* out of our tinder boxes.

(From W. FERGUSON, to a Friend in England, 1 November 1842)

      b. Here we were joined by a Mr. Anderson, one of the ship's carpenters,
          who was going to the vessel, and by a Mr. Box, who was going as far as
          Buccarra, and here our labours *begun*.

(From W. FERGUSON, to a Friend in England, 1 November 1842)

In the *Freiburg English Dialect corpus* (FRED), the forms with the historical plural
stem in <u> are still surprisingly frequent (attested from south-eastern, south-
western as well as some northern dialects, see Anderwald 2007: 274). They are
thus not clear indicators of a particular regional dialect but rather markers of non-
standard usage. The problem with these instances is that they come from the same
letter, which, additionally, is written in a generally high register that occasionally
contains some colloquial syntactic patterns (see Section 3.2 above). They are thus
further examples of stylistic mixing rather than regional variation.

The only other example of variation in the verb paradigm is that of the verb *show*, which has a variant *shew* (three attestations in my data). *Shew* is still used as an archaic form of the verb today, and, moreover, it is not an indicator of regional variation, either. Overall, the letters are regionally rather neutral. They do not provide evidence of grammatical patterns that Ihalainen (1995: 213–15) lists as dialect markers, such as second person singular verbs (*tha knows*) or the Northern Subject Rule as examples of northern regionalisms, nor uninflected *do* and *have* (*he don't know, it have happened*) as southern dialect features.

3.4 Recessive constructions

The letters contain a number of syntactic constructions that were no longer part of the core grammar at the time, such as negation without *do*-support, or at best recessive patterns, such as the *be*-perfect. Another example of a recessive pattern is the passival (and the innovative progressive passive). I will look at these in turn.

3.4.1 Negation without do-support

During the Early Modern period, negation of lexical verbs with auxiliary *do* became more and more widespread (see Ellegård 1953; Warner 1990). In Present-Day English, *do*-less negation can still be used with marginal modals such as *need* or with lexical *have*. These uses are also attested in the New Zealand letter collection:

(24) With money you *need not* undergo the least hardships worth speaking of, and you can get almost everything you want from the commencement.

> (Extracts from a Letter from the REV. CHARLES W. SAXTON, to Mr. BROMFIELD, 13 July 1842)

(25) I confess I was very much disappointed at first at our not having a harbour, but then we have so many advantages which the other settlements *have not*, that I am quite reconciled to it.

> (From ALEXANDER AUBREY, ESQ., to WILLIAM BRIDGES, ESQ., 10 May 1842)

Do-less negation of lexical *have* is actually quite a common pattern in the data (9 out of the 20 examples of *do*-less negation). There are three instances of *do*-less negation of *need*, but, more importantly, neither lexical *have* nor modal *need* are attested with *do*-support in the data.

Throughout the Late Modern Period, negation without *do*-support is clearly a recessive pattern. According to Denison (1998: 195), this usage becomes ungrammatical only towards the end of the nineteenth century. So it does not come as a surprise that the letters contain evidence of *do*-less negation of verbs such as *know*, *fear*, *doubt* and *care*:

(26) a. Of the 100,000 acres, of which *I know not* exactly how many sections
          have been given out – say 70,000, [. . .].

(Extract from a Private Letter to H. S. Chapman, Esq., 30 August 1842)

      b. [. . .] when once I get a little settled to have a spring crop, I *fear not* <u>but</u>
          my house will be the house of plenty, [. . .].

(From MR. WILLIAM CULLEN, formerly of Huish Episcopi, near Langport,
Somerset, 3 July 1842)

      c. *I doubt not* <u>but</u> I may get good land, as the greatest number of choosers
          are for people in England, [. . .].

(From MR. WILLIAM CULLEN, formerly of Huish Episcopi, near Langport,
Somerset, 3 July 1842)

      d. *I care not* who may boast of the hardships they have had to undergo in
          these new colonies, [. . .].

(From MR. D. MOORE, who went out to New Zealand as a Master Builder, to
his friends in Yorkshire, 19 June 1842)

Of these, only *doubt* (3) and *fear* (2) occur more than once; furthermore, four of
these five instances are followed by a concessive clause introduced by *but*. Among
the verbs that are attested without *do* in negation, only *doubt* and *know* are also
used with auxiliary *do* in my data. While there is only one instance of negated *doubt*
with *do*-support in the letter collection (from an official letter),[15] *do*-supported
negation is actually the default pattern for *know* (eight with *do*-support vs. only one
do-less negation). More importantly still, *know, doubt, fear* and *care* are all quite
often negated without *do* until the nineteenth century (Denison, p.c.), and the
letters thus represent current usage of the time rather than a particularly archaic or
innovative language use.

3.4.2 *Present (past) perfect with* be *as auxiliary*

The perfect construction in the Late Modern Period has a recessive variant with an
auxiliary *be* when the verb is a motion verb or a mutative verb. The *be*-perfect is
on its way out, particularly in the second half of the nineteenth century (see Kytö
1997), but it is still attested occasionally with verbs of motion such as *go* (27), *come*
(28) or *arrive* (29):

(27) a. [. . .] for if she is not here in eighteen months, I shall very likely *be gone*
          away from here.

(From WILLIAM DENT, one of the labourers of the Preliminary expedition to
Nelson, 10 September 1842)

      b. her husband *was gone* about ninety miles into the country to barter for
          pigs with the natives.

(From JAMES BARTON, to his Parents, 9 July 1842)

---

[15] This may simply be due to the limited size of the sample.

c. Some Scotch [. . .] *are gone* down to Wellington to fetch their baggage, and set to work among us.

> (From one of the earliest settlers at Wanganui, and the largest Landowner there, to the Editor of the *New Zealand Journal*, 5 May 1842)

(28) a. I have sent this letter by the Clydeside, that has been under repair at Wellington, which *is come* direct to England.

> (From WILLIAM DEW, to his brother, MR. JAMES DEW, Ham, Surrey, 25 December 1842)

b. [. . .] and although the spring *is not come on*, I am leaving off wearing flannel, &c.

> (From W. FERGUSON, to a Friend in England, 1 November 1842)

(29) Stanton and Tunnicliffe *are just arrived* by the ship Clifford.

> (Extract from a letter from MR. ROBERT BODDINGTON, to Mr. W. BODDINGTON, Coventry (brother), 28 May 1842)

With *gone* the letters still have an even split of *be*- and *have*-perfect constructions (five instances each), whereas with *come* and *arrived*, the *have*-perfect prevails (nine out of a total of eleven and seven out of eight hits, respectively). One of the likely reasons why perfect *be* was eventually replaced by forms with auxiliary *have* is that *be* was doing double duty as the auxiliary for the perfect and the passive, so that some instances are ambiguous between an aspectual and a (stative) passive reading:

(30) [. . .] we arrived safe to this place and *were landed* 20th September 1841, after a very prolonged voyage.

> (From JAMES THOMAS SHAW, formerly Shipwright in the Dockyard at Devonport, to a Friend in Plymouth, 16 February 1842)

The letters contain two more examples of *landed* with the auxiliary *be*, but also an unambiguously passive example with the additional auxiliary *have*:

(31) Two cargoes of horses, cattle, and sheep, *have been* recently *landed* here;

> (From Mr. TUCKETT, Chief Surveyor, to the New Zealand Company, February 1842)

Without more reliable quantitative data, however, it is difficult to assess whether the usage of the *be*-perfect in the New Zealand letters is particularly conservative or innovative.

3.4.3 *Passival vs. progressive passive*

In Late Modern English, it was still possible to use the present progressive with a passive meaning, especially if the patient noun in subject position was inanimate. According to evidence from the ARCHER corpus (Hundt 2004: 104–5), the passival shows a slight increase in the first half of the nineteenth century and still outnumbers the progressive passive when the settlers migrated to New Zealand. It is therefore not at all surprising that the letters contain a few passivals (four altogether):

(32) a. Great preparations *are* at present *making* for the whaling season [. . .].

> (From ALEXANDER PERRY, Esq., to his Father, Dr. PERRY, of Glasgow, written after a year's experience of Port Nicholson, 10 June 1842)

  b. While dinner *was preparing*, H—— and myself lay along the floor, and overcome with fatigue, fell asleep.

> (From W. FERGUSON, to a Friend in England, 1 November 1842)

  c. [. . .] a chapel, a public school-room, and a library *are building*.

> (From JAMES BARTON, to his Parents, 9 July 1842)

  d. In the third year a cruel stop *is putting* to agricultural exertions just at spring time.

> (Extract from a Private Letter to H. S. Chapman, Esq., 30 August 1842)

The syntactic newcomer – i.e. the progressive passive – is also attested, but it is not used more frequently – and even though the data in this very small collection of texts do not allow us to subject them to statistical modelling, at least they do not contradict the general development at the time. The progressive passive, while being an established pattern by the mid 1800s, is used relatively infrequently.[16] Note that in example (33c) the progressive passive could be regarded as a variant of the mediopassive[17] rather than the passival.

(33) a. they *are*, however, *being* fast *destroyed*, or *driven away*.

> (From a Gentleman at Nelson, to his Father in Warwickshire, 16 May 1842)

  b. [. . .] roads, bridges, and drains *are being made*.

> (From G. FELLINGHAM, journeyman printer, to his parents, 12 March 1842)

  c. [. . .] (the price at which it *is being retailed* at present is £2, carriage included) [. . .]

> (From MR. FRANCIS JOLLIE, to WILLIAM BLAMIRE, Esq., London, 20 December 1842)

In some instances, a prepositional phrase is used that allows the writer to avoid the choice between a passival and a progressive passive altogether. Example (34b), incidentally, occurs immediately after the passival quoted in (33b) above, and in (34d), the passive-like reading has additional support in the agentive *by*-phrase:

---

[16] There is only one instance of a progressive passive in the Cherry Valley letters, which will be discussed below: 'But there is the dreadful picture – the countrey *is* always *being drained* of the able-bodeyed men to fill the ranks of the Army [. . .]' (Thomas Buckley to his children, 5 December 1864).

[17] Note that mediopassives, e.g. '[. . .] they have *sold well* at 6d. 4d. 3d. each, according to size' (From WILLIAM DEW, to his brother, MR. JAMES DEW, Ham, Surrey, 25 December 1842), at a total of 16 instances, are much more frequent than the progressive passive. This might be some indication that mediopassives were a relatively frequent pattern in the input to New Zealand English grammar (for the frequency of the mediopassive with *screen* in Present Day New Zealand English, see Hundt 1998: 115–16).

(34) a. Several farms are already occupied and *in process of occupation.*

> (From CAPTAIN ARTHUR WAKEFIELD, R. N.; Company's Agent at Nelson, to the Secretary, 21 August 1842)

b. There are, at the present time, several brick houses *in course of erection,* [. . .]

> (From G. FELLINGHAM, journeyman printer, to his parents, 12 March 1842)

c. We have two or three schools on foot, and a library, and a literary and scientific institution; several brick houses *in course of erection*, and a number of respectable wooden ones.

> (From a letter received from Nelson by MRS. CATHERINE TORLESSE of Stoke, by Nayland, 9 June 1842)

d. A road to it is *in progress* of formation by the Company.

> (From a respectable settler at Wellington, who had recently visited New Plymouth; from a private Letter received by the Secretary of the New Zealand Company, 5 June 1842)

Denison (2007: 118), who also found a surprising absence of progressive passives in his letter corpus, discusses other avoidance strategies, such as the use of a plain passive.

To sum up, none of the variants discussed in this section appear to be particularly marked regionally or socially at the time. The recessive features that are attested in my letter collection therefore do not provide evidence that the written language of the migrants was particularly conservative or innovative.

4. A close-up on relative clauses

The New Zealand letter collection contains a number of relative clauses that are worth looking at. These would have fitted into some of the sub-sections of Section 3 but will be treated here under one heading. Relative clauses that have a personal pronoun as their antecedent, for instance, could have been discussed in the context of recessive features: according to Denison (1998: 111, 274–5) they are obsolescent in Late Modern English and archaic (or very formal) in Present Day English, especially with a third person pronoun. My letter collection yields four instances of this obsolescent pattern:

(35) a. I shall not benefit by any one's coming, but I should be glad to see any one from home, and *they that do not come*, I hope, by the blessing of Almighty God, to return and see, [. . .].

> (From MR. WILLIAM CULLEN, formerly of Huish Episcopi, near Langport, Somerset, 3 July 1842)

b. Dear friends, I am happy to say, that the people behaved very kind to all the passengers that came out in our ship; for **they** *that came out in the first ship* had some houses up to receive us.

> (From A. and E. HOSKIN, to their Parents, 19 February 1842)

c. [. . .] the natives sing and pray in their way; they make a fire, and say
    'that if any do curse or tell lies they will burn in that fire, and **they** *that are*
    good will go up to the stars.'

> (From THOMAS DODSON and GEORGE DODSON, to F. W.
> JERNINGHAM, Esq., Southampton, September 1841; note the Biblical quality
> of this example)

d. **They** *that work for private individuals* have 6s. a day.

> (From JOHN and ANN FRENCH, working emigrants, to their parents, near
> Ashburton, in Devonshire, 28 February 1842)

The last example does not appear stylistically marked and, maybe somewhat surprisingly, stems from a letter written by labouring emigrants. Note that, in an
alternative analysis of these examples as nominal relative clauses, the pronoun could
be viewed as part of the relative clause rather than its antecedent (see Denison 1998:
275).

Occasionally, the writers use the non-standard relative markers *what* and *but*
what, but they are all from letters that provide us with very little background
information on their authors:

(36) a. We are now expecting a cargo of sheep and bullocks from Sydney, *what*
         Captain King is gone after.

> (From A. and E. HOSKIN, to their Parents, 19 February 1842)

b. I should say that the wages and gifts *what* she gets by sewing is not less
    than £40 a year.

> (From JANE CROCKER to her Father, MR. SAMUEL CROCKER, Revelstoke,
> 7 February 1842)

c. There is not one Coventry man here *but what* is doing well, and has a
    house of his own.

> (Extracts from a Second Letter from JAMES BARTON, to his Parents,
> 13 September 1842)

On the social connotations of *but what*, in particular, see Denison (1998: 283).
In one instance, *what* looks like a non-standard relative marker *but what* actually
introduces a hypothetical clause:

(37) It is a great pity *but what* some person was out here with a machine to dress
     it: they might make a fortune in a short time.

> (From G. FELLINGHAM, journeyman printer, to his parents, 12 March 1842)

Denison (1998: 288) mentions the possibility of blending relative clauses and conditionals, but the examples he mentions are of a different kind, i.e. they are actual
blends of the two types of clauses, whereas in the example above we find a relative
marker that occurs in the position where we would expect *if* as a subordinator.

Not surprisingly, perhaps, preposition stranding in restrictive relative clauses is also attested in my data. The first one (38a) is from a letter that contains other non-standard features whereas the second (38b) is from an official letter (where it co-occurs with Latinate words such as *commence* and *contiguous*):

(38) a. We can get them from the natives for blankets, or for 'money gold' as they call it, which we call sovereigns; the last lot we bought was from a ship that brought pigs for sale; we bought as many as came to £77. 10s. which, thank God, we have had a good sale *for*.

> (From A. and E. HOSKIN, to their Parents, 19 February 1842)

b. They are steady, honest folks, that I consider myself lucky in meeting *with*.

> (From MR. FRANCIS JOLLIE, to WILLIAM BLAMIRE, Esq., London, 20 December 1842)

There are also some instances without prepositions that could be classified as 'non-standard' (both examples, incidentally, are from letters that contain other non-standard features):

(39) a. They had twenty yards of ground given them to build on for two years, ø *which Peter's was not finished*.

> (From A. and E. HOSKIN, to their Parents, 19 February 1842)

b. I have a good crop of cauliflowers, ø *which I have had the praise of the colony for second beauty*.

> (From WILLIAM DEW, to his brother, MR. JAMES DEW, Ham, Surrey, 25 December 1842; contents suggest that he is a carpenter)

In an alternative reading (Denison, p.c.), these might be interpreted as vague relatives, i.e. as continuative rather than relative clauses proper, with *which* functioning as a coordinating conjunction rather than a subordinating one (see Denison 1998: 286). Continuative relatives are attested elsewhere in my data, probably a feature of a comparatively 'loose' style:

(40) a. They are going on dressing the flax, which, if it answers, will be a great interest to the colony; it makes employment for the children, *which at present there is none for them*.

b. Our wheat is now in bloom; there is about 100 acres of wheat in the colony this year, *which is most of it among the poor people*.

> (From WILLIAM DEW, to his brother, MR. JAMES DEW, Ham, Surrey, 25 December 1842)

c. I we have a plenty of every thing to make ourselves comfortable, *which it will be much better* when Captain King's fat cattle comes from Sydney.

> (Letter from ARTHUR HOSKIN, to his Father, Mr. JOSIAH HOSKIN, Wheelwright, Holsworthy, Devon; 2 March 1842)

   d. There was one tree, which they call the cherry-tree, nineteen feet round, *which **it** is a thing impossible for me to tell* how many feet there is in them where they stand.

(Letter from ARTHUR HOSKIN, to his Father, Mr. JOSIAH HOSKIN,
Wheelwright, Holsworthy, Devon; 2 March 1842)

Zero relatives also occur quite commonly with subject antecedents in my data, another construction that is considered non-standard:

(41)   I had *a master ø offered me* 8s. per pair for making high shoes.

(From JAMES HARPER, a settler at Nelson, to his friends at Wootton Bassett,
17 April 1842)

Denison (1998: 281) points out that they come closer to standard usage when they are used in existential *there* sentences, which is in fact the most commonly attested context in my data with five out of seven instances; some also have indefinite pronouns as antecedents:

(42) a. There is *fine wood ø grows here* [. . .].

(From PAUL INCH, Shoemaker, to a friend at St. Malin, near Bodmin,
Cornwall, 2 March 1842)

    b. There is one *Mr. Butt, ø has sold his acre* for £900, with *six maori ø built houses* on it.

(From J. PHILPS, Brickmaker, to his brothers and sisters, 15 December 15 1842)

    c. [. . .] there have been *three ships ø come here* from England since I left.

(From. S. and W. CURTIS, to their relatives at Bodmin, Cornwall; 10 February
1842)

    d. There is a *man ø been to Mokou* after pigs [. . .].

(From JANE CROCKER, to her father, MR. SAMUEL CROCKER, Revelstoke;
26 February 1842)

    e. There is *some here ø would make £100.* each if home in England.

(From PAUL INCH, Shoemaker, to a friend at St. Malin, near Bodmin,
Cornwall; 2 March 1842)

    f. I don't think that there would be *many ø return to England* if free passages were given them.

(From Mr. S. GILLINGHAM, to his Brother, Mr. ROBERT GILLINGHAM, of
Camfield House, Shaftesbury, Dorset; 1 October 1842)

   Like the other features discussed, the evidence from the usage of relative clauses indicates that there is a certain amount of non-standard usage in the letters of the early New Zealand emigrants. In fact, relative clauses provide one of the most non-standard usages in my data. On the whole, however, the letters are surprisingly standard and conform largely to the written norm of their time.

5. Edited letters and their value for the study of linguistic variability

In order to be able to evaluate the perceived homogeneity of the New Zealand letters in my collection, it is important to assess the degree to which variability might have been edited out of the original letters. In order to do so, I will compare evidence from the New Zealand letters with an edition of roughly contemporaneous letters that were edited in 1991, and where we have more background information on the impact that the editorial process is likely to have had on the variability of the data.

One of the drawbacks of the New Zealand letter collection I used is that it was edited and published by the New Zealand Company, and little is known about the extent to which the editors changed the original letters. Spelling is the most likely aspect of the letters that would have been homogenised, and spelling variation was therefore not investigated. But the question remains as to whether the editors also adapted the grammar of the original letters. An indirect way of assessing the reliability of the New Zealand letter collection is by comparing it with a similar set of letters that were edited more recently and where we do have information on the extent of homogenisation that took place. I will use the Cherry Valley letters described in Section 2. We will first take a look at two longer examples that illustrate a higher degree of orthographic variation than that found in the New Zealand letters. From there, we will proceed to look at grammatical variability, including a close-up on patterns of negation.

5.1 Qualitative analysis

The first letter in the Cherry Valley collection (with the original line breaks) shows that the editors obviously did not modernise the original spellings (spellings that diverge from PDE conventions are italicised):[18]

(43)
[To Ralph Buckley]

June 1845

Dear Son and Daughter

I take this opportunity[19] to *adrefs* a few lines to you *hopeing* they will find
you all well as by the *blefsing* of God they leave us all at *presant*. I
received yours on the 20th Int. *wich* gives *caus* of joy as well as grief. Joy
that your *Brother* is *safly* landed, grief to *here* I am now the only son of my

---

[18] Note that the editor chose to transliterate the long <s> from the original autographs as <f> (e.g. *adrefs* instead of *adress*).

[19] Even though the editor seems to have generally transliterated the original spelling of the autographs, there are some (unconscious) normalisations in this electronic letter collection, too. The autograph of this letter is included in the published version of the letter collection (Dennett 1991), and the word *opportunity*, for instance, in the autograph is spelled <opertunity>.

Father. I feel glad you have sent me a few lines in *wich* you state you have
much to say but you cannot say it now. If your *Brother* be not set off I
should be glad if you <u>will</u> communicate all your mind by letter along with him.
I shall say I never intend to induce anyone to come to this country because
the change is so great both as regards the climate, the way of living and the
customs of the *Inhabitants* so that at first it makes *People* to mourn and grow
homesick and then to blame all who have given them any advice but I am of
opinion that there is a better chance to bring up a family here than there is
in England and am sorry I did not come 20 years sooner for things *where* better
then than they are now though trade is good. One thing I dislike is the con
stant *moveing* about of the working *claſs*. The wages of the common hand is but
low but Frank can tell you all about the country and climate.
Though I should be very glad to see all my children near me yet I would not
for a world induce any to come here against their own mind lest they should be
discontented and lay the blame upon me. We are expecting a change here
shortly as Mr Bottomley is going to sell the Factory at *wich* I now work, they
say next Wednesday and what will be my lot I cannot tell.
Pollard is not staying in York State we expect he is now working about
24 miles from us.
If you wish to know anything about *Releigon* or any other thing ask Frank – if
Frank be not set off I should wish him to write and let us know when he is
setting sail and the *Name* of the *Ship*. I am sorry I did not send for a good
cloth coat as the making is so high here. Sally wants him to bring a lether
girdle to put round David's *wast* – tell Frank *Fancy Makeing* is not as brisk as
it has been but *Broad* cloths are rather better.
Now we must commit you to God and the *Word* of His *Grace, hopeing* He will keep
you through *Grace* unto *Eternal Life* as we may never see each other more in the
flesh. This is the only way we can commune with each other so no more at
present, but conclude by giving our best wishes and *moes* sincere respects of
your ever loving and affectionate

Father and Mother
T & M Buckley

A letter from Thomas and Martha's son Frank shows that the letters in the collection
are from people with varying degrees of schooling: Frank appears to be a somewhat
less skilled letter writer in that his writing shows more internal variability, and he
even transferred hypercorrect *h*-insertion to the page:[20]

[20] That *h*-deletion is part of the local dialect is evidenced in the following sentence from a letter by Thomas and
Martha Buckley to their children Ralph and Sarah: 'But thank God she *as* been enabled still to bear up and
through great care and the good nursing of a fond Mother she is now much better' (13 September 1846); see
also Thomas Buckley to his children: 'my *ealth as* been good through the Winter, and is still good for my age'
(14 May 1872). Note that *h* is frequently dropped from *has* (84:59 for *(h)as been*) but never from *have* in present
perfect constructions in the data.

(44)

Millbury April 28th 1846

Dear Brother & Sister

I hope you *hare* well, as *thefs* [these] few lines leave *mee* at *preasent*. I have to in
form you that I *ham* working for the same *mastor* that I worked for before I
came to England. I *ham* working as a *mecanick* in the *mecannick's* shop. My
wagous are 9 shilings per day, or, in your *monney*, 6 per day. I *all so gow*
out *in to* the *countorey* to start looms. For *thifs* I have all *expenos* [expenses] and
board. Besides, I work 11 hours a day now; I ask you if *thifs* is not better
than *stoping* in *ingland*.
I *hame* going to have Thomas bound *prenties* in the same shop as I *hame* in. I
cannot say *mutch* about my father and mother or Charles and wife *becoas* I *doo*
not *now mutch* about them. When I got home from England I stayed *thair* 2 weeks
befour I went to work, and *aftor* I went to work I *wafs* 7 *munths befure* I
shaded *thair* door *whith* my *preasance*, and *wee* are not on the best of *tirms*
yet.
The reason is *becoas* as *soown* as *wee* got home, Sarah Ann began to set *summ*
disturbance, and I thought that I would *bee* out of the way. I have only seen
Salley once since I came, so from *thifs* you will see that I *hame*
alone, and, as it *wair*, *whithout aney* of our folks near me. Trade is *verrey*
good and wages are good. *Povition* is *rathour* sour than it was last *Sumour*.
I should like to know how you are *geting* along and *wair* you are, and in *wat*
state things are in *whith* you. I would write you a large *lettor* if I thought
that it would not *hirt* you to *loouse* it, but I will now *coclude*. Give my love
to all inquiring friends, and *axept* the same from your brother.

Frank Buckley

Despite the fact that the Cherry Valley letters show a greater variability in
their spelling, they are surprisingly standard in their use of grammatical patterns.
In particular, the Cherry Valley letters are remarkably similar to the New Zealand
letters in that they do not yield evidence of grammatical regionalisms. In the Cherry
Valley letters, we might expect features of Northern English, but features such as
second person singular verbs are only used in contexts where religious language is
quoted in the letters[21] and there are no instances of the Northern Subject Rule or
any of the regional features discussed in Ihalainen (1995). The Cherry Valley letters,
just like the New Zealand letters, contain a few instances of irregular verbs, but
again, these few irregular forms do not make them particularly non-standard.

---

[21] Another, equally marked, context is in a letter by Thomas Buckley's father to his son (14 December 1851),
reporting the utterances of some deceased members of the family that they conversed with in a spiritual session;
the reported speech is in verse and thus not part of the language of the letter writer.

(45) a. We *have wrote* to you two or three times, and have not heard a word from
          you, nor can we asertain wether you are alive or not.

                              (Thomas and Martha Buckley, to their children, 22 April 1849)

      b. I have seen stormes and *been drove* by the furious winds of the sea to seek
          shelter in soom peaceful harbour.

                                  (Thomas Buckley to his brother and sister, 14 December 1851)

      c. I have no need to fear want, nor of being *beholden* to any friend for a
          little while.

                                      (Thomas Buckley to his children, 13 December 1863)

      d. We have a good place to work at and *have* not *light up* at all this week . . .

                                 (Thomas and Martha Buckley, to their son, 25 February 1852)

      e. When it began to be cooler wether, I felt better and my appetite *begun* to
          improve – so now I feel much better and stronger.

                                      (Thomas Buckley, to his children, 26 December 1866)

      f. I have been a long time, and not got a letter form anny one, so I *begun* to
          think I was altogether forgotten.

                                      (Thomas Buckley, to his children, 15 November 1873)

      g. Jefse *is begun* to work, and David is now fit for work.

                                 (Thomas and Martha Buckley to their son, 2 September 1850)

      h. But you will say 'How as this *sprung* up?'

                                  (Thomas Buckley to his brother and sister, 14 December 1851)[22]

5.2 A case study on negation

The two letter collections are very similar in their use of negation patterns. As in the
New Zealand letters, multiple negation is curiously absent from the Cherry Valley
letters: there are no co-occurrences of other negative particles with *no*, *never* and
nothing. Likewise, the Cherry Valley letters contain the patterns of *do*-less negation
that are typical of the second half of the nineteenth century: lexical *have* and
need are both used without *do*-support (eight and thirteen instances, respectively).
As in the New Zealand data, both verbs are not attested with *do*-support.[23] The
Cherry Valley letters also contain other examples of lexical verbs negated without
do-support, namely *bloom*, *boast*, *come*, *doubt* (2×), *judge*, *know* (8×), *tempt*, *pour*,
say and *think* (2×). One difference between the two letter collections is that *know*
occurs more often with *do*-support in negation than without (21:8), including the
following example:

---

[22] Other examples of 'Bybee verbs' (*rung* and *sung*) are attested in hymns that are quoted in the letters.
[23] In addition to *need*, *dare* and *ought* are also negated without *do*-support in the Cherry Valley letters. Interestingly,
       inflected examples of *need* and *dare* (*needs not*, *dared not*, *durst not*) are also attested.

(46) I doant know yet.

(Thomas Buckley to his brother, 4 May 1847)

The orthography of the auxiliary in (46) is idiosyncratic, but the grammatical form is not. In other words, variability of negation in the Cherry Valley letters, overall, tends more towards the pattern evolving in the twentieth century than the New Zealand emigrant letters.

6. Conclusion and outlook

The letters from settlers and labouring emigrants that I investigated were written too soon after the establishment of the first settlements to possibly show any signs of dialect mixing or levelling. My aim in this chapter has therefore been to establish a part of the (written) base that went into the mix from which, eventually, standard English in New Zealand developed.

Due to the limited size and skewed composition of the letter collection, the analyses had to be of a qualitative rather than a quantitative nature. The close reading of the letters produced evidence of some idiosyncratic, some informal as well as the occasional non-standard grammatical patterns; other constructions fit the general stage of development of standard English at the time. The main result is that, with the exception of relative clauses, the letters are, on the whole, surprisingly standard and homogeneous. The letters, moreover, do not yield evidence of the non-standard features discussed in Hundt *et al.* (2004) for Present Day New Zealand English.

Comparison with the Cherry Valley letters shows that the high degree of homogeneity in the grammatical structures used in the New Zealand letters cannot be attributed to the editing process. The orthography of the Cherry Valley letters was much more variable, but, in terms of grammatical variability, this letter collection also proved to be surprisingly 'standard'.

The perceived standardness of the letters might have to be attributed, in part, to avoidance strategies – in cases of debated usage, for instance with the passival and the progressive passive, writers use prepositional phrases that express the same idea without having to make the choice between a construction that might have been felt to be already somewhat archaic and a construction that had only very recently been introduced into the grammar of English. Grammatically, then, the letters by both the New Zealand emigrants and the Cherry Valley settlers are surprisingly close to the standard English of the time, even though the latter exhibit a fair amount of orthographic variability, some of them betraying the regional origin of the writers. Regional grammatical markers, on the other hand, are conspicuously absent from the data, as are lexical items. One may suspect that it is the written medium that makes the authors (regardless of their social background) opt for regionally unmarked grammatical patterns and words.[24] The avoidance of regionalisms might be one aspect of what Fairman (2007a: 40) has aptly called 'letteracy'. In the case of the New Zealand letters, it would therefore be interesting to compare the results of this study with the spoken material available at the ONZE project.

---

[24] Tony Fairman (p.c.) similarly found a dearth of regional lexical material in the letters by his mechanically schooled writers (see, e.g., Fairman 2007a: 38).

CHAPTER 6

Emerging standards in the colonies: variation and the Canadian letter writer

Stefan Dollinger

1. Introduction[1]

Not too long ago, the Late Modern English (LME) period was considered to be a time when 'nothing much happened in the English language' (Tieken-Boon van Ostade 2009: back flap). Yet this period falls squarely into what Mesthrie and Bhatt (2008: 16) call the 'third crossing' of English, which, after the occupation of Britain by the Anglo-Saxons in the fifth century (first crossing) and the colonisation of Ireland in the twelfth century (second crossing), saw the further expansion of English as the language of the British Empire. Comparatively little is known, however, about former 'Colonial Standards', to use Mesthrie and Bhatt's term, or the non-UK Inner Circle Englishes, to employ Kachru's (1985) familiar model.

While work on Late Modern British English varieties has proceeded quickly in the past decade, which is perhaps best illustrated by the emergence of general textbooks on the period (e.g. Beal 2004; Tieken-Boon van Ostade 2009), the study of colonial varieties lags behind. There are, of course, notable exceptions, e.g. American English as the oldest New World variety and, more recently, as the result of the fortuitous discovery of early sound recordings (Gordon *et al.* 2004), New Zealand English. For Canada and its 'other' North-American variety – Canadian English (CanE) – the situation is particularly problematic as real-time studies are especially rare (Dollinger 2012). What is well developed, however, is a broad categorisation that describes CanE language history externally and relates it to assessments of probable linguistic practice (e.g. Chambers 1991; Bailey 1982). This allows a rudimentary classification of Canada in Schneider's (2007: 240–50) Dynamic Model in a top-down approach. For bottom-up theory building, linguistic data are sparse (but see Dollinger 2008a; Dollinger and von Schneidemesser 2011). The present chapter offers real-time data from early Ontario, the Canadian province that acted as the springboard for the settlement of much of the Canadian west and is therefore of prime importance in the foundation of Canadian English norms.

Much of the discussion on CanE has focused on the issue of the homogeneity of a CanE standard accent (see, e.g., Avis 1973; Boberg 2008; Dollinger and Clarke 2012a; and contributions in Dollinger and Clarke 2012b). From the point of view

---

[1] Thanks go to Marianne Hundt and Merja Kytö for their feedback on earlier versions of this paper, to anonymous reviewers and to Richard J. Watts for presenting an earlier version, but especially to Anita Auer for her belief in unconventional ideas. All shortcomings remain, however, entirely my own.

of twentieth-century urban middle-class speakers, this perspective seems to be adequate and is usually explained by means of extensive Canadian networks, both private and business-oriented, along the east–west axis that reinforce Canadian norms. For other linguistic levels, most notably spelling, considerable heterogeneity exists to this day (e.g. Ireland 1979; Heffernan *et al.* 2010), and there is good reason to assume that in earlier periods even greater heterogeneity existed, some of which becomes evident in the letter data to be presented in Section 4.

The present chapter aims to provide linguistic data that illustrate the process of new-dialect formation, i.e. the koïnéisation process that affected early CanE and led to the establishment of Canadian norms that come to be distinct from norms of British and American input varieties. Section 2 introduces the letter data at the core of the empirical part of the present chapter, while Section 3 examines the guidelines for first person *shall* and *will* in three of the most prevalent grammars in early Ontario. In Section 4, usage from letter data will be contrasted with the standard print data that are usually found in corpus studies. It will be shown that, firstly, the letter data are superior compared to the print data and, secondly, that grammars in early Canada offer little evidence for actual usage.

2. The letter data and the variable

The letter data come from the *Corpus of Early Ontario English* (*CONTE-pC*) and were found under the heading MS-563 (Reel 1–36) in the Archives of Ontario, Toronto. The common denominator of these letters is that they represent the incoming and outgoing mail to the Surveyor-General or the Commissioner of Crown Lands from the late eighteenth century to around 1900. The Surveyor-General and Commissioner were in charge of administering land grants, and as such the correspondence includes important documents to establish legal ownership of land in Ontario. While the outgoing letters were written exclusively by educated, middle-class or lower middle-class clerks, the incoming letters represent some of the best available evidence of the vernacular in early Ontario, or at least of writers who wanted to relocate to Ontario. In these letters, a wealth of texts by people writing to the Government of Ontario (Upper Canada) can be found. Writers ask for land grants, report (as land surveyors) on their work carried out in the field, or argue over the proper implementation of a settlement policy. Linguistically most interesting are the minimally schooled writers who aimed to acquire land in Canada.

By applying the criterion of adherence to standard English norms at the time, the letter material can be divided into middle-class (or lower middle-class) and lower-class writers, as Table 6.1 shows. The lower-class writers were identified by their writing style, diction and by the subject matter.

Fitting for the business context of these letters and for a frontier community at the time, but very regrettable, is the fact that evidence for female writers is almost non-existent. The letters in period 1 consist of forty-eight authors, only four of whom are female; in period 2 only two out of forty-two authors are female; and

Table 6.1 *Ontario letter data, 1776–1849, by number of words*

	1776–99	1800–24	1825–49
Middle-class writers	11,600	14,000	12,000
Lower-class writers	3,200	1,000	3,100
Total	14,800	15,000	15,100

Table 6.2 *Origins of letter writers in* CONTE-pC, *identified writers in percent*

Origin	1776–99	1800–24	1825–49
Scottish	18.2	17.4	6.3
Irish	9.1	8.7	25.0
English	27.3	13.0	18.8
American	36.4	52.2	25.0
Canadian	9.1	8.7	18.8
Welsh	0	0	6.3

in period 3 merely two out of sixty-four authors are female. These letters, which are all manuscripts on microfilm, may be classified into two groups:

- petitions from private persons applying for land grants or support;
- intra-governmental communications.

While the second group is highly uniform, the first displays a remarkable amount of linguistic variation. Table 6.2 shows the heterogeneous origin of the authors that could be identified.

Results from these letter data will be contrasted with traditional print-based corpus material from the *Bank of Canadian English* (*BCE*) (Dollinger, Brinton and Fee 2006–) in Section 4. The *BCE* is a much larger quotations database than the letter corpus, with 2.25 million words, ranging from the sixteenth to the twenty-first century.

The linguistic variable to be studied here is the use of *shall* and *will* in first person declarative sentences. The metropolitan English standard has codified the use for these two modal verbs functioning to indicate future time in the following way, as stipulated in Johnson's dictionary in declarative sentences, the first person uses *shall* as the modal auxiliary to mark the future, in the second and third persons *will* fulfils this function.

Non-compliance with the 'rule' had serious consequences. Sundby *et al.* (1991) classifies first person *shall* and *will* as a heavily commented variable. Beal (2004: 97) refers to deviant linguistic behaviour in this regard as a 'shibboleth of Scots speech', Görlach (1999: 84) stereotypes it as Irish, while Wales (2002: 53) identifies the Northern English as users of first person *will*. Most recently, McCafferty and

Amador-Moreno (2014) provide one of the most coherent accounts on the spread of first person *will* and, using data from Dollinger 2008a, argue for a regional English English origin. A glance at popular grammars in early Ontario will offer a point of departure for the empirical part.

3. Guides to a norm: early grammars in Canada

Looking back from today's perspective, Anglophone Canada acquired its linguistic autonomy fairly recently. The long history of the movement towards CanE autonomy is best illustrated by the very late development of endonormative language standards. Only in the second half of the twentieth century were important linguistic developments towards an autonomous standard made and important hallmarks of linguistic autonomy produced. Among those were the first high-quality Canadian dictionaries (since 1962), scholarly dictionaries (Avis *et al.* 1967), guides by the Canadian Press syndication for journalists (since 1940, Pratt 1993: 53), and, fairly late, reference grammars (Fee and McAlpine 2007 [1997]). It was not until 1967 that the first, fully Canadianised desk dictionary (*Gage Senior Dictionary*, Gregg 1993) was made available.[2] These benchmarks cast some doubt on the classification of Phase IV (Endormativity) as *ending* around 1970 (Schneider 2007: 245–7), suggesting instead that this process was merely beginning at that time.

However, for much of the eighteenth and nineteenth centuries, Canada was looking towards London, England, for its linguistic models. At the same time, the overwhelming majority of its speakers spoke a North American dialect and accent (Avis 1973), and it is here, at the intersection of a Late Modern American linguistic input layer and a thorough helping of positive British sentiments, that the perplexing Canadian split of language standards emerges. For those language features that are consciously accessible *and* that were noticed by prescriptivists, the sociolinguistic situation at the time can be described as a North American base with a British upper layer. While CanE originated in AmE varieties, the prestige variety until the mid-twentieth century was the 'Queen's' or 'King's' English, the language of the English public schools and of Oxford and Cambridge. Chambers (2004) has called this Canadian sociolect, the affected language of those Canadians aspiring to 'out-English' the English, Canadian Dainty, which is described as a 'superimposition on the indigenous Canadian accent of a British layer that came, for the next century [mid-nineteenth to mid-twentieth century, SD] to represent good breeding and good taste' (Chambers 2004: 229). One would expect such sentiments to be reflected in the popular grammar books of the time.

---

[2] The *Canadian Oxford Dictionary* (1st edn 1998, 2nd edn 2004), which won the PR battle with Gage, now Nelson, in the late 1990s and early 2000s is no longer Canadian. The mother publishing house, Oxford University Press, decided in October 2008 to close the entire Canadian dictionary unit in Toronto (see Dollinger 2008c). Considering the inactive state of the *Gage Canadian Dictionary* since 1997, CanE has reverted to a de facto exonormative status as it pertains to desk dictionaries.

Table 6.3 *Print run (and, implicitly, copies sold) of*
Davidson's Canada Spelling Book

Year publ.	1840	1845	1850	1860	1864
Copies sold	0	42,000	121,000	157,000	175,000

Three of the key texts in wide circulation in early Ontario were Alexander David-son's *Canada Spelling Book*, which was first published in 1840, Samuel Kirkham's 1831 *English Grammar* and Lindley Murray's *English Grammar* from 1795. Murray's grammar was chosen because it was published early and is deemed to have had a great influence on early North American English.[3] Davidson's *Canada Spelling Book* seems to be one of the most influential works if one looks just at its circulation. The figures for various print editions shown in Table 6.3 provide the number of copies sold, according to information on the inside covers of the book.[4]

Even if these numbers are only approximately correct, Davidson's book was bound to have had a staggering influence. In 1851, at the time of the first Canadian census, about 2 million[5] people lived in the entire country, about 950,000 of these in Ontario. Apparently, more than 120,000 copies of the book had been sold by that time, which would yield a considerable rate of dissemination through about 6% of the population. These data pale in the face of the sales figures for the best-selling present-day *Canadian Oxford Dictionary*, which has sold about 250,000 copies since its publication in 1998 and is widely considered an enormous commercial success for a Canadian population of 30–33 million from 1998 to the 2008 closure of the Toronto OUP reference unit. Even without factoring in the lower literacy levels, Davidson's 121,000 copies sold by 1850 must have been a spectacular commercial success.

Davidson was born in Northern Ireland in 1794 and came to Upper Canada (Ontario) in 1821, well beyond his formative years, where he lived until his death in 1856. He was a man of many talents, a teacher, an author, a journalist and a newspaper editor, a businessman, a politician, and he held many public offices in SW Ontario, from Port Hope to Niagara-on-the-Lake. When he started teaching in 1822, he 'disliked the extensive use of American textbooks in Upper Cana-dian schools. He noted in June 1828 to . . . the civil secretary at York, that in his

---

[3] Note that Webster's speller is not discussed in this chapter because its importance in the present context appears to have been minimal.

[4] It is assumed that the numbers on the covers give a somewhat reliable representation of a print run. For practical purposes, I will equate the printed copies with the copies sold. The figures find indirect corroboration in Davidson's sales figures when matched with the print run offered in his editions. By 1847 'Davidson could enthusiastically report that 43,000 copies of the book had been sold, and by 1856 that figure had tripled' (Wilson 2000).

[5] Upper and Lower Canada's population amounted to close to 1.85 million alone (Board of Registration and Statistics 1853: v).

```
┌─────────────────────────────────────────────────────────────┐
│                    First Future Tense.                        │
│  1. I shall or will love,        1. We shall or will love,    │
│  2. Thou shalt or wilt love,     2. Ye or you shall or will love, │
│  3. He shall or will love.       3. They shall or will love.  │
│                                                               │
│                   Second Future Tense.                        │
│  1. I shall have loved,          1. We shall have loved,      │
│  2. Thou wilt have loved,        2. Ye or you will have loved,│
│  3. He will have loved.          3. They will have loved.     │
└─────────────────────────────────────────────────────────────┘
```

Figure 6.1 Davidson's (1845: 153) treatment of *shall* & *will* ('etymology' section)

experience nine out of ten books in use were from the United States' (Wilson 2000). Davidson identified himself as Canadian, which was not a given at the time, when he wrote that British books were 'to *us* necessarily defective, not being suited to our scenery and other localities' and that 'books of a foreign origin [i.e. American] are liable to more serious objections'. This sentiment apparently gave him the impetus to write his own speller, and in 1829, while resident in Port Hope on Lake Ontario, he completed 'The Upper Canadian spelling book' (Wilson 2000). Despite making many efforts to gain government support in aid of publication, he only managed to publish the book eleven years later, under the title *The Canada Spelling Book*.

While *The Canada Spelling Book* was to become the first copyrighted book in Upper Canada, Davidson could not get it approved for use in schools by the Ontario Superintendent of Education. One can assume that copyright fees acted as a deterrent for Superintendent Ryerson to adopt the book, but pedagogic reasons may have played a role as well (Curtis 1985). As pointed out above, the print run was impressive and it would be highly unlikely if at least some copies were not used in schools.

Besides Davidson, Murray's grammar is another interesting book. It is sometimes claimed to have had a profound impact on North American linguistic norms (Finegan 1998b: 373–4; cf. Beal 2004: 116, who considers Murray's grammar 'the most influential grammar until the last quarter of the [nineteenth] century'). Davidson's speller and Murray's grammar share a few key characteristics, including their treatment of modal auxiliary verbs. Murray and Davidson presented the modal auxiliaries in the etymology section, which, according to the conventions of the day, dealt with 'the different sets of words, their derivation, and the various modifications by which the sense of a primitive word is diversified' (Murray 1795: 19). Davidson's treatment of *shall* and *will* is shown in Figure 6.1.

This is all Davidson and Murray had to say on *shall* and *will*: *I shall or I will*, and *We shall or we will*. Crucially, when to use the one or the other (as discussed, for example, in Boyd and Boyd 1980; Tieken-Boon van Ostade 1985) was left unaddressed. Such paradigms, which were ubiquitous in grammars and spelling books of the day, give no guidance on when to use *shall* or *will* in the first person. Corpus studies have shown that the verbal paradigm in these grammars does not reflect late eighteenth- and nineteenth-century usage (e.g. Fries 1925; Dollinger 2008a: ch. 9). Instead, it represents an antiquated model and is a good reflection of the chasm between prescriptive grammatical statements in upper- and middle-class circles and the language use of the masses.

It is in this context that Kirkham, the 'American' grammar, offers a fresh departure from old lore. In a comment to the 'received wisdom' of the time, as shown in Figure 6.1, Kirkham states:

> NOTE. What is sometimes called the *Inceptive* future, is expressed thus; 'I am going *to write*,' 'I am about *to write*.' Future time is also indicated by placing the infinitive present immediately after the indicative present of the verb *to be*, 'I am *to write*,' 'Harrison is *to be*, or ought *to be*, commander in chief;' 'Harrison is *to command* the army.' (Kirkham 1831: 140)

Kirkham features a description of newer periphrastic forms expressing the future, the immediate future, the *going to* future. For *shall* and *will*, however, even Kirkham reiterates the conventional knowledge of the time.

To summarise, we can say that, first, three widely used and popular reference guides offer no guidance for the use of first person *shall* & *will* to the Canadian student, and, second, that some grammars included a descriptive element, which seems to have been a novelty in the Canadian context (but see Beal 2004: 113 on Joseph Priestley's [1761] non-prescriptive attitude) and, third, that rules and norms in this area were, most likely, handed down orally by the teacher if the teachers offered such guidance at all.

4. *Shall* and *will*: making the case for letter data

In this section, I present data from first person *shall* and *will* in early Canada from both print and letter data. I will first look at traditional print data, which will then be contrasted with letter data; this will highlight how letter data play a crucial role in establishing the LME vernacular. As shown in Section 2, British English has traditionally embraced first person *shall* as the standard form in declarative sentences with future tense reference.

Table 6.4 shows the data from more traditional, historical corpus linguistic sources, represented by the *Bank of Canadian English*, which is largely comprised of print sources. All reported tokens, here and elsewhere, stem from declarative sentences. What is noticeable is that despite being a much larger text collection than the letter corpus, first person *shall* does not occur prior to 1850.

If the print data are taken at face value, one would need to assume that first person *will* was the standard form in the early nineteenth century and from 1950 onwards,

Table 6.4 *First person* shall *and* will *in BCE print data (n). Declaratives*[6]

BCE	First person *shall*	First person *will*
1750–99	0	0
1800–49	0	3
1850–99	4	5
1900–49	5	4
1950–99	3	25
2000–9	2	26

Table 6.5 *First person* shall *and* will *in Canadian letters, declaratives. Percent (n)*[7]

	shall	will
1776–99	73.3 (22)	26.7 (8)
1800–24	54.5 (18)	45.5 (15)
1825–49	48.1 (13)	51.9 (14)

when *shall* only appears in stylised contexts. Moreover, the print data suggest a linguistic effect concerning first person *shall* and *will* that correlates with 'Canadian Daintyism' in the period 1850–99. At the time when Canada was becoming a country in its own right, a 'Dominion' in 1867, a linguistic 'link' to Great Britain is shown in first person *shall* uses. From 1950 onwards, we see that *I/we shall* is holding some ground by 'specialising' in semantic functions, taking on undertones as a marker of quaintness/playfulness, which is illustrated below with an example from the *Nanaimo Harbour City Star*, a small local British Columbian paper:

> In return I promised her that if she succeeds in this high calling, I shall send her for one whole month, all expenses paid, to the sunny LaLa Land, where oranges grow on apple trees. (*Harbour City Star*, 27 September 2003: A9)

Overall, though, these marginal uses make clear that *will* had become the Canadian standard.

If we compare the print data in Table 6.4 with letter data, a much more nuanced picture is unfolding. Table 6.5 presents the data for first person *shall* and *will* from the Canadian letter data, which yields quite a different distribution for the variants.

---

[6] Instances of *'ll* (of which there are 206 instances of first person *'ll* in that version [2009] of the BCE) were ruled out, as it is not clear whether they represent *shall* or *will*.

[7] One-tailed chi-square results (hypothesis: *will* superseding *shall*): p (btw. 1776–1779 and 1800–1824) = 0.099; p (btw. 1776–1779 and 1825–1849) = 0.046; hypothesis confirmed in the long run – between period 1 and 3.

Table 6.6 *Period 1: first person* shall *&*
will *in letters, declaratives. Percent (n)*[8]

1776–99	shall	will
CanE	73.3 (22)	26.7 (8)
NW-BrE	55.3 (131)	44.7 (106)
St-AmE	68.2 (15)	31.8 (7)
St-BrE	62.5 (25)	37.5 (15)

We see earlier attestations of *will* in period 1, 1776–99, which was not available in the more formulaic print styles in the early Canadian print sources, where direct speech, a speech act fostering first person *shall* and *will*, hardly occurs. In the frontier context, newsprint is used as a medium of announcement, which favours the third person. In the first half of the nineteenth century, the letter data offer a more heterogeneous picture than the early print sources. At this point, first person *shall* and *will* are roughly split in half, which is in marked contrast to the categorical use in the print data of first person *will* from 1800 to 1849.

A comparison of the use of first person *shall* and *will* with letters of British and American provenance[9] reveals further insights that are beyond the reach of print sources (see Table 6.6). Compared with three other letter corpora, Table 6.6 shows that in period 1 CanE is more conservative in its more prevalent use of first person *shall* than letter writing in the BrE standard at the time, the American standard and a regional variety of BrE letters. Combined with the diachronic data in Table 6.5, a change in the frequency of first person *shall* can be observed: from a large majority form prior to 1800 (more than 73%), to a small majority in the first quarter of the nineteenth century to slightly under 50% in the second quarter. The direction of the change in the first part of the nineteenth century is remarkable, given the immigration stream into Ontario from the British Isles which peaked around those years. Yet, regardless, first person *will* was clearly gaining ground during that time. The print data from the *BCE* in Table 6.4 do not allow such a detailed diagnostic, which is evidence of the versatility of letters.

The letter data allow an additional point to be made. When the provenance of the letter writers is considered, the apparent mismatch between British in-migration and the establishment of first person *will* as the emerging Canadian norm becomes clear. Canadian Dainty was a lifestyle of linguistic consequence that is captured

---

[8] One-tailed chi-square results (hypothesis: St-BrE more conservative than all other varieties in the adherence to *shall*): p (St-AmE and CanE) = 0.46; p (St-BrE and CanE) = 0.24; p (St-BrE and NW-BrE) = 0.25; no statistically significant differences.

[9] The abbreviations in Table 6.6 stand for the following: 'NW-BrE' is the North-Western British English letter corpus compiled by Van Bergen and Denison (2007). 'St-AmE' and 'St-BrE' refer to the letter section of ARCHER-1.

Table 6.7 *Letter data from SIN (Scottish, Irish and Northern English) immigrants to Canada*

First person	1776–99	1800–24	1825–49
shall	4	0	0
will	0	3	4

in a 1956 poem by Irving Layton, entitled 'Anglo-Canadian'. Kingston, Ontario, mentioned in the poem, lies at the heart of United Empire Loyalist country:

> ANGLO-CANADIAN
> A native of Kingston, Ont,
> – two grandparents Canadian
> and still living
>
> His complexion florid
> as a maple leaf in late autumn
> for three years he attended
> Oxford
>
> Now his accent
> makes even Englishmen
> wince, and feel
> unspeakably colonial.
>   (Layton 1992: 87)

Canadian Dainty was a strategy to overcome one's colonial inferiority by 'out-Englishing' the English, a phenomenon which was still widespread among the Canadian elite in the mid-twentieth century, so that the date of publication is no coincidence. There is little wonder that Canadian Dainty-ism was doomed to be superseded by something more lasting, i.e. the emergence of a Canadian identity in its own right, which includes an accent and dialect that is native to Canada (this development is mirrored in Australia and New Zealand in the abandonment of 'colonial cringe', e.g. Leitner 2004: 87–106).

In the light of the Canadian Dainty hypothesis, the prevalence of first person *will* at the height of British immigration in 1825–49 in the letter data in Table 6.5 seems at odds with British norms. While the 'swamping' of Canada with speakers from the British Isles after 1815 until the 1860s brought in hundreds of thousands of immigrants from Britain and Ireland, more than 90% of them did not speak a south-eastern English dialect (Dollinger 2008a: 93). This is a crucial distinction, and it appears that the immigrants from Scotland, Ireland and Northern England (SIN) had the effect of reinforcing existing majority patterns towards first person *will*. The limited letter data from SIN writers helps to illustrate the point, as shown in Table 6.7.

As outlined in Section 2, SIN regions have been known to operate differently in terms of *shall* and *will* as a regional characteristic, but it is here that lower-class speakers almost categorically would not apply the English English *shall* & *will* distinction in the first person. And even the middle-class writers in early Canada do not adhere in the majority to the first person *shall* 'rule'. Only in the third period, 1825–49, do the middle-class writers exhibit more first person *shall* than the lower-class writers (Dollinger 2008a: 241).

Montgomery (1995) points out that letters from the semi-literate are hard to obtain. In this vein, Table 6.7 shows sparse data whose only compelling feature is their categoricity, which suggests a shift in use of SIN immigrants' usage around 1800 that can be explained by the immigrants' background. Earlier immigrants were often educated, such as clerks and civil servants who helped to establish a colonial hold on the country, while later, post-1800 immigrants were lower-class writers with limited education. The fact that letter corpora of the period generally allow the compiler to identify at least a proportion of the letter writers offers a highly localisable diagnostic that is, especially in the case of writers of limited schooling, indicative of regional usage.

These letter data, however, not only enlighten the discussion of input varieties and the amalgamation of input dialects into a Canadian standard. They go beyond the immediate local context and contribute to the discussion of other LME dialects. In the normative literature, *shall* and *will* have been among the key areas of research starting with the ME period, and yet, for LME, we are confronted with conflicting statements. More precisely, the Canadian letter data presented offer a layer of detail to the situation in Late Modern Ireland. In a recent textbook, Tieken-Boon van Ostade (2009) assesses the existing literature as follows:

> If the Irish ever had belonged to that category [Samuel Johnson's category of 'faulty users' of *shall* and *will*], by the nineteenth century, according to Facchinetti (2000), their usage wholly agreed with the normative structure of the eighteenth-century grammarians. (Tieken-Boon van Ostade 2009: 90)

This would imply that the Irish would use first person *shall*. The Canadian letter data do not concur with this account, since the SIN speakers, including the Irish, did not use first person *shall* at that time (1800–49), or at least not much. Looking at Facchinetti's (2000) data, which consist of reprints of Irish material in English newspapers, we can gauge that there are better-suited sources for a study of Irish English, such as letters. When Facchinetti (2000: 130) writes that the 'data suggest that, at least in the first part of the nineteenth century, the Irish employed *shall* with first person subject even more frequently than the English', we are dealing with all kinds of standardisation processes in the print media, including Irish printers, English printers and, possibly, Irish hypercorrections, so that it is impossible to reconstruct authentic Irish usage from it. Here, letters offer a set of data that serves as a corrective which would not be accessible with print sources.

In the light of these data, it is probably safe to say that Irish English speakers were using first person *will* in the first part of the nineteenth century. While a larger CanE letter sample would doubtless produce some forms of first person *shall*, there is reason to believe that the (non-upper-class) SIN speakers, the 'provincials', did not abide by the 'rule' that the first person future in declarative sentence demands *shall*. This is explicit in the letter data in Table 6.7 and implied in Table 6.5.

5. Homogeneity out of heterogeneity?

The present chapter has aimed at interpreting changes in use of first person *shall* and *will* from a bottom-up perspective. The findings can be summarised as follows: first, existing letter data have been shown to offer a much richer spectrum than the most extensive print corpus data for the variety. Second, grammar books in widespread circulation in Ontario at the time offered no clues for the heterogeneous practice in early Canadian letters, which establishes a need towards more letter data from other Canadian regions. Third, the case has been made that colonial varieties are not just a mere addendum, but a crucial part of the study of LME (see Watts and Trudgill 2002, McCafferty & Amador-Moreno 2014). Fourth, without letter data, the limitations of existing studies would be more difficult to identify.

These findings have repercussions for the modelling of Canadian English, which has usually been carried out from a language-external point of view or from top-down approaches. Based on such data, Schneider (2007) places Canada in the fifth and final phase of the formation of new Englishes (Phase V, dialect diversification), when it can be argued that previous stages, such as Phase IV (endonormative stabilisation), are not yet complete and dialect diversification has not yet begun (Hoffman and Walker 2010). Letter data from early Canada would certainly go a long way towards providing valuable clues, which are presently only partially available.

Common wisdom pertaining to Canadian heterogeneity in other linguistic areas, such as spelling, may probably be replaced by more precise accounts. One traditional take is the following expert statement on the sociolinguistic situation of a Canadian standard. Chambers goes so far as to suggest that being part and parcel of the Canadian make-up, Canadian linguistic tolerance is the cause for heterogeneity in spelling and usage found today:

> Education, policy-makers, linguists and others in many countries have apparently found it worthwhile and perhaps even interesting to consider matters of language standards and standard dialect and standard accent in their countries. You will be hard-pressed, I think, to find any counterpart for Canada. I do not think that the gap is accidental – that is, it is not due to anyone's neglect of duties, or to academic malaise, or anything negative like that. I think, rather, it is because there is a sense in which the notion of standards is alien to – perhaps even repugnant to – our national character. (Chambers 1986: 2–3)

Such an assessment seems to be unthinkable for nineteenth-century Canada. Egerton Ryerson, Superintendent of Education from 1844 to 1876, who spent his long tenure in office standardising textbook usage, would have protested vehemently.

The reason why language standards today vary across Canada might be found in an education system that dealt with numerous oddities in a young frontier society that fostered regional standards and focused on 'the big issues' such as political allegiance. That linguistic matters, apart from select spelling preferences and some other features, would take a back seat in such contexts is not surprising. Likewise, the Canadian elites provided little impetus towards the creation of a Canadian standard as they looked towards England for their models. Of course, only those who could afford it would attempt to do so, while the largest section of the population spoke a North American dialect. By 1956, it was fine for a poet to poke fun at those who did not. Concerning first person *shall* and *will*, however, *will* was on its way towards becoming the Canadian standard by the mid-nineteenth century.

What this case study shows is that CanE needs to be studied throughout its entire history on two levels: a British English superstratum and a North American substratum. As the literati in Canada tended to have ties with Britain and looked across the Atlantic for linguistic models for the most part of Canada's history, their writings tend to skew representations of the 'language of the people' disproportionately. We therefore need to look even more carefully in the archives for letters by immigrant or early Canadian writers, who have provided the bulk of the population input and the substratum that tends to be overlooked. For first person *shall* and *will*, regional letters provide valuable clues that allow a more coherent interpretation of variation. As an addendum, Canadian data can illuminate other LME variants, and vice versa. As Watts and Trudgill (2002) demonstrate, today there is no excuse not to treat English varieties beyond England. I hope to have shown that colonial varieties such as Canadian English are worth studying not only for their own sake, but also for the insights they give us on LME in general.

CHAPTER 7

Linguistic fingerprints of authors and scribes

Alexander Bergs

1. Introduction

One of the methodologically most challenging tasks in historical linguistics is to find out who actually produced the linguistic material which is available to us today. In other words: who is – linguistically speaking – responsible for the manuscripts and texts that have survived? Whose language do they represent? How much influence did scribes actually have on the final product?

These questions seem particularly interesting and important from the viewpoint of historical sociolinguistics (see Bergs 2005; Nevalainen 2012), which aims at describing and understanding language variation in context, i.e. in relation to speakers. On the one hand, we need to think about who actually produced the material we see before us now. As any sociolinguistic textbook today shows, it certainly makes a big linguistic difference if speakers are male or female, old or young, rich or poor. Both stable and dynamic social factors (e.g. gender and membership in a community of practice, or network) play an important role in the use of linguistic variables. There is no reason to believe that this was any different in the past, though we need to establish, of course, which factors were actually relevant at a given point in time (see Bergs 2012 on the risk of anachronism in historical sociolinguistics). In order to gauge the importance of any factor, we need to know who was actually responsible for the linguistic output we are analysing. Furthermore, we should not forget that manuscript production itself is an important social practice, and subject to a number of constraints that need to be investigated (see Fairman, Chapter 4 this volume). Both micro-level variation and macro-level modes of production are important questions in historical sociolinguistics, but both can only be studied productively if the exact source and context of linguistic performance are documented, or at least critically discussed.

This chapter focuses on methodological issues regarding the identification of scribal influences on authors' language. In particular, it discusses the distinctions between authors, scribes and the modes and context of production in historical letter writing. It uses the late Middle English Paston letters (*c.* 245,000 words by eleven male and four female Paston family members between 1421 and 1503) as an exemplary database to show that it can be very productive to distinguish between the different language levels when it comes to scribal influences. It will be shown that the influence of scribes (we can identify at least twenty-two different hands in the letters!) on the level of morphosyntax is rather limited. It is assumed that morphosyntactic variability in language is located right between conscious and subconscious language use in the sense that speakers are often aware of variables, different variants and their contextual value or function, but that, on the other hand, some of the variability goes unnoticed in concrete online processing. One example from present-day German is the infamous question of word order in subordinate clauses introduced by *weil* 'because'. We find variability here between verb final (standard) and verb second (innovative) order. The latter has been associated with greater subjectivity (see Keller 1995). Variability in this case has been attested across the board, and yet few if any speakers are even aware that they do show variability in their language use here.

This in turn can mean that historical scribes were often but not always aware of the language they heard from their authors, and that they probably attached some importance to the different forms they noticed (or, in some cases, maybe even ascribed to certain speakers/authors). In order to demonstrate this, it will have to be shown that scribes actually were very flexible when they wrote for different authors. If this is so, this will lead us to the conclusion that, at least on the level of morphosyntax, what we see in the letters really represents their authors' and not their scribes' linguistic habits. This means, in turn, that in historical sociolinguistics we need to pay careful attention as to whether we wish to discuss the language of authors or scribes. But then we might have a small window on the language of people who did not write themselves, as their language (or at least morphosyntax) would even be represented in dictated letters.

2. Authors, scribes and literacy in medieval England

Before about 1500 only a fraction of English society was literate. Cressy (1980: 177) estimates that on average 10% of the male population and only 1% of the female population had something like signature literacy, i.e. they could write their own name. In the Paston letters (see below for details), for example, this becomes very clear. Davis (1971: xxxvii), in his introduction to the authoritative edition of the letters, explains that there is no evidence whatsoever that any of the hands that wrote the letters by female authors could be the hand of the authors themselves. Three letters by Margery Paston are very illuminating in this respect: while the letters themselves are written in a normal, clear and skilled hand, they have subscriptions 'Be yowre seruant (and bedewoman) Margery Paston', all in the same distinctively halting and uncontrolled hand, as of someone beginning to learn to write (nos. 417, 418, 420). 'These must be by Margery herself, making a rather ineffectual effort to sign her letters in her own hand as the men so often did' (Davis 1971: xxxviii). Davis sees this as evidence that Margery was probably the only woman in the family capable of writing her own name. We do not know, of course, to what extent people unable to write were also unable to read. Reading and writing were taught as separate skills in the Middle Ages, so it might well be possible that some people were only able to read, but not to write. However, this fact is primarily interesting when we think about reading and writing as social practices; it only concerns the topic of this chapter insofar as speakers who were able to read could actually check what the scribes had written. Unfortunately, we have little to no evidence about the ability to read of many historical speakers, so this question will have to remain an open one.

Another group of people we are concerned with here are those who are able to read and write, but who, for one reason or another, did not want to write themselves. In Antiquity, Quintilian generally pointed out that handwriting was a menial and wearisome task, but at the same time also offers a very detailed differentiation between the different purposes of writing:

> XXVIII. Non est aliena res, quae fere ab honestis neglegi solet, cura bene ac velociter scribendi. Nam cum sit in studiis praecipuum, quoque solo verus ille profectus et altis radicibus nixus paretur, scribere ipsum, tardior stilus cogitationem moratur, rudis et confusus intellectu caret: unde sequitur alter dictandi quae transferenda sunt labor. XXIX. Quare cum semper et ubique, tum praecipue in epistulis secretis et familiaribus delectabit ne hoc quidem neglectum reliquisse. (Quintilian, *Institutio Oratoria*, 1.1.28–9)

> [XXVIII. The art of writing well and quickly is not unimportant for our purpose, though it is generally disregarded by distinguished people. Writing is of the utmost importance in the study which we have under consideration and by its means alone can true and deeply rooted proficiency be obtained. But a sluggish pen delays our thoughts, while an unformed and illiterate lacks understanding, a circumstance which necessitates another task, namely the dictation of what is to be copied. XXIX. So you will always and everywhere be at your ease, but particularly in secret or intimate correspondence, if you have not neglected this point.]

So, while copying (whole) works was absolutely dispreferred, the handwritten letter to a friend would certainly be appreciated. We do not know exactly what the medieval situation was, though it can be assumed on the basis of the data that we have (most authors did not write their own works, even when they were literate) that handwriting was not considered to be a valuable and intellectually rewarding task.

People who needed to write something, but were unable to or did not want to write themselves, therefore hired scribes who put their words in writing. This could be done in a number of ways (see Davis 1971: xxxviii): sometimes they dictated directly, sometimes they told scribes what they intended to say and the scribes later composed the documents 'more or less freely on the basis of instructions given by the author' (*ibid.*). The issue of drafting and copying also needs to be considered. Sometimes people drafted letters themselves or let scribes draft them in order to have them copied later on. Again, the Paston letters are very interesting here. Most of the letters to addressees outside the family are now only available as drafts; the original fair copies that were posted are lost. The drafts that we have usually show heavy corrections. Only two letters still exist both as draft and as fair copy (no. 42

and no. 209) and can show us the quantity and quality of revisions. There are some letters written to family members, however, which were sent off directly without previous drafting. These are also very illuminating with respect to the production of written language, and Davis (1971: xxxix) characterises some of them as being 'in a very untidy state'.

All of this makes the sociolinguistic analysis of historical texts very difficult if not impossible in some cases. If we want to contextualise the producers of language and talk about the influence of external factors such as education, gender, social strata, social networks, place of living, we need to know whose language we are looking at. How reliable, for instance, are representations of female speech when there are no female writers/scribes, but 'only authors'?

Let us assume that the influence of scribes on the language of particular documents is not an issue of all-or-nothing, but may rather be something gradual, depending not in the least on the linguistic level we are looking at. For example, it is fairly obvious that the actual spelling in the manuscripts is mostly that of the scribes and not that of the (maybe even illiterate, i.e. non-reading and non-writing) authors. It is of course conceivable that literate (at least reading) authors checked the final product (including its spelling) before it was sent off, but this surely was extremely rare. But depending on how the letters were produced (i.e. dictated directly or composed from memory) and how carefully the authors monitored the production process and checked the final product, scribes may have had some influence on the level of morphology or morphosyntax. They may have substituted a third person singular <-th> by <-s>, or may have used single instead of multiple negation. They may have preferred a particular word order pattern – which the author did not use, perhaps did not even have in his or her linguistic competence. And they may, of course, have had influences on the wording and textual level by changing single words or even rephrasing complete passages (e.g. when writing from memory).

To my mind, it seems intuitively unlikely that scribes changed many words or phrases when authors dictated directly. Usually, authors were in a more powerful position than their scribes, and so scribes probably did not dare to change their words 'on the fly'. Similarly, it seems unlikely that authors would have accepted changes or corrections from their scribes after their dictation, unless the scribes were regarded as 'coaches' in terms of linguistic forms and norms. This would have been the case, for example, when female speakers (even when they were socially more powerful) acquiesced in situations where the scribes were the experts. But surely this was not often the case. Changes on the macro-level would usually only be possible when scribes wrote down what they had heard from memory or maybe from notes.

Morphology and morphosyntax, however, appear to be different, as has been pointed out above. These more structural micro-levels could allow for changes on both a conscious and a subconscious level, i.e. changes that would go unnoticed by the author – perhaps even the scribe – in direct online dictation, but which may also be intentionally changed in later revisions, for example. And since language structure is affected here, it would not even be unlikely that scribes unconsciously used their own forms when taking down a certain letter or document online, as they had to work under time pressure and perhaps did not pay close attention to the forms they were hearing, but rather to the macro-structure. In what follows, because of the Janus-headed nature of morphosyntax, we will therefore focus mostly on morphosyntactic elements, and how these could have been influenced by scribes.

3. The Paston letters as a database

The collection of *Paston Letters* as edited by Norman Davis in 1971 contains 421 documents with about 245,000 words authored by fifteen family members, eleven male and four female, between 1421 and 1503. The letters survived because of a legal issue that made it necessary that the documents be kept in public archives. The Pastons were a well-known and well-to-do family of Norfolk landed gentry. While the family history actually spans several hundred years, the best-documented period and the one that concerns us here is the time between 1421 and 1503. There are numerous historical studies that describe the Pastons and their life during this time (e.g. Gies and Gies 1999). Today, we have documents from three generations of family members: the founding generation, represented by William I and Agnes Paston; Generation 2 represented by John I, his wife Margaret, Edmond I, Elizabeth, William II and Clement II; and Generation 3 with the two brothers Johns II and III, Margery, Edmond II, Walter and William III. As an overview, Figure 7.1 shows a family tree and the biodata of the family members:

Table 7.1 below lists the different authors and their share in the total number of letters and words. The list mentions 422 documents as one letter exists in exactly the same form as a draft and as an actual letter, and was counted twice by Davis in his authoritative edition. For current purposes, however, we will work with 421 actual, different documents.

The number of autographed and dictated letters varies considerably across the collection. Most of Clement's, John II's, John III's, Walter's and William III's documents were autographed. Practically none of the letters by female authors were autographed, confirming Cressy's claim that female illiteracy was extremely high in the Middle Ages. Davis (1971, 1954, 1971) was able to analyse and identify a large number of hands, some of them personally (e.g. as the hand of James Gloys, a servant, family chaplain and clerk), others just as anonymous Hand A, Hand B, etc. Table 7.2 below summarises Davis' findings.

4. Linguistic variables and methodology

As mentioned before, the present study focuses on morphosyntactic variation in the Paston letters. It describes and analyses two salient variables in late Middle English: the third person plural pronoun forms and relativisation patterns.

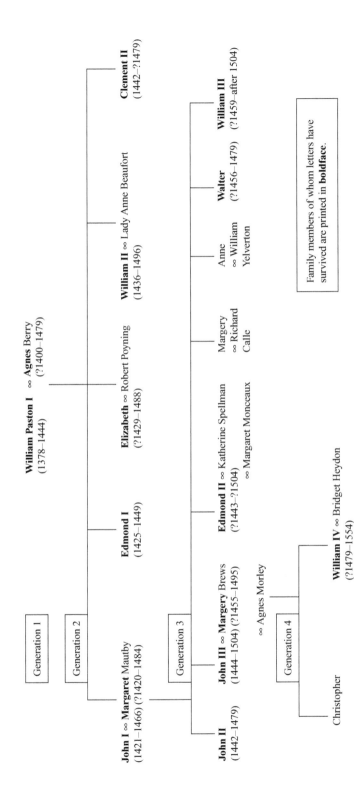

Figure 7.1 Family tree and biodata of the Pastons, 1421–1503

Table 7.1 *Authors, texts and approximate word frequencies in the Paston letters*

Author	Texts	Words	Author	Texts	Words
Agnes	22	7,746	Margaret	107	67,305
Clement	7	3,254	Margery	6	2,634
Edmond I	2	569	Walter	4	1,305
Edmond II	8	3,813	William I	12	8,132
Elizabeth	3	3,958	William II	33	15,311
John I	44	33,092	William III	9	4,508
John II	86	48,603	William IV	1	127
John III	78	43,490	Total	422	243,847

Table 7.2 *Scribes in the Paston letters*

Scribe	No. of letters	Scribe	No. of letters
Anonymous	64	William III	8
John III	87	Clement	7
John II	69	William I	6
Hand G	24	Richard Calle	5
James Gloys	23	James Gresham	5
John Pampyng	17	Thomas Playter	4
John Wykes	12	Edmond I	1
John Daubeney	11	William IV	1
William II	11	William Lomnor	1
Edmond II	11	John Mowth (Molet)	1
Hand C	9	William Ebesham	1

4.1 Personal pronouns in late Middle English

The Viking invasions in the Old English period led to various changes in the English language. Among them was the borrowing of new personal pronoun forms in the plural. The pronoun forms in Old English (i.e. Anglo-Saxon) were *heo* 'they', *hem* 'them' and *here* 'their'. These were gradually replaced in the Middle English period by the new, innovative *th*-pronouns *they, their, them* (see Thomason and Kaufman 1988; Watts 2012a). The development can be summarised as in Table 7.3.

It is not quite clear today whether all of these three forms were actually borrowed from Old Norse, or whether it was only the subject form *they* that was borrowed, followed by analogical extension of the *th*-form in English dialects. The problem is that most of the changes that go back to Old Norse influences only become visible after the Vikings disappeared (Werner 1991: 381). What we do know is that (a) in Middle English, the individual pronoun forms were substituted gradually and (b) direct language contact with the Vikings was only a factor in the north of the country. For the south, the spread and adoption of the new forms must

Table 7.3 *Development of plural pronoun forms in English*

	Old English	Middle English	Present-day English
Nominative	hi(e)	thei	they
Genitive	hire/heora	here(e)/their	their
Dative	him/heom	hem/them	them
Accusative	hi(e)	hem/them	them

have been a matter of dialect contact, rather than contact with the actual donor language. We find that the twelfth-century *Ormulum* text (Ms Bodleian Junius 1, *c.* 1175 from South Lincolnshire) only has *they* in the nominative and about 83% of the possessive forms are *their*. *Them* as an object pronoun is rare with only 7% new forms (Greul 1934; Morse-Gagné 1992). In contrast, the south was a lot slower in its adoption. The proclamation of Henry III in 1258 has only Anglo-Saxon *heo* and *heom*. In Chaucer we usually find *they*, but also *here* and *hem* (see Benson 1987: xxxii). This mixed paradigm even extends into the fifteenth century and can be found, for example, in Hoccleve and Lydgate. Even in the late fifteenth century we still find *hem* occasionally, for example in Malory (*c.* 1469) and Caxton's *Troye* (*c.* 1471). Eventually, this means that we can expect a great deal of linguistic variation in the pronoun forms when we look at the fifteenth-century Paston letters written by authors from East Anglia, despite the fact that the latter was actually part of the original Danelaw area.

4.2 *Relativisation in (late) Middle English*

The second variable that this chapter seeks to investigate is the relative pronoun system. Fischer claims that 'in the thirteenth century *that* stood practically alone as relativizer' (Fischer *et al.* 2000: 91; cf. Morris 1882: 198, who sees this point about 100 years later). Watts (2012a, p.c.) sees this in connection with the changes in the article system. For him, the disappearance of 'the' left a gap in the relativiser system which was filled by 'that'. This means that the modern English relativiser system with a group of *wh*-relative pronouns (*which, who, whose, whom*), an invariable particle *that* and zero as options developed between the fourteenth and eighteenth century (if we wish to see Addison's 'petition' in *The Spectator* 1711 against the upstart Jack Sprat *that* as some kind of endpoint in the development). Like the personal pronoun system, the relativiser system also did not develop in one single step, but gradually, possibly as a consequence or at least in the wake of the changes in the determiner system. First, we see the spread of *whose* and *whom*, often in non-restrictive relative clauses, following a preposition and with animate antecedents. '*Which* began to supplant *that* only in the fifteenth century' (Fischer *et al.* 2000: 92). *Who* was introduced in the late fifteenth century. Its lag is still one of the great puzzles in the history of English (Kivimaa 1966; Traugott 1972:

154; Rydén 1983; Fischer 1992: 301). Romaine (1982) conducted one of the first sociohistorical investigations of this phenomenon, and she finds that accessibility, style and addressee were crucial factors in the use of the new *wh*-relativisers. Thus, factors that have been discussed in this context are sociohistorical aspects such as style and text type, psycholinguistic constraints such as accessibility hierarchies and language contact. Bergs (Bergs and Stein 2001: Bergs 2005) offers the idea that the development may have had to do with semantico-pragmatic factors, i.e. pragmatics which effects semantics, with ultimate consequences for morphosyntax (cf. Watts' 2012a Innovation>Diffusion>Actuation model): the first instances of *whose* and *whom*, and later *who*, were in religious contexts, often with the deity as antecedent. Over time, these contexts were expanded, and these specially marked relativisers were also used for highly respectable people, then for friends and finally for anything animate. *Whose*, eventually, does not even have this constraint anymore. This process was defined as markedness reduction and (in some sense) also grammaticalisation of these relative pronouns. New forms are innovated as 'extravagant' highly marked constructions in order to (pragmatically) signify especially marked contexts or referents (such as the deity). Over time, however, as in grammaticalisation, this extravagance wears off and gives way to regular (more or less unmarked) semantic factors (such as human or animate) until we finally end up with straightforward morphosyntactic constraints. Eventually, this may be described as grammaticalisation in the widest sense, as pragmatic, extralinguistic elements eventually are integrated into the grammar of a language, i.e. pragmatics becomes morphosyntax (cf. Bergs 2004; Watts 2012a).

There is one more form that needs to be discussed here. In Middle English we find one particular relative construction which again disappeared in the Early Modern period: *the which*. This combination of article and relativiser may have arisen through language contact with French (as Einenkel 1887 suggests) or through the fusion of Old English *se* 'the' and *swa hwylc swa* (as Curme 1912: 153 suggests). In Middle English, *the which* is particularly common in non-restrictive relative clauses which are further away from the antecedent and thus need especially 'strong' grammatical marking (see Fischer 1992: 303). Again, it is fairly obvious that the history of this construction can and should be linked to the development of the determiner system. However, most of these developments had already reached completion by 1400, i.e. by the time of our data in this chapter. What remains is a system where we find more or less 'complex' or 'explicit' grammatical markers such as *the which* next to more or less unmarked forms such as *that*. Current psycholinguistic research (such as Hawkins 2004) suggests that grammatical complexity correlates with information complexity, so that we can expect more explicit structures to be more common in more complex constructions, e.g. with further removed antecedents. At the same time, we should not forget that, even without standardisation as we know it, speakers probably also attached certain sociocultural values to the respective forms. *The which* was perhaps borrowed from French (which still may have enjoyed prestige), and yet showed redundant morphosyntactic marking (*which* may have already been dispreferred). On the other hand, spoken online discourse seems to have clear morphosyntactic marking, so that *the which* may have been the preferred form here. To cut a long story short, sociohistorical investigations in morphosyntax face a number of complex problems which go back directly to the very nature of the variables themselves. As Garcia (1985) has already shown, establishing synonymic equivalence for grammatical variables is extremely hard and sometimes impossible so that we may have to content ourselves eventually with functional equivalence.

As with the personal pronouns discussed in Section 4.1 above, the relativisation system of fifteenth-century English is highly variable and dynamic so that we can expect to find sufficient material here to investigate the role of authors and scribes, and perhaps even the sociohistorical context of writing and reading as such. This will be the topic of the next sections.

5. Analysing the Paston letters: Who did it?

Obviously, autographed letters do not pose a problem for the present study, or even in general. With these, we know exactly who composed and actually wrote them – even though we may not always know many biographical details about that person. We are primarily interested in authors who have not left any letters, or only a few, and whose language might be influenced by their scribes. The Paston letters are a great opportunity for such a study, since some of the family members occasionally acted as both authors and scribes, e.g. male family members wrote for female family members who could not read or write. This allows us to form the following hypothesis: if one author also acted as scribe for another speaker, the writings of that particular speaker either contain or do not contain features that we find with that particular scribe/author. If they contain features that do not show up in the author's own writings, but only in the dictations that he took down, we may assume that these come from the speaker who dictated the document. And vice versa: if the language of a particular author is more or less the same in his own writings and when he acts as scribe for somebody else, we may assume some greater influence here.

5.1 Personal pronouns

Edmond II, John II and John III acted as scribes for their mother Margaret and wrote letters as authors themselves. Table 7.4 shows their use of pronoun forms. It contrasts the use of the individual pronoun forms in autographed letters by these three speakers with letters which these three only wrote down as scribes.

The traditional pronoun forms only appear when Edmond II acts as scribe for his mother. He never uses them when he is writing for himself. John II also has a comparatively high rate of *hem* when writing for his mother (50%). Only about 2% of his own object pronouns have this traditional form; the vast majority are

Table 7.4 *The use of third person pronoun forms by Edmond II, John II and John III when acting as authors and scribes*

Scribe	Author	hem	them	here	their	Total
Edmond II	Edmond II	–	8	–	1	9
	Margaret	5	9	1	–	15
John II	John II	3	98	–	15	116
	Margaret	4	4	–	3	11
John III	John III	60	77	2	57	196
	Margaret	21	11	4	4	40

modern. The figures for John III are superficially different, but essentially show the same pattern. When he is writing for himself, he uses *hem* about 40% of the time. When he is writing for his mother, *hem* is almost twice as frequent as modern *them*. The possessive forms are even more illuminating. Only about 4% are traditional when he is the author, but when he acts as scribe for Margaret, traditional and modern forms are on a par.

In sum, all three speakers were much more conservative when they wrote for their mother. Unfortunately, the observed frequencies are too small to allow for statistical significance tests, but one cannot avoid the impression that the actual author of the letters played a much greater role in the selection of the pronoun forms than the scribe. How else could we explain the reasonably clear preferences that the scribes show in their own writings and which differ from the choices that we see in the dictated letters? What we could and should think about, though, is whether the choice of pronoun forms on the part of the scribe was guided by the actual language of the author, or what the scribe thought the author should sound like. Perhaps women generally were supposed to sound more conservative, and the scribes were inclined to represent that assumption, despite the fact that Margaret actually showed different forms in her oral performance? Unfortunately, since we lack any data in this respect, this will have to remain a matter of speculation. What is interesting, however, is that Margaret's language (or the representation thereof) also changes over time. While she always showed both traditional (conservative) and innovative language forms, the latter became much more common in and around 1468, roughly the time when her husband died (in 1466). As Figure 7.2 below shows, she consistently used more *th*-forms from then on. This may have to do with three different factors:

1. Her language may simply have changed over time.
2. Her social role and thus also her language changed after her husband's death. She is now the head of the family.
3. She is accommodating to different people and their expectations. While her husband probably expected more conservative language, her sons can be shown to be more innovative (and therefore also more tolerant?) in some respects.

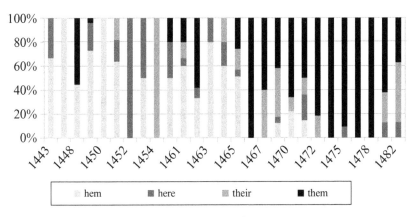

Figure 7.2 Pronoun forms (*hem* vs. *them*, *here* vs. *their*) in Margaret Paston across time (based on Bergs 2005: 112)

What can be excluded as an explanation are scribal influences. She had nineteen scribes in twenty-nine years in more than 100 letters; no scribe was solely responsible for the early or the late letters and there were no generational shifts. It thus seems highly unlikely that the scribes were directly responsible for the observed changes. However, we have no accounts and no secondary evidence that could help us in guessing what exactly lies at the heart of this phenomenon. All we can say is that scribal influences on the language that we observe today seem to have been fairly limited.

But let us come back to the methodological question that lies at the heart of this chapter: how can we tell whose language we are actually looking at? A second group of letters that is particularly interesting consists of letters by different dictating authors (say, John I and his wife Margaret) that were actually written down by one particular scribe (say, James Gloys, a servant and chaplain for the family). The hypothesis is the same as the one just outlined: if the language in the letters were that of Gloys, they would be linguistically very similar, despite being dictated by different authors. If they are different, this can only be due to the authors' choices, since the scribe was the same. And indeed, the findings are quite illuminating.

Gloys, when writing for John I, used the possessive pronoun *her(e)* nine times in 1449 (letter no. 36, 1,062 words) and modern *their* only once. When he was writing for John I's wife Margaret in 1469, he used *their* nine times and *her(e)* not at all (letter no. 200, 874 words). These figures need to be taken with a pinch of salt, however. The temporal distance of twenty years between the letters may also have played a role. As Bergs (2005) shows, the changes in the family happen very rapidly and people change their language drastically within ten years and less. It is particularly noteworthy in this case that the letter from Margaret from 1469 shows so many innovative *th*-forms, despite the fact that she seems to have been fairly conservative. Nevertheless, the findings are still not implausible, particularly when compared with the letters that John II wrote for Margaret, where we also find some innovative forms, particularly in the possessive. We also need to bear in mind that Margaret's role as a female speaker could have changed over time. Before the late 1460s she was first and foremost the wife of John Paston I. In this role she probably acted and spoke (and was supposed to act and speak) quite conservatively. It can therefore be expected that her language (or rather the language that scribes ascribed to her) was indeed more conservative. This changed dramatically when she became head of the family. On the one hand, perhaps she felt more at ease to accommodate to what she heard all around her; on the other hand, people would perhaps tolerate (and even expect) more innovative (or better: contemporary) language use from her.

Let us compare the findings for Gloys with those for another scribe, John Wykes. Wykes wrote both for Margaret Paston and for John Paston II, Margaret's son. He used the object pronoun form *hem* twice, but *them* only once when writing for Margaret in 1465 (letter no. 190, 1,069 words, to her husband John I), in 1469 when writing for John II he used *hem* only once, *them* twice (letter no. 242, 1,308 words, to Walter Writtle). Unfortunately, the figures are really very low here and certainly do not allow for any definite conclusions. Still, they point in the same direction as those presented above, and they suggest the same tendencies, namely that scribes did not (always) compose letters in their own style, but actually paid attention to the forms that the authors used (or at least which they believed to be appropriate for certain authors, e.g. male or female, young or old, conservative or modern). The advantage that we have when we compare the two letters written by Wykes is that the letters are of comparable length and written roughly at the same time.

5.2 Relativisation

Let us now turn to our second variable, relativisation structures. As we have seen above, here we can expect variability between the traditional form *that*, on the one hand, and the new *wh*-structures on the other. Needless to say, the same caveat applies as with the personal pronouns discussed in Section 5.1 – perhaps even more so. On the one hand, we need to take into account language-internal factors that may have had an influence on the use or non-use of a particular form with a particular speaker (such as restrictiveness or the close association of *who* with Deity-invoking formulae; cf. Bergs and Stein 2001; Bergs 2004). On the other hand, it has been pointed out before (Romaine 1982; Bergs and Stein 2001; Bergs 2004, 2005) that the new *wh*-relativisers were probably stylistically very marked (as high-style Latinate constructions). This, in turn, may have had an effect on the question as to the type of person for whom it was appropriate to use these forms. So it might well be possible that female speakers did not use one or more of these forms (at least in writing) because they were not appropriate for female language. Or, just as with the personal pronouns, some scribes may have thought that it is not appropriate to use a particular form for a particular kind of speaker – and therefore changed them.

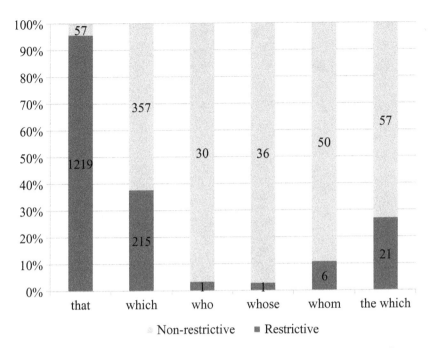

Figure 7.3 Relativisers in restrictive and non-restrictive relative clauses in the Paston letters
(based on Bergs 2005: 151)

So do we see the tendencies that we saw with personal pronouns confirmed? Do the relativisation strategies in the Paston letters rather represent the language of the authors or that of the scribes? Or maybe even both? Figure 7.3 above summarises the use of the major relativisation strategies in the letters and categorises these according to their use in restrictive versus non-restrictive relative clauses (we will exclude zero as a relativisation strategy for methodological reasons).

Figure 7.3 shows quite clearly that the majority of relative clauses was (still) introduced by *that* (1,276 = 62% versus 774 = 38%). In present-day English, *that* is on a par with the *wh*-relativisers in conversation only. The latter outrank *that* in fiction, news and academic prose (Biber *et al.* 1999: 610–11). This in turn suggests that in the fifteenth century we are looking at the lower part of the S-curve of development which leads to the present situation where the *wh*-forms are clearly more dominant on the whole but have not completely ousted *that* (in other words we are currently witnessing the upper part of the S). With regard to restrictiveness as a factor, we also see some differences between the fifteenth century and the present day. *That* is already clearly preferred in restrictive contexts (83%), the *wh*-forms dominate in the non-restrictive domain (more than 90%). Nevertheless, a few (57 out of 587) non-restrictive relative clauses introduced by *that* can still be found. Bergs (2005: 209) has even been able to document the loss of *that* in non-restrictive

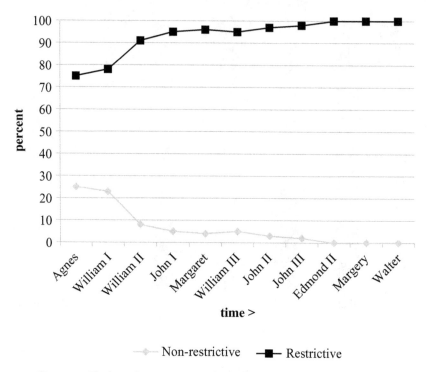

Figure 7.4 The loss of non-restrictive *that* across time (in %) (Bergs 2005: 209)

context across time by looking at the language use of different family members from different generations (Figure 7.4).

Animacy of the antecedent has been identified as one of the most influential factors for present-day English. The same cannot be said about late Middle English. We do not find any significant correlation between *which* and inanimate antecedents, or *who/whom* with animate ones. Still, the former was very common with inanimates (at a ratio of about 3.5:1), while the latter is (still) most common with deity antecedents in formulaic expressions. This picture also confirms what has been said above: what we are seeing here is the incipient phase of the (S-curve like) development of the relativiser system.

The which seems to be a special case, though. Its origins are still disputed (French loan vs. determiner plus relativiser?) and its general distribution can only be described as messy. Mustanoja (1960: 199) claims that in fifteenth-century prose *the which* was far more common than simple *which* and, indeed, in the Helsinki Corpus we find 49% (n = 31) *the which* for the time period 1420–1500. Yet in the Paston letters there are only 80 (11%) instances of *the which* versus 601 instances of simple *which*. One explanation might be that *the which* was associated with 'lower-class' language. Raumolin-Brunberg (2000: 218) shows that in the *Corpus of Early English Correspondence* (*CEEC*) the group of Merchants and Non-Gentry were the strongest users of *the which* (with 96% usage in 1480–99!) while 'Royalty,

Nobility and Gentry' only used it 34% of the time. These figures are, of course, much closer to what we find in the Paston letters. And yet Raumolin-Brunberg herself cautions against simple interpretations: the data for the 'Merchants and Non-Gentry' group derive almost exclusively from the Cely Letters – a family of London wool merchants. Caxton, a contemporary London draper, for instance, is a strong user of *which*. So while we might believe that *the which* somehow could have smacked of 'bad language' in some sense, there is no hard evidence for this.

What makes matters even more complicated is the fact that both Raumolin-Brunberg (2000) and Bergs (2005) do not find any clear and unambiguous language internal correlates for *the which*. While Raumolin-Brunberg speaks of 'disorderly heterogeneity', Bergs (2005: 167) suggests that there might be a preference for *the which* to occur with full NP antecedents; but this, too, is not statistically significant. Surprisingly, it does not correlate with syntactic distance between antecedent and relative clause, as might have been expected on the basis of current studies on syntactic complexity and grammatical explicitness (see Rohdenburg 2003; Hawkins 2004). So what actually triggered the use of *the which* still remains a mystery that needs to be solved in the future.

Against the backdrop of this general picture, let us come back to our original question: do we see the language of the authors or that of the scribes when we read the Paston letters? It was suggested that, in the domain of morphosyntax, it is actually the authors' language (or maybe the language the scribes attributed to the respective authors). This means that we should find similar patterns and phenomena in the use of the personal pronoun variables and that of the different relativisation constructions.

We can use the same two letters by John Wykes to get a first impression. In letter no. 190 (for Margaret), John Wykes uses *that* nine times, 'modern' *which* not even once. In letter no. 242 (for John II), he uses *that* three times, but *which* seven times. So this use of the relativisers essentially aligns with our findings for the personal pronouns. The scribe does not have a clear preference for particular forms which we then find across the board. Rather, the use shifts with every (dictating) author. If the author is more innovative (such as John II, see Bergs 2005) we find more innovative forms such as *them*, *their* and *which*. If the author is older and/or more conservative (such as Margaret) we find more conservative forms such as *hem*, *here* and *that*. This is confirmed by what we see when we analyse the language of fifteenth-century women and men on the communal level. In the Paston letters, male authors clearly prefer *which*, female authors *that* (see Bergs 2005: 180–1). This is indeed very interesting considering the fact that the same female authors also prefer *the which* (see Nevalainen 1996: 82, who also reported the preference of Sabine Johnson, the wife of a sixteenth-century wool merchant). What this means is that female authors seem to prefer a more traditional form (*that*) and a form that could have been associated with lower-class language use (*the which*), while males preferred the new *wh*-forms *which* and, even more importantly, *who* (which is almost never used by female authors). This appears to be a direct consequence of the presumably Latinate nature of these relativisers (see Romaine 1982). Perhaps these were reserved (in some sense) for male authors with a classical education; or at least they were used in such a way as to distinguish between male and female speakers. But this story still has a twist. As we have discussed before, female speakers do use some *wh*-relativisers, and they do so in a quite remarkable way. Agnes, Margaret and Elizabeth[1] were among the strongest users of *which* in connection with inanimate antecedents. Sixty (= 81%) out of Margaret's seventy-four uses of *which* are with inanimate antecedents; Elizabeth uses six (86%) out of her seven uses of *which* with inanimate antecedents; Agnes has an astonishing seventeen out of seventeen (100%). Most male authors do not exceed 70 to 75%. So while male authors use *which* more often, female speakers use it more progressively. Unfortunately, the same pattern cannot be found with the loss of non-restrictive *that*. Here, as has been shown above, female authors do not show any deviation from the community norm and simply follow the general developments.

All this is interesting in itself, but it also leads to an important point concerning the relationship between authors and scribes. Scribes, needless to say, were male. This means that it is unlikely that these had any major impact on the language of female authors as represented in their letters. If they had had any influence, we would have seen greater similarity between male and female language use, especially with regard to such subtle and probably even subconscious developments as the constraint on the use of *which* with different antecedents. This is probably something that passes the scribe by and escapes correction. Or, alternatively, *that* does not get inserted deliberately. We can also expect some differences when it comes to major noticeable constructions such as the use of *who* in formulaic language. This is one of the traditional phenomena where language use is often constrained by social factors such as gender, class, style and decorum. So it is not surprising that male and female authors show different language use and that, perhaps, scribes used different constructions to represent their different authors when they were not taking down dictation verbatim. This is the other side of morphosyntactic variability, which is clearly conscious and deliberate, where speakers/writers have to make deliberate choices, and where they are probably aware of the different values attached to the individual variants – not unlike traditional lexical variables, one might add.

6. Summary and conclusion

What does this mean? As I pointed out before, the figures are nowhere near what we would expect from present-day data regarding statistical validity. Nevertheless, they suggest certain interpretations, which can be evaluated according to their plausibility. One such suggestion is that scribes had only very little influence regarding the morphosyntactic and lexical shape of the letters, even when authors did not dictate directly. The morphosyntax and lexicon that we find can be seen as the null

---

[1] Note that none of them left any autographed letters.

hypothesis, i.e. unless they can be shown to come from other sources, this must be regarded as the authors' and not the scribes' personal language use. And this, in turn, opens up new ways for the cultural and sociological interpretation of those language uses. However, despite the fact that the data presented above suggest this conclusion, matters might not be that straightforward after all. On the one hand, it might well be possible that what we see actually is the authors' language; on the other hand, it might also be the case that what we see is the language that scribes wanted to see from certain authors. In other words, scribes, being experts in language and appropriate language use, may have used the language which they thought was appropriate for a certain kind of author. Morphosyntactic variables are particularly suitable for this, it seems, as they oscillate between conscious and subconscious language use. On the one hand, some variants can easily go unnoticed especially in fast online processing; on the other hand, other variants can also be very noticeable when used in a particularly marked context. One example of the former could be the new pronoun forms. These could, of course, be noticed, but it would be no surprise if scribes subconsciously changed them in particular ways. Relativisers, being phonetically and grammatically more prominent, are a different matter. While the introduction of a new relativiser or the crass 'misuse' of one would certainly be noticed, subtle changes such as the use of *which* only with inanimate antecedents are probably imperceptible to readers or hearers. And this takes us back to the language change model developed in Bergs (2005). Here we find a distinction between noticeable and unnoticeable changes (see Figure 7.5 below).

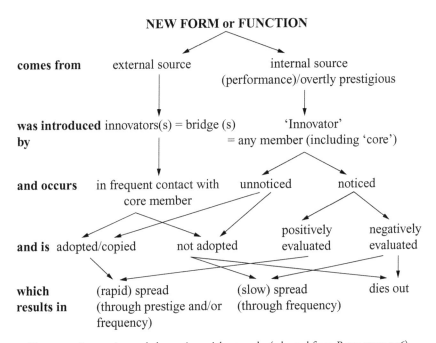

Figure 7.5 Innovation and change in social networks (adopted from Bergs 2005: 256)

When new forms (or forms in new functions) are introduced to the linguistic community, it makes a big difference whether they occur unnoticed or noticed by others. If they occur unnoticed, they may be (subconsciously) copied (adopted) by others, or they simply die out. Alternatively, they are noticed by other speakers, in which case, they undergo evaluation. If this evaluation is positive and the new variant is found to be cool, interesting, empowering, prestigious or something like this, it also survives and spreads through the network. If it is evaluated negatively, it is not propagated further and dies out (or spreads only very slowly through sheer frequency).

What this means is that scribes in late medieval England could have had a central and most important role for the development of the language. What we do find in their writings is perhaps not the pure language of the authors, and also not that of the scribes, but it might be exactly the sort of language scribes attributed to certain groups or types of authors. It could represent the sociocultural image or ideal that society held regarding certain people and authors. So it might well be that Margaret (who in all likelihood should have used more new forms in her spoken language) did not all of a sudden change her language in the mid-1460s, but that it became acceptable, or even desirable to let people see and hear that she uses new forms and new constructions. When written language is a slow and tedious form of communication, but at the same time is also the only means of communication across long distances – there is no fast travel, no telephone, no email – every single word and every single form probably carries a tenfold amount of communicative weight and value as it would in today's emails and text messages. Unfortunately, we still lack data and sociocultural interpretations from historians, but I believe that collaboration between linguists and social-historians will provide us with many new insights in this respect in the not so distant future.

CHAPTER 8

Stylistic variation

Anita Auer

1. On stylistic variation

Stylistic variation plays a pivotal role in the field of sociolinguistic variation in that it sheds light on speakers' strategies with respect to external variables and allows linguists to observe ongoing linguistic change (see Labov 1966; Eckert and Rickford 2001; Schilling-Estes 2002). Stylistic variation can be observed between speakers (inter-speaker variation) as well as in the speech of individual speakers (intra-speaker variation). As Schilling-Estes (2002: 375) notes, a range of different types of variation are associated with intra-speaker variation, 'including shifts in usage levels for features associated with particular groups of speakers – i.e. DIALECTS – or with particular situations of use – i.e. REGISTERS'.

Over the last forty years, intra-speaker variation (from a synchronic perspective) has been approached in a number of different ways. It is noteworthy that discussions on how to define stylistic variation are ongoing (for selected studies, see, for instance, Eckert and Rickford 2001; Auer 2007). To date, three major approaches to stylistic variation can be identified, namely (1) Attention to Speech, (2) Audience Design and (3) Speaker Design (see Schilling-Estes 2002). The first, i.e. Attention to Speech, is strongly associated with William Labov's New York City study (1966), which launched quantitative research on language variation. In this study, Labov 'established that stylistic variation constitutes a crucial nexus between the individual and the community – between the linguistic, the cognitive, and the social' (Eckert and Rickford 2001: 2). He showed that the use of sociolinguistic variables is closely connected with social-class variation and that the stylistic repertoire of each speaker may be seen as a continuum within the socioeconomic hierarchy. The upper end of this continuum charts the 'prestigious' realisation of the speaker's speech, which may be seen as the result of more careful, formal speech, while the lower 'stigmatised' end can be considered the result of more casual and unmonitored speech. The speaker's stylistic choices are thus closely associated with the socioeconomic hierarchy, i.e. in particular with the speaker's place within it and his/her strategies with regard to the hierarchy. Of central importance in Labov's theory is the degree of attention that speakers pay to their speech.

The second major approach to stylistic variation, the so-called Audience Design model, was first proposed by Bell in 1984. This model may be seen as a further development to social psychological work in speech accommodation theory (e.g.

Giles 1973; Giles and Powesland 1975), which revealed that the speaker's orientation and attitude to the addressee are of great importance in choosing speech styles. According to Bell (1984), stylistic variation may be interpreted as a response to the speaker's audience, which can be the actual addressee, third persons present (such as auditors, overhearers and eavesdroppers), as well as non-present audience members, i.e. so-called referees, that could influence style shifts. As topics are associated with audience types, the latter are seen as fundamental in topic-based style shifting.

The third major approach to stylistic variation, the Speaker Design approach, differs from the Audience Design approach in that it does not view style shifting and thus stylistic variation as a reactive phenomenon but as resources that speakers use to create and recreate speaker identity (see, for instance, Coupland 1985, 2001; Mendoza-Denton 1997; Eckert 2000). Rickford and Rickford (2000), for instance, focus on performativity in style, which suggests that 'variability can play a role in the performance of the speaker's own social affiliations and identity' (Eckert and Rickford 2001: 5). All in all, Speaker Design models assume that language and society are co-constituted, i.e. that linguistic features and patterns are seen as 'resources speakers use to shape and re-shape social structures such as class and gender groups, as well as their positioning with respect to these structures and with respect to one another' (Schilling-Estes 2002: 389). The latter approach is thus closely associated with an individual's social identity and his/her maintenance and negotiation of social relationships.

While this is only a brief overview of approaches to stylistic or intra-speaker variation within variationist sociolinguistics, what can be observed is that the focus has broadened over time, e.g. a wider range of factors are considered to influence stylistic choice, more types of features, i.e. not only phonology but also morphosyntax, lexis, as well as pragmatics, are looked at, and paralinguistic elements such as intonation and non-linguistic elements of style are considered.[1] All of these different and changing views on stylistic variation are based on spoken language in the first instance. The question thus arises as to how stylistic variation is reflected in written documents, i.e. in particular in written records from earlier stages of a language.

Depending on the type of document, it is possible to make a distinction between different levels of formality, their proximity to speech, as well as a range of communicative determinants such as participant relationships and communication situation (see Kytö 1991: 37–44). In fact, over the last thirty years it has been shown that sociolinguistic methods employed to investigate synchronic phonological variation can be successfully transferred to the study of grammatical variables in diachronic linguistics. In this field of sociohistorical linguistics, the notion of genre has played a central role (see Romaine 1982; Nevalainen and Raumolin-Brunberg 1996, 2003). For some time now, the text type 'letters', its sub-genres, e.g. business letters, love letters, pauper letters, and the process of letter writing have generated a great amount

---

[1] For a more detailed overview of studies on stylistic variation, the different approaches and their limitations, see, for instance, Eckert and Rickford (2001) and Schilling-Estes (2002).

of interest (see Vandenbussche and Elspaß 2007: 146). Not only is this particular text type considered to be more speech-like and therefore prone to foster linguistic innovation (see Elspaß 2005; Nevalainen and Raumolin-Brunberg 2003),[2] it also allows sociohistorical linguists to gain access to the language use of different social ranks, notably also the lower social strata in the later Modern period.

For the English language, the focus on letters is reflected in the number of (electronic) corpora that have been compiled and the publications based on these resources.[3] All of the letter corpora in the reference section at the end of this volume contain correspondence written during the Modern English period (1500–1900), i.e. a time during which education and the skill of letter writing obtained through education were socially stratified. In the early part of the period, education was restricted to the upper layers of society, and illiteracy may be seen as 'a special characteristic of the poor' (Nevalainen and Raumolin-Brunberg 2003: 35). Even though educational opportunity increased at all social levels, it was still the 'higher ranks and upper levels of the middling sort' that had easy access to education. However, during the Late Modern English period, letters were no longer only an important medium for the upper layers of society, but also for people who received less schooling (see, for instance, Sokoll 2001; Fairman 2003; Whyman 2009; Allen this volume; Fairman this volume; Laitinen this volume). While we have access to language use from all social layers during the Late Modern English period – albeit restricted to letters and sometimes diaries – it can be assumed that social differences and opportunities, which affect education and literacy, equip language users with different linguistic repertoires that have a great bearing on stylistic variation (see Nurmi, Nevala and Palander-Collin 2009: 12).[4]

In this chapter, I shall be concerned with social variation and its effects on stylistic variation in Late Modern English letters. Firstly, I will focus on education opportunities and literacy at all layers of society during the Late Modern English period. Secondly, special attention will be paid to epistolary norms that prevailed at the time and thus contemporary perceptions of how letters should be written and, more specifically, which styles were recommended – as laid down in letter-writing manuals and style guides. Thirdly, the focus will be on linguistic repertoires and style shifting as reflected in selected letters written by people who are considered representative of the different social layers, notably the elite, the middling orders and the labouring poor.

---

[2] Biber and Finegan (1989) have demonstrated that 'personal letters are among the most involved and therefore oral of written genres' (Romaine 1998: 18).

[3] For a selection of letter corpora and work based on these corpora, see the Primary Sources section of the List of References, this volume.

[4] With respect to multivariate analysis applied to the *Corpus of Early English Correspondence* (*CEEC*), Nevalainen and Raumolin-Brunberg (2003: 191) formulate an implicational hypothesis which states that 'social variation is greater and hence more fundamental than stylistic variation according to addressee in personal letters', thus 'social variation > register variation according to addressee (> register variation according to auditors > overhearers > eavesdroppers) > register variation according to topic'.

2. On education opportunities and literacy in Late Modern England

When studying the art of letter writing, and language use in general, in the Late Modern English period, one must necessarily consider the fact that education and, therefore, literacy were socially stratified. Until the introduction of compulsory elementary schooling (1870 Education Act) and even for some time after this landmark event, education, also within the different social groups, was far from uniform. For the elite of the country, education and training was of great importance. The boys received formal instruction, i.e. classical education, either at home and/or at a prestigious public school. While home tutoring was still common at the beginning of the eighteenth century, education in public schools predominated from the middle of the century onwards. As Henry (2002: 315) notes, 'elite boys in particular not only acquired similar knowledge, attitudes, manners, dress, speech, behaviour and accomplishments, they also forged a close and exclusive network of friends, and equipped themselves for their leading roles in society and government'. In the public school curriculum the main focus lay on the classics, which were considered conducive to acquiring a strong sense of British patriotism. Other subjects taught, whose aim it was to breed polite and cultured members of society, were art, music, poetry, language and public speaking. In order to instill social manners and habits into the future British gentlemen, the boys were given lessons in dancing, fencing, drawing and riding. In addition, team sports were considered important as they inculcated values such as courage, competitiveness and resilience (Henry 2002: 316–17). The education of girls born into the elite layer of society differed greatly from the education their brothers received. In fact, the kind of education girls received may be described as peripheral, and it largely depended on their parents' attitudes. Female education in higher social classes was carried out at home either by the parents or a tutor, or in a boarding school, and was largely confined to practical and religious training that would prepare the young ladies for their domestic role. Education for girls was thus mostly informal and varied greatly in terms of quality (Henry 2002: 315).

With regard to the education of the so-called middling orders, the sons of the richest members of this social stratum were sent to elite public schools. As these schools were not necessarily conducive to profitable business careers, many sons received home tutoring and/or were sent to grammar schools or dissenting academies. A common trajectory was school attendance for a few years, followed by an apprenticeship in trade or business (Lawson and Silver 1973; Rogers 2002: 174). According to Lawson and Silver (1973: 195), grammar schools, which continued the classical tradition of education in the Late Modern English period, admitted boys at the age of seven or eight. Some of these boys still had to be taught reading and writing. The most important part of the curriculum was the teaching of grammar, which included 'some rhetoric, classical history, geography and mythology, and . . . religious knowledge gained largely through Latin' (Lawson and Silver 1973: 117). Dissenting academies developed a more comprehensive curriculum in comparison to traditional grammar schools.[5] In addition to the classics, modern and utilitarian subjects were introduced, e.g. 'English grammar, arithmetic, accounts, geography ("the globes"), history ("chronology"), elementary science ("natural" or "experimental philosophy") with French, music and dancing taught by visiting masters' (Lawson and Silver 1973: 204). As well as the general curriculum, dissenting academies could also provide very different subjects such as specific vocational and professional courses in surveying, navigation and military science, as well as commerce. As regards the education of daughters from the middling sort, only a few possibilities for formal education existed in the eighteenth century. Apart from home schooling, private boarding schools, which were established in the course of the seventeenth century, provided some formal instruction; the latter mostly 'taught reading, writing, music, dancing, needlework, household skills, and perhaps some French and Latin (with visiting masters)' (Lawson and Silver 1973: 122, 208).

Female education was a popular topic during the eighteenth century, which is reflected in numerous publications. What most of the treatises have in common is that they favour moral training and genteel accomplishments over intellectual content; after all, the prime object was, according to Edgeworth and Edgeworth (1815: 111), 'to increase a young lady's chance of a prize in the matrimonial lottery' (see Kamm 1965; Lawson and Silver 1973; Skedd 1997).[6] The varied education possibilities for women, both in the elite and middling ranks, suggest that the levels of literacy women could attain would also have varied to a great extent.

Before taking a closer look at the education opportunities of the labouring poor, it is noteworthy that the ruling elite in the eighteenth and the first half of the nineteenth centuries was of the opinion that 'too much literacy among the population at large was a danger to the established order' (Lawson and Silver 1973: 179). The social system, which was considered to be divinely ordained, required many servants and labourers. Providing them with education above their place in society could potentially lead to dissatisfaction and social disruption. The ruling classes therefore decided that 'elementary education for the poor should be minimal, designed to inculcate mainly practical religion, social obedience and low-level occupational skills' (Lawson and Silver 1973: 180). Access to education was given to the poorer layers of society in Sunday schools, charity schools and dame schools. Apart from these institutions, some members of the labouring poor taught themselves and each other (Lawson and Silver 1973: 189–95, 238–50). The view of education in charity schools as well as the close association with religious and social obedience is well reflected in the orders that had to be given to the pupils' parents. One of the rules, as reprinted in Lawson and Silver (1973: 183) states the following:

> VI. And that this School may not only serve for the Instruction and Benefit of the Children, but also of their Parents, particularly of such who cannot Read; They for

---

[5] For more details on nonconformist education, see Lawson and Silver (1973: 164–8).
[6] Ramsbottom (2002: 214) notes that '[a]t any level below that of the gentry, women would also have been directly engaged in the education of young children'.

their own sakes, as well as their Childrens, are frequently to call on them at Home
to Repeat their Catechism, and to Read the Holy Scriptures, especially on the Lord's
Day, and to use Prayers Morning and Evening in their Families; so that all may the
better be informed of their Duty, and by a constant and sincere Practice thereof,
procure the Blessing of God upon them.

While reading and writing, as well as sewing and housecraft for the girls and
accounts for the boys, were part of the curriculum, as pointed out above, the main
focus was on religious discipline and social subordination. The Bible served both
as a primer and as a source for religious discipline. Similar to charity schools,
industrial schools focused on religious education and the very rudiments of literacy,
and some schools also provided industrial training (Lawson and Silver 1973: 181–9;
Vincent 1989: 64–5, 73–9). The method used to teach children letters, as reflected
in primers written for early charity schools, proceeded from teaching the alphabet
to lists of disconnected syllables, e.g. 'ka ke ki ko ku', to lists of monosyllabic
words, bisyllabic words, and so forth until they reached reading lists of words with
seven syllables. The teaching of writing, which originally consisted of instructions
on how to hold a pen and to copy graphs and words, became more sophisticated
with the introduction of the 'Mulhauser method', where a letter was divided into
four parts, namely 'lines, curves, loops and crotches' (Vincent 1989: 76–7).[7] The
approaches used to teach the lower classes differed from those for the upper layers
of society in that the reading of literature and grammatical training were not part
of the curriculum. Vincent (1989: 67) appropriately summarises the situation in
stating that '[t]he most striking characteristic of the procedures adopted to teach
children their letters up to the imposition of universal and compulsory elementary
education between 1870 and 1880 was their sheer variety'.[8] In addition to the variety
of teaching methods, one must also consider that literacy cannot be seen as a unity
but that it is determined by an interplay of different factors such as technological,
distributional and sociocultural components (Levine 1986: 11–13).[9]

   In order to establish literacy rates across the country, the Hardwicke Marriage
Act of 1753, which required that all marriages were recorded in a marriage register, is
considered of great importance by educational historians. It is the ability to sign or
mark the marriage register that is taken as the criterion of literacy (see also Fairman,
this volume). As Houston (1982: 200) notes, '[t]hose writing their full names are
deemed literate, those making a mark or initials are taken as illiterate'. Based on the
assumption that reading preceded writing in the learning process, evidence from
the nineteenth century 'suggests that ability to sign is associated with a reasonable
proficiency in reading, thus marking a rough mid-point in the spectrum of literate

---

[7] Fairman (2008a) refers to the approach used to teach the lower orders as mechanical schooling as opposed to
grammatical schooling.

[8] For instance, Rose (2010) and Whyman (2009) provide examples, based on letters and diaries, that illustrate
how selected members of the labouring poor stratum have used literacy as a means to earn a living/create a better
position for themselves.

[9] For a detailed discussion of these factors see Auer (in prep.).

accomplishments' (Houston 1982: 200). Even though the criterion of literacy is imperfect and one can criticise the approach, it may be seen as a good indicator of trends over longer periods of time (see Sanderson 1995: 9). According to More (2000: 58), literacy rates, namely 66% of men and 40% of women, did not change much in the period between 1750 and 1840, but after 1840 literacy rates rose rapidly.[10]

3. On epistolary norms

The art of letter writing, which formed part of rhetoric, can be traced back to classical times. Attempts to standardise the *ars dictaminis* in letter-writing manuals had been made since *c.* AD 1000 (Austin-Jones 2007: 16). One of the first manuals in English was William Fulwood's *The Enemie of Idlenesse* (1568), which was translated and then adapted to English from a French work that is attributed to Jean de la Moyne (1566). In comparison to earlier Latin manuals, which were used as scholarly aids, Fulwood's letter writer 'was more concerned with everyday life and domestic matters' (Austin-Jones 2007: 16). The model letters contained in the manual, which cover a wide range of topics and situations, also take into consideration the variety of people writing letters as well as different addressees, e.g. wife to husband or gentleman to a noble captain. The first book (or chapter) of the manual provides instructions on how to indite epistles and letters and also contains some advice on epistolary style that ought to be employed.[11] First, Fulwood notes that an epistle or letter 'is nothing else but an Oration written, containing the mynde of the Orator or wryter, thereby to giue to understand to him or them that be absent, the same that should be declared if they were present' (1571: 1). He then distinguishes between three groups of addressees, namely superiors, equals and inferiors, and particular ways in which to write to the respective groups. Fulwood's advice on how to address members of different social standing is as follows:

> If we speake or write of or to our superiors, we must do it with all honour, humilitie and reuerence, bring to their personages superlatiue and comparatiue termes: as most high, most mighty, right honourable, most redowted, most loyall, most worthy, most renowned, altogether according to the qualitie of their personages. (1571: 2)

> If we adresse our speech to our equall, we must speake with a certain familiar reuerence, bring positiue and comparatiue termes and very fewe superlatiye, as wyse, sage, honourable, worshipfull, discrete, renowned, etc. (1571: 4)

> If we speake to our inferior, we must use a certayne kynde of modest and ciuill authoritie, in giuing them playnely to understand our intent and purpose. (1571: 4)

Fulwood appears to be most concerned with address formulae in the case of superiors and equals. With inferiors, it is the plain way of conveying the letter writer's

---

[10] After that date government funding had become available and the parents' incomes had increased, which was conducive to the rise of literacy rates (More 2000: 59).

[11] Note that the term 'style' is not used in Fulwood's chapter.

intent rather than forms of address that is being emphasised. Moreover, the letter writer is advised not to 'write to them that be simple and ignorant by termes that be straunge and unknown, for so should they haue iust occasion to suspect that we deride and mocke them' (1571: 6). The choice of the appropriate lexis is thus of importance. Similarly, the letter writer himself should avoid touching upon higher matters than his understanding or knowledge can comprehend. Another piece of advice is to 'wryt succinctly and brefly', irrespective of how pleasant the subject matter is, to people who do not enjoy reading (1571: 4). Fulwood's manual appears to have been very popular in the Early Modern English period, as reflected in the great number of editions contained in the database *Early English Books Online*, and it must have started a trend, as many more letter-writing manuals were published in numerous editions during this period. This trend was continued into the Late Modern English period (see Myers 2003: 373; Fens-de Zeeuw 2008: 165; see also *Eighteenth Century Collections Online*). After all, these guides not only taught 'proper forms, styles and contents for letters of different kinds' but also 'proper social, professional, commercial and domestic conduct' (Bannet 2007: 13). Accordingly, the book market offered letter-writing manuals for businessmen as well as for ladies.[12] The prospective readership, as indicated by the authors of these manuals, can vary greatly. Searches on *Eighteenth-Century Collections Online* (*ECCO*) reveal that most of the manuals printed during the eighteenth century are addressed to 'young Gentlemen, Ladies, Tradesmen, &c.' (Tavernier 1762) and thus to the elite and the middling sorts. Manuals that are explicitly directed at a lower-class audience are less common. A manual that also considers the labouring poor as prospective readers is Revd. Thomas Cooke's *The Universal Letter-Writer; or, New Art of Polite Correspondence* (1775), which contains 'the complete petitioner; Containing, Great Variety of Petitions on various Subjects, from Persons in low or middling States of Life, to those in higher Stations'. In fact, the manual contains a model pauper letter (1775: 215):

(1)   From a poor Woman whose Husband was lately dead, soliciting for a weekly
       Pension from the Parish.

       To the Minister, Church-wardens and Overseers of the Parish of B.
       The humble Petition of A. B.
       Sheweth,

       That your petitioner's late husband was a laborious,
       and industrious honest man; that he was both by
       birth and servitude one of your parishioners. That
       whilst he enjoyed his health, it was his constant practice
       to do every thing in his power for the support of his family:

---

[12] *The Ladies Complete Letter Writer*, published in 1763, is considered to be the first English letter-writing manual for women; it did, however, draw on earlier compilations (Brant 2006: 40).

that he was lately seized with a violent fever, which,
after two weeks illness, terminated in his death. That
your petitioner was left entirely destitute with three help-
less children: that your petitioner is willing to do every
thing in her power towards their support by her own labour,
but that being insufficient, she has presumed to present
a state of her case to you, humbly praying, that
a small matter may be allowed her weekly, which with the
profits arising from her labour, will enable her to bring up
her children useful members of society.
   And your petitioner, as in duty bound, shall ever pray.

Even though model letters for paupers exist, one very rarely comes across letters based on these models in archives. The historian Thomas Sokoll, for instance, has only found one letter in the Essex archives that is clearly based on a model letter (2001: 193–4):

(2) 133* From Ann Marsh in [Shoreditch] London, [11 October 1824]

  To the Churchwardens & Committee of the Parish of Chelmsford
  This Humble Petition of Mrs Ann Marsh of Sugarloaf Court Long Alley
  Moorfield Sheweth
   That your poor Petitioner is a Parishioner of Chelmsf^d and is left a Widow
  with 7 Children 6 of whom are dependent on the poor pittance; which the
  kindness of a few neighbours supply her with; by sending her a few
  cloathes to Mangle for them which at present is so trifling that they are
  now literally half starving; and in winter time she knows from past experience her supply will be near wholly cut of, as her few employers do not
  Mangle in the Winter season as in Summer So that she has now a long
  dreary Winter to look forward to with numerous infants whom she fears
  will be crying to her for Bread; which it will not be in her power to provide.
  She therefore is impelld humbly to beg your pity & humanity to assist her
  utmost endeavour; this Winter, to provide for her numerous infant charge,
  (without which) She never can keep them from Starving,) 4 of them being
  under 9 years of age which She hopes will claim your kindest Sympathy,
  which She will ever acknowledge with grateful thanks to her kind
  benefactors

          Your very Humble Supplcant
          Ann Marsh

As Sokoll also found other letters signed with the name Ann Marsh (see also Section 5.3 in this chapter) and compared them, he was able to draw the conclusion that the petition above 'was quite clearly neither written nor composed by Ann Marsh' but by a professional scribe, which is reflected in the choice of vocabulary (the linguistic repertoire), the layout of the letter as well as the copperplate handwriting (2001: 48). The lack of these types of letters in actual archives, as also noted by the 'Letters of Artisans and the Labouring Poor' project group, indicates that paupers did not use letter-writing manuals as models for their letters to the parish overseers.

When looking at the actual content of letter-writing manuals from a chronological perspective, it can be observed that the authors largely relied on each other – if they did not adopt parts of the works completely, they were at least inspired by earlier epistolary manuals. To illustrate this, I will also take a look at a Late Modern English letter writer, namely *The Art of Letter-Writing* (Anon.: 1762), and the way in which epistolary style is defined. The ground rule that is often repeated by the anonymous author is 'to write as we speak' (1762: 3).[13] Further elaboration on this ground rule shows that the author does not in fact suggest that actual speech should be put on paper; instead, the letter writer is advised to aim for a natural style that should not be packed with 'great and sounding Words, or a Swell of pompous Thought' (1762: 4). If a letter writer hopes to be regarded as knowledgeable and polite, he ought to express himself in an easy, simple and natural way combined with elegance and delicacy. By contrast, if the epistolary style contains unnatural phrases and lacks beautiful simplicity, it will be concluded 'that he is a Man of scanty Knowledge and of a very ill Taste' (1762: 5). The advice given points towards the choice of lexis – the more elaborate (foreign) words, the more unnatural the writing style appears to be. In addition, '[t]he antiquated may be well set aside, and those newly coined adopted with Precaution' (1762: 8). Apart from this advice, a polite person should make a distinction in style between letters addressed to 'well-bred persons' as well as the range of different subjects that can be treated in letters. It is thus of the utmost importance that the letter writers suit their 'Expressions to the Nature of Subjects and the Rank of Persons'. As for the different ranks of addressees, the letter writer is advised to 'rise nobly, when [. . . writing] to Persons of great Consideration by their Condition of Life; and, on the other Hand, descend to more familiar Ways of Speaking, when [. . . communicating his/her] Thoughts and Opinions to intimate Friends' (1762: 5). With respect to diversity of style and different subject matters, bombastic style as well as figurative thoughts and expressions, comparisons, fables, history, proverbs, flattery and servile complaisance should be avoided. Moreover, the writer is advised to keep the letter short and concise, which is done with business and society letters as well as compliments. In summary, according to letter writing manuals, the choice of style depends on (a) the kind of person the letter writer aims to be seen as, which may be interpreted as creating a social identity, (b) the rank of the person the letter is addressed to and (c) the subject matter of the letter. Accordingly, the letter manual consists of a wide range of letters that

---

[13] Interestingly, the author argues that 'nature . . . forms Poets, and Art Orators', and it is thus nature that helps master the epistolary style. For those writers who were not born with this talent, the author suggests the following: 'We must read much, and transcribe often such Collections of Letters as are most in Request for their Beauty of Thought and Elegance of Diction: And thus we shall form ourselves by Degrees, and Art and Study will supply the Defects of Nature' (Anon.:1762: 3).

illustrate letters to different addressees and/or on different subject matters. With regard to the linguistic level and stylistic options, the choice of lexis is touched upon only when the letter writer is warned against the use of inkhorn terms.[14] Syntax is not commented on in the manuals that I investigated. It is noteworthy that some of these manuals, particularly in the eighteenth century, were accompanied by a brief grammar. According to Fens-de Zeeuw (2008: 189), extensive grammar sections were no longer included in nineteenth-century manuals but restricted to capitalisation or punctuation at the most. In fact, it appears that a rather relaxed view was taken on letter writing during the heyday of normative grammars. For instance, the grammarian Lindley Murray (1795: 203) accepts the elliptical style 'in conversation and epistolary writing, yet, in all writings of a serious and dignified kind, it ought to be avoided'. Then again, the epistolary style was meant to obey grammatical rules. Hodson (2007: 38) rightly points out that advice on letter writing was somewhat contradictory in that the letter writer should aim for naturalness and plainness, but this requirement was simultaneously undermined 'by insisting upon a precise and elevated style'. How letter writers dealt with this conflicting advice will be looked at in Section 4 of this chapter. Another question that arises with regard to letter-writing manuals is whether letter writers were in fact aware of the advice given. As mentioned earlier, the proliferation of letter-writing manuals throughout the Modern English period and up to the present day is a strong indication that there was and is a market for these guides. Austin-Jones (2007: 18), for instance, argues that letter formulae, which can be traced back to letter manuals, are a sure sign that letter writers were used. Examples of letter formulae are (a) address forms (see Fulwood's recommendations above), (b) opening formulae like 'I take this opportunity to write you a few lines' or 'I take up my pen' (Austin-Jones 2007: 18) and (c) health formulae, i.e. enquiring about the addressee's health. Then again, the formulae used in letters are not necessarily those recommended in letter-writing manuals. In particular with regard to lower social ranks, it can be assumed that these manuals were not purchased (see also discussion above); instead, letter writing may have been taught in schools or by community and family members. Received letters may also have been adopted as models for letter writing.

4. On epistolary practice at different social layers

At this point I will provide examples of stylistic variation as found in letters written in the first half of the nineteenth century. The focus will be on letters written by selected women representing the elite, the middling order and the labouring poor respectively. Important criteria in selecting the letters were that they were addressed to different people, thus reflecting different types of relationships, i.e. one closer and one more distanced, and that the letters touched upon different

---

[14] For an overview of different approaches to style, see Jucker (1992: chapter 2).

topics that required different tones (see Traugott and Romaine 1985).[15] During
the Late Modern English period, i.e. the codification stage in the standardisation
process of the English language, plenty of grammars, dictionaries, spelling books and
letter-writing manuals were available for purchase or to borrow in lending libraries,
but, as discussed in Section 2, education opportunities and literacy, particularly for
women, still varied greatly. Even though the tools for practising writing had already
been available to all the different layers of society, not everybody had the chance or
the means to make use of these tools. Ultimately, the opportunities for education
in combination with informal instruction by family or friends as well as self-help
determined the different linguistic repertoires a person had and therefore also the
different styles they had at their disposal. The focus of the three case studies will
be on how style/s was/were employed for self-presentation and to negotiate social
relationships.

4.1 Style shifts in selected letters of Mrs Fitzherbert – the elite

To represent the upper layer of society in the Late Modern English period, I have
chosen two letters written by Mary Anne Fitzherbert, née Smythe (1756–1837), who
is best known as the unlawful Roman Catholic wife of George IV (1762–1830). Mary
Anne was born into a Catholic landowning family that had kept the old religion as
well as their estates during the persecution. Because of this strong Roman Catholic
family background, and the fact that a Catholic education was not available in
England at the time, Mary Anne was sent to France in order to receive formal
schooling. It is believed that from the age of twelve onwards she attended as a boarder
at the convent school of the Conceptionists, the Blue Nuns, which is an English
Order in Faubourg St-Antoine. Mary Anne received part of her education from
the Benedictines at Dunkirk. As regards the curriculum taught at convent schools,
the French language would have been taught, alongside subjects such as ancient
history, geography, literature and heraldry. It is unlikely that she was taught classical
languages, but other European languages may have been offered as an option. Other
subjects taught were drawing, embroidery, music, singing and deportment. This
combination of subjects was to provide a good 'balance between acquiring useful
knowledge, practising social graces, and gaining an understanding of, and love for,
their religion, all in preparation for their future place in society' (Irvine 2005: 8; see
also *ODNB* under 'Maria Anne Fitzherbert'). It may be concluded that she received
a good education and was well trained in reading and writing. In 1774, at the age of
eighteen, Mary Anne Smythe was introduced to London society. In the same year,
she met the young, wealthy Catholic widower Edward Weld who was sixteen years
her senior. Mary Anne and Edwald Weld got married in July 1775. The marriage
was short lived as Weld died three months later. As Weld had not signed a new will,

---

[15] Nurmi and Palander-Collin's use of the term 'register' is similar to what is often referred to as 'style', i.e. their
'concept of register variation, defined in terms of the relationship between writer and recipient in the two cases
makes for very different stylistic selections, and a considerably different degree of formality' (2008: 26–7).

the young widow was forced to remarry as soon as possible. She agreed to marry the young Catholic gentleman Thomas Fitzherbert of Swynnerton from Staffordshire in the early summer of 1778. Mary Anne became a widow for the second time in 1781. Shortly after the death of her second husband, she entered London high society, which is where she was introduced to George, Prince of Wales. The young prince, who had become infatuated with her, was able to convince her to marry him. The marriage, which was celebrated in December 1785, was illegal under the Act of Settlement of 1701, the Act of Union of 1707 and the Royal Marriages Act of 1772 (Irvine 2005: 33; see also *ODNB* under 'Maria Anne Fitzherbert').[16] After many ups and downs, which included affairs on the Prince's part, the couple split up in 1794. In April 1795, Prince George married Caroline of Brunswick for financial reasons. Only a few years later, Mary Anne and the Prince reunited, i.e. after the Vatican had agreed to her being the Prince's canonical wife. Their relationship, which hit the rocks again in 1806, when Prince George embarked on another affair, never recovered. Mary Anne Fitzherbert died and was buried in Brighton in 1837 (for more detailed accounts of Mrs Fitzherbert's life, see Munson 2001; Irvine 2005; *ODNB*).

As for the two letters selected for closer investigation, the first letter from 1784, according to the postmark, is addressed to her uncle William Fermor and refers to the 'the poor little man', who appears to be the Prince of Wales. The second letter from 1812 is addressed to the Prince of Wales. After the couple's final break-up, it was agreed that for the rest of her life Mary Anne should receive an allowance of £6,000 a year and that she should live as a private person. As a higher amount, namely that of £10,000, had originally been promised to her parents and her uncle, and she had become used to an expensive lifestyle, she tried to get a higher allowance (Munson 2001: 326; Irvine 2005: 137). The two letters are provided in full below, followed by the analysis.

(3)   Letter 1 (addressed to Mary Anne's uncle William Fermor; Legg 1939: 56–7[17]):

1   My Dr Mr Fermor   [5 August, 1784]
           Every Post day I have been expecting a line from you, you
        promis'd to write to me, and I take it exceedingly ill of you for-
        getting me so soon What can you be about that you could not
5   find one Quaterr of an hour to bestow upon me, it is not flatter-
        ing I must allow. I cannot help adding you cannot employ an Idle
        moment in a way that will be more thankfully acknowledg'd, to

---

[16] Both the Act of Settlement (1701) and the Act of Union (1707) excluded 'a prince or princess married to a Catholic from succeeding to the throne'. According to Irvine (2005: 33), '[t]he Royal Marriages Act, passed in 1772, forbade any Prince or Princess descended from George II, and under the age of twenty-five, to marry without the consent of the ruling monarch. Should one of them wish to marry without royal approval after the age of twenty-five, he or she could apply to the Privy Council, and could then marry a year later, provided neither the Lords nor the Commons had raised an objection.'

[17] I was not able to compare Legg's transcription to the original letter and therefore need to trust that this is a faithful transcription.

have the satisfaction of hearing that you and yours are well, will
allways give me the greatest satisfaction, and if you have not quite
10   forgot that there is such a being existing, perhaps I may flatter
myself w^h you know how much pleasure it will give me you will
not refuse me the pleasure of Hearing from you.

/I have been here three weeks these last four days this place [p. 2]
has been crowded being the Races, but cheifly consisted of Men,
15   there are very few people staying here that I am acquainted w^th
a great Mixture of Company wch is always the case in these sort of
places. I live very quiet and very reliev^d I am now laying in a
stock of Health for the next champagne I get up (wonderfull to tell)
at eight oclock every morning and Bath every day in the sea dine
20   at half past four and go to bed regularly at Eleven I am certain this
style of life will prolong my life at least ten years.

I am sure you will be glad to hear that my poor little Man and
I settled our affairs in the DARK perfectly to my satisfaction dark
I took care it should be and I believe he will remember it for some
25   time for in going out of the Room he had like to have put an end
on himself by tumbling over one of the Chairs, and although I was not
dis'pos'd to laugh yr verses and nonsense/came immeadiatly [p. 3]
to my assistance and I thought I would have expir'd upon the Spot
I was not able to Speak for Laughing I think this history will
30   entertain Mrs Fermor I am not quite clear wether she wont be angry
at me for behaving so ill – pray give me† kind love to her and to
all y^r Generous [?] Circle – I often wish to give a peep at you and
were I quite at liberty I should certainly do it wth the greatest pleasure I have wrote so many letters by this post that I can scarce
35   see a stroke I make, excuse this horrid scrawl, and pray burn my
letter otherwise the History of my little Man and me may perhaps
become quite scandalous and those that only know that we have met
and that in the Dark I must own appearances would be much against
me pray take care of my Reputation and indulge me wth either
40   lighting y^r fire or to Occupy a place where I once found Candide
tho' I sh^d wish to be dispatch'd as soon as possible perhaps you
would be good natur'd enough to make a pilgramge† on purpose to
that shrine/I shall feel extremely gratefull to you if you do and [p. 4]
I hope you will not feel the worse for it. Adieu bon Soir ever y^rs
45   affectionately   [unsigned]

Direct for me Brighton Sussex.
[Addressed: –] William Fermor Esqr
Tusmor
Brackley
Northampthonshire.

(4)   Letter 2 (addressed to the Prince of Wales after their final breakup)[18]:

1   Sir Octr 25 1812
              It is with no small
         degree of mortification that
         I find my last letter to you still
5   unnotic'd, I cannot add any ~~thing~~
         stronger arguments to what that
         letter contain'd, Moments of reflection
         must recall to y^r. Royal Highness
         recollection that what I there
10   repeated, I had in your own
         hand writing and signature –
         I am confident Sir my letter was
         perfectly respectfull & written
         with great good feeling towards
15   y^r R.H. Do not Sir by a contemptuous
         silence compel me for my own
         justification to appeal to the
         opinions of impartial persons
         by shewing them my letters to
20   you on this occasion that they
         may judge whether or not I have said
         [new page]
         any thing in them to merit
         the treatment I have met
         with, I still wait your R.H.
25   pleasure to know the cause
         of this delay, & when it is to
         cease. I have the Honor of
         subscribing myself yr R.H.
         very obd. Hum^ble Servant
30   M.F.

The two selected letters by Mary Anne Fitzherbert reveal that the letter writer Mary had a wide repertoire that allowed her to create different social identities in her correspondence. The first letter, addressed to her uncle William Fermor, shows the young, carefree and playful Mary, who finds herself at great ease with her uncle (and aunt) and considers him her confidant. In the first ten lines of the letter (ll. 2–12), she teasingly complains about her uncle not having sent her a letter. Following a brief account of how she spends her days (ll. 13–21), she assures her uncle that she

---

18   This letter is transcribed from the original, which can be found on http://rpmcollections.wordpress.com/2011/
     02/01/letter-from-mrs-fitzherbert-to-the-prince-of-wales/

has settled the affair with George IV, and in a lighthearted tone continues that this letter ought to be burnt so that nobody finds out about the affair, and that her uncle should take care of her reputation. Mary's starry-eyed, carefree and playful nature is not only reflected in the content of the letter but also in her letter-writing style. For instance, she actually writes as she speaks: she does not use punctuation marks consistently and does not strictly adhere to existing grammatical advice, which, even though it does not fully concur with advice for the perfect letter writer, creates a feeling of intimacy, familiarity and social proximity. It may also be observed that she capitalised some words randomly and used archaic spelling (based on *OED* evidence), e.g. *allways* (l. 9), *cheifly* (l. 14), *wonderfull* (l. 17), *immeadiatly* (l. 27), *gratefull* (l. 43). Similarly, the use of the past participle *forgot* (l. 10) instead of *forgotten* may be interpreted as archaic language use (see Gustafsson 2002). The letter also reveals that she received a good education, e.g. as reflected by her general use of vocabulary, and that she was aware of epistolary conventions, e.g. formulae and abbreviations such as wth for 'with', wch for 'which', y^r for 'your', $reliev^d$ for 'relieved', sh^d for 'should' and *dispatch'd* for 'dispatched'. The latter two observations, i.e. that of her being educated and familiar with epistolary conventions, are particularly prominent in letter 2, addressed to the Prince of Wales some time after their final breakup, in which she tries to get a higher allowance, which had in fact been promised to her. As the former couple had a strained relationship for some time, the letter does not testify to any intimacy and familiarity; instead, she presents herself as rather distanced and worried about the agreement, but at the same time deeply hurt by the Prince of Wales' silence and his treatment of her. Similar to letter 1, she complains in the opening formula about the fact that her letter had not been noticed. However, this has been done in a much more succinct and formal way in letter 2, i.e. 'It is with no small degree of mortification that I find my last letter to you still unnotic'd . . .' (ll. 2–5). The formal and distanced tone is also reflected in the address formulae used and particularly in the choice of vocabulary, which contains many Latinate words such as *mortification* (l. 3), *contemptuous* (l. 15), *compel* (l. 16), *justification* (l. 17). In addition, the second letter, being less conversational, appears to adhere more strictly to letter-writing norms, i.e. in particular to sections that give advice on how to address people of a superior social standing (see Fulwood 1568).

Even though the letters were written at different stages of Mrs Fitzherbert's life, they reveal that her wide repertoire of vocabulary and also her familiarity with letter-writing conventions and her wide use of them, allowed her to create different social (epistolary) identities and to vary and adapt her style according to the person she was addressing and the topic/s covered in the letter.

4.2 *Style shifts in the letters of Mary Wordsworth (1770–1859)*

Mary Wordsworth (née Hutchinson), who has been selected to represent the middling sort, was the wife of the poet William Wordsworth (1770–1850). Details about

Mary Hutchinson's upbringing and her life can be retrieved from her memoirs and her numerous letters. As stated in her memoirs (Burton 1958: xxi), Mary, like the Wordsworths, had her roots in Penrith. At the age of eight, she moved to her grandparents in Bishopston, where she stayed for the next four years. Shortly after her return to Penrith, both her mother and father died, and Mary, who was then the oldest at thirteen, formed a household with four siblings and their great-aunt Gamage. It is known that Mary and her sister Sara attended primary school in Penrith at the same time, namely in 1776 and 1777, as William and Dorothy Wordsworth. While we know details about the education the Wordsworths received after primary school, little is known about Mary Hutchinson's educational training. In 1788 Mary and Sara Hutchinson settled with their brother at Sockburn. On 4 October 1802, Mary and William Wordsworth were married in Brompton Church. They had five children, two of whom died at an early age. Mary Wordsworth died on 17 January 1859 (see *ODNB* under 'William Wordsworth').

Two letters written by Mary Wordsworth will be discussed here,[19] the first of which is addressed to Edward Moxon, who was William Wordsworth's publisher after 1834. The second letter, written on 10 November 1847(?) is addressed to Fanny Eliza Wordsworth (1821–88), the wife of Mary Wordsworth's youngest son William (1810–83).

(5)   Letter 1 (sent to Edward Moxon, William Wordsworth's publisher):

1   My dear Mr Moxon

      If the parcel to Rydal is not already forwarded, please to add to its contents 6 ~~Vols~~ copies of the Excursion, 6 [Du] Sonnets, & 6 of the Yarrow Revisited – and six selections – We want them for our Village Bookseller, a Worthy Woman who seems to have a considerable demand – & the Kendal Booksellers only allow her ½ profit with themselves – So that it is an object to her to have

5   them as you charge them to us, and the trade.

      Mr W. reached home well & in good spirits last Saturday, tho' he is still annoyed by the sprain or weakness in the

      [new page]

      ancle, which confines him to our own grounds.

      If the books are not already sent off to Hereford I hope that they are nearly ready – should you not

10   have heard, which I trust has not been the case, from Dr. C. Wordsworth about them will you be

---

[19] The letters written by Mary Wordsworth were retrieved from the website http://collections.wordsworth.org.uk/. I have adopted the transcriptions provided on the website; while the transcriptions are faithful, they do not adhere to the line breaks found in the original letter.

kind enough to send to remind him, by asking for the list – as it is of great consequence to my nephew that as little delay as possible should interfere with his receiving them.

I was very sorry to hear from Mr W. that you had not

[new page]

been well enough to fulfil your intention of accompanying him to Oxford – I hope you are ere this

15 better, & that Mrs & Miss M. & the children are all well.

Hartley Coleridge tells me he is nearly ready for you. I wish you may find this really to be the case.

Believe me dear Sir with best regards from all here to yourself & Mrs M – to be sincerely Yours M. Wordsworth

Rydal Mount June 22 d.

[new page]

Your parcel just arrived – send the books required separately if you please immediately

Edward Moxon Esqre

44 Dover Street

(6)   Letter 2 (addressed to her daughter-in-law, Fanny Eliza Wordsworth)

1   My dearest Fanny

I have to thank you for 2 letters – & much as I was pleased to received them, each brought the its own disappointment – for in neither do you mention your own health which is what I am anxious about – Wm. has not written lately so that I have had no report thro' him. I was thankful to hear

5   from you that you thought him better.

Thank you of for your report of Jane & for your kind attention to her & notice of her friends – I have not received her letter, & shall be glad to hear from her, tell her with my love – she will excuse my writing

[new page]

to her as she can hear all about us from you – but she must tell me when the school breaks up – so

10   that I may apprize Mr Robinson who kindly holds himself to be in readiness to be her Escort to the

North – I do not know how the plan for your return, or continuance at Brighton is arranged – but if you are still there at their departure & are so steadily well as to render your coming home adviseable – we you may

be sure will all rejoice that you should make one of the travelling Party.
I have had a letter from Mr R this mg who only left Brighton on
Thursday – I could not obtain his

15 Brighton address or I would have

[new page]

sent it you – but I wrote to him directing to Russell Sq. to be forwarded
& he just reached home to receive the note – & says he was sadly vexed
for ~~almost~~ at the last hour of his being in B. he was told by his Landlady
or Hostess there that she had seen Mrs W.W. in the town – & with the
chance of losing the train he was <u>about to</u> run to call upon you – when
she ½ corrected her words by

20 saying 'Don't be disappointed if I am wrong, for I am not quite sure but
I think it was she' – this checked his intention, & now finding you are
really there he is sadly vexed.

As we are expecting Dr & Mrs Ch: Wordsworth tomorrow & who say
they are to be in Carlisle tomorrow on their way

[new page]

(where they hope to see you & Wm) I am half to hope that Wm may
return with them – as the

25 Collection must now be over, & Mr Carter when he went away said he
should propose to Wm to remain at Carlisle a while to allow Wm to
come to see us.

I think this will be accepted by him for the sake of seeing a little more of
his Cousins – Yet on 2d thoughts he will scarcely like to quit Carlisle till
after the sale of the house he spoke of. His Father does not enter into the
idea of the purchase as he would do, had he more confidence that the

30 residence in the Town would be suitable to your health &c And should
you be <u>Possessors</u> of a house, you would have too strong a motive for
keeping to it – whether

[new page]

it quite agreed with you or not – so that he fears unless, it were bought
at such a rate as to be a good investment – it would, as Houses are in
themselves a bad Property, only be an entanglement. I have no doubt
but that Wm will act prudently.

35 We have the boys still here & cannot spare James to take them home,
till after our visitors are gone – Who [purpose] to give us a week of their
precious time. I suppose they are upon a tour of visits – We were
surprized by the announcement of their intention of coming to us. –
John also has a guest staying with him – an Old College friend.

You will easily conceive that with such a family my

[new page]

40   hands & my thoughts are kept busy – for poor Father continues in the
same sad state – indeed the broken weather increases this – for he
cannot walk so much as he did at Briscoe – H Cookson only left us
yesterday – to give way for our preparing the room for our expected
nephew & niece I feel a great loss of her, as you may easily suppose.

Now dearest Fanny you will excuse this worthless note & with our joint
remembrances to yr.

45   Father & Br & with earnest wishes for your improvement – & desire, at
all events, you will tell me how you are in all particulars believe me to
be your anxiously loving Mother M.W.

[new page]

I cannot see to read what I have written so you must correct as you go
on.

In the two letters, Mary Wordsworth presents herself in two different roles,
namely as assistant to and wife of William Wordsworth in letter 1, i.e. the letter
addressed to her husband's publisher Edward Moxon, and as a caring mother-
in-law in the second letter, which is addressed to Fanny Eliza Wordsworth. Even
though the letters to Moxon are the most formal of Mary Wordsworth's correspondence contained in the Wordsworth Trust collection, it is striking that her writing
style does not differ too much from her personal correspondence. In terms of
content, she deals with business matters but also touches upon personal issues
in her letter to Moxon, i.e. when she writes about William Wordsworth's or
Mr. Moxon's health. While letter 2, addressed to Fanny Eliza, opens by thank-
ing her for the letters and worrying about Fanny Eliza's health, in letter 1 she
gets straight to business without any introductory formulae, e.g. health formulae.
What both letters have in common is, for instance, the use of dashes alongside
full stops, the former of which seem to indicate either a pause in her 'written speech' or a change of topic. In comparison to Mrs Fitzherbert's letters (see
Section 4.1), one cannot observe a marked difference in vocabulary choice and
syntactic constructions. It is also noteworthy that not many abbreviations are used
in the letters, e.g. & (both letters) and *mg* for *morning* (l. 14, letter 2), and there are
no grammatical solecisms, i.e. apart from a missing *have* in *I was pleased to received*
(l. 2, letter 2), which may just have been a slip of the pen.

    The similarities in terms of writing style in both of Mary Wordsworth's letters
under investigation, and also supported by her other correspondence, may be
interpreted in two ways. Either her relationship to both addressees is not too
dissimilar, i.e. they are both relationships of familiarity and social proximity, which
then may explain the lack of stylistic variation in the letters, or her linguistic
resources in writing were restricted and therefore only allowed her little room to
manoeuvre. Considering that Mary Wordsworth was surrounded by members of
her husband's literary circle and their written works, she would have been aware

of nuances in language use and she would have most likely applied them, when appropriate, in her own usage.

4.3 Style shifts in the letters of Ann Marsh – labouring poor

When we are dealing with pauper letters, it is difficult or next to impossible in most cases to find out background information about the letter writer, and one therefore has to rely on information given in the letter itself. The two letters selected for investigation were written by Ann Marsh, the single mother of six children, in London in 1824 (Sokoll 2001: 190). The first letter, signed with the name *Ann Marsh*, is addressed to her brother Robert and her sister:

(7) 1   1824   London July the 26

  Dear Brother & Sister

     I hope this will find you all well we are but verry poorly here I Received
  Your Letter and was Glad to here You were then well Thos Marsh is
  5   Married and is no assistance watever to Me I hope You will Go to the
  Committe and You will Show them the oth<er> Side I Can asure You if
  Something is not d<one> I must Come to the parish I hope You will rite an
  Answer as Soon as You Can
     Ras[on] Desire thir Love to You and my Duty to My Mother and Love
  10   to all

  From Y^r
  Ann Marsh

The second letter is addressed to the overseers of Chelmsford, which was most likely Ann Marsh's legal parish of settlement:

(8) 1   To the Oversears of Chelmsford

     Gentelmen Since the time that I was down at Chelmsford I have tried all
  in my power to Maintain my family wich is Six fatheless Children the
  Little work I have is not Suffient to find them in Bread I have been Obliged
  5   to part with the Chief of my things for our Support Gentelmen I hope You
  will take this into Your Serious Consideratton and allow Something as in
  Your wisdom may think proper Towards the maintenance of so Large a
  family if Something is not Done I must with my family apply to to be Sent
  home to My parish

  10   Gentlemen I Rem^n Your &. Ann Marsh
  London July 26 1824

The language use, i.e. in particular the spelling, suggests that the author received basic training in writing. Even though the letter writer did not fully master all the skills that are requisite to writing, which are mechanical and calligraphic skills, orthographic, grammatical and lexical skills, the examples above show that it is not necessary to have a perfect command of all of these skills as long as one has a rudimentary mastery sufficient to get one's message across (see Ludwig 1998: 150). The fact that Ann Marsh only received basic training in writing, i.e. in comparison to Mrs Fitzherbert and Mrs Wordsworth, already strongly suggests that her resources for expressing herself in writing are restricted. In the letters, Ann Marsh takes on two different social roles, namely sister and also daughter in letter 1, and starving pauper mother who insists on her right to receive out-relief in letter 2. Both letters reveal that the writer, who may or may not have been Ann Marsh, was aware of letter writing conventions in that the person knew how to start and end letters appropriately. For instance, the beginning of the letter addressed to Ann Marsh's brother and sister contains a health formula – 'I hope this will find you all well' (l. 3) and the closing formula 'Desire thir Love to You and my Duty to My Mother and Love to all From Y^r Ann Marsh' (ll. 9–12). The more formal letter addressed to the overseers starts with 'Gentelmen' (l. 2) and gets right to the point when it states that she had done all in her power to maintain her family. The letter closes with the formal phrase 'Gentlemen I Rem^n Your &. Ann Marsh' (l. 10). Apart from that, the letters have many similarities in that they lack punctuation marks, words are randomly capitalised, they contain non-standard orthography; at the same time, the more official letter addressed to the overseers contains certain Latinate words that Ann Marsh uses in order to make her case, e.g. *maintain* (l. 3), *suffient* ('sufficient', l. 4), *Obliged* (l. 4) and *Consideratton* ('consideration', l. 6). As these terms are frequently found in pauper letters, one may consider them register-specific vocabulary, i.e. a repertoire of words that is typically found in pauper letters (see, for instance, also letter sample (2) in Section 3, which shows a model letter petition signed with Ann Marsh's name). Through the use of these terms, she is able to present herself as a serious petitioner whose application should be taken into consideration by the overseers. In comparison to Mrs Fitzherbert's stylistic changes (Section 4.1), Ann Marsh has clearly less room to manoeuvre. In the latter case, it is primarily the use of address and other letter-writing formulae, i.e. apart from the register-specific terminology, that allows Ann Marsh to create different social identities.

5. Concluding remarks

Through a discussion of educational opportunities and levels of literacy at different social strata in Late Modern England attained through education, combined with a qualitative analysis of letters written by women from different places in the social hierarchy, it was my aim to show that stylistic variation in Late Modern English letters is largely determined by the written linguistic repertoire one was able to accumulate by way of formal and informal instruction as well as by self-improvement and practice. As pointed out, for instance, in the discussion of letter-writing norms (see Section 3; cf. Nevalainen and Raumolin-Brunberg 1996, 2003), the choice of style in letters depends on various factors, such as the aspirations of the writer him-or herself, the addressee as well as the topic. If we take it that style plays an important role in the determination of an individual's social identity as well as the maintenance and negotiation of social relationships, it may be argued that the possibilities for a letter writer from the lower social scale will be a lot more restricted when writing. After all, the construction of a linguistic repertoire including different stylistic nuances and thus variation requires months to years of training and fine-tuning. For instance, Ann Marsh created different social identities, i.e. that of sister and that of pauper petitioner, by way of adapting the address formulae and other letter-writing formulae and by using register-specific vocabulary in the letter addressed to the overseers. The better the schooling and the writing practice, the greater the stylistic variation will be. This variation was particularly well reflected in the letters written by Mrs Fitzherbert, who represented the highest layer of society. What does this mean for language change? Based on the small-scale qualitative study carried out here, one would assume that linguistic changes in written Late Modern English are more likely to be actuated in the language use of the elite and the middling sort as these writers can be more creative with language and have the repertoire that allows them to choose different styles and vary between styles. This hypothesis, however, remains to be tested with more letter material from the different social layers.

CHAPTER 9

English aristocratic letters

Susan Fitzmaurice

1. Introduction

There is a wealth of recent historical sociolinguistics research on what the personal letters of women, of 'men of letters' and of various networks of writers tell us about the role of individual language use in language practices, variation and change (Nevalainen and Tanskanen 2007; Pahta *et al.* 2010). In particular, the uncovering of a rich seam of paupers' letters in the archives of England's parishes has afforded the opportunity to examine the writing (and by extension the language use) of the unlettered (Fairman 2007b; see Fairman, Auer, Laitinen, Allen this volume). In contrast, although the letters of the high-born – the aristocracy – in the eighteenth century have been studied as historical evidence for particular constructions of political and economic historical narratives, they are not generally considered to be of any interest to the historical sociolinguist as potentially illuminating witnesses of language variety and use in a period. This chapter seeks to redress the situation by exploring the extent to which the letter-writing practices of noblemen and aristocrats shed light on the nature of variation in English literate culture in the first half of the eighteenth century, before the heyday of prescriptivism. It is also concerned with the extent to which stylistic variation and varieties of practice convey information about the self-positioning and social stance of the writers within this particular literate community in the early eighteenth century.

The aristocratic letters that are the subject of this study are produced by men who dominated Whig politics and court society in the early eighteenth century. They defined the powerful Kit-Cat Club, an aristocratic London dining club that Brewer (1997: 41) notes 'included most of the most powerful Whig grandees of taste and no fewer than ten . . . dukes'. The Kit-Cat aristocrats were immersed in written language culture. It might seem obvious that, because they lived in a culture that was both constructed and conducted through written language and, particularly, print culture in the form of the periodical, the published essay and poetry, these men's language would probably occupy the standard end of a standard–non-standard continuum. However, because the men in the community that I focus on are active before the codification project is really embedded in the second half of the eighteenth century, it is important to consider the extent to which it is appropriate or productive to connect them with standard language ideology in the same way that we might connect the professional writers who produced the periodicals, newspapers and poetry that defined the literate culture of the period. It is possible that their language provided the (negative and positive) reference for the models adopted in the codification projects undertaken by their clients.[1] To ascertain the place of aristocratic letters in English literate culture in this period, I examine the nature of written-language culture and the manner in which aristocratic men interacted with and participated in this culture. To understand their place within the broader context, it is necessary first to inspect the representation, treatment and reception of the English aristocracy and the perception of aristocratic values in the popular press of the period as well as in the larger literary world of the eighteenth century. The relationships among the Kit-Cat aristocrats and their non-aristocratic counterparts as they were played out in the public discourse of the time provide the critical context for discovering the manners in which their language choices convey social meanings, including the ways in which they mark out their place within the complex political and social hierarchies that shape their worlds. Then, in the second part of the chapter, I discuss the variation of style, syntax and idiom in a selection of aristocratic letters and situate their meanings in terms of the ways that aristocrats treated letters and letter writing in their writing lives. To this end, I investigate the ways in which individuals' epistolary practices are used to negotiate their relationships with their addressees and, in so doing, shape identities tailored to those relationships. In this way, I draw upon Third Wave approaches (e.g. Eckert 2005, 2008) to the analysis of sociolinguistic variation in terms of the interpersonal meanings that become associated with what Eckert (2008: 456) calls 'persona style' in particular social contexts.

2. The English aristocracy and the Kit-Cat Club

Until 1714, English politics was dominated by a minute group of highly influential aristocratic statesmen, known as the Whig Junto. The Junto, which exemplifies the status and the interests of the aristocracy at the beginning of the period, was the heart of the Whig party, their 'hard core' (Handley 2004c). The Junto's club was the Kit-Cat Club, whose membership assured its enduring influence on the culture and ethos of English party politics in the period. This rather personal 'empire of towering politicians' was a very small group of immensely powerful and immensely rich aristocrats who formed an oligarchy (Porter 1990: 55). The Kit-Cat Club aimed, according to Brewer (1997: 40), 'to shape the arts by creating an elaborate web of influence and patronage, and by creating a sympathetic climate for writers it favoured'. The club was also distinguished by its anti-Tory politics and its dedication

---

[1] The would-be codifiers I am thinking about are men who all sought the patronage of the great men I discuss here: for example, Joseph Addison, whose *Spectator* 135 discusses abbreviations and the omission of relative markers; Charles Gildon, who published *A Grammar of the English Tongue* (1711), and Jonathan Swift, whose *Tatler* contribution rails against the ill usage of the most popular authors. However, it is clear that these clients – professional writers and polite authors – themselves provided illustrations of bad and occasionally good models of language for the codifiers of the second half of the century.

to the Hanoverian succession, 'serving as a social and financial network drawn from the three main, and most influential, elements of the party at Westminster' (Carter 2005). Essentially, the aristocratic members of the Kit-Cat Club sponsored its literary members and contributed to broader cultural projects. The Kit-Cat Club paid for John Dryden's funeral in 1700, and its members collectively contributed to the building of the Queen's Theatre in Haymarket (1704), and they individually took out subscriptions to pay for the publication of the non-aristocratic Kit-Cat writers' work.

The Kit-Cats were almost all involved in parliamentary Whig politics. The Whig Junto included the career politician Thomas Wharton, first Marquess of Wharton, the lawyer John Somers, Baron of Evesham, Edward Russell, Earl of Orford, the financier Charles Montagu, Earl of Halifax and Charles Spencer, third Earl of Sunderland. Wharton (Honest Tom to his friends and fellow partisans) was also the Whig Junto's chief election manager, and he spent a great deal of his own fortune on his election campaigns.[2] Their fellow Kit-Cat peers included diplomats like Charles Montagu, fourth Earl of Manchester, lawyers like William Cowper, first Earl Cowper, courtiers like Charles Howard, third Earl of Carlisle, and army officers like Charles Mohun, fourth Baron Mohun. In addition, the involvement in the Club's activities of the great Whig magnates Charles Lennox, Duke of Richmond and of Lennox, Thomas Pelham-Holles, first Duke of Newcastle upon Tyne, Charles FitzRoy, second Duke of Grafton, John Montagu, second Duke of Montagu, and Charles Seymour, sixth Duke of Somerset assured its influence on the culture and ethos of English party politics in the period.

The relationship between the aristocratic Whig grandees and the men who worked as junior civil servants in the great men's offices continues to be of interest. These relationships were patron–client connections demanding a particular mode of humiliative discourse (Fitzmaurice 2002a, 2002b, 2003).[3] The lesser Kit-Cats included Joseph Addison and Richard Steele, the men behind *The Spectator* and *The Tatler*, the diplomat poet friends of Charles Montagu, Earl of Halifax, Matthew Prior, George Stepney, the dramatists William Congreve and John Vanbrugh and, of course, the club's founder and secretary, the publisher Jacob Tonson. The behaviour of the lesser Kit-Cats indicates a somewhat ambivalent relationship with and attitude towards great men, particularly the Junto Lords who were among the Kit-Cat grandees and also their sometime patrons. A measure of the lesser Kit-Cats' recognition of the importance and influence of the aristocratic Kit-Cats is the prevalence of public dedications in which they praise their patrons' virtues and might. While these texts are instrumental in memorialising their subjects, they are also important evidence of the weighty and correct judgement of their authors

---

[2] '[Wharton] had a great income of £16,000 after his second marriage. Yet he spent so much on his election campaigns that by 1708 he was close to the brink of bankruptcy, with bailiffs descending on his Dover Street house to distrain the furniture' (Holmes 1993: 331).

[3] I have also considered the relationships between specific prominent individuals and their junior counterparts (Fitzmaurice 2008).

in making these dedications. Accordingly, the more sententious and elegant the dedication, the more likely its writer was to be recognised.

The first collected editions of *The Spectator* in octavo and duodecimo volumes were gilded by dedications to Lord John Somers, William's Lord Chancellor, Charles Montagu, Earl of Halifax, former Chancellor of the Exchequer and founder of the Bank of England, the Duke of Marlborough, the Whig party manager, Thomas Wharton, and Charles Spencer, 3rd Earl of Sunderland. Addison had dedicated his 'Poem to His Majesty' (1695) and his *Remarks on Several Parts of Italy, &c. In the Years 1701, 1702, 1703* (1705) to Somers in the attempt to gain his patronage. For Addison, Somers represented a perfect patron, a man whose own learning and superb taste qualified him to recognise excellence in others. His dedication to the first volume of *The Spectator* notes:

> None but a Person of a finished Character can be the proper Patron of a Work, which endeavours to Cultivate and Polish Human Life, by promoting Virtue and Knowledge, and by recommending whatsoever may be either Useful or Ornamental to Society.
>
> Your Lordship appears as great in your Private Life, as in the most Important Offices which You have born. I would therefore rather chuse to speak of the Pleasure You afford all who are admitted into your Conversation, of Your Elegant Taste in all the Polite Parts of Learning, of Your great Humanity and Complacency of Manners, and of the surprising Influence which is peculiar to You in making every one who Converses with your Lordship prefer You to himself, without thinking the less meanly of his own Talents.[4]

Addison dedicated the second volume of the collected *Spectator* to Charles Montagu, Earl Halifax in 1711 when the latter was fifty years old, in a similar vein:

> While I busy myself as a Stranger upon Earth, and can pretend to no other than being a Looker-on, You are conspicuous in the Busy and Polite world, both in the World of Men, and that of Letters; While I am silent and unobserv'd in publick Meetings, You are admired by all that approach You as the Life and Genius of the Conversation. What an happy Conjunction of different Talents meets in him whose whole Discourse is at once animated by the Strength and Force of Reason, and adorned with all the Graces and Embellishments of Wit: When Learning irradiates common Life, it is then in its highest Use and Perfection; and it is to such as Your Lordship, that the Sciences owe the Esteem which they have with the active Part of Mankind. Knowledge of Books in recluse Men, is like that sort of Lanthorn which hides him who carries it, and serves only to pass through secret and gloomy Paths of his own; but in the Possession of a Man of Business, it is as a Torch in the Hand of one who is willing and able to shew those, who are bewildered, the Way which leads to their Prosperity and Welfare.[5]

---

4 *The Spectator*, Volume 1. London [1712–15] [1713]. *Eighteenth Century Collections Online*. Gale. University of Sheffield. 15 August 2011 http://find.galegroup.com.eresources.shef.ac.uk/ecco/CW3312985557.

5 *The Spectator*, Volume 2. London [1712–15] [1713]. *Eighteenth Century Collections Online*. Gale. University of Sheffield. 15 August 2011 http://find.galegroup.com.eresources.shef.ac.uk/ecco/CW3312986037.

These dedications highlight the fact that both patrons were regarded as men of learning and culture as well as men of society and politics.

3. Context: literate culture and the aristocratic letter

We scrutinise the world of the grandees to consider the extent to which there is any evidence to suggest that their own communicative practices and forms were shaped or affected by some notion of and adherence to particular norms of epistolary behaviour, on the one hand, and to standards of language and standard language practices, on the other. To do this, we need to consider the role of letters in their world. We have a good idea of the place of the letter in the discursive practices of what I have labelled the lesser Kit-Cats. For these men, the letter and letter writing were part of their daily writing routines; they also participated in the milieu's literary culture by writing poetry and plays. Their literary products and their reception provide evidence of their familiarity with the discursive rules of and adherence to the practices of the literate discourse communities of the period, whether essayists, playwrights or poets. These practices included the reliance on the epistle form in a range of genres, particularly those used for political and social satire. Addison and Steele, for example, used the letter form extensively in their periodical essays for *The Tatler*, *The Spectator* and their own individual periodical projects, including *The Freeholder* and *The Englishman* (Fitzmaurice 2010). They also wrote personal letters to their friends as well as letters seeking patronage to the grand men listed above (Fitzmaurice 2002a, 2002b). The letters that the Whig diplomat and Kit-Cat George Stepney regularly sent to his Whitehall masters and his Kit-Cat patrons from the courts of England's European allies provide important evidence of the extensive role of the letter in professional communication. The diplomatic letter was the principal means of reporting to the key state committees and department heads the progress of or obstacles in negotiating the best possible terms of peace (Fitzmaurice 2006). But the diplomatic letter was also capable of conveying more confidential, impressionistic observations and subjective political interpretations of those diplomatic negotiations (Fitzmaurice 2006). What marks these diplomatic letters is evidence of careful attention to the rank of the (usually superior) addressee as well as of acute awareness of the difference in rank. George Stepney also wrote business letters to associates and literary letters to friends in which he employed a more direct and frank manner of address (Fitzmaurice 2011).

The aristocrats we are interested in require similar examination. What kinds of writing did they engage in, and what can we infer about the role of letters in their writing lives? It is possible that the only kind of writing they ever did was letter writing because the letter was the written register for conducting political, financial and diplomatic business.[6] Many of them had secretaries or amanuenses who took

---

[6] This is certainly true of non-aristocratic businessmen like Edward Wortley Montagu, husband of Lady Mary Wortley Montagu.

dictation or made fair copies of the rough drafts of the communiqués exchanged, and so the task of making the letters was split into encoding and copying (Dossena and Fitzmaurice 2006). Now, even if the only writing the Kit-Cat aristocrats ever did was letter writing, their experience would have been markedly different from lower-class, largely ill-educated and perhaps illiterate people in the same period for whom writing a letter might have been a major task undertaken very rarely as the only form of writing ever practised. The reason is that the Kit-Cat aristocrats were immersed in a literate culture of which letter writing was an integral part. Many of them attended public schools such as Westminster, or other schools such as cathedral schools, even for a brief period, before either going to one of the universities or travelling abroad. If, like Charles Montagu, they went to Westminster in the second half of the seventeenth century, their education would have been firmly rooted in classical languages and literature (Fitzmaurice 2011).[7] However, if, like Charles Talbot, Duke of Shrewsbury, they were educated abroad, they would have become highly fluent in modern as well as the classical languages. Richard Busby, headmaster of Westminster until 1695, introduced mathematics as well as instruction in modern and oriental languages to the school. A classical education in England included instruction in colloquial Latin conversation, Greek philology, as well as cultivated epistolography for professional needs, for example, notarial letter-writing (Witt 1982; Lerer 1997: 10–11; Magnusson 1999).[8]

Apart from familiarity with letters and letter writing as part of a humanist classical education, some of the Kit-Cat aristocrats were also practising poets. The grandest and most senior patron of the Kit-Cats, Charles Sackville, 6th Earl of Dorset, was a libertine poet whose verse satires and songs were widely circulated in manuscript by scribal publication right up until the end of the 1690s (Love 1993: 270–1). The practice of scribal publication, which involved the compilation of a collection of documents into a manuscript copy for presentation to important people, and circulation among a selected circle of readers or for preservation for posterity tends to be associated with the production and transmission of literary texts in the late sixteenth and early seventeenth centuries. There were several main reasons for writers to employ a scribe to create a very limited set of copies of their work instead of seeking print publication for wider dissemination. These writers opted for a mode of circulation that they were able to control in order to be able to share controversial political material without automatic prosecution for treason, or being sued for libel, or falling foul of obscenity laws. Dorset, then known by the courtesy title, Lord Buckhurst, following in the footsteps of Donne, Katherine Philips, Carew, Cotton and Marvell, wrote primarily for scribal publication (Love 1993: 4).

---

[7] Charles Montagu, Earl Halifax, was the younger son of the 1st Earl of Manchester. He attended Westminster School, where he met Matthew Prior, and then Trinity College, Cambridge.

[8] For discussion of the impact of classical education on early eighteenth-century literary culture in England, see Fitzmaurice (2011), specifically on the practice of writing Latin verse, translating Latin and Greek poetry, and writing vernacular verse using classical models, such as Horace and Virgil.

Although writers may not themselves have committed their work to print, their work ultimately found its way there. A search of databases like *Eighteenth Century Collections Online* (*ECCO*) and *Early English Books Online* (*EEBO*) reveals palpable and enduring interest in Dorset's reputation as a Restoration wit. For example, in 1714, the notorious Edmund Curll published a collection, *Poems on Several Occasions. By the Earls of Roscommon, and Dorset, &c.*, an anthology that includes a political lampoon attributed to Dorset and dated 1686, titled 'A faithful catalogue of our most eminent ninnies'. Love characterises this as 'the longest and most vituperative essay in the [lampoon] genre' (1993: 235), a poem that was copied in a range of versions in manuscript anthologies in the 1690s.[9] Dorset's name was also connected with a collection of model letters printed numerous times between 1669 and 1698.[10] In addition, Dorset was also associated with political and military treatises – which appeared only in 1753, pointing to the other element of scribal publication, namely, the tendency for parliamentary papers and 'separates' (newsletters) to be published in manuscript collections which appeared in print only much later (Love 1993: 9–10).

Charles Montagu, first Earl of Halifax, Matthew Prior and George Stepney were known as 'Dorset's boys', because Charles Sackville had encouraged their literary ambitions when they were young men in the 1680s. Montagu's commemorative verses on the death of Charles II, published in *Moestissimae ac laetissimae Academiae Cantabrigiensis affectus* (1685), drew Dorset's attention. In consequence, Dorset brought Montagu to London and introduced him to 'the society of the Wits' in London (Eves 1939: 22). Once immersed in the literary circles of the most powerful men in the land, Montagu acquired what Sarah Churchill, Duchess of Marlborough, labelled 'a great knack at making pretty ballads' (*Private Correspondence*, 2.144, cited by Handley 2004a). In 1687 he and Matthew Prior collaborated to write a parody of John Dryden's *Hind and the Panther*, entitled *The Hind and the Panther Travers'd to the Story of the Country Mouse and the City Mouse*, in which they substituted a mouse for the hind, a choice that earned him the nickname 'Mouse Montagu'. This kind of literary lampoon recalls the political antics of their patron Dorset in the Restoration period. But the levity of this practice sits somewhat uneasily with the increasing gravity of Montagu's public life in the 1690s. In 1690, Montagu underlined his indebtedness to his patron, Dorset, by writing *An Epistle to the Right*

---

[9] Love (1993: 352) shows how the variations in the manuscript copies made through the 1690s change the *ad hominem* and temporal references in the poem to fit the manuscript's period. He notes that moving a particular couplet results, for the 1690s scribes, in a 'perfectly apt, if somewhat oddly phrased, comment on the state of Ireland in the aftermath of William's invasion. In this case a sexual insult in a poem attacking members of the court of James II has been metamorphosed into a sneer at Anglo-Dutch conduct in Ireland'.

[10] *The New academy of complements erected for ladies, gentlewomen, courtiers, gentlemen, scholars, souldiers, citizens, country-men, and all persons, of what degree soever, of both sexes: stored with variety of courtly and civil complements, eloquent letters of love and friendship: with an exact collection of the newest and choicest songs à la mode, both amorous and jovial / compiled by the most refined wits of this age.* London: Printed for Samuel Speed, 1669.

Honourable Charles Earl of Dorset and Middlesex, Lord Chamberlain of His Majesties Houshold.[11]

By 1693, Montagu was in the heart of the Treasury and rising rapidly in the financial administration as instrumental in the founding of the Bank of England. He was soon appointed Chancellor of the Exchequer, First Lord of the Treasury and a member of the ruling Whig Junto in quick succession. In these roles, Montagu, created Earl of Halifax in 1700, was now a patron himself, attracting in turn verse epistles from younger men seeking his patronage.[12] His own literary life gave way to the serious writing that is central to government. However, a search of *ECCO* indicates that booksellers like the ubiquitous Edmund Curll collected and published his poems together with hastily compiled biographies in posthumous volumes to capitalise on his name recognition. These collections were in print and circulated for years after his death in 1715. The only other published work that is recorded in the databases as authored by Halifax before these posthumous verses is a two-page pamphlet, *Seasonable Questions Concerning a New Parliament*, printed in 1710. This collects the questions asked in parliament from the opposition benches about the early dissolution of the 1710 parliament, citing its disastrous consequences for the war against France.

Halifax's published oeuvre is thus quite mixed, consisting of early satirical verses as well as formal commemorative poems on state occasions, on the one hand, and parliamentary notes, on the other. His written oeuvre is far greater, of course. He wrote a large volume of letters that survive in autograph as well as in fair copies made by amanuenses. He also collected in-letters from well-known figures, from his patron, Dorset (considered below), to literary figures like Jonathan Swift and Daniel Defoe, to would-be clients such as Charles Gildon (see Fitzmaurice 2008 for fuller discussion). His political letters to his colleagues and superiors during his time in different offices in the first decade of the eighteenth century are preserved in various volumes of state papers. Among those are the *Portland Papers*, the collection of manuscript documents for the Earls of Portland, beginning with the first earl,

---

[11]
        WHat? shall the King the Nation's Genius raise,
        And make us Rival our great *Edward*'s Days;
        Yet not one Muse, worthy a Conq'ror's Name,
        Attend his Triumphs, and Record his Fame?
        Oh, *Dorset!* You alone this Fault can mend
        The Muses Darling, Confident, and Friend!
        The Poets are your Charge, and, if unfit,
        You should be fin'd to furnish abler Wit;
        Oblig'd to quit your Ease, and draw agen,
        To paint the Greatest Heroe, the Best Pen.

[12]
        For example, An epistle to the Right Honourable Charles Montague,
        Chancellour of the Exchequer, &c. upon the general peace,
        London: printed, and are to be sold by E. Whitlock, near Stationer's-Hall, 1698.

William Bentinck (1649–1709), the *Calendar of Manuscripts of the Marquis of Bath*, a volume published in 1907 of documents held at Longleat.[13] The letters of Charles Montagu, Earl of Halifax, are thus distributed across the collections of most major figures of the period. We will examine an illustrative example of Halifax's working epistolary practices in the form of a letter to King William's confidant and advisor, the Dutch-born Willem Bentinck, who was created Earl of Portland in 1689 on the accession to the English throne of William of Orange.[14]

In contrast to Halifax, whose early literary career made him a fellow poet and friend of the lesser Kit-Cats, Charles Talbot, Duke of Shrewsbury was not a literary man. However, playwrights like Thomas Shadwell dedicated their works to him in the hopes of attracting literary patronage.[15] Shrewsbury was not a Kit-Cat but he was a political associate of many of them, including the members of the Whig Junto. His life and political career were both colourful and controversial; born a Roman Catholic, Charles II was his godfather; he succeeded to the dukedom at the age of eight when his father was killed in a duel with his mother's lover, the Duke of Buckingham. He did not have an English public school education like the men of the generation that succeeded his. Instead, he was sent to study in France at the age of fourteen and, after volunteering to fight against France in Flanders in 1678, returned to England where he converted to Protestantism. He was called to the Lords when he was just twenty and took a position in the court of Charles II which lapsed upon Charles' death and the accession of James II.[16] After the Glorious Revolution, Shrewsbury and the 2nd Earl of Sunderland were trusted advisors to William, providing an important bridge between the court and the Whig Junto throughout William's reign. He was a close associate of Sydney Godolphin and the Duke of Marlborough, too. However, the pressures and stress of office took their toll on his health, and in 1700 he travelled to the Continent, visiting Paris and

---

[13] For example, this includes a letter from Charles Montagu, Earl of Halifax, to Earl Rivers, dated January 27, 1706/7.

[14] 'An act of naturalisation for Bentinck and his children was passed by parliament on 8 April 1689, and the following day he was created Earl of Portland, Viscount Woodstock and Baron Cirencester. He was introduced into the House of Lords on 15 April, and in early May was given the estate of Theobalds in Hertfordshire. At court he was appointed groom of the stole, first gentleman of the bedchamber, treasurer of the privy purse, and privy councillor, receiving apartments adjoining the king's in the palaces of Whitehall, Kensington and Hampton Court. Portland's duties in his English offices were in some ways similar to those he had undertaken for the past two decades at The Hague. In daily conference with the king, he remained his closest adviser and secretary, the intermediary between William and the British political nation, and the person to whom the bulk of state correspondence was addressed' (Dunthorne and Onnekink 2004).

[15] Shadwell dedicated his comedy *The Amorous Bigotte* with the Second part of *Teague O Divelly, a Comedy* to Shrewsbury in 1690. He dedicated another play, *Bury Fair, a Comedy*, to the Earl of Dorset in 1689. See Gerard Langbaine, *The lives and characters of the English dramatick poets also an exact account of all the plays that were ever yet printed in the English tongue, their double titles, the places where acted, the dates when printed, and the persons to whom dedicated, with remarks and observations on most of the said plays / first begun by Mr. Langbain; improv'd and continued down to this time, by a careful hand.* 1699. *EEBO.* Accessed 11 August 2011.

[16] Handley (2004b) notes that Shrewsbury was initially loyal to James, but that his disagreement with his religious policies made him a prominent opponent of James and an active supporter of the intervention of William of Orange.

Geneva before settling in Rome in 1701. Shrewsbury returned to England in 1705 to resume political duties and, despite intermittent ill-health and a signal reluctance to side permanently with any party, continued to be a critical player in government as a conciliator, mediator and negotiator among the opposing sides. For instance, at the time of the death of Queen Anne in 1714, he held the offices of Lord Treasurer, Lord Chamberlain and Lord Lieutenant of Ireland.[17]

In 1710, the chronicler of parliamentary affairs Abel Boyer praised Shrewsbury as 'a Person who borrows less Splendor from his Illustrious and Heroick Ancestors, than repays to them by his Shining Qualities and Political Virtues' for his loyalty to the Queen as Chamberlain and his association with Harley.[18] Handley (2004b) assesses Shrewsbury as 'the embodiment of the courtly aristocrat', whose 'grace and charm made him attractive to the monarchs he served', but whose 'prevailing character trait would appear to have been caution'. Shrewsbury was a prolific and catholic correspondent to judge from the voluminous and varied correspondences he conducted with the most prominent figures of his age, including Willem Bentinck, the first Earl of Portland, Henry St John, Lord Bolingbroke, the diplomats, Alexander Stanhope and George Stepney, as well as with Charles Montagu, Earl of Halifax.

4. Aristocratic letters

If the Kit-Cat aristocrats were immersed equally in print culture and epistolary communication, it would seem reasonable to assume that they were so familiar with the currency of educated forms of spoken and written language that the notion of a 'standard' language variety was irrelevant. I consider this proposition by examining three aristocratic letters in some detail, as listed below (and transcribed in full in the appendix):

1. Grand patron and Kit-Cat, Charles Sackville, 6th Earl of Dorset, to Halifax (27 August/7 September 1706) (Halifax's letter-book, BL Add. MS 7121)
2. Charles Montagu, Earl of Halifax, to Willem Bentinck, 1st Earl of Portland (19 February 1707) (Portland Papers, University of Nottingham, PwA945)
3. Charles Talbot, Duke of Shrewsbury, to Halifax (24 September 1701) (Halifax's letter-book, BL Add. MS 7121)

The Earl of Halifax is the addressee of two of the letters: Dorset's letter (written in 1706, a year before his death) and Shrewsbury's letter (written in 1701 while abroad), and writer of one, to the now retired Earl of Portland, in 1707. The questions

---

[17] P. 35, *The Annals of King George, year the first: Containing not only the affairs of Great Britain, but the general history of Europe, during that time. With an introduction in defence of His Majesty's title, and an account of his descent from all the Royal families that ever reign'd in this island.* London, 1716. *Eighteenth Century Collections Online.* Gale. University of Sheffield. Accessed 10 August 2011. http://find.galegroup.com.eresources.shef.ac.uk/ecco/CB3326984751.

[18] Pp. 30–1, Boyer, Abel. *An essay towards the history of the last ministry and Parliament: containing Seasonable Reflections on I. Favourites II. Ministers of State. III. Parties. IV. Parliaments. and V. Publick Credit.* London, MDCCX. [1710]. *Eighteenth Century Collections Online.* Gale. University of Sheffield. 11 August 2011. http://find.galegroup.com.eresources.shef.ac.uk/ecco/CW3305585844.

to consider are whether the form and language of the aristocrats' letters register the differences among their addressees, and whether their letters are situated in terms of the tasks being performed and the behavioural norms governing epistolary communication. Focusing exclusively on the letters of aristocrats arguably allows us to consider the extent to which matters of relative rank, social and political authority and familiarity might shape their practices. I will look at the letters at several levels in order to ascertain the extent to which their writers adhere to identifiable norms, of form, style and presentation (such as those identified in Fitzmaurice 2008). The first level is that of the autograph text, the level at which writers' idiosyncratic or personal habits are likely to be evident in spelling and abbreviation preferences.[19] The second is the level of the epistolary frame, where writers' uses of salutations, acknowledgements and ritual compliments may indicate choices in line with relative rank, degree of familiarity and the private or public nature of the purpose of the letter. Finally, we look at grammatical complexity and choice of vocabulary and expression in the context of the addressee's own background, circumstances and location. For example, in a period when matters of succession and religion took the business of government outside the domain of England to Europe, the letters directed abroad to senior government members necessarily acknowledged their roles in an international ruling elite concerned with the ways in which European wars and dynasties affected the government and economy of England.

4.1 The autograph text

This is the level at which we are likely to see evidence both of individuals' idiosyn-cratic choices and of their adherence to group norms of practice. It is also the level at which we may recognise sociolinguistic style being enacted to perform a persona identity. In some respects, as it is the most material level, it is therefore the easiest to examine. In this discussion, I compare the practices of our aristocrats with those of the commoner Kit-Cats (discussed in Fitzmaurice 2008). This comparison will allow us to consider the extent to which the aristocrats themselves form a distinct subgroup within the community of practice that is the Kit-Cat Club as a whole. The letters share a set of common abbreviations, listed below in Table 9.1.

The abbreviations for basic function words like *which, with, what, would* and the pronoun *your* are quite transparent. Just as conventional is the use of what we represent as a <y> in the abbreviation for *the* and *that*. Of course, this is the descendant of the thorn character from Old English, and although it is to all intents and purposes visually <y> rather than <th>, the abbreviation has become symbolic by this period and routinely used regardless of the hand. Other common abbreviations include the use of a tilde or wavy line above a letter to indicate a

---

[19] I will not consider handwriting in any detail in this paper; I have looked at Dorset's handwriting in some detail elsewhere (Fitzmaurice 2008).

Table 9.1 *Common abbreviations*

which	wch
the	ye
that	yt
with	wth
what	wt
would	wd
your	yr (also less commonly: y)
without	witht

missing letter or letters, usually <m> or <n>. Typical lexical expressions that carry this abbreviation are *command, common*. The use of a superscript <t> at the end of a word to stand for *-ment* or *-ant* is common, as *Parliam^t* 'Parliament' (Halifax). Occasionally, there are recognisable yet less frequent abbreviations, such as *agst* 'against' (as used in Shrewsbury's letter). All three letter writers employ abbreviated forms indicated by a colon, or a colon plus a superscript often produced directly underneath the superscript letter, in titles like Lord <L^d:> or Lady <L^a:>. Titles are routinely and conventionally abbreviated. Accordingly, we find <L^d> for 'Lord', *Lord^{sp}* for 'Lordship' and *Maj^{ty}* for 'Majesty'. Shrewsbury also adopts abbreviations for place names, such as *Eng:* 'England', and *Sp:* 'Spain'. Some of the writers adopt conventional visual and phonological contractions (Fitzmaurice 2004). Chief among the visual contractions are the use of *tho* or *thô* to represent 'though', and the omission of <e>, with its optional replacement of an apostrophe in words ending in <-d>. Phonological contractions include *'em* for 'them'. These contractions are not used with any consistency within the same document.

Punctuation in the letters tends to be idiosyncratic, as Vivian Salmon remarks (1999: 52) of practices in seventeenth- and eighteenth-century manuscripts, despite the fact that writers had opportunity to seek guidance on the appropriate use of punctuation. Some practices, however, seem to be conventional. For example, the colon or semicolon tends to be used to indicate the end of a sentence, and round brackets tend to be used in place of the modern comma to mark out a phrase. The hyphen, represented as an equal sign (=), is used at the end of a line to indicate a break in a word; some writers use the sign at the beginning of the next line to mark the continuation of the word. Preston and Yeandle (1992: x) remark that word-breaks rarely occur in 'legal documents or manuscripts written by scribes familiar with legal practices'. While Dorset follows the convention of using an equal sign both at the end of the line and the beginning of the next to mark word-breaks across a line, and Shrewsbury uses it at the end of the line, Montagu adopts the modern practice of using a hyphen at the end of the line.

Compared with the spellings apparent in the working-class letters examined by Fairman (2007b) and others (this volume), the spelling preferences exhibited in the aristocrat letters are remarkably uniform. Among what appear to be quite conventional spellings is the <ei> sequence in words like *freind, beleive* and *yeild*, the use of <e> instead of <o> in *shew*, the omission of a second <e> in *agreable* and the use of <w> instead of <u> in words like *perswade*. Many writers do not use double consonants in words that now require them, as in *od* 'odd' and *sudain* 'sudden'. And conversely some writers use double consonants in places where modern spelling does not have them, as in *wellcome, deffending, verry*. There are also spellings that appear to be old-fashioned if not quite archaic by the first decade of the eighteenth century. These include *haue* in place of *have*, *obiect* in place of *object*, particularly evident in Shrewsbury's letter to Montagu.

4.2 The epistolary frame

The aristocrats adopt a very simple epistolary frame. All three letters exhibit a straightforward pattern of opening salutation, namely, 'My Lord', and all adopt the modern form of the second person pronoun as the preferred form of address, *you*, unmarked for number. The closing salutations or subscription formulae are more elaborate. They vary in degree rather than in form. The most common expressions include the attribution *your Lordships*, followed by one or more of the following adjectives – *obliged, obedient, faithful, humble* – and then the expressed commitment of service to the addressee through the conventional term *servant*. Each aristocrat signs off using his title rather than his surname, thus we see *Dorset, Halifax* and *Shrewsbury* in their respective letters.

In previous work (e.g. Fitzmaurice 2002b, 2006, 2008), I considered as part of the organisation of the epistolary frame, conventional epistolary acts including salutation and justification for writing and, in begging letters, the request or appeal, its justification and the closing salutation. The aristocrat letters exhibit rather different components, as they do not seem to be designed to gain professional, personal or political advantage for the writer. Accordingly, the selection of opening compliment, ritual expressions of gratitude and expressions of friendship appear to be conditioned less by the motive in writing and more by the relative seniority of the addressee to the writer.

As Halifax's erstwhile patron, Dorset was highly regarded by the younger man. At the same time, by the date of this letter, written in 1706, Dorset was sixty-eight years old, and in the last year of his life. Thus we have a letter from an old master and patron to his protégé, now a powerful public figure and patron in his own right. As fellow Kit-Cats, they were members of a community of practice that relished the conviviality of the exclusive dining club with politically empathetic friends who shared the same literary pursuits and leisure activities. His opening salutation offers a conventional excuse for not writing sooner, and he follows swiftly to assure his correspondent that their shared acquaintances 'both old and young' have asked 'verry kindly' (interpolated) after him. Dorset's stance is one of a man who takes the close and easy relationship he enjoys with his correspondent for granted as he gossips about the goings-on in the Hanoverian court. Indeed, Dorset offers two tid-bits of court gossip that appear designed to amuse and to flatter his addressee respectively. The first is the titillating news about the mystery of the identity of a woman companion of the Electress Sophia, which Dorset appears to relish announcing, in vague albeit vigorous terms, as 'our little Robust freinds Bastard'. The second is a story about the outcome of a gift of swords that Halifax had made to two pages who had attended him in Hanover. In his treatment of this 'snotty point', he adopts a teasing tone while never relinquishing the conventional form of address to somebody of Halifax's rank, namely *your Ld^{sp}*, in the episode. He prefaces his closing signature with an assurance of the 'humble services' of his fellow Englishmen, Lumley and Smith, and then invites his correspondent, conventionally enough, to 'lay your commands' on him should Halifax consider that he is able to serve him abroad. Dorset's conventional and gracious signature contrasts with the familiar, jocular body of his letter to his younger friend.

Halifax's letter to Willem Bentinck, the Earl of Portland, in 1707 is quite different in purpose and tone. This letter is designed to inform this highly influential but now retired statesman about the goings-on in court and parliamentary circles in the session in which the Act of Union that would create Great Britain was debated. Portland retired formally from government in 1699 to his Buckinghamshire house, Bulstrode Park, but he continued to represent the interests of the English crown abroad. During the reign of Queen Anne, Portland's political activities and interests as a European player continued as he acted on behalf of the English government with her allies as a senior negotiator in the war against France in 1706.[20] He continued to attend the House of Lords, and men like Marlborough and Godolphin, for whom he served as an informal means of communication with the Dutch republic, continued to seek his diplomatic advice. In addressing this senior statesman, Halifax does not exactly place himself in the position of supplicant. His opening address conveys a conventional acknowledgement of the happy receipt of a letter, and he takes the liberty of interpreting the letter as signifying Portland's 'confidence' in him. He plays with the polysemy of 'confidence' as he expresses his estimation of Portland's act of confiding in him as immensely valuable. He draws attention to his interpretation by underscoring the salient expressions:

(1) I received the Honour of Your Lordships
     Letter of the 17th with a great deal of pleasure and satis-
     faction, it seemed to me, as a mark of your Lordships
     confidence, towards a <u>Man that truly values yours</u>.

     (ll. 2–5; Halifax to Portland)

Halifax's address is therefore designed to convey the impression that he was well aware of his own very prominent public standing relative to Portland's private

---

[20] His biographers note that 'as a Calvinist sympathetic to the fate of the Camisards during the revolt which broke out in the Cévennes in 1702, he conferred with the Dutch states general in 1704 about ways to assist them, while in 1706, at the height of the war against France, he was among those subscribing to a loan of £250,000 to the emperor' (Dunthorne and Onnekink 2004).

retirement at the time. Accordingly, he adopts a confidential stance in expressing his attitude towards the breakup of the 'triumvirate' of Sydney Godolphin, John Churchill, the Duke of Marlborough and Robert Harley, the Tory speaker of the House of Commons. According to Speck (2007), the 'triumvirs' served the queen as advisors and brokers between her and Tory leaders, on the one hand, and the Whig Junto, on the other. By 1703, they were meeting regularly to discuss cabinet business. Halifax's letter alludes to the irrevocable breakdown in relations between Harley and the other 'triumvirs' in December 1706, when party interests finally trumped court loyalties within the triumvirate. After the elections of 1705 resulted in a hung parliament, Godolphin had replaced Harley (with the latter's agreement) as speaker of the House of Commons with a Whig, John Smith. In October of that year, Godolphin had appointed the Whig Lord Cowper as Lord Keeper of the Great Seal, now to the disapproval of Harley. The final straw for Harley was when Marlborough and Godolphin secured the Secretaryship of State for the South for another Whig and Kit-Cat, the 3rd Earl of Sunderland (Speck 2007). Halifax discusses these matters with Portland on the presupposition that it is not necessary to spell out the details of events and participants. He employs the euphemism 'our Great Men' for the treasurer Godolphin and the war hero, the Duke of Marlborough, and refers to Harley simply by the initials *M.H.* His stance is evidently that of a partial Whig observer, taking care to reassure his correspondent that none of his associates was likely to have been involved. Halifax is careful too to intimate to Portland that, while he is unable to expand upon 'this intricate matter, wch will have a strange appearance abroad', he is anxious that his correspondent will be able to explain the situation diplomatically to their allies in Europe. In closing, Halifax draws attention to the difference in their situations. He first adopts the stance of one who is familiar, even intimately so, with his correspondent's circumstances, in the assumption voiced that Portland may well regard him as a city man rather than one with any fondness for the 'Country'. He then protests his desire ('great Inclination') to visit Portland at his country estate. Halifax thus underlines the fact that while Portland is enjoying his retirement, Halifax continues to toil, albeit in the highest levels of government.

Shrewsbury's letter to Halifax, written in 1701, is also interesting in terms of the relationship it apparently indexes between the two men. Shrewsbury fashioned a political career that put him at the centre of power in the last decade of the seventeenth century. He was sought by William as a link between the court and the Whig Junto, he was appointed twice to the office of Secretary of State, and in the reign of Queen Anne he was recruited (unsuccessfully) as a diplomatic mediator with the French. In 1701, Shrewsbury was travelling in Europe having escaped the tedium of office ostensibly because of ill health. His opening salutation to Halifax follows something of the pattern of Halifax's to Portland, in acknowledging the receipt of a letter as a mark of Halifax's 'kindnesse & friendship' to him. His promise not to 'trouble you with . . . news' is consistent with his reluctance to be engaged in discussion about government business. However, he also asserts for anybody who might happen to read the letter as it is likely 'to pass so many hands', that it would be 'improper' to do so. He does, however, take the trouble to respond to an observation that Halifax had evidently made on a recent controversy. This concerns Halifax's impeachment, together with the Earl of Portland, Lord Somers and the Earl of Orford by the House of Commons for 'high crimes and misdemeanours' on 14 April 1701.[21] The case collapsed, and the impeachment was discharged in June. It is evident that Shrewsbury feels an obligation to register his view of the 'frivolousness' of the charges against his correspondent and to express his admiration for the way in which he has borne the case. This necessary assurance completed, he continues with the altogether less grave but detailed accounts of his crossing the Alps to Italy and his experiences of European city culture. Shrewsbury's closing salutation acknowledges the (undue) length of his letter as a justification for omitting the highly conventional business of elaborate compliments. He nevertheless ignores his own conceit and ends his letter in the expected conventional fashion, expressing the 'hope' that his correspondent should 'never doubt' the sincerity with which he signs himself as his 'most faithfull and obedient humble servant'.

4.3 Grammatical complexity

All three letters deal with topics and people that are familiar to the correspondents and present in their shared worlds. Dorset's and Shrewsbury's letters to Halifax are largely narrative, colloquial and informal. Their grammatical repertoires – marked by coordinate syntax and parataxis – might be argued to reflect the personal communicative purpose of their letters. Halifax's letter to Portland is less narrative and more discursive, but he also deploys some colloquial and informal expressions. At the same time, they observe 'standard' grammatical practices in terms of the variety and complexity of the constructions employed. The letters exhibit to varying degrees the grammatical as well as temporal organisation of information. What this means is that the writers choose constructions (such as passives, conditionals, relative clauses and adverbial constructions) that permit variation in word order to effect the backgrounding and focusing of information. So in addition to coordination and compounding, the aristocratic writers opt for complex sentences (Rissanen 1999: 280). However, in doing so, they do not avoid the constructions that would become shibboleths in the second half of the eighteenth century. These include zero relatives (represented as [Ø] in the examples below) and the use of *that* instead of a *wh*-pronoun in relative clauses, as well as preposition stranding and sentence relatives. These constructions tend to do the work of circumlocution as the writers

---

[21] The indictment contained six articles, most of which referred to the procurement of grants, but which included as the most serious charge Halifax's role in the first partition treaty, which James Vernon had communicated to him in August 1698. *England and Wales. Parliament. House of Lords. The several proceedings and resolutions of the House of Peers, in relation to the lords impeached or charged.* London, 1701. *Eighteenth Century Collections Online.* Gale. University of Sheffield. 10 August 2011. http://find.galegroup.com.eresources.shef.ac.uk/ecco/CW3307986261.

strive to avoid explicitly mentioning the detail and substance of sensitive topics just
in case the letters should be read by people other than their addressees. Accordingly,
in examples (2a) and (2b), the zero relative clauses are adopted in allusive references
rather than descriptive comments, both in Halifax's letter to Portland:

(2)   a.   The matters [Ø] your Lordship desires to be informed of, are more fit for
           discourse, than a Letter

                                                         (ll. 5–6, Halifax to Portland)

      b.   this is all the light [Ø] I can give your Lordship into this intricate matter,
           wch will have a strange appearance abroad

                                                        (ll. 34–5, Halifax to Portland)

   In (2b), the allusive zero-relative is followed by a non-restrictive relative with
which to create a contrast of what can be barely glossed with an assessment of the
impact of its news. In discourse terms, from a reader's perspective, the zero-marked
relative clause serves to alert the interlocutor that attention should be paid to the
nature of the impact the writer expects the 'matter' to have. In view of the fact
that the feature would be increasingly vigorously proscribed in the latter half of the
century, the use of zero relatives contributes to the tone of informality in the letters.
This is particularly true of the letters written by the older men, Shrewsbury and
Dorset, to Halifax as illustrated in (3a–e):

(3)   a.   the comon transactions [Ø] Mr Yard is very punctuall in sending me

                                                    (ll. 9–10; Shrewsbury to Halifax)

      b.   the share [Ø] wee all had in that matter was so small

                                                    (ll. 27–8; Shrewsbury to Halifax)

      c.   there was an od woman that was Continually with the Electress

                                                        (ll. 18–19; Dorset to Halifax)

      d.   the Swords [Ø] you sent to the two pages that waited upon you

                                                        (ll. 31–2; Dorset to Halifax)

      e.   this may seem very extraordinary even to your L:^P that has some
           knowledge of 'em

                                                        (ll. 50–1; Dorset to Halifax)

   The aristocrats also deploy *wh*-relative clauses. Shrewsbury uses *wh*-relatives in
quite an old-fashioned way. In the extract in (4a), the antecedent is separated from
its pronoun by the predicate to postpose the relative clause. This extract also exhibits
a string of explicit as well as implicit anaphoric references to the NP 'our Countrey',
including a *wh*-pronoun (indicated by the subscript indices):

(4)   a.   I can not but thinck those$_i$ are happy [who$_i$ haue least to do in our
           Countrey$_{ii}$], [which$_{ii}$] if it$_{ii}$ had a little more sun [Ø]$_{ii}$ were very good to
           live in, but very bad to gouern in.

                                                    (ll. 31–4; Shrewsbury to Halifax)

   b. this year, the variety [Ø] removeing from place to place affords, is very diverting to me who am alone

(ll. 36–8, Shrewsbury to Halifax)

   c. I hope you Lay your commands upon one who would be glad of any opertunity to shew with how much sincerity he is

(ll. 55–8; Dorset to Halifax)

Shrewsbury uses a zero relative followed by a *wh*-relative in reference to himself in (4b). Dorset's somewhat conventional use of a *wh*-relative in his closing salutation is illustrated in (4c). The choice of the *wh*-relative pronoun *who* in self-reference in these two cases seems to draw the interlocutor's attention to the state and status of the writer. Halifax adopts *wh*-relatives in detailed commentary about events and people of mutual interest. In (5a), in a restrictive relative clause headed by the fronted preposition *for* and *wh*-relative pronoun *whom*, he elaborates on the relationship of the 'great Men', namely Marlborough and Godolphin, with Harley ('a Man'):

(5) a. How our great Men came on a sudain to proceed to extremitys against a Man [for whom they had such fondnesse and Partialitys before], is a mistery to us.

(ll. 11–14; Halifax to Portland)

   b. the Ministers may be supported, and the Government carried on steadily, if those, [who are not concerned] think fit

(ll. 41–42; Halifax to Portland)

In (5b), Halifax adopts a *wh*-relative in subject position to refer rather obliquely to the Whig politicians put into key positions by Godolphin and Marlborough to balance the Tory interests in the hung parliament. Halifax's style is markedly complex in several parts of his letter, using relativisation and complementation, on the one hand, and clefting on the other in order to foreground his opinion about the topic discussed. For instance, in extract (6), the direct object of the verb *determine* is fronted as a heavy complex subject NP (indexed as NP$_i$), which affords the sentence-final verb more emphasis:

(6) Whether they were jealous of Him, as their Rival in favour, or convinced at last, of that which every body else saw long a goe, is what I can not determine:

(ll. 14–17; Halifax to Portland)

'Whether they were jealous of Him, as their Rival in favour, or convinced at last,

of that [which every body else saw long a goe],]$_{NPi}$ is [what]$_{NPi}$ I can not determine [Ø]$_{NPi}$

'I cannot determine whether they were jealous of him(. . .) or convinced (. . .) of that (. . .)'

Halifax also uses complement clauses which reflect the complexity of the argument constructed. In extract (7), he is at pains to assure his correspondent that he does not believe that Dorset's associates were involved in creating the rift between Harley and Godolphin and Marlborough. However, he is unable to dismiss completely the possibility of their having had some effect on the situation, and expresses this in the form of a complex nominal which is co-referenced with the dummy subject *all* specified by the zero relative *I know*:

(7)   . . . all I know is, that your friends had no hand in it, unlesse their not having so much submission to the Court this year as formerly, made the Ministers more sensible how little assistance, those sort of gentlemen gave them in carrying on their businesse.

(ll. 17–21; Halifax to Portland)

'I know [that your friends had no hand in it]$_X$ unless [their not having so much submission to the Court this year as formerly,]$_Y$ made [the Ministers]$_Z$ more sensible how [those sort of gentlemen gave them little assistance]$_W$ in [carrying on their businesse]$_P$
= I know all[that X, unless Y made Z sensible how W in P]'

All the letters also exhibit some of the characteristics of colloquial discourse, such as the use of comment clauses that give the impression of an involved and conversational style, as in Shrewsbury's story of his journey down the mountains by chair (8):

(8)   this I confess was uneasy to me, and
especially it hapning to raine at that time, the
soil and the stones were slippery, and at the very
first one of my mens heeles flew from under
him, which abated in my opinion \of/ that
Infallibility which they pretend to of stepping
sure, thus farr one may reasonably assure
ones self, that in a long time that this way of
carrying in Chaires has been practised, no ill
accident has been known to happen.

(Shrewsbury to Halifax; ll. 55–64)

At the same time, this extract shows how the 'train of thought' can become derailed in an additive style that combines narrative with commentary executed online, as it were, without careful prior planning.

Dorset also adopts a style of composition that relies on the accumulation of clauses through concatenation or addition rather than subordination.[22] In extract (9) below, he uses the connectives *and* and *but* to link clauses. In this style, Dorset

[22] Dorset also uses the old-fashioned *be*-perfect construction with the verb *get*, as in 'you were got into England' (ll. 6–7).

plays with word order in order to vary his narrative focus. In his conclusion to the story about the pages and the swords, for instance, he preposes the direct object 'story' to signal a shift from the narrative to his comment on the episode:

(9)   and this story he told me when I came to town
        and at this time thought the matter was quite
        over, but upon enquirey it seems the Counsel is
        once more to meet about it, and the poor boys
        are still in pain least it should go against
        them

                        (ll. 44–50; Dorset to Halifax)

The grammatical repertoires exhibited by the letter writers are quite varied, including parataxis as well as hypotaxis, with a range of strategies for foregrounding and elaborating the points they regard as important to the communication.

4.4 *Vocabulary choice*

It is possible that the language adopted by the aristocrats might betray their classical education, for example, in the choice of vocabulary and diction. Specifically, if their choice of vocabulary were consistently Latinate rather than Germanic, it would be reasonable to infer that their language use is profoundly informed by their experience of the literate culture and classical learning of their time. In fact, the styles of all three writers are characterised by vocabulary that owes its origins principally to Old French or Latin. In addition, they all exhibit a preference for nominalisation, choosing expressions like 'have a strange appearance' (Halifax, l. 34) instead of the verbal 'appear strange'; 'want your assistance here, and your explaining \to/ them' (Halifax, l. 36) instead of something like 'want you to assist here and to explain to them'. Thus the nominal style is evident in the syntax as well as the vocabulary. The writers frequently adopt polysyllabic nouns ending in *-tion* derived from verbs, compared with nouns ending in *-ance*. Similarly, they choose nouns ending in *-ity* derived from adjectives more often than nouns ending in *-ness*. Examples taken from all three letters (indicated by D; H; S) are listed in Table 9.2.

Halifax uses doublets, each consisting of a noun with an English suffix and one with a Latinate suffix, for example, *fondnesse* and *Partialitys* (ll. 13–14) and *steadinesse* and *Resolution* (ll. 30–1). His lexicon is quite formal compared with that of his correspondents, yet it is highly expressive at the same time. For instance, he adopts a range of adjectives, including *surprising, unexpected, jealous, sensible* (*OED* s.v. *sensible* sense II.7a; obs. 'capable of feeling or perceiving'), *intricate* and *effectual* to characterise his own attitudes and responses to events as well as those of other actors in the events he discusses. His lexicon situates his discourse squarely in the first part of the eighteenth century, too. Firstly he chooses the

Table 9.2 *Derived nominals in the letters*

Nouns ending in -ion	Nouns ending in -ity	Nouns ending in -ness	Nouns ending in -ance
affliction (D)	inormities (D)	fondnesse (H)	assistance (H)
invention (D)	sincerity (D)	steadinesse (H)	appearance (H)
mortification (D)	extremitys (H)	kindnesse (S)	assurance (S)
intention (D)	Partialitys (H)	frivolousness (S)	continuance (S)
satisfaction (H)	necessity (H)		
submission (H)	facility (S)		
Resolution (H)	Infallibility (S)		
inclination (H)	familiarity (S)		
transactions (S)			
Justification (S)			

word *complaisance* in the phrase 'by an universal complaisance' to describe Harley's operating practices. This has a specific reading, namely, 'obligingness; compliance with or deference to the wishes of others' (s.v. *complaisance*, sense a; *OED*). He also uses the adverb *trimmingly*, after crossing out the word *simmingly*, to characterise the negative political practice of pursuing 'a neutral or middle course between opposed principles or parties, especially when this is done to stand in favour with both' ('*trimmingly*, adv.'. *OED*. June 2011). The *OED* attests this adverb as derived from the adjective *trimming* as late as 1719, which suggests that Halifax's use in 1707 was highly contemporary, even innovative. The cumulative effect of Halifax's formal, Latinate lexis and complex syntax is a letter designed both to impress the elder statesmen to whom it is addressed and to highlight Halifax's own powers of formal eloquence. In other words, the letter embodies the construction of an identity type that Halifax aims to have his reader recognise and accept.

Shrewsbury and Dorset exhibit some idiosyncratic lexical preferences that contribute to their distinctive epistolary styles. For instance, Shrewsbury's lively description of his travels over the Alps and his engaging appraisal of the people and cultures he encounters, the landscapes and cities he visits are marked by an evaluative and subjective view. His choice of nouns like *frivolousness* to describe his judgement that Halifax's impeachment was based on spurious evidence and *infallibility* to characterise the foolish fearlessness of the men who bore his chair over the mountains indicates his efforts to entertain his correspondent. Similarly, his suggestion that the 'Alps are not so horrid as some haue represented' prepares the reader for his assessment of the 'descent towards Piedmont' as 'much \more/ dreadfull', with a 'Precipice on one side of a prodigious height', building to a narrative climax only to undercut it at the end. Shrewsbury plays a game of one-upmanship with himself as he first challenges contemporary descriptions of the Alps as *horrid* 'rugged, rough' ('*horrid*, adj. and adv.'. *OED*. June 2011), and then declares the descent he takes to be *dreadfull*, 'formidable, dangerous, exciting fear' ('*dreadful*, adj., adv., and n.'. *OED*.

June 2011. sense 3).[23] He describes the 'Palaces' as 'wonderfully noble and magnificient', contrasting their grandeur with the expensive but miserably kept gardens. He attends to his correspondent's English perspective by characterising the social mores and habits of his Genevan hosts as more French than English in practice. He is particularly struck by the fact that the gentlemen 'visit & converse with the Ladys, much more freely than wee do in England' (ll. 79–80). He also notes that Continental noblemen and women enjoy 'a freedom of living with one another which is not much practised among the lower rank of people' (ll. 95–6). These observations indicate the extent to which Shrewsbury scrutinises his surroundings and company for the benefit and entertainment of his correspondent.

Dorset's letter is similarly designed to entertain and engage his correspondent. He creates an atmosphere of mock gravity through the use of the language associated with the law courts to relate the story of the swords. Accordingly, he notes that the 'Counsel ajorn'd' and after a 'considerable debate', the Ministers 'deputed' Baron Knyston to investigate the possible nature of Halifax's 'intention' in the case (ll. 39–43). He introduces the episode in bathetic fashion, as a 'snotty point', a paltry matter that has unaccountably to be solved. Dorset also shows a tendency for comic overstatement, describing the 'great affliction' caused by the departure of a friend, on the one hand, and the 'greater mortification' caused to a friend by the realisation that nobody remembered him, on the other. When he introduces the salacious matter of the Electress' 'od' woman companion, he similarly spices the story through his lexical choice. He notes that 'our little Robust freinds Bastard' was 'forc'd' to leave Berlin and go to her father 'incognito' because of the 'inormities' she was supposed to have 'committed'. His choice of the current term *incognito* (< Italian, first attested 1676, sense a, 'unknown; whose identity is concealed or unavowed, and therefore not taken as known', *OED*) seems designed to provoke further inquiry. His mischievous choice of the word *inormities* plays on two current senses: one has to do with irregular, eccentric or extravagant behaviour (sense 1a, *OED*) while the other has to do with a deviation from moral rectitude (sense 2a, *OED*), both no doubt designed to titillate the reader.[24] He also shows some fondness for the adverb *pretty*, using it twice in the letter, first to assert that he was pretty sure his correspondent had returned to England (l. 6), and second to describe the identification of his friend by 'certain marks pretty peculiar to himself' (l. 16). Thus Dorset's vocabulary shows considerable variety, from his preference for

---

[23] The *OED* attests John Evelyn's use of the adjective *horrid* in his *Diary* (1654, III, 103), as follows: 'There is also on the side of this horrid Alp, a very romantic seate.' Its use to describe the Alps suggests that this characterisation must have been a well-known commonplace, and that Shrewsbury alludes to it in his challenge. The *OED* illustrates the colloquial sense, 3, of *dreadful* as a strong intensifier, with another quotation describing the Alps, taken from Lady Mary Wortley Montagu's letters, (12 September (1965) I. 434, *I intend to set out to morrow to pass those dreadfull Alps, so much talk'd of*).

[24] The *OED* illustrates the first sense with a quotation from *The Tatler* (No. 250. 1710), attributed to Addison: 'Enormities in Dress and Behaviour'. *enormity*, n. Second edition, 1989; online version June 2011. http://www. oed.com.eresources.shef.ac.uk/view/Entry/62536; accessed 15 August 2011. Earlier version first published in *New English Dictionary*, 1891.

Latinate nouns (see Table 9.2) to his fondness for contemporary slang. This stylistic variety suggests that, unlike Halifax, for example, Dorset has the freedom to move among (historical) identities he has fashioned for himself in his letters, without being worried about their effect on his interlocutors.

5. Aristocratic letters: some concluding remarks

The three letters considered afford a glimpse into the writing practices and habits of aristocratic men at the beginning of the eighteenth century. The witty letters written by the two older men Dorset and Shrewsbury to their younger peer Halifax exhibit the extent to which they were versed in the polite epistolary art of pleasing their correspondents in writing. Their situation was different from that of their addressee Halifax, of course. They were both travelling abroad and were both apparently at leisure to communicate their observations and assessments of their societies and surroundings without having to be concerned about any official repercussions of their choice of topic or their treatment. However, Shrewsbury was still in the public mind, even if he was out of sight in 1701; it is possible that he wrote to Halifax with the expectation that, despite the fact that his letter is entirely social and sociable, it was still likely to be subject to official scrutiny if other hands happened upon it. In contrast, as a more private citizen in late retirement, Dorset appears to exercise more freedom in tackling slightly salacious topics in an enthusiastic style. However, he does so in such an oblique and jocular manner that one infers that he was not unduly concerned if his letter were to fall into the wrong hands.

The letters examined in this chapter exhibit all the hallmarks of standard language practices, but their language also provides grist to the mills of the prescriptivists because it does not embody a variety that is codified to any degree. All three letters exhibit the co-occurrence of features that would acquire negative social meaning in the standard language ideology that would be codified and championed in the second half of the eighteenth century (for example zero relatives), together with features that would increasingly be regarded as emblematic of the correct way to speak (for example, *wh*-relatives). Their combination does not indicate that these writers were consciously or intentionally asserting a particular persona style in their letters. Indeed, it is arguable that their grammatical style suggests a degree of indifference or disregard for the elevation of style that would seem to be warranted by their status and background. This variety is not true of the use of the letter form itself and the conventional epistolary patterns used. These are well established, and these aristocrats exhibit complete adherence to the models no doubt instilled in them as schoolboys.

At the same time, each of the letter writers studied uses the letter as an opportunity not only to maintain a particular relationship with his interlocutor, but also to perform a particular persona and thus express a particular identity for that interlocutor at the time of writing. Importantly, as the relationships between the writers and their addressees changed over the course of their lives, the letters that we have as records of the history of these relationships also mark how the men themselves change in the ways they fashion their personae.

Ultimately, these aristocrats' epistolary practices are deeply embedded in the literate culture of the period. The Kit-Cat aristocrats are part of a community of practice shared with the Kit-Cat commoners. However, the letters considered here suggest that the literate aristocrats of which these are exemplars are members of a broader English aristocratic discourse community whose membership is marked by a common set of educational, political and social experiences assured through privilege and patronage.

Appendix: Transcripts of the letters

1. Grand patron and Kit-Cat, Charles Sackville, 6th earl of Dorset, to
    Halifax Hanover Aug:27/Sept: 7
    My Lord
    Tis now something more then a week
    Since we came hither, and I should not have fail'd
5   writeing to your L:ᴾ sooner but that I was willing
    to refer it till I could be pretty sure you were
    got into England therefore with:ᵗ desending to par=
    =ticulars I shall begin with assureing you yᵗ every
    body enquire'd \verry kindly/ after your L:ᴾ both old and young,
10 vans Barr is in town, but to my great affliction
    Bel Barr, went into the Country the day before our
    arrival, you may depend upon all Falliso's letters
    from 'em, to be entirely his own invention, and
    to his greater mortification I can assure you, they
15 neither remembred him nor his name, till describe'd
    him by certain marks pretty peculiar to himself
    I can't help telling you that when I first came hither
    there was an od kind of woman that was Continually
    with the Electress and hardly ever seen any where
20 but in her Closet, twas the business of the whole
    Court to find out who she was, but she seemes
    was so well kept that no creature could give any
    account of her till after she was gone, and then
    it came out that she was our little Robust
25 freinds Bastard, who for having committed
    some inormities at Berlin, was forc't to leave
    y:ᵗ place with an intention to go over to
    her father incognito; the Ministers here look
    as Solem as ever, they are at present employ'd

30 about a snotty point entirely oweing to your L:ᵖ
    the Swords you sent to the two pages that waited
    upon you, Oberg desire'd that a stop might be
    put to the delivery of them till they had met about
    it,
35 and accordingly when they were assembled he urge'd
    that in his opinion the Swords had better be sold, and
    the value of 'em equally distributed to all the pages
    however nothing was resolv'd that day but the Coun=
    =sel ajorn'd to \yᵉ/ next and then they order'd bothe the
40 swords so laid before them, and after a Considerable
    debate, they deputed Baron Knyston and on other
    to go to M:ʳ How and ask him what he im=
    =magine'd to be your L:ᵖˢ intention, you may
    be sure 'X he was verry clear in the matter, and
45 this story he told me when I came to town
    and at this time thought the matter was quite
    over, but upon enquirey it seems the Counsel is
    once more to meet about it, and the poor boys
    are still in pain least it should go against
50 them, this may seem verry extraordinary even
    to your L:ᵖ that has some knowledge of 'em
    but I'le assure you tis true to a Letter,
    M:ʳ Lumley[25] and M:ʳ Smith both present their
    humble services to you, and if I can be any way
55 serviceable to your Lᵖ in these parts, I hope you
    Lay your Commands upon one who would be glad
    of any opertunity to shew with how much sincerity
    he is
    Your L:ᵖˢ
60 Most oblidge'd
    humble servant
    Dorset
    If your L:ᵖ favours me with a Letter pray
    Direct it to Drummonds in Amsterdam.

            * *

---

[25] This is likely to be Henry Lumley, an army officer, who, in July 1704 as a lieutenant-general in Marlborough's army, took part in the bloody assault on the Schellenberg, at Blenheim, and afterwards fought at Ramillies, Oudenarde, and Malplaquet (Archbold 2004).

2. Charles Montagu, Earl of Halifax to the Earl of Portland, 1707
   \<PwA945>
   My Lord
   I received the Honour of Your Lordships
   Letter of the 17th with a great deal of pleasure and satisfaction, it seemed to me, as a mark of your Lordships
5 confidence, towards a <u>Man that truly values</u> yours. The
   matters your Lordship desires to be informed of, <u>are more</u>
   fit for discourse, than a Letter, and I do assure you I
   am at a losse my selfe, how to understand them; the great
   changes that have been of late were as new as surprizing
10 and as unexpected to me, and some other of your friends
   here, as they were to your Lordship at Bulstrode. How
   our great Men came on a sudain to proceed to extremitys against a Man for whom they had such fondnesse and Partialitys before, is a mistery to us. Whether
15 they were jealous of Him, as their Rival in favour, or
   convinced at last, of that which every body else saw long
   a goe, is what I can not determine: all I know is, that
   your friends had no hand in it, unlesse their not having
   so much submission to the Court this year as formerly, made
20 the Ministers more sensible how little assistance, those
   sort of gentlemen gave them in carrying on their businesse.
   While by an universal complaisance all things went on
   smoothly, and the most difficult affairs were made easy,
   M. H. had opportunity of making it beleived He did every
25 thing, and at last I beleive, our Great Men found, He did
   nothing for them, but play'd a double game for him
   selfe; and then they saw there was a necessity to get rid of
   Him; this step has once more united all the Whigs in the
   House of Commons, and if right measures are taken they
30 may be kept together, but whether some people have stead
   -inesse and Resolution enough to manage this as it ought
   to be, will be seen in a little time: this is all the light
   I can give your Lordship into this intricate matter, w^ch
   will have a strange appearance abroad, and I must
35 put you in mind that at the beginning of this winter, I told
   you, that this session many things would happen that would
   want your assistance here, and your explaining \to/ them abroad.
   The Parliam^t is now drawing to an end, and upon the whole
   wee may say, the supplys are very great, and will be effectual
40 the prospect of the new Parliam^t is very good, the Ministers
   may be supported, and the Government carried on steadily, if

those, who are not concerned think fit, If the Allys will
act vigorously, and make a push this year, wee may do the
businesse, but if they act cautiously abroad, and XsimminglyX
45   trimmingly at home, wee shall be very low next winter.
I know you do not believe me when I speak of
the Country, therefore I will not say much, but I assure you
I have a great Inclination to spend a day at Bulstrode.
I am
50   My Lord
Your Lordships most Hum^{ble}
and most Obed^t Servt
Halifax
19 Feb^{ry} 1707.
* *

3.   Charles Talbot, Duke of Shrewsbury, to Charles Montagu, Earl of
Halifax, 1701
My Lord
I recieved the favour of your Ld^{ps} of the 11th
of Aug: this day sevenight at Geneva, the day
before I left that place, it could bring no news
5   more wellcome to me than the assurance of the
continuance of your kindnesse & friendship, &
if your Lo^p will sometimes confirm that to me
it will be a great comefort in my absence, and
I desire to trouble you with no news, the comon
10   transactions Mr Yard²⁶ is very punctuall in
sending me, and any thing els would be impro=
per for a Letter that is to pass so many hands
I agree with your Lo^p that it is a great Justi=
fication to the Lords Just: that after so long
15   a ministry, nothing els could be obiected to
them, and I think you had singular an aduan=
tage in that particular & by the frivolousness
of the M: agst you, that it has very much
turned to your honour, I am satisfyd if the others
20   had had the XXX opportunity of deffending
themselves, it would yet have been more
advantageous, however it is no small Justification

---

²⁶ Robert Yard (1651–1705), a career government administrator in a nascent civil service, became chief clerk in
the office of the Secretary of State under Shrewsbury in February 1689. In March 1694, Yard was made under-
secretary, again serving under Shrewsbury. In 1698 Yard became secretary to the lords justices by using the
patronage of Shrewsbury and Lord Chancellor Somers (Marshall 2004).

to perceive how ready one side was to be tryd &
how unwilling the other was to come to ye printes

25 As to what your Ld^p mentions relating to my
self, I assure you for severall reasons I never
had one unquiet thought about it, the share
wee all had in that matter was so small, that
I never expected it would have been obiected by

30 any, but it is so plaine that when people have
a mind, any pretence serues, that I can not but
thinck those are happy who haue least to do in our
Countrey, which if it had a little more sun were
very good to live in, but very bad to gouern in.

35 It is certain you could haue no thoughts of leaving
Eng: this year, the variety removeing from place to
place affords, is very diverting to me who am
alone, & would be much more so in good company, but
I find already since I have crossed the Alps, that the

40 want of a facility of speaking the Language, tho I
understand Italian, is very inconuenient.
I have not seen many things yet worth giving
you the trouble to relate; The Alps are not so
horrid as some haue represented them, and yet

45 they are a prospect that afford variety to consider
the ascent from Savoy XXX is not difficult,
the plaine upon Mont Cenis, being now at this Season
free from snow, is a fertile good feeding country for
Cattle & a noble pond or Lacke at the top of the hill,

50 the descent towards Piedmond is much \more/ dreadfull
I was caryd back up & down in a Chair by men, who
for the nearer way will sometimes take a narrow
path where they step hastily from stone to
stone, with a Precipice on one side of a prodigious

55 height; this I confess was uneasy to me, and
especially it hapning to raine at that time, the
soil and the stones were slippery, and at the very
first one of my mens heeles flew from under
him, which abated in my opinion \of/ that

60 Infallibility which they pretend to of stepping
sure, thus farr one may reasonably assure
ones self, that in a long time that this way of
carrying in Chaires has been practised, no ill
accident has been known to happen.

65 I made a short stay at Turin, all the men of
that Court, at least of my acquaintance, were in

the army, the Queen of Sp: was iust upon her
departure the dutchesse I was told had expressed
her self very unsatisfyd with our \nation/ upon account
70 of our Act of Parl: upon the whole matter I stayd
but 2 days in towne & slipped by without making
my compliments to that Court.
I arrived at Geneva when most of the Company was
at their Countrey houses, but Giustiniani & some
75 others I had known in Eng: being in towne they
shewd me what Company was \to/ be seen, and I surmise
they live there much after the French liberty
there are societys euery might in severall places
& they visit & converse with the Ladys, much more
80 Freely than wee do in England, the buildings of
their Churches, but especially of the Palaces exceed
what I expected from them, they are wonderfully
noble & magnificent, but continued within
so that they are better to see than to live in
85 Some of their gardens haue cost a great deal of
money, but are miserably kept, their furniture
is extream rich, it is a towne where if the air
were good one might pass ones time well inough
This little sister Comonwealth follows muc
90 the same fashions they converse at Societys with
great familiarity, and there are severall very
handsom women in this XlittleX City, both here or
at Geneva the nobles men & women converse
onely among themselves and they have introduce
95 a freedom of living with one another which is not so
much practised among the lower rank of people
I will not lengthen this long letter with compli=
ments, because I hope you can never doubt,
but that I am what I have so much reason to be
100 My L^d
Your Ld^ps
most faithfull and
obedient humble servant
Shrewsbury
105 My La: Westorland sends me word
she is very happy in your Ld^ps
neighbourhood & Ld Carlisle is my Cosin
it is the best part he ever gaue to his
good eyesight

CHAPTER 10

Early nineteenth-century pauper letters

Mikko Laitinen

1. Introduction

It is clear that the diachronic material sources in English linguistics have expanded considerably over the last decades. Sources through which scholars can access speakers' vernaculars include, for instance, online databases like the *Old Bailey Corpus* of spoken English from the eighteenth and nineteenth centuries (Huber 2007), collections of historical writings like the American English writings in the *Corpus of Older African American Letters* (Siebers 2010), and dialogue corpora like the *Corpus of English Dialogues 1560–1760* (*CED*) (Culpeper and Kytö 2010). Moreover, personal letters, which tend to reflect everyday language use, have long been used as the material in studies modelling the social embedding of variability (Raumolin-Brunberg and Nevalainen 2007). Despite this progress in capturing vernaculars, it might not be too far-fetched to claim that English historical linguistics is still biased towards the upper social layers.

To illustrate this fact, England at the beginning of the nineteenth century was a country with some 9–10 million inhabitants (Hilton 2006). The upper strata, with an income of over £800 per year, consisted of less than 100,000 people, and roughly one-third of the population belonged to the middle order, earning over £10 per month. The great majority, some 7 million people, earned less than £10 a month. They form the overwhelming majority, yet their voices, not to mention those at the bottom end of this majority, are not too often represented on a large scale in diachronic corpora.[1]

There are at least two reasons for this focus. Firstly, we have the practical question of the survival of written materials. They survive by chance (Nevalainen 1999), and the chances are higher for the top social layers whose materials tend to be over-represented relative to their sizes in the whole population. Secondly, research questions have obviously favoured certain social groups: historical (socio)linguistics has in many instances focused on tracing the emergence and development of the standard language, i.e. the social dialect of the most powerful layers in a society.

---

[1] For instance, Culpeper and Kytö (2010: 26) point out how upper-rank men 'are generally better represented in the majority of the texts' in the *CED* 1560–1760, a fact which applies to all historical English corpora. Of the five dialogue types in the *CED*, only witness depositions contain a substantial amount of material from low-ranking people.

Increasing efforts are being made in English historical linguistics to unearth and
digitise vernacular materials, as this volume shows. My chapter will discuss one
early nineteenth-century textual source that broadens the material basis towards the
bottom of the income scale. The material consists of the so-called pauper letters, i.e.
applications for economic relief sent by the labouring poor who resided outside their
home parishes (Hitchcock, King and Sharpe 1997). These pauper letters have so far
received only limited attention in English historical linguistics, with the exception
of the detailed studies by Tony Fairman (1989, 2000, 2002, 2006, 2008a).[2] The
letter material has survived as a lively record of the old poor law (Act for the
Relief of the Poor 1601) in England (Hitchcock, King and Sharpe 1997).[3] These
documents survive in the record offices around Britain and have been edited by
social historians (Sokoll 2001; Levene *et al.* 2006). The material used in this study
consists of Sokoll's (2001) edition of pauper letters from Essex. People whose letters
of application survive in this collection belonged to the lowest social levels in the
early nineteenth century.

The main argument here is that the increased availability of vernacular materials
calls for an expansion of the theoretical bases for research. This is particularly true
with these pauper letters, which often crossed considerable socioeconomic boundaries from the applicants to parish overseers, who belonged to the middling sort
in their communities and were responsible for distributing the relief. It will, therefore, be useful to draw from the theoretical insights of scholars who have explored
similar types of socially uneven communication in other contexts. Questions such
as control over norms, imagined standards and the selection of available linguistic
and stylistic resources play a considerable role, and one needs theoretical tools when
assessing their normative value. Furthermore, the broader sociocultural context of
industrialisation could be expected to play a considerable role in understanding
the use of linguistic resources in the early nineteenth century. The social impact
of this revolution was considerable (Hobsbawm 1962: 45–50), and one concrete
consequence was mobility, as shown by Tieken-Boon van Ostade (2009: 10–11).
Mobility affected all layers of society; people moved towards the industrial centres,
and if they felt economic hardship, the poor laws forced them to establish connections with their home parishes in writing. In more formal terms, they were using
linguistic resources across various social and physical spaces.

To suggest concrete solutions for expanding the theoretical bases of historical
sociolinguistics, this study draws from the present-day sociolinguistics of globalisation and mobility (Blommaert 2010; Blommaert and Rampton 2011), which
offers an interesting framework for two reasons. Firstly, this perspective explores
mobility/migration through vertical social spaces and focuses on people making
use of linguistic resources that are valued differently in various spaces. Access to

---

[2] There are numerous studies that focus on non-standard varieties in the US (Schneider and Montgomery 2001)
or on people with limited literacy in Yorkshire (García-Bermejo Giner and Montgomery 2001).

[3] A key factor in pauper legislation was the Removal Act of 1795, which *de facto* forced people in distress to apply
for pauper aid and led to an increase in the written pauper applications sent to parishes across the country.

forms and their normative control is always unevenly distributed, and language use always has a built-in normative dimension, since some forms and pragmatic solutions are always more valuable than others depending on the social situation anchored in the time and space where they occur (cf. present-day asylum seeker discourses in Maryns and Blommaert 2001). Secondly, migration and indeed the entire enterprise of the sociolinguistics of globalisation are sometimes associated only with present-day societies (Vertovec 2007; Blommaert and Rampton 2011). This chapter aims to illustrate how linguistic diversity on an almost equal par with the so-called 'super-diversity' of today also concerns the history of English and is particularly important in the Late Modern period.[4] These applications for poor relief provide records of the early phases of globalisation. The social diversity (and the injustices) of the early twenty-first century have their roots in the emergence of nation-state hegemony and industrialisation at the time when these letters were written and sent. The framework therefore provides an interesting testing ground for this material.

The poor relief system enabled people on a large scale to move elsewhere, and the home parish was responsible for providing relief as long as an individual applied for it in writing (or face-to-face) and provided sufficient evidence to support the application. Sending these applications meant crossing physical and social spaces, which in many instances must have been a new way of communicating for many individuals. The pauper letters are authentic accounts of how people had to make use of written vernaculars to negotiate with the established societal system, and the applicants had to engage in a process of socialisation of developing one form of genre literacy (cf. Taavitsainen 2010 on the evolution of genres in medical writing). In other words, sociocultural changes forced applicants for pauper aid to make use of new linguistic and stylistic resources in a social and cultural setting that was different from the immediate environments of the (often) poorly paid labourers.

The study provides another angle to Fitzmaurice's (2002a) study on humiliative discourse in Late Modern literary networks. Even though my informants represent the lowest social levels, the letter-writing context and the mobilisation of the best linguistic resources here are similar to the networks in her study. Pauper letters are, of course, highly idiosyncratic, but they nevertheless constituted a formal communicative setting because of the social distance between the applicants/recipients and because of the importance of pauper aid for the applicants.

Section 2 introduces the sociohistorical context and elaborates on the theoretical framework. In Sections 3 and 4 I will present a set of characteristic features of these pauper letters. The objective is that these features might be able to serve the purpose of suggesting paths for future research that would combine methods commonly used in English (socio)historical linguistics and the sociolinguistics of globalisation.

---

[4] O'Rourke and Williamson (2000) present a wide range of opinions on when globalisation actually began, and they conclude that there is sufficient evidence supporting the view that the world economy was fragmented and deglobalised prior to the nineteenth century.

2. Local and translocal styles in pauper letters

The old poor laws of 1601 gradually had substantial social consequences. Prior to them, each village took care of those needing assistance, and Rule (1991) argues that changes were small up to the mid-eighteenth century, since applicants and overseers often knew each other. Changes started taking place towards the end of the century (see footnote 3). They were brought about by the growing population in rural areas, seasonal employment opportunities in developing industries and legislative changes, all of which contributed to mobility. Socially disadvantaged people were required to develop new types of social knowledge, including new forms of written interaction that were essential for their survival. These new written forms were those that could be used in translocal, impersonal and decontextualised communication, as opposed to local, personal and momentary face-to-face interaction. The concepts are discussed in more detail towards the end of this section.

An integral concept in pauper relief was legal settlement in a parish,[5] which meant a parish issuing a certificate which stated that an individual together with the family and future issue belonged to them. If a person became chargeable to the new parish, the home parish was responsible for supporting them through pauper relief or taking them back at its expense.

The need for pauper relief was obvious: Lindert (1997) estimates that the proportion of the early nineteenth-century population forced to apply for poor relief was as high as 10%. By the early nineteenth century, the majority of parishes provided non-resident relief schemes (Sokoll 2001: 10–11). They came to an end when the Poor Law Amendment Act was passed to reform the system in 1834 (Hitchcock et al. 1997), and applying for relief through writing letters gradually ceased. There is, however, a time span of a few decades from the mid-1790s to the mid-1830s during which plenty of vernacular material from the lowest social levels was produced.

The following illustration provides a glimpse into the lives of some of my informants, seen through the overseer's eyes. This overseer's letter from Norwich describes the living conditions of William Wilsher,[6] a legal resident of St Peter, Colchester:

(1)   I look'd in upon Wiltshire last night. There is misery and wretchedness, with
        poverty plainly apparent in their house but I found he had that day obtained
        a peice of work, but the manufatoring is so slow that those who have
        constant work are [ob]liged to play three or four days betw[een] [paper
        torn] . . . I find he is indebted a half years rent all but 13 shillings, which is

---

[5] The criteria for settlement were strict and aimed at attracting those who had proved their worth and gained experience through longer hirings. These included renting a property (worth at least £10 per annum) or paying taxes on such a property. Working for a legally settled inhabitant for continuous periods of 365 days also paved the way for a settlement, as did seven years of full apprenticeship. Women changed their legal settlement on marriage.

[6] The overseer calls the applicant 'Wiltshire' but the name used in the letters is 'Wilsher' (Sokoll 2001: 503).

2 guineas, and a few shillings to their doctors, – Perhaps they might save a few shillings in the Summertime, but that is a thing which does not enter their heads as they (situated as they both are in respect to health) are sure you must relieve them . . .

(Sokoll 2001: 503)

The sociocultural information in this letter is twofold. Firstly, Wilsher was clearly a labourer whose livelihood depended upon the ups and downs of manufacturing and who belonged to the great majority in early nineteenth-century England. Secondly, the applicants were not simply powerless objects, because the legislation guaranteed relief, and Sharpe (1997) points out that paupers often possessed a confident attitude towards relief.

The Essex letters in Sokoll (2001) are reliable material for studying language use of the lowest social groups. The edition has been favourably reviewed by historians (Rose 2002), and its textual criticism and editorial principles, as Raumolin-Brunberg (2003) points out, have been carefully documented. Certain restrictions exist (Fairman, this volume), one of which is the question of authorship, which is difficult to establish. Even though literacy in the early nineteenth century was low among the labouring masses (Vincent 1989), there were enough literate people in one's immediate family or neighbourhood to ensure that a literate person was available to scribble a letter of application. Hitchcock *et al.* (1997) show that writing applications for pauper aid did not involve crossing one's sociocultural boundaries but was 'for the most part performed within the social and cultural milieu of the labouring poor themselves' (Sokoll 2001: 65).

The picture shown in Figure 10.1, a detail from a painting in 1850, illustrates writing being performed in a middling-sort family setting in the mid-nineteenth century. Though not depicting a pauper family, it nicely illustrates how writing letters involved those family members (or people in the neighbourhood) who could contribute to the task.

The introduction to this chapter briefly touched upon the concepts of centres and peripheries when using linguistic resources (Blommaert 2010: 39–41, 63–100). We will nevertheless have to make a distinction between geographic and sociocultural localities. On the geographical level, the parishes from which the people migrated constitute peripheries. Employment opportunities existed in the industrial hubs, and many had to migrate towards the centres to survive. However, on the social level, the centre was located in the geographic peripheries, i.e. in the home parishes where the parish overseers were responsible for deciding upon and distributing the relief. These people were the 'leading farmers and shopkeepers within the local community', upon whom the paupers depended (Sokoll 2001: 11).

But why are centres and peripheries important when studying pauper letters? Language practices that develop (and have developed) among the most powerful are often those that are needed to survive in a society. In other words, those applying for pauper aid had to learn a range of speech habits, develop genre

Figure 10.1 Nineteenth-century letter writing in immediate sociocultural milieu (Image from James Collinson's *Answering the Emigrant's Letter* (1850). Reproduced with the kind permission of the copyright owners, the Manchester City Galleries.)

literacies and understand social values of linguistic forms.[7] The applicants had to develop competence in writing applications, and they had to participate in a process of socialising into genre conventions of this particular genre. They were forced to learn, to quote Taavitsainen (2001: 139), the inventory of 'inherently dynamic cultural schemata used to organize knowledge and experience' through written linguistic means. The inventory of linguistic items studied here aims at moving beyond formulaic phrases that imitate what is appropriate and polite in a context (see Nevalainen 2001 on the challenges in filtering the expression of politeness through contemporary etiquette). Rather, the objective is to draw from the concepts of local and translocal communication in a socially and geographically polarised environment.

The extracts below illustrate two types of language practice relevant to pauper letters here. The first consists of local, personal forms and momentary stylistic choices, and the other of translocal forms and more decontextualised choices.

---

[7] Underprivileged people have been very good at this task throughout history. Mandler (1990: 1) argues that the poor have always understood the rich and powerful better than the other way around. For the poor, this skill is essential for survival, whereas for wealthier people social knowledge is only a luxury.

These are illustrated in (2) and (3) respectively, showing extracts from two letters sent from London to Essex in the 1820s. These applications were sent by older men, both born in the mid-eighteenth century. They illustrate variability not only in spelling and grammar, but more importantly also in the mobilisation of linguistic resources, all of which have varying normative values among the overseers, who act as evaluative authorities in the social centres:

(2)   Honoured Sir

This is to Inform you I have sent Two letters before – wich I am suprised I have not Receved anney Ansur This is to Inform you I cannot stop Anney longer without you send the Monney – as I am tormented by the Peple that I ow it two – pray Sir be So kind as to send as soon as Possable – as I am In great Destress for want of at – or I must Come Down – pray Sir Cosider wat trouble And Expence it will be for me to Come It is Seven Deus last Saturday the 5 June Wich I hope you will not fale Sending it by Mr French as I am In great wants of it –

(from Sokoll 2001: 183)

(3)   To the overseers and offises of the Parish of Chelmsford

Sheweth that I Samuel Hearsum late of the Little farm of Moulsum Common rated Fifty Pounds a year have Lost in the year 1813 and Optained my Livly hood by Labour in the Regents Park untill afflicted with a fill of apable etery the 12 of May 1820 and near 76 of Age which renders me incable of geting a Livelyhood, Should be very Thankfull for a small Trifle of Money If it is only 2 Shillings per week, and am Gentlemen you most Humble Obedeint Servant.

(Sokoll 2001: 266–7)

The task of applying for aid is accomplished by indexing two functions. They include introducing oneself as a legal resident of the parish, and describing one's living conditions to convince the overseers of the necessity of assistance. Apart from these basic functions and the fact that they both contain numerous signs of deference, the letters are highly different. The example in (2) is a direct plea in which the stylistic choices do not support the position of the applicant. This directness is apparent in the fact that the applicant introduces himself by anchoring the letter with the previous correspondence and then proceeds with an adverbial stance clause presented in a forceful, if not hostile, tone 'wich I am suprised I have not Receved anney Ansur'. The relief itself is labeled as a definite NP, 'the Monney', and the relief remains the topic throughout the letter through an anaphoric chain, as it is repeated three times, at first implicitly ('to send as soon as Possable'), and then explicitly twice through pronouns ('want of at' and 'wants of it'). The uses of these linguistic resources (i.e. local, personal and momentary) provide evidence for Sharpe's (1997) observations that the applicants were in many instances aware of their rights. This is also further emphasised when the applicant resorts to a frequently used threat of returning to the home parish (see below).

The micro context of (2) was such that the applicant's aid had been reduced heavily a few months earlier when he was considered to have received some money for his employment of distributing notices in London (Sokoll 2001: 184). This letter, it seems, is his effort to try to save the situation, but the selection of the less acceptable linguistic resources, in the eyes of the overseers, did not lead to the intended result. The letter-ending plea framed with a stance marker, 'I hope', is not enough to turn the scale in his favour. One reason might be because it is followed with a direct request that does not support the applicant's subordinate social role.

The linguistic resources in (3) are more indirect than those in (2), and thus the consequences turned out to be different. The parish records show that the applicant's pauper aid had been discontinued because he was thought to be employed in selling tea in London (Sokoll 2001: 179). With this letter, he was able to convince the overseers of the necessity of relief, and the parish accounts show that the applicant's aid doubled some three weeks afterwards.

A close look at the use of linguistic resources shows that Samuel Hearsum manages to use forms and stylistic solutions that had a higher value on the addressee's side. The letter opens with an introduction which establishes him as an original resident of a parish, and which, one might assume, was high on the indexical orders of the addressees because it was the key judicial requirement. Hearsum argues that he had been part of the middling sort of a rural community some two decades ago. The intended meaning of this introduction suggests that he is on a social par with the parish overseers in that he used to belong to the same social layer. According to Boulton (2000), referring to one's past as a minor rate payer is a frequent strategy, because these rate payers were responsible for financing the greater part of the system. Pauper relief is labelled as 'Money' and is modified with two adjectives to diminish the speech act of asking for aid. The actual asking takes place through a declarative '[I] Should be very Thankfull for a small Trifle of Money', in which the modal is clearly honourable from the speaker's point of view. The applicant highlights this by suggesting that the pauper relief is 'only 2 Shillings per week'.[8]

The two illustrations above are important because they show first of all how applying for poor relief was a complex task on the individual level. Secondly, they illustrate the two poles, one local and the other translocal, that have varying normative values with real life consequences. It is important to bear in mind that the normative dimension refers not only to individual linguistic items, such as idiosyncrasies in spelling, morphosyntax or face-saving phraseology (like 'pray Sir be So kind as to send as soon as Possible' that is found in the local letter (2)), but also to stylistic elements and argumentative structures as they are illustrated here and discussed in the following section.

---

[8] The pauper relief of 2 shillings per week would result in the annual sum of over £5, well above the average aid of £3.92 per recipient in the early nineteenth century (Lindert 1997).

3. From mobility to diversity in linguistic resources

This section focuses on how linguistic functions are organised in these letters and how understanding the structure may help to identify local and translocal elements. A close reading of the hundreds of pauper letters shows that there is no standardised letter form, which is understandable if one takes into account their chronological scope of a few decades and their geographic spread. Yet, as the letter extracts below illustrate, the applicants perform a range of similar functions that place the material within the genre of request letters (see Barton and Hall 2001). The applicants first identify themselves as legitimate candidates for pauper aid (i.e. they seek to secure good will) and then provide sufficient evidence of their living conditions (through a narrative). The narrative, which may include an overt act of asking for financial aid, typically offers a rich source of vernaculars, and it is the part in which the applicants often shift back and forth between local and translocal elements.

This mix of linguistic features and stylistic resources is illustrated in the following letter (4) from Sarah Albra to the overseers in Chelmsford. The letter is the only one from Sarah surviving in the collection and, despite the stylistic variation, it was written in a single hand:[9]

(4)   Sir   London 16th April 1829

I have taken the liberty of Addressing those few Lines to you hopeing you will not feil it to much Truble to lay befour your honourabl Bord I Sarah Albra Wife of James Albra of Chelmsford Bookbinder My husbam has bin ill 3 mounth not bin able to ham a fathen and I am Left destude with 4 yong Children and back with my Rent and in the Great Drestress my husbann is at Chelmsford With is mother at the Royal Oke in the Back Street Ware you Can Inquire And if you dute Wot I Say if you any o Gentleman in town to inquire I Live at N° 12 Dorrington Street Brooks Market Holbom or at my Landlords Mr Holmes N° 10 in the Same Street Which i how for Rent 1-10-0 which I hope Si[r] you and the rest of the Gentleman will do Same think for me or Else I Shall be Compell to Come Down With my Children and throw myself and Children on the perish So Si[r] I Wait your answair

I am You[r] Humble Ser[t] Sarah Albra
I hope Mr Crimer you will Do Some think for me

(Sokoll 2001: 282)

The salutation is followed by a formal opening phrase that forms the early contact between the applicant and the overseer. Its tone is apologetic, and it continues with a modal of volition ('you will not feil it'), and the board of overseers is premodified with an adjective. The opening also contains two phrasal clusters, the first consisting of 'I have taken the liberty of Addressing', and the second one where she lays her

---

[9] The letter was manually checked by the author at the Essex Record Office in February 2004.

application before the board. The social meanings of these elements indicate that she attempts to negotiate with the overseers, much like the applicant in (3) above. Many of these resources may be learned stylistic patterns.

The first major discourse function after the initial greetings, not explicitly separated from the opening, is a formal, testimony-like naming in which the applicant identifies herself as a legal settlement holder of the parish:

I Sarah Albra Wife of James Albra of Chelmsford Bookbinder

What follows is the longest section, the narrative, in which the use of linguistic and stylistic elements lingers between local and translocal. She refers to her children; a solution which, despite being a personal reference, is clearly a more decontextualised solution than referring to an unspecified group of people, as was the case in extract (2) above. The applicant continues using translocal elements in her actual request for help and naming the relief. This takes place after the circumstances have been described, and she proceeds to take up the topic of her rent:

... Rent 1-10-0 which I hope Si^r you and the rest of the Gentleman will do Same think for me ...

In the speech act of asking, she appeals not only to the overseer, but also to the board, and frames the request with a stance marker 'I hope'. The act of asking is carried out through the verb 'do', as she asks the overseers to 'do Same think' [i.e. 'thing'] for her. The actual sum is realised through an anaphoric generic noun, 'thing', and not by naming the sum for the second time or through the object ellipsis. There are two possible readings for 'Same think': the first is the communicatively unlikely 'same thing', which is nevertheless supported by the spelling 'Same street' only a few words earlier. The second ('something') would be more appropriate semantically, but note the indefinite pronoun 'Some think' in the closing line.

Speculating about the intended meanings of idiosyncratic spellings is, however, a minor detail. Instead, one has to bear in mind that the naming practices in the three illustrations so far have been variable, ranging from the most local in (2) ('the money') to 'a small Trifle of Money If it is only 2 Shillings per week' in (3) to the almost covert asking for aid in (4). One interesting area for future studies is to examine changes in naming practices throughout the four decades of pauper letters.

It is in the last part of the narrative where the applicant shifts to local situated style when she points out the possibility of moving back to Chelmsford. This is the third time in this short letter that the applicant opposes the overseers' point of view. The first moves (i.e. the opening clauses and the act of asking for help) are apologetic in tone, but on this third occasion there are no traces left of the early unpretentiousness, as she points out how she will throw herself, together with the children, on the parish care. The selection of a concrete object form for the verb 'throw' emphasises the number of people that could become the parish's responsibility.

The mix of stylistic resources used in (4) suggests that the applicant may be able to see how certain discourse features are indexed as socially more acceptable than others. In addition to the almost nonchalant forms of asking for and naming the aid, the short narrative makes a number of connections between the context and situation itself (i.e. Sarah applying for relief) and the social order in the poor relief system. The narrative section indicates her awareness that the overseers' decisions are based on the information at their disposal, and she willingly provides detailed information of the whereabouts of her husband in Chelmsford and of the landlord, but she is nevertheless unable to continue the translocal style from the early part of the application.

The letter in (5) was sent to Colchester some two years earlier than Sarah's letter. Both letters were sent about a half-mile from each other in London, yet they display a great deal of variability in the identification and in the actual naming and asking for relief:

(5)　Gentlemen friend Ireceived your letter at the present time ihave Nothing to take to Nor any thing ican make Sixpence of only the kindness of my landlady Assisting me my illness in an inward Complaint wich as afflicted me 5 months and of that nature that icant Explain to the Gentlemen and if they please to send they will find what ihave Stated to be true and if the Gentlemen dont do something for me imust come home as my landlady cant let me Stay any longer.

(Sokoll 2001: 345)

Compared with the letters above, (5) is more idiosyncratic in spelling. Despite the idiosyncrasies, the two main discourse functions are present. Firstly, the identification is implicit, as the applicant refers to previous correspondence to support her legal status. Secondly, the narrative provides factual support for the application, and it is in this part where she also requests relief. The identification and the narrative illustrate the complexity and creativity of this type of communication for applicants who were barely literate. In this case, the creativity is illustrated in the shift of deictics that separates the two parts. The applicant first addresses the overseer in person ('your letter') and turns the point of view in the address to third person uses ('if they please to send they will find'). The narrative aims at speaking directly to the board of overseers rather than to the addressee.

The naming and asking for relief resemble the practice shown in (4). Even though no specific sums are mentioned, the narrative anchors the application to the concept of financial relief. It becomes the main topic right after the introduction and identification. It is referred to as 'something', and the act takes place indirectly, making reference to the landlady and not to the applicant herself. This is again a concrete illustration of how applicants are able to recognise the social values of certain expressions and resort to translocal, decontextualised communication. The applicant selects stylistic resources that are high in the indexical order on the addressee's side. The small landowners in the home parish, i.e. those in charge of deciding upon pauper relief, must have been able to relate to the problematic situation of the unknown landlady in London, more so than to the pauper's situation.

4. Variability in naming practices

The previous section shows that applying for pauper aid was a complex enterprise that consisted of selecting forms that could be expected to have normative validity at the overseers' end. In this section I take a closer look at a set of fifty letters in Sokoll (2001), focusing on the speech acts of asking for aid. I will look at how naming practices co-occur with select features of humiliative discourse. Some of these features are characteristic of the pauper letters illustrated above, and some have been adopted from Fitzmaurice (2002a).

The three most frequently used forms in naming are the items appearing in Examples (2)–(5) above. They consist of nouns or noun phrases in which the head noun is either 'trifle' (13 instances), 'money' (13 instances) or the assertive indefinite pronoun 'something' (10 instances). The applicants rarely asked for specific amounts. Indeed, when this takes place, the purpose of using the money is often stated in the context. Rachel Brown writing from Clerkenwell in London is one of the very few in this sample to refer to a sum:

(6)   . . . but as i am in wants Of Som Cloathing as my Fathers income Is not
       Enugh to Supply us Both with Nessarys . . . I therefore Beg the favour of you
       to Solisset the Gentelmen for me If they would have the Goodness to send
       me $1^{£}0^{s} 0^{D}$ i should be very thankfull as i want A gown and other
       nessurys . . . .

                                                                  (Sokoll 2001: 241)

   This practice suggests that despite the fact that the applicants were aware of their rights, the practice of labelling the assistance carries considerable social meaning. The fact that the semantically weak generic terms and indefinite pronouns are frequently used suggests that naming the aid was loaded with values. The applicants seem to have been sensitive about the social distance between themselves and the recipients, and it was not a common practice to be too demanding in this type of discourse, but rather to provide sufficient grounds in those cases in which specific sums were asked for.

   In addition to the most commonly used forms in naming, there is of course considerable variation in the sample. What is noteworthy is that this variability in the naming practices occasionally involves broader shifts in stylistic choices on an individual level. The changes in naming practices are occasionally part of a more extensive stylistic shift in which the applicants move from using local, here-and-now resources to more translocal ones. One such case is illustrated below through two letters from Thomas Carritt. There are altogether six of his letters in the collection, all written in a similar hand but sent from various locations in London and in

Cambridge in the 1820s. These letters contain plenty of variation with respect to the stylistic choices and interactional features. The changes are illustrated in (7) and (8) below.

The extract in (7) is an earlier letter (sent in 1828), and it illustrates an application that is not more informal in its phraseology than the later applications, but which nevertheless clearly relies on more subjective and contextualised resources:

(7)　. . . I have Frinds in 3 or 4 places who promise to do something for me – & I do hope in afew days some one of them will be enabled to get me into some Kind of employment – I trust you will be Kind enough to assist me in the Money way – I will await the Arrival of Mr Frenchs Coach on monday morning – when you can either give the money to the Coach Man or make a parcel of it – I will write you again in time for the Committee on Thursday – could you see Mr Bacon – he had something in view for me . . .

(Sokoll 2001: 269)

It contains stylistically formal phrases like 'I trust you will be Kind enough to assist me', but overall it draws from local, individual-level resources. These local resources refer to 'friends' in several places getting him 'some Kind of employment', and the relief itself is first called 'the Money way' and then repeated twice in the instructions that Thomas provides for the overseer, even though he is not in a social position to provide them.

About a year later, he continues using formulaic phrases, but he has developed his genre literacy and is now able to be more effective, translocal in his argumentation for relief. For instance, he draws from the institutional and community-level norms to motivate his pauper aid, as shown in (8) and is able to put himself in the position of the overseers. He provides specific information of his employment history, and introduces the topic of his family to motivate the overseers:

(8)　Not having one day employ since 11st January last it is with extreme regret that I am compell'd to apply for pecunary aid – I hope you can so arrange that I may receive a weekly Stipend until I again git into employ – when you shall immediately hear from me it will give me as much satisfaction to get off your funds, as it not grieves me to compelled to come on them I have put off waiting to the very last extremity and we are now in very distressed circumstances and quite destute of money, *Food*, and any thing to pledge to procure *food* – an early reply or at foot will much oblidge Gentlemen

(Sokoll 2001: 285)

These two letters show that the applicant has been able to perform a 'scale jump', if we accept Blommaert's (2010: 35) terminology, as he draws from institutional and community-level norms to motivate aid. This is apparent, for instance, when he points out that his future employment will result in the 'satisfaction to get [i.e. the applicant] off your funds'. In other words, the earlier letter is more local, personal and specific whereas the later one has argumentative validity beyond the here-and-now.

In several instances the head nouns are premodified with determiners ('some'), adjectives ('small/little', etc.) or a combination of both ('some little'). Such a pre-modification is an indication that the applicant aims at diminishing the act of asking for aid. There are, however, a few exceptional applicants whose letters are surprisingly direct, and this is also reflected in the ways in which the aid is labelled. Such cases are illustrated below by extracts from two women, one residing in the western parts of Essex near London and the other in Ipswich. Both resort to 'my money' in their letters, and the first of these, shown in (9), even uses the term 'my half years pay':

(9)   . . . I should be much obliged to you if you would send me my Money as soon as It is due I received my last money on the fifth of December my half years pay will be due on June . . .

(Sokoll 2001: 286–7)

(10)   I take the present opportunity of beging the remitance of my Money – as the time is Expired. necessity oblige me to be exact to the time as the person have calld on me for some Money . . .

(Sokoll 2001: 312)

Despite the directness in the naming, both extracts show that the applicants are able to use stance markers, such as conditionals and indirect sentences, which aim at imitating humiliative discourse in this type of communication. Unfortunately, the textual marking on the original letters does not indicate whether the applicants were granted relief.

A question closely related to naming is the verb form that is used in requesting action. Table 10.1 displays the distribution of the most common verbs in the sample. The most frequent verb is the concrete 'send', and the other alternatives are minor variants compared with the most frequent one. A less concrete 'allow', which points to permission and ability more than to necessity, appears surprisingly infrequently, yet it is the second most frequent item. Example (11) below shows an extract from an application that is a lively description of the living conditions and in which the applicant labels the aid with an indefinite pronoun and resorts to the verb 'allow':

(11)   . . . i have found the one pound that was lost i had it last tusday i was in deet for rent ten shilens and i wors forst to pay it if i had not paid it we should all bean turned out of dores and i hoed 6 shilens for Bread i paid it out of the pound and the 2 Leters cost me 2 shilens and 4 pence and i have no Worke to do pleas to alow us sumthing a weeak til i get sum worke to do for i do not like to keep riten so every weeake . . .

(Sokoll 2001: 339)

Table 10.1 *Verbs used in the speech act of asking for pauper aid*

Verb form	Frequency
Send	29
Allow	4
Do	3
No explicit verb	3
Grant	2
Relieve	2
Advance	1
Answer	1
Forward	1
Help	1
Pay	1
Remit	1
Render	1

A noteworthy fact in Table 10.1 is that there are a few letters in the sample in which the speech act of asking for aid takes place either indirectly or is to be implicitly understood on the basis of the information in the application. The first, an indirect speech act, is shown in (12), in which the asking takes place when the applicant describes his/her living conditions and begs the overseer twice to answer their needy request:

(12)   I am Sory to inform you we have Nothing to take Two And pray take our destressed Case into Considerrashion And Earnestly think what me And my husband And Family Can do had not Mr Wyatt Lent me 2 Shilling we Could not have Broak our Fast But we Cannot Exspect to think our marster Can or will Lend us money And my husband Not Able to work nor I do not know when he will and if you most wordy Gentellmen Do not think proper to Answer our needy Request we must Be Brought home For wheare no money Can Be Earnt no Living Cannot Be had therefore pray Answer our needy Request and Answer our needy Request with Speed ...

(Sokoll 2001: 179)

Pauper aid is clearly the topic of this application, but the applicant never directly asks for parish aid.

A highly implicit application, with no explicit verb of asking, is shown in (13). The applicant combines the two main discourse functions by first pointing out that the letter is an application, and then anchoring herself with the parish with the adverb 'again' that signals previous correspondence (and thus also possible legal status). The narrative describing the living conditions does not contain a direct speech act of asking for help:

Table 10.2 *Frequencies of the four discourse features in Essex pauper letters*

Form	Frequency
Hope/wish + (non)-finite clause	25
Persuasive threat	20
Conditional	16
Third-person pronoun address	4

(13)   It is with great regrett that I am Obdleged to Petition to you again fer Some
       Little relief from you as I am in Very great distress at this time for I have
       been Confined to my Bed fer this Last three weeks with a Bad fever . . . I
       have not a Penney to get any thing to help me out off the trouble that I am
       in I thearfore thought it better to lett you know the distress that I am in then
       to trouble the Parish that I am in hear thear fore Sir I hope you will take my
       requst into Consideration . . .

                                                                    (Sokoll 2001: 388)

Extract (13) also illustrates the use of at least two common discourse features in
pauper letters. The first of these is the stance marker 'I hope', and the second is the
threat of returning back to the home parish. It is noteworthy that the threat may
also be used as a desperate aim to resort to institutional norms. So in other words,
the threat could be interpreted as a signal of attempting to cross to the recipient's
point of view, i.e. an attempt at crossing scales from local to translocal.

Table 10.2 presents a quantitative perspective towards a set of stylistic features in
these letters. Three of them have been adopted from Fitzmaurice's (2002a) study
on humiliative discourse in literate circles and one, the letter-ending persuasive
threat, is a feature characterising pauper letters. The most frequently used discourse
feature is the use of 'hope/wish' used as a stance marker followed with either
a *to*-infinitive or a finite clause. Half of the applications in this sample make
use of this feature, and such cases are illustrated for instance in (4) and in (13).
Surprisingly for the applications that cross considerable social boundaries, the
persuasive threat of returning back to the home parish is the second most frequent
discourse option of the four features. Many of the extracts above illustrate the various
forms of threat. A question for future studies could be to provide a comprehensive
inventory of these forms and discuss the various discourse functions they might
have.

The frequencies suggest that the third person pronoun use in addressing the
recipient overseers, shown for instance in (5), is an infrequent variant, as most of
the letters address the recipients in the second person.

5. Conclusions

The Essex letter material discussed here and other similar letter sources that contain the language of the masses, i.e. artisans and labouring poor, make it possible to catch a glimpse of the lives, fates and language use of ordinary people in early nineteenth-century England. These materials therefore clearly take us closer to observing ordinary people's vernaculars and contribute to making more materials available for historical linguists. They thus correct some of the social imbalance in the material sources in this field.

The individuals whose words appear in the Essex letters are those who are not typically represented in (standard) histories of (standard) English. There is of course a great deal of variability, and many applicants, as seen here, barely crossed the threshold of being literate, whereas some were more skilful letter writers (or they had a skilful person in the vicinity to write the applications for them). The material is a living record and evidence of vernacular speech at the time when the general ideology of standard English was being formed by the privileged and the most powerful (cf. Crowley's 2003 account of public debates on a standard language). This time period was also a time of social change that forced people on a large scale to resort to written communication, and not just any form of leisurely writing among individuals, but highly significant communication through vertical social spaces.

What I have presented should be taken as programmatic, as an illustration of one perspective to language from below that, I feel, deserves further research. With this I mean that the Essex pauper letters illustrate the kinds of material that have already become available alongside the more socially prestigious materials. These material sources enable access to people's vernaculars, but more than that, they enable scholars to study the actions of individuals who struggle to make sense of the new social orders and social contexts in which they find themselves.

I have presented one perspective to understanding a select set of informants, the social context of writing letters of application and sending them to parish overseers for poor relief. I have aimed at providing an account of the discourse practices in letters that have been described as open and direct by social historians. I hope to have been able to show how there is directness in the material but, more importantly, there is heterogeneity in them, and creative ways of expressing the various functions through various linguistic forms, all of which deserve further study.

A non-standard standard? Exploring the evidence from nineteenth-century vernacular letters and diaries

Barbara Allen

1. Introduction

In most general discussions about English, what is assumed without question is that the subject matter is the variety linguists refer to as 'standard English', although non-specialists probably never consider the matter and rarely specify. However, the term 'standard English' reveals ideological attitudes, since it is not neutral. For nearly 200 years, notions about the standard dialect have been wrapped up with a range of social attitudes, often to do with correctness, appropriateness, morality, respectability, intelligence, decency, achievement, worth, importance, acceptability, merit, ethics, honesty and principle. To this list, particularly for the nineteenth century, we might add exclusiveness and superiority, especially class-based superiority.

In discussing standard English and exploring aspects of homogeneity and heterogeneity in usage, there are currently two widely-held meanings of the term:

1. The standard dialect is largely invariant.
2. The standard dialect is a model.

By the beginning of the nineteenth century a fixed standard, as both an invariant system and a model, had emerged. It was the variety prescribed by grammarians, and its rules were abundantly published; 187 prescriptive grammars appeared in the eighteenth century (Alston 1965; Michael 1991; Fitzmaurice 2000). Görlach (1998) lists many more for the nineteenth century, and Finegan (1998a: 543) observes that the target and compass of these texts were broadly similar. The English prescribed in them was modern, in the sense that the many archaisms still present in regional dialects had been eradicated and formal, meaning that it was correct, rather than colloquial and ungrammatical (Fitzmaurice 2000: 198). The standard was a manifestation of contemporary grammatical and stylistic perfection. And as such it appeared in print, in books and in the newspapers and periodicals which were beginning to circulate in increasing numbers at the beginning of the century.

In exploring nineteenth-century educated handwritten standard English, however, it is immediately apparent that invariance was not a characteristic of the system. The variety of the standard which was to be found in print adhered most closely to the rules formulated by the grammarians. The variety of the standard found in educated handwriting, in business and personal correspondence and diaries, for example, was different from that found in printed matter, deviating from the Lowthian rules in a number of features, although in his personal correspondence even Robert Lowth himself did not always obey the rules he promulgated in his grammar (Tieken-Boon van Ostade 2011). Sentence length, punctuation and capitalisation in particular were markedly different from that seen in print. Nevertheless, in general terms, educated handwriting conformed to the conventions of the standard in the sense that it was grammatical and generally correctly spelt.

Not only was a degree of variation tolerated within the standard between print and handwriting; the standard did not stand still. Evidence for changes to the standard which occurred during the course of the century is to be found in a comparison of printed matter over time. What is meant by 'standard English' at any one time therefore needs defining, and assessments of the extent of uniformity or variation need to have careful regard to date and data. Even as a fixed system, nineteenth-century standard English changed. As a model, too, it was a moving target. Out in the shires, older members of the rural gentry struggling to keep pace with orthographic fashion were satirised by authors like George Eliot (1819–80):

> Mr. Tulliver did not willingly write a letter, and found the relation between spoken and written language, briefly known as spelling, one of the most puzzling things in this puzzling world. (*The Mill on the Floss, 1860*)

2. Vernacular writing

Beyond the versions of standard English which appeared in print and educated handwriting is a range of material in the form of letters and diaries in vernacular English. The importance of these writings is now recognised beyond the small group of scholars working in what Vandenbussche and Elspaß have referred to as 'the German sociohistorical tradition' (2007: 145). These vernacular writings are vital, though, in contributing evidence to a full account of nineteenth-century English. To ignore them is the equivalent of describing only the upper classes in a text on nineteenth-century English society. Whilst published collections of working-class writings in English have been around for some time, by Burnett (1974, 1982), Vincent (1981), Burnett, Vincent and Mayall (1984), Jenkins (1997), Cameron *et al.* (2000), for example, and some quantitative studies of nineteenth-century literacy have been undertaken, notably by David Vincent (1989) and David Mitch (1992), there is much qualitative work still to be carried out. These vernacular writings, so long ignored, reveal a great deal about language use amongst a group of people little esteemed by society, who saw small worth in their literary endeavours and accustomed themselves to apologising for their hard-won abilities. The aim of this chapter is to attempt some contribution towards a qualitative description of sociocultural aspects of nineteenth-century vernacular English, exploring what those writings reveal about the extent to which the authors were aware of the standard described above and attempted to emulate its conventions, concluding that it is not only educational level that compromised their ability to match that standard (Allen 2007).

The fifty-two letters and diaries[1] discussed here were written in the nineteenth century by working-class individuals living in the Sussex Weald, then a relatively remote and backward area. Some of the items are collections or groups of letters by an individual or members of a family, which are especially useful for ascertaining that the features exhibited are not merely scribal errors (see Bergs, this volume). For all of the diaries and some of the letters something is known of the writer. Five other items are by educated individuals from the same area and within the same time-frame, in order to justify the claims of difference.

3. The extent of non-standardness

The purpose of this chapter is to investigate the data – the letters and diaries described above – to provide a description of the non-standardness of the written English they contain. I want to suggest that classifying the variety of English used in these writings simply as 'non-standard' over-simplifies and over-generalises to the point at which the term becomes meaningless. At first sight there appears to be a large, haphazard quantity of non-standard items in both the letters and diaries, and yet it is soon clear that those features are not random, but are to some extent systematic, and therefore predictable. Since that is the case, it begs a question: was there a non-standard standard? Was there, in any sense, a non-standard model?[2]

In an attempt to describe non-standard writing, I want to posit a continuum, from a variety close to but recognisably different from the educated standard at one end, to extreme non-standard at the other, from acrolect to basilect, to borrow terminology from creolists. At the acrolect end of the continuum are those writings which suggest that the author had a relatively close acquaintance with the formal grammar and orthographic systems of the English language. At the basilect end of the continuum are the documents written in ways that diverge extensively on a number of features from the general norms of the standard.

For the most part, amongst the group of writers whose writing is acrolectal, from whenever in the nineteenth century the writing dates, the syntax and spelling largely reflected contemporary standard norms. In many items of this type, though, there are usually one or two features which reveal the writer as schooled, rather than educated.[3]

---

[1] The fifty-two letters and eight diaries, almost all unpublished, were collected as data for a PhD thesis (Allen 2006).

[2] Cf. Pietsch, this volume.

[3] I use the term 'educated' here to mean having received a classical education, at one of the public schools such as Eton or Winchester, at a grammar school or at home with private tutors. The term 'schooled' indicates that the pupil attended a local school. The level of education received by pupils at local schools varied enormously.

The schoolroom, of whatever sort, was the context in which the ability to write was acquired. Literacy might be acquired at a school or at home; a local private school or academy at which grammar was taught was undoubtedly the context in which the grammatical rules had been inculcated by writers at the acrolect end of the continuum. Private education was more likely in the first half of the century; there were twice as many private as state-subsidised schools in this period, and many parents preferred them (Laqueur 1976b; Digby and Searby 1981). Academies or local charitable schools were vocational, and the boys who studied there until the age of thirteen or fourteen were destined for apprenticeships in the skilled trades. Although Kenyon (1992: 4) states that 'at some schools boys were instructed in practical literacy and numeracy-related skills such as business letter writing', it was not the job of the local academies to teach their pupils to write in a style befitting a social class to which they could not aspire.

For most nineteenth-century rural working-class children, education took place in small village schools. According to Best (1979: 174), such schooling varied in quality 'from the wantonly cruel to the acceptably good'. Church-run schools, established in the 1830s, offered a generally better standard of teaching than dame schools, which were unregulated, and in some cases taught little. Not only did the quality of instruction vary in village schools, the need for children to contribute to household income often prevented their regular attendance.

When the writing of educated and schooled individuals is compared, it is handwriting which most immediately exposes the differences between them. The former covered sheets of paper in luxuriously expansive script. The handwriting of the schooled writers is, by comparison, small, often cramped, with narrow margins and little space between lines.

Principally, however, it is lexis and syntax that distinguish the educated and the schooled authors. The former use an extensive range of Latinate vocabulary (see Fairman 2012: 219), and their writing is characterised by complex clause constructions, neither of which occur in the writings of schooled authors. Examples from the data exemplify both points:

(1) A local landowner's agent wrote to his employer in 1802:
     'Previous to the meeting I called upon Luck, who I understood to be the person who most ostensibly opposed the alterations of the road . . . '

(2) A solicitor wrote to his client in 1823 about an estate in the West Indies:
     'I have not a sufficiently distinct recollection of the [details] to be able to make any accurate estimate of the Value of the property – nor, situated as matters are at present, does it appear to me an easy task.'

An extract[4] below from a letter written by Polly Pinyon, an educated woman writing to a friend in 1841, demonstrates the characteristic handwriting, layout, lexis and syntax typical of educated authors:

(3)   A brief extract from Polly Pinyon's letter:

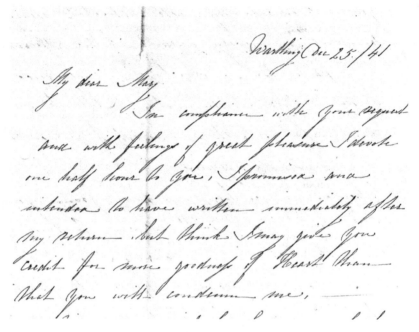

Transcription:

Wartling Dec 25. / 41

My dear Mary
            In compliance with your request
and with feelings of great pleasure I devote
one half hour to you, I promised and
intended to have written immediately after
my return but think I may give you
credit for more goodneſs of Heart than
that you will condemn me, –

4. The continuum of non-standard writing

Just like educated authors, schooled authors' writing was characterised by a variety of particular features. At the acrolect end of the continuum, the number and variety of the stereotypical features is far less than at the basilect end.

---

[4] The author is grateful to the Sussex Postal History Society for permission to use letters from which Examples (1–3) above are taken.

There was a comparative absence of Latinate vocabulary and less complex sentence structure in vernacular writing than in the writing of educated authors. Typically, the schooled writers of this data set composed sentences consisting of single clause, past tense declaratives, with sophistication of construction being achieved by joining two such clauses with conjunctions such as 'and' and 'but'.

There are also other features which identify the schooled authors. Misspellings are relatively rare amongst authors at the acrolect end of the continuum. Those educated in the local academies usually learnt to spell correctly; errors are rare in their writing, and therefore of particular note. Spelling rules were rigidly drilled and spelling manuals for schools were published in increasing numbers from the 1820s. At the basilect end of the continuum, not only are misspellings frequent, but writers also demonstrate a high level of misunderstanding of word structure and morphology, producing such forms as *silom* for 'asylum' (in Sophia Miles' diary[5]) and *setteld in* for 'settling' (in William Oxley's letter[6]).

The quarter-page extract below, with transcript, is from a letter[7] written in 1850. The writer, Thomas Dann, was well schooled. Except for the word 'their', which he rendered throughout as *thier*, every word in this four-page letter is correctly spelt and most of it is grammatical:

(4)   A brief extract from Thomas Dann's letter, 1850

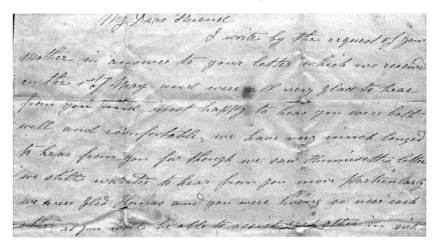

Transcription:

> My Dear Friend
>   I write by the request of your
> Mother in answer to your letter which we received
> on the 1st of May and were all very glad to hear
> from you and most happy to hear you were both

---

5 Privately owned, part-published in *Sussex Family Historian* Vol. 12, 6.
6 East Sussex Record Office PAR 492/26/8.   7 Privately owned, unpublished.

> well, and comfortable, we have very much longed
> to hear from you for though we saw Hunnisettis letters
> we still wanted to hear from you more particularly
> we were Glad Thomas and you were living so near each
> other as you will be able to assist each other in sick-

An intriguing item in Thomas Dann's letter is the possessive form *Hunnisettis*. It could have been simply an error, but the possibility of a *his*-genitive cannot be ignored. Although the *his*-genitive was a feature of late Middle English, Baugh and Cable (2002: 241–2) cite Robert Baker's 1779 polemic against Samuel Johnson on the topic, showing that its demise was slow. To find an example in a letter dated 1850 is, however, somewhat unexpected.

At the acrolect end of the continuum, then, sit the writings of individuals like Thomas Dann. Another is Joseph Blake,[8] whose twenty-year diary is generally grammatical and generally spelt according to the norms of the time at which he was writing, apart from some contracted forms and, like Thomas Dann, *thier* for 'their'. Close as their style was to that of educated writers, it was not close enough to be indistinguishable from it; indeed, a brief inspection of a few lines is sufficient to identify both Thomas Dann and Joseph Blake as products of local academies. They both knew and could use standard English. They both read newspapers and periodicals and were acquainted with a formal, educated style, even if they did not use it themselves in the items that survive. There would be little point, however, in Thomas Dann writing to friends in formal, standard English, a style to which they might not have been accustomed, and a diary such as Joseph Blake's is such a personal form of writing that as evidence for styles which the writer can command, it reveals little.

Further along the continuum, the letters contain a far wider range of non-standard features. In the mesolect range, the letters reveal a general awareness of standard forms, of a model, of conventions, but it is clear that insufficient familiarity with the norms of the standard makes its use impossible. Every letter demonstrates some acquaintance with letter-writing practice. Letters conform to a conventional shape on the page, and it is clear that writers knew that it was customary to inscribe the date of the letter and place of origin at the top of the page, which is not necessarily the case with letters at the basilect end of the continuum. It is also clear that authors knew that there were proper forms and formulaic phrases for beginning and ending letters, although their choices might often have been considered inappropriate by those higher up the social scale. Vernacular writers frequently comment on or apologise for lack of writing skill, and it appears to have been polite to express self-effacing opinions about one's own abilities; no such comments occur in the letters of educated or acrolect writers, nor those at the basilect end of the continuum.

---

[8] See Allen (forthcoming).

A considerable range of non-standard features characterise letters at the mesolect point on the continuum. Most exhibit a large number of non-standard spellings and few writers write any grammatical sentences at all. Punctuation and capitalisation were the two least fixed features of the standard in the first years of the nineteenth century, and variation in these areas is to be seen across the spectrum.

All of the letters and diaries in the data between the mesolect and basilect ends of the continuum suggest that spelling was the feature of written English most at variance with the standard. This is hardly surprising. Spelling is the most fixed feature of the language and the easiest to get wrong. But dates are important; some forms appeared in print and were used by educated writers at the beginning of the century and cannot be considered non-standard at that time. Contracted past tense *-ed* endings were sometimes written *-'d*, *-d* or *-t*, occasionally in superscript. In the early years of the nineteenth century, spellings such as *stopt* and *dress'd* appeared in the published works of Jane Austen. A vernacular letter of 1801 exhibits two such spellings, *Baptisd* and *Faild*, which may have been acceptable at the time. However, the same author also wrote the grammatically incorrect *bornd*. In an 1831 business letter, the schooled author wrote *sign'd* and *enclos'd*, but by then, midway through the century, none of the business letters by three educated men exhibit this type of spelling. Contractions such as *-'d* no longer appeared in print by this date, suggesting that acceptability of these variants was declining from the early years of the century. The last date on which they appear in the data is 1839.

The range, extent and type of spellings that varied from the standard at the time they were written suggest a number of possibilities: imperfectly learned systems, a misunderstanding of word structure or a failure to remember correct spellings. The fact that words were very often spelt differently in the same document suggests that writers did not notice inconsistency, or did not think it important if they did. Inconsistency in spelling indicates that authors were not in the habit of referring to what they had written earlier, simply writing down their nearest guess at the correct form on each occasion. It is unlikely that any of the authors were accustomed to checking spellings or consulting a dictionary, even if they had the means to do so.

Many of the non-standard spellings exhibited in the documents appear to be systematic. Particular features caused confusion: diphthong spellings; homophones; words containing some consonant clusters or sounds, particularly /tʃ/; unstressed syllables, aspirated or non-aspirated words, words beginning /w/ and /ʍ/. Where any of these features were combined or occurred in common words, variant spellings were frequently the result. Regularly confused forms include:

- *here* and *hear*, occasionally *heare*,
- *to, too* and *two*,
- *there* and *their*, *where* and *were*,
- *has* and *as*, *his* and *is*.

In addition we have the following:

- 'right' appears in documents as *rite, right, write, wright* and *whright*;
- 'write' appears in a number of documents as *write, rite* and *wright*;

- the past tense of some irregular verbs, e.g. 'write' which in addition to *wrote* appeared as *rote, wroat* and *whroat*;
- the regular past tense form for the past participle, e.g. *wrote, drove*;
- 'much', 'ditch' and 'fetch' appear as *much, mush, mutch, dich* and *fech*;
- 'which' appears as *which, whitch, witch* and *wich*;
- *whith* was written for 'with';
- *wether* appeared for 'whether' and *wheather* for 'weather';
- 'what' was sometimes *wat*, 'when' appeared as *wen* and 'why' as *whey*;
- '-ing' appeared as *-en*.

Any of these spellings might co-occur in the same document.

The spellings above are frequently to be found in documents at the mesolectal point on the continuum. There are not enough tokens of some words in the data to suggest that they are the subject of spelling confusion, but where they do occur misspelt, they usually fit into the pattern described above. For example, one author spelt 'see' as *sea*, but six words later he wrote *see*. Emigrant Benjamin Jeffery wrote both *quear* and *quere* for 'queer'. He usually spelt 'are' as *ar*, but occasionally he wrote *are*. Another emigrant, Robert Manktelow, an extensively non-standard speller, wrote his daughter's name differently on the same page: *Bartha* and *Bertha*. He spelt 'there' as *thear, ther* and *thar* within a few lines. Part of his letter is reproduced below, page 4 on the left and 1 on the right:

(5)   Robert Manktelow's letter, 1878[9]

---

[9] The author is grateful to the Sussex Postal History Society for permission to use Robert Manktelow's letter.

> Dear Brother and sister
>
> We received your kind letter and was glad you was all well I must tell you Bartha as Been ill But is Better Clark as lost four of his with the same deses the four younger all dide in two weeks he as Bought a acker of land for sixty dollars But he as not Pade acent yet he Put up a hut onit one Room now the Roads run north and south east and west some Farms have 50 ackers and some 100 2 men and 2 horses do the work on fifty ackers exsept in harvesten Bill works a Farme on a half he as all the work to do thear not much to be made in that
>
> Bill and wife and littel girl are quit well her fok's come from Goudhurst and her mothers come from Crambruk thear not much doen hear for wheal rits and Blaksmith it all don in a larg Cale Eliza sase tell Ester she don't like this Cuntry and never shall ther churches hear But small of diferent soiteys you must wright and let us naw all the news you can give my love to Willy and all of them and thay must wright to us I must now conclude wishing you a merry Christmass and a happy New Year From Your Affectionate Brother and Sister Robert and Eliza manktelow

The principal problems with spelling for authors like Robert Manktelow appear to have been uncertainty about and unfamiliarity with the standard written form, compounded with the frequent lack of correlation between spelling and pronunciation (Baugh and Cable 1993: 12). Some non-standard spellings suggest that the writers had only ever heard the word spoken and had not seen, or did not remember seeing it written or printed, so their spelling was a representation of the sound of the word as they pronounced it, based on their understanding of the orthographic system of the language.[10] Writers attempting unfamiliar words produced phonetic forms such as *silom* ('asylum'), the initial unstressed syllable unnoticed or analysed as the determiner *a*. Robert Manktelow wrote *nek's* for 'next'. Addressing his employer as *Onned Sir*, another writer requested the services of the *Sovair* (surveyor). Elsewhere writers produced *emty waggin* ('empty wagon'), *now* ('know'), *beyound all reson* ('beyond all reason') and *deses* ('disease'). One writer, in various letters over a three-year period, wrote *sluvinly*, *Shugar*, *raimainder*, *woful* and *govorment*. All these examples demonstrate writers' unfamiliarity with the morphological structure of the words and the standard written forms.

---

[10] Hall (1987: 52) cites Henderson's (1980) research showing that children learning to spell go through stages, one of which involves writing words in accordance with the phonemic feature indicated by the alphabetic letter name, producing forms such as *lef* for 'leaf'. Later, silent vowels are added, often resulting in forms such as *lefe* for 'leaf'. It appears possible to suggest that the writers of these documents may not have stayed at school long enough to progress far beyond the second of these stages, accounting for some of the spellings exhibited in these data.

Whilst a level of education insufficient to acquire the standard forms might account for many of these spellings, it might not be the whole story. The number of years between completion of schooling and writing is also a factor. If the writer had not been in the habit of writing since leaving school, the ability to spell would decline. The limited number of years spent at school, as well as irregular attendance, militated against learning to spell. But the deeper significance of the misspellings in vernacular writing should not pass unnoticed. Spelling for the practised and well educated is easy and relies mostly on memory. Those whose education has not equipped them to depend on their memory have to apply what they know about the principles of spelling in order to write the word they want to use. Most of those responsible for education today regard the ability to apply learning as far more important than the ability to recite from memory and to that extent the schooled writers, whose education was far less extensive than those higher up the social scale, used their knowledge successfully in attempts to communicate via the written word.[11]

5. Spelling as evidence for oral forms of the language

Some of the spellings in the letters appear to indicate a Sussex pronunciation. Benjamin Jeffrey, an 1871 emigrant to New Zealand, describes the beginning of his sea voyage in a letter[12] to his mother, saying 'the thams poilet Left us at deal and now we have a Channel poilet on bord' possibly indicating his use of the diphthong /ɔi/ where Received Pronunciation would have required /ai/, the former still being a pronunciation feature of rural Sussex speech today. The *Linguistic Atlas of England* (*LAE*; Orton *et al.* 1978) maps the /ai/ diphthong, showing, for some words, an isogloss very close to Little Horsted, where Benjamin Jeffery grew up. Most common throughout Sussex and on one side of the isogloss the given form is /əi/, on the other it is /ɔi/. How he pronounced 'pilot' cannot be known, but when it came to writing the word, Benjamin Jeffery would have selected the best orthographic representation of the word as he pronounced it. However, the /ai/ diphthong is not represented phonetically as /ɔi/ in any other of six letters by Benjamin Jeffery. Another 1871 letter, from American emigrant Robert Manktelow, describes the local churches of different *soiteys*. The unstressed first syllable of 'societies' and Sussex pronunciation might account for this spelling, but, like Benjamin Jeffery, Robert Manktelow's letter exhibits no other spelling which suggests he pronounced the /ai/ diphthong as /ɔi/. His letter contains a large number of misspellings of words with the /ai/ diphthong, for example, he wrote *dide*, *hier* and *fier* for 'died', 'hire' and 'fire'. Non-standard spellings in other letters, like *gitt*

---

[11] Discussing children's misspellings, Barton (1994: 155) suggests that these often originate from 'hypotheses about the nature of language' which 'reflect a sophisticated knowledge of the English sound system'. The same applies to the writers of the letters and their misspellings.

[12] Original letters on the open shelves at East Sussex Record Office, unreferenced.

('get'), *close* ('clothes') and *naw* ('know'), the last in Robert Manktelow's letter, may reflect the authors' pronunciation of those words. The *Survey of English Dialects* (*SED*; Orton and Dieth 1967) shows a range of Sussex pronunciations of these forms.[13]

One writer spelt 'beautiful' as *butiful* and another wrote *sute* for 'suit', possibly representing their respective pronunciation of /buːtifʊl/ and /suːt/, but also possibly because of the pronunciation of the letter name 'u'. The High Weald pronunciation of 'suit' is shown as /uː/ in the *LAE*, and Coates (2010: 45) notes that in the pronunciation of the Sussex dialect postconsonantal /j/ is lost after some fricatives, citing 'suit' as his example. The *SED* shows that responses for Sussex speakers to 'suit' include /sɪuːt/, /sɒuːt/ and /suːt/. Benjamin Jeffery spelt 'few' as *fiew*, which accords with the *LAE* report of the pronunciation of 'few'.

It is not only spelling that characterises the writings at the mesolect point of the continuum, there are also a number of syntactic features. Although each of those listed below is only present in a few items, they do suggest that standard English was not the model for these writers:

- inconsistent or absent copular *be*, as in a letter of 1831: 'I left home 10th Aug for New York it more than 300 Miles it not much trouble to go 3 or 400 miles in this country';
- adjectives as adverbs, for example: 1853 'Mother had the spasms very bad'; 1865 'She writes so very nice for her age';
- *-th* verb endings, occasional and not consistent. Example from 1831: 'Jno hath got a good place' and later in the same letter 'his father hath given his word';
- absence of auxiliary verbs, occasional and not consistent, e.g. from 1846: 'theare Been A Blight Among Potaters This year In England They Been selling 6s Pr Bushel';
- *come* and *see* as past tense forms, 1833 'when we landed at New York we see many English friends'; 1865 'we had such a summer last year as we never see before'.

Some non-standard syntactic features occur more frequently than the items listed above. Concord is one feature more than any other on which writers did not emulate the standard, but since lack of concord is a widespread feature of dialects in the English-speaking world, its failure is predictable. In the following examples, the third person singular verb form has been used where nineteenth-century standard English required the third person plural. Blake states that it was one of the issues tackled by grammarians: '[C]oncord between the subject (especially when it was

---

[13] *gitt SED*: most Sussex informants had /gɛt/; one had /gɪt/. *close SED*: (form: ordinary 'clothes'). All Sussex informants had /ð/. One had /klɔʊðz/, all the others had /klɒʊðz/. (Form: 'clothes basket'), all Sussex informants except one omitted the /ð/. *naw SED*: form not given, but Sussex informants produced /ɹɒʊd/, /ɹɒɒd/, and /ɹɪuːd/ for 'road'. The *Linguistic Atlas of England* shows that in all of Sussex and most of Kent the vowel in 'mow' is pronounced /ɔʊ/, which might suggest a pronunciation of 'know' to result in a spelling *naw*.

compound) and the verb was insisted upon so that sentences like *John and I was there* were not acceptable' (1996: 264).

(6)   1801   my Brother and Father is very well at preasant
      1831   his letters was very short
      1833   Mrs Roſe would be better if some of her friends was hear
      1833   we was in no danger
      1837   Since the 1st Jany there has been About 300 failures in the City of
             New York
      1850   George and Ann was mared
      1861   there is no hops this year
      1872   there is three hundred and four passengers on board
      1873   I wish you was not so far away that I could come and see you
      1878   we received your kind letter and was glad you was all well

Baugh and Cable (2002: 344) note that 'schoolmastering of the language' resulted in the emergence, in about 1820, of singular *you were* where previously the more logical *you was* had been the accepted form, as exhibited above in the letter of 1873.

Another syntactic feature which appears in several items is the construction *a-[x]ing*, a non-finite verbal clause, the centre of which is the participial form of the verb with *-ing* occurring occasionally as *-en*. In a ten-year-old boy's diary of 1829 there are several examples: one reads 'Father went down to Mr Aylwin a Hog Ringen'. Various *a-[x]ing* constructions appear in other items, some of which, like the example above, appear purposive, for example, 'at present i are a Choping of Wood for fireing' (1833 emigrant's letter); 'I know of a party that are a coming out there next spring' (a young lady's letter to her emigrant fiancé, 1854). Both Baugh and Cable (1993: 287) and Beal (2004: 80) suggest that the *a-[x]ing* construction was an intermediate stage in the evolution of the passive progressive verb form *be+ing*, and Bailey (1996) comments that the new form began to be used extensively in the eighteenth century, despite the protests of Samuel Johnson and others. By the early nineteenth century, the *a-[x]ing* construction had disappeared from educated writing. After 1865, no instances of the construction appear in these letters, but since negative evidence is unreliable, it is not possible to state anything more than that their absence might indicate that the form was beginning to be abandoned or stigmatised even in vernacular writing.

The use of relativisers, which had largely become standardised by the nineteenth century, is another feature on which vernacular usage occurred concurrently with standard usage. Denison (1998) states that before the end of the eighteenth century *who* and *which* took over the ground lost by *that* in written English. From the nineteenth century, *who* was used in standard written English for animate nouns and *that*, *which* and zero relativiser Ø for inanimate nouns. Of the ten examples below three have animate nouns, only one of which uses the relative pronoun *who*:

(7) 1809   the roade wich Is impossebel to Pas
     1839   Jhon Brought the Letter Ø you Sent to him
     1846   thees few lines that I received from you
     1850   In answer to your letter which we received on the 1st of May
     1854   I know of a party that are coming out there next spring
     1855   My sister-in-law often asks me questions Ø I cannot answer
     1862   Mr Fox is married to a young woman that has been living with him
            for some time
     1871   It is all the paper Ø we have got to night
     1872   a Channel poilet on bord that will leave us when we get to Plymouth
     1892   She has gone to see my brother who we expect to hear every post has
            passed away

6. Punctuation and capitalisation

Despite the strictures of some grammarians – Lindley Murray (1795) described in detail both the qualities and conditions for forming sentences and the importance of punctuation – both educated and schooled writers frequently wrote long sequences of language with associative, sequential and contrastive connections between them. Occasionally a letter contained only one sentence-type sequence in one paragraph. Amongst the schooled writers there is very little in the way of punctuation of any sort. Absence of full stops in much of the writing affects structure and therefore capitalisation; if there is only one sentence, only one capital letter at the beginning is required. The example below is a transcript of the first page of an 1823 letter from an educated young man to his father. He punctuates with commas, but in a two-page letter there is not one full stop, nor are there any obvious sentence ends:

(8)
Honoured Sir,
        I had not an opportunity of seeing you on Saturday when at Eastbourne but I have been given to understand that it is your Intention to allow Frederick £3 for him to go to London in search of a Situation which Journey I Shall consider fruitless as I have written to a Gentleman (of the name of Johnson a branch Pilot in the East India Service) who has promisd that the first Situation that offers to view he will not fail to let me know, and as the East India Fleet does not sail till January there is plenty of time as yet and as you know we are not over stocked with money I think it might be applied to a Much better purpose . . . (etc.)

If educated authors wrote lengthy sequences of language, it is difficult to argue that absence of full stops was non-standard. In print, however, although sentences were often longer than would be found today, full stops were certainly a regular and reliable feature of composition.

Apostrophe usage is a good barometer of changing practice over time. Bauer (1994: 133) suggests that apostrophe rules 'have been breached ever since they were set down'. Jane Austen's use of some possessive apostrophes would be considered incorrect today, so it is clear that this punctuation feature had not fully matured by the start of the nineteenth century.[14] Apostrophe usage marks out the difference between the educated, who were taught to use them, and the schooled, most of whom were not. The educated writers also use an abundant range of punctuation marks not found in schooled writing: full stops, commas, colons and dashes. In the vernacular documents there are very few apostrophes used at all and only two used correctly, one to indicate an elided letter and the other to mark the possessive case. The first is in a letter of 1823: 'please to be so kind as to send it directly as their's a shop selling of cheap'. The second is in Thomas Dann's letter, the only item in the data where an apostrophe is used correctly to mark the possessive case: 'Mrs Hunnisett has been over to your mother's to see your letter'. It is the same author, however, who wrote the possessive *Hunnisettis*, referred to earlier. Robert Manktelow's letter also contains apostrophes. He writes 'he think's som of working By the day nek's summer' and 'Bill and wife and littel girl are quit well her fok's come from Goudhurst', but these are not possessives and they do not mark an omitted letter in the normal sense. The use of punctuation in line with standard English is often difficult for people with far more education than most of these writers received, so it is not surprising to find so few punctuation marks such as apostrophes used in these letters.

Throughout the documents the application of capital letters appears to be random. Most writers capitalise place names and people's names, although Robert Manktelow signed his own surname with a lower case <m>. Others are not systematic. Benjamin Jeffery, for example, does not capitalise days of the week, nor some other proper names, such as *thams* (Thames), and place-names *deal* and *beachy head*. On the other hand, he capitalises *London, Channel, Gravesend, Plymouth* and *Dunedin*. In several letters by various authors the first person pronoun appears as lower case <i>, which had become non-standard by the mid-eighteenth century (Görlach 1999). Few of the writers capitalise in ways which had become standard by the nineteenth century, suggesting that they were not aware of this aspect of formal practice, or did not apply it to their own writing if they were. An example of

---

[14] *Pride and Prejudice* published 1813, Penguin Classics Edition (1985: 227): 'I am under the necessity of relating feelings which may be offensive to your's', and from *Mansfield Park*, published 1814, Penguin Classics Edition (1996: 126): 'it was now generally admitted to be her's'.

extreme over-capitalisation is the Richard Miles letter, a part transcription of which appears below:

(9)   Transcription of Richard Miles' letter, 1846:

January th 4 1846
    Deare Brother
In Answer To thees Few Lines
That I Received from you I See That
you Arived Safe After A Passage of six
Weakes Whitch I am Glad to Heare hoping
That This Will Find you In good health
As it Leaves us At Present Thank god
I Rite to Let you know That I Not seen
John Brooker But That Letter Came to
Forrest Row And Brother John Brought
In Down to me In November And He Not
Paid His Arraires In the Bank At That time
But With A Faithful Promise To Pay It
Inn At Crismase Without Fail He Done
the Repairse To the Barne But Not To
Cottage Wheare Waters Lives Nor Throne The
Timber But Will In the Spring I Not Been
Up To Forrest Row Last Spring to see
How They are getting on since Last Spring
But Think of going Up Next spring
If Please God spares my Life I Now Living
Under Lord Ashburnham now 3 Miles
Further Down then I was When you
Came to England. . . . . (etc)

7. Basilectal writings

Amongst the subset of items at the basilectal end of the continuum are those containing the highest proportion of and most extreme non-standard features. There are too few items to enable any generalisations to be made about the forms of non-standardness, except that in addition to those already discussed, which also appear in these writings, it is possible to add a misunderstanding of English morphology as a major cause of error. This point is best exemplified by a letter, reproduced below, with a transcription:

(10) William Oxley's letter, 1812:

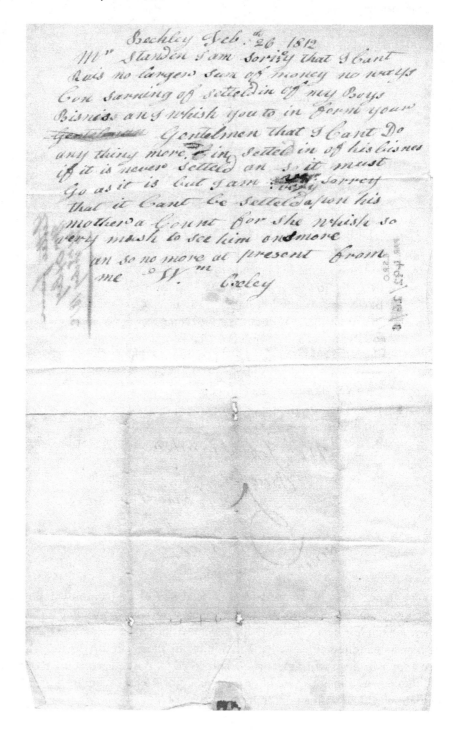

Beckley Feb. th 26 1812
Mr Standen I am Sorriey that I Cant
Rais no larger sum of money no ways
Con sarning of setteld in of my Boys
Bisniss an I whish you to in form your
Gentelmen that I Cant Do
any thing more in setteld in of his bisnes
if it is never setteld an so it must
Go as it is but I am very sorrey
that it Cant be setteld apon his
mother a Count for she whish so
very mush to see him onsmore
an so no more at present from
me Wm. Oxley

William Oxley was probably not accustomed to either reading or writing letters, since this one shows no attempt to emulate layout conventions. Clearly, though, he had an important message to convey, and despite the shortcomings in production, the recipient would have been in no doubt about its meaning. There are many non-standard grammatical forms, but it is intelligible and unambiguous. The handwriting is legible. Many words are misspelt, but the majority are spelt correctly. He misunderstood the morphological structure of several words, such as 'concerning', 'inform', 'settling' and 'account', and the phrase 'once more', which he rendered *con sarning, a count, in form, settld in* and *onsmore*, but none is so garbled as to be incomprehensible. Neither his possessives nor his contractions contain apostrophes, but nor did those of many other schooled authors. He knew that a formulaic phrase was the correct way to conclude a letter, although his choice was inappropriate. The letter may have been written in haste and *in extremis*, as suggested by the crossings out. William Oxley may have been an old man whose memory of little-used written forms was beginning to fade. Without knowing something more of the author than is the case here, it is difficult to say with any certainty that his style was typical or representative.

There is one item in this collection of data which is far more non-standard than William Oxley's letter, although it is a diary and the original has not been seen. In this case, however, something is known of the author. Sophia Miles, wife of an illiterate labourer, kept a diary for twelve years, recording the day-to-day events of her life. The family was poor and Sophia received parish pay; nevertheless she found the time and materials to write letters as well as the diary. In this collection of data, Sophia Miles was the writer least well acquainted with standard English-spelling norms, if the published version of her diary is any guide, and there is no reason to suppose that the transcriber has made the diary appear more non-standard than the original. Sophia Miles' tenuous grasp of the spelling system is revealed by entries which need a gloss, such as for 3 August 1860 *sod som cubege ceed* ('sowed some cabbage seed'). The extent to which she is representative of basilectal writers is difficult to establish without a larger quantity of material to work with:

(11)   Extract from Sophia Miles' diary

       1851

Feb 1	Alfred Miles was born
April 11	to hoing been at Clarks
April 13	George sow pared
May 3	Cow carved
May 29	don hoing beens at Clarks
July 19	a leter from Epsom
Aug 2	Georges cow to bul
Aug	William died August 17
	bered at Keymer Aug 20
Nov 18	I had my half bots

8. Absent features

Having considered the range of forms and features found in vernacular letters, missing evidence should also be considered. There are several features which might be expected but are not found. For example, none of the spellings suggest phono-logical features reported to be typical of speech in nineteenth-century rural Sussex. Genuine original nineteenth-century Sussex dialect writings, on which such expec-tations are based, are few (Coates 2010). The 'Jernal' of John Burgess, a glover from Ditchling who emigrated to America, is the best example of the uneducated natural written form of Sussex speech from the late eighteenth century. James Richards, born in Hailsham in 1866 of working-class parents, wrote in the Sussex dialect as 'Jim Cladpole', but wrote other works in standard English. In contrast to Burgess' journal and letters, Richards' writing consciously evokes the Sussex dialect. In the foreword to *De ABC Psalms*, Richards writes:

(12)   When I fust begun to put dese A.B.C. Psalms into de Sussex
       dialect I onny thought dere was sebn of hem.
       (Cladpole, in the edition by Coates 1992: 1)

Most prominent among the phonological features of the Sussex dialect is the use of /d/ for /ð/, seen in *dese, de* and *dere* in the extract above, but also word medially, as in, for example, /mʌdər/ for 'mother'. This feature is consistent throughout Richards' writing as 'Jim Cladpole', and appears in other Sussex dialect writ-ings, such as those by Richard Lower (Wales 2000).[15] Prominent though this

---

[15] In a letter (Sussex Archeological Society library, uncatalogued) to an acquaintance, A. W. Fuller, Richards stated that he used to hear 'mother' and 'father' pronounced as (his orthographic convention) 'moder' and 'fader', but

feature is reported to have been in Sussex speech in the nineteenth century, it never appears in any of the vernacular letters, indicating that however the writers pronounced /ð/, they knew that the correct written form was <th> and not <d>.

Rhoticity was only rarely a feature of educated speech in the nineteenth century (MacMahon 1998); in rural dialects it was far more common (Hogg 2006), and it is unlikely that *r*-lessness was a feature of speech amongst the vernacular writers. There is little spelling evidence amongst the letters to support that claim, although there are slight hints in one of the diaries that unfamiliar place names were spelt in a way that suggests a rhotic pronunciation; for example, in the ten-year-old boy's diary, *Herringly* was consistently written for 'Hellingly', *Bareship* for 'Boship' and *Furrell* for 'Firle'. Another diary writer spelt the place of his birth as *Isveil* (Isfield), reflecting not a rhotic accent but the typical Sussex pronunciation of /v/ for RP /f/ (Parish 1875, edn 2001: 20).

Not only are phonological features that might be expected to appear absent from the data, but Sussex dialect words are also conspicuous for their rarity, occurring in only three of the diaries. Diaries provide a very different sort of data from letters. They might not be written for others to read at the time, as letters are. They might contain forms that letters, which were often widely circulated, would not, since no disgrace for poor writing standards or stigmatised vocabulary is visited upon those who write only for themselves or future readers. As with pronunciation, there appears to be a conscious avoidance of writing dialect words in letters, perhaps providing some evidence for the view that a correct, proper form was considered appropriate for letter writing, a form developed in the schoolroom, and not the form used in the home or in the village street.

The impression that there was considered to be a correct form for letter writing is strengthened by the almost total absence of another feature common in all dialects – double negation. Stigmatised in the schoolroom, double negation appears to have been successfully eradicated from vernacular writing throughout much of the continuum, showing the powerful impact that schoolroom English rules had on writers. In support of the point, one example of multiple negation occurs, in the basilectal letter of William Oxley: 'I am Sorriey that I Cant Rais no larger sum of money no ways', although he also writes 'I Cant Do any thing more'.

The absence of *do*-support – a feature becoming established in standard English by the nineteenth century (Han and Kroch 2000) – in the vernacular letters is noticeable. But *do*-support is only variably present in the letters of educated individuals; for example, Polly Pinyon's 1841 letter contains the line '[I] had not that relish for...' and another educated author writes 'I have not a sufficiently distinct recollection of...' (1823). Perhaps the absence of *do*-support in every letter in the data can be accounted for by noting that their authors do not use negative or interrogative constructions in which it would be found.

also commonly with a medial /v/. Although he homogenised the /d/ spelling in his dialect writings it was an artifice, not intended to imply a universal Sussex pronunciation.

8. Conclusion

Over forty years ago Uriel Weinreich, William Labov and Marvin Herzog suggested that 'linguistic variation is characterised by "structured heterogeneity"' (Weinreich, Labov and Herzog 1968: 99). They argued that speaker choice is not boundless, but constrained by both the grammatical system of the language and by the social organisation of the community in which it is used (my paraphrase). If speakers are so constrained, then vernacular writers in the nineteenth century were the more so, having an extra layer of school-generated rules applied to their choices which limited further the range of available variants.

In this chapter I have posited a continuum of non-standardness. I have suggested that vernacular letters can be categorised by the extent and variety of the non-standard features they exhibit, which can be used to attach them to a specific point on the continuum. All other items in the same slot will display non-standard features from the same set, and share characteristics in terms of type of variant. The fact that a set of features characteristic of vernacular writing can be identified, and the variant forms of those features predicted, suggests that we can extend Weinreich *et al.*'s description. Within their concept of 'structured heterogeneity', which applies to all linguistic output, spoken and written, a degree of structured homogeneity in vernacular writing is recognisable. That homogeneity must have been the consequence of an implicit acceptance by authors of a model not of prestige forms, but of uniformity. At each of the points along the continuum, writers must have had some idea of what a letter looked like, some notion of how news was conveyed, what it was important to write. There was tolerance of variant spellings, especially since the recipient was no more likely to be able to spell the word than the sender.

I began by seeking to explore whether within vernacular writing there was any notion of a standard, in the sense of either uniformity or a model to aspire to. My conclusion is that there was a considerable degree of uniformity; vernacular writers used a common set of features. Many of the vernacular writers would have been used to reading the letters of others, and, however successfully or not they reproduced it, schooled English, as it appeared in letters from peers, was their conscious model. But lessons learnt in school are only remembered and enforced with regular practice. For many of these authors, the act of writing a letter was a relatively infrequent event, and for those at the basilect end of the continuum it must have been rare. Schooling might have been brief, time dims memories and unused skills rust; individually these letters do not reveal even circumstantial evidence about authors' abilities, but collectively they provide evidence for some description of a non-standard standard.

CHAPTER 12

Archaism and dialect in Irish emigrant letters

Lukas Pietsch

1. Introduction

This chapter reports on a newly created corpus of historical non-standard written Irish English, the *Hamburg Corpus of Irish English* (*HCIE*).[1] It is based mostly on private letters written to and by Irish emigrants abroad between the late seventeenth and early twentieth centuries. While the corpus has been designed and used so far mostly from the perspective of contact linguistics, i.e. in order to gain insight into specific grammatical issues of Irish English related to the language contact situation between English and Irish, the material also poses interesting questions regarding the more general issue of the linguistic use of historical written material of a non-standard character. The nature of the written language in private, sub-literary texts, especially letters produced by writers of limited schooling and literacy, has in recent years been discussed from the perspective of a 'language history from below' (Elspaß 2005; see also Fairman 2003 and contributions in Vandenbussche and Elspaß 2007; Elspaß *et al.* 2007), leading to the realisation that such texts require a wholly new approach to the classification and interpretation of their status within the spectrum of varieties beyond the traditional terms of 'standard' and 'dialect'.

The present chapter will concentrate on one observation that has also been previously pointed out by Elspaß (2005: 49) in his seminal study of comparable German emigrant letters: the surprising persistence of some conservative grammatical features in the written production of less schooled writers, which in some cases match neither the prescriptive literate standard of the time, nor what can be known of the spoken regional dialects that their writers would have spoken natively. The existence of such features underlines the necessity to consider the nature and provenance of regional norms specific to these sub-literary writing practices, their modes of transmission and preservation and their interactions with both the spoken dialects and the prescriptive standard variety.

The feature I will analyse to illustrate this phenomenon is of some interest both from a historical and from a dialectological perspective and also has interesting parallels in non-standard varieties of other Germanic languages: the free use of

[1] I gladly acknowledge the generous support of the German Science Foundation *(Deutsche Forschungsgemeinschaft)* in funding the research program during which the creation of the corpus, and initial research based on it, were carried out, in the framework of the Collaborative Research Centre 538 Multilingualism at the University of Hamburg.

periphrastic *do* in unstressed assertive contexts. Certain uses of periphrastic *do* are well attested in the spoken dialects of Ireland, especially as a habitual aspect marker. However, as will be demonstrated below, the corpus material of late eighteenth- and nineteenth-century letters shows a fairly widespread use of *do* in other environments as well, where one would not expect it according to the patterns of the spoken dialects. However, these usages appear to reflect grammatical patterns familiar from the emergent standard English of a much earlier period, which in the educated written standard had become obsolete by at least the mid-eighteenth century.

2. Letter writing and formulaic imitation

In a light-hearted book of *Gossip about Letters and Letter Writers*, the Scottish genealogist George Seton (1870) included a chapter on the 'less elaborate effusions of the humbler classes'. Among the most prominent features he ascribed to this group, and especially to emigrant writers, was the frequent use of stereotyped, formulaic expression (Seton 1870: 140–1):

> The touching simplicity and warmth of affection so frequently displayed in the letters received from emigrants to distant lands . . . cannot fail to interest the most callous reader. References to the mutual health of the parties constitutes one of the most prominent features of the correspondence under consideration, and the style usually adopted forcibly reminds us of the classical *præloquium* . . . 'I write these few lines to say that I *hop* you are well, as this, thank God! leaves us at preasant' – a very creditable translation of 'Si vales, gaudeo; ego valeo'. Perhaps the most objectionable characteristic of these unpretending epistles is the superfluous statement with which they almost invariably close: 'No more at present, but remains, etc.'

Indeed, both of the characteristic letter-writing formulae mentioned here, the 'as this leaves us' formula and the 'no more but remains' formula, are part of a well-established inventory of stereotyped elements that are ubiquitous in letters of writers of lower educational background in the nineteenth century (see Dossena 2007). Austin (1973, 2000, 2004) has located the sources of some of them in letter-writing manuals and literate models that can be traced back 'to the fourteenth and fifteenth centuries' or sometimes even further, noting that they had 'largely disappeared from the letters of literate and literary persons' by the late eighteenth century (2000: 52–3). Austin goes on to ask:

> How was it that these formulae survived? Letter writing does not seem to have been taught in schools, certainly not in elementary schools, until the late nineteenth century, so the explanation is probably that they were passed down by family tradition. (2000: 54)

Letter writers thus relied on the use of stylistic models that were handed down to them through a practice of imitation, a social practice that was self-contained and effective enough to keep some linguistic forms alive for decades or even centuries after the demise of their original models in the standard English of more literate writers. The existence of these formulae, however, is only one sign of a more general phenomenon of stylistic conservatism, which includes not just stereotypes of phrasing but, as I will try to show in the remainder of this chapter, also features of grammar. The situation may be particularly complex in cases where features of vernacular grammar and features of an archaic 'intended' standard accidentally overlap or mix with each other.

   One instance of such a mixture may be observed in the 'no more but remains' salutation formula mentioned above, which in the writing of nineteenth-century Irish and Scottish emigrants not only represents an example of archaic wording, but also regularly displays a conspicuous non-standard grammatical feature: the use of the verbal *-s* on the final verb (typically *remains, concludes* or similar). It is typically part of a subjectless clause linked to the preceding context by a coordinating device (*but* or *and so*), with the writer as the understood subject (often, but not always, with an anaphoric reference to an overt instance of a subject *I* in a preceding clause). In letters from more literate English writers of the late seventeenth and early eighteenth centuries, when the formula was still part of the educated repertoire, the verb regularly appears in the *s*-less base form, in accordance with its grammatical status as an intended first person singular form as in Examples (1–3):

(1)   I apprehended it my Duty to give your Lordship the soonest Advertisement
       thereof I could; and so remain Your Lordship's Most humble and faithful
       Servant, – E. Mountagu

                                           (1660, in Cobbett and Wright 1808: 53)

(2)   In the mean time, I beseech you to let me learn by degrees to be without
       that agreeable conversation, which I value more than I can express. I can say
       no more; but conclude with assuring your Grace that, use me as you will, it
       is not in your power to make me otherwise than your Grace's, &c.

                                    (Thomas Coningsby, 1712, in Marlborough 1838: 87)

(3)   a. I had sooner tendered my services herein, which I leave to yor
           consideration, <u>and rest</u> – Sʳ yʳ humble servant, John Jones.
                              (*Corpus of Early English Correspondence* [=CEEC], 1659)
       b. whereof I thought fitt to give you this intimation by your owne
           messenger, and remayne – Sir, yoʳ humble servant, Jo. Jones.

                                                               (*CEEC*, 1659)

The same is still true for letters found in less educated writers in late eighteenth-century England, as shown in examples (4a–c), from the *Corpus of Late 18th Century Prose* (= *CL18CE*):

(4)   a. All at Present, but remain Your, Humble, Servant. James Swindells

(*CLi8CE*, 1772)

b. I hope your good Famely are all well so Conclude my selfe your Humb:
Sarᵗ &c John Robinson

(*CLi8CE*, 1785)

c. Pray Except of my Best wishes for your and your family and remane your
much abligd humble Serent Sarah Bavin

(*CLi8CE*, 1788)

On the other hand, inflected verb forms in *-s* in this position occur in Scots
writing in the early seventeenth century, as shown in Example (5) from the *Helsinki
Corpus of Older Scots* (= *HCOS*). In this context the *-s* form comes as no surprise, since in Scots it was conditioned in this position by a regular syntactic
pattern, the so-called Northern Subject Rule, which licenses *-s* in all verbs that are
not immediately adjacent to a personal pronoun subject (see Montgomery 1991,
1994).

(5)   a. So leuing to truble you and my self both longer this lait nicht, I commit
you to God his holy keiping, for euer rests, your faithfully affectionit vyf
til deith, – D. Juliane Ker

(*HCOS*, 1613)

b. and nocht hauing farder for this present, bot to wish yiow all happines,
restis your lordships maist affectionat to serue yiow, – Lord Bruntiland.

(*HCOS*, 1614)

In the letters of the *Hamburg Corpus of Irish English* (= *HCIE*), the verb also
quite regularly appears in the *-s* form, just as it apparently did in the emigrant letters
that the Scotsman George Seton had in mind. Example (6a) comes from a Belfast
citizen, John McKeown, writing in 1881, while (6b) is from John Sinclair, a farmer
from Ulster, writing in 1872:

(6)   a. So may God Bless you and watch Over you untill we meet again no more
at present But Remains your Affectionate Father & mother till Death

(McKeow01, 1881)

b. I have nothing more to say at present But Remains your – Truly John
Sinclair

(SinclJ01, 1872)

It is not entirely clear from these letters what exactly motivates the *-s* form in these
contexts. Is it simply the effect of the dialectal northern *-s* rule, which was part of the
local vernacular in much of Ireland and would have been available to many of the
writers in the corpus, just as it was to the Scots writers in the seventeenth-century
examples in (5)? However, the 'but remains' formula is also found in the letters

of writers whose English is otherwise fairly close to the standard, and who avoid non-standard verbal *-s* elsewhere. The verbal *-s* form tends to appear with much greater regularity in the salutation formula than it does elsewhere in the letters. Or is the usage to be explained as a syntactic reanalysis, such that the salutation formula was felt to be a subject–verb inversion structure, with the writer's signature acting as a postposed grammatical subject, hence demanding a verb in the regular third person singular form? Did the availability of verbal *-s* in the vernacular and its occurrence in perceived models of standard English reinforce each other to produce this stereotyped usage? Whatever the motivation, the crucial fact is that we are dealing with a structure that is neither part of the authentic local vernacular nor of authentic contemporary standard English, but part of a specific, localised practice of letter writing, which had its own linguistic rules.

In this chapter, we will explore the possibility that such specialised, text-type-specific grammatical patterns may permeate not just individual, lexically specific formulaic phrases, but may also be employed productively throughout a text. The object of this investigation will be the use of free periphrastic *do*, a grammatical feature that is of considerable interest because it constitutes a place of accidental overlap between archaic standard English and vernacular English in Ireland.

3. The corpus

The study is based on a corpus of private letters written from and to Ireland between the early eighteenth and early twentieth centuries, mostly in the context of emigration to America and Australia, the *Hamburg Corpus of Irish English* (Pietsch 2009b). Private letters have of course played an important role in the study of non-standard varieties for a long time, and Irish emigrant letters in particular have been at the centre of several important studies of the Irish English dialects and their development (Montgomery 1995, 1997; Filppula 1999; McCafferty 2003, 2004; Hickey 2007). The *Hamburg Corpus of Irish English* was compiled in order to enable studies of this type on a larger scale than was previously possible, representing a geographically and diachronically varied sample of private, sub-literary and non-standard texts written by individuals of limited literacy or with limited access to educated standard English.

The corpus comprises some 510,000 words, in just under 1,000 texts from 400 different writers from all parts of Ireland. Most of these were collected by the present author from various archives in Ireland and the United States. In many cases, the search for these documents followed up on references in works such as Miller *et al.* (2003) and others. The corpus material collected from archival documents was complemented for the present study with a number of texts published in print. In addition to several items published in Miller *et al.* (2003), this includes letters from Fitzpatrick (1994) – material which has also previously been used for similar linguistic purposes by Filppula (1999) and McCafferty (2004) – as well as texts from O'Connell (1980), O'Farrell (1984), Houston and Smyth (1991) and

Sullivan (1921–57). Letters written in the context of emigration form the bulk of the material. They are the most plentiful type of text suitable for the purpose and available today because mass emigration, in the eighteenth and even more so from the mid-nineteenth century onwards, was the main factor that prompted substantial numbers of individuals of lower social status and limited literacy to write, and caused their writings to be preserved for posterity; many of these individuals would otherwise have had little or no cause to produce any lasting written output.

For the purposes of dialect comparison, all texts (except for very few where such information was unavailable) were assigned a geographic point of provenance within Ireland, wherever possible down to the level of baronies or at least counties. This was possible in many cases on the basis of information about the writers' or addressees' places of residence or other place names mentioned in the texts, or on the basis of biographical information provided by the archival sources or the published editions. In a few cases, writings by second-generation emigrants were included, where these letters formed part of a larger set of correspondence also involving first-generation emigrants or Irish residents from the same family. Here, too, the texts were counted as representative of the family's place of provenance within Ireland. On the basis of a quantitative comparison of the distributions of several grammatical key variables, locations were grouped into four areal clusters, which correspond approximately to relevant dialectal divisions within Ireland (for a dialectological overview, see Hickey 2007). The four areas are: (a) north-east Ulster, corresponding largely to the northern coastal strip identified by dialectologists as the area of 'Core Ulster Scots' (see Gregg 1972); (b) the rest of Ulster (for dialectological details, see Barry 1981); (c) the south-east, roughly corresponding to the province of Leinster, including coastal and midland areas characterised historically by early anglicisation; and (d) the south-west, roughly corresponding to the provinces of Connacht and Munster, including many areas of late anglicisation and long retention of Irish.

While the corpus aims to cover all areas of Ireland and all time periods between the early eighteenth and the beginnings of the twentieth century, a fully balanced and representative coverage of all areas and periods could not be achieved for practical reasons. The earlier sub-periods, in the eighteenth century, are much less well represented than the nineteenth century, with the bulk of the material clustering between *c.* 1840 and 1900. In addition, the north is somewhat over-represented compared to the south, especially in the earlier parts of the corpus. A full account of the distribution of corpus material, with word counts cross-tabulated for area and time period, is given in Table 12.1.

4. Vernacular periphrastic *do*

In the following section I will focus on one example of how features of vernacular speech and features of what writers perceived of as part of an intended standard norm may interact in letter writing. It concerns the use of non-standard free periphrastic *do* in nineteenth-century letters in the corpus. At the centre of our interest is the

Table 12.1 *Distribution of word counts across areas and time periods in the* Hamburg Corpus of Irish English *(HCIE)*

Period	NE Ulster	Central Ulster	South-East	South-West	(unknown)	Total
–1780	8,896	31,029	12,740	1,766	916	55,347
–1820	18,523	14,834	11,808	12,043	749	57,957
–1840	22,025	7,082	7,060	8,543	594	45,304
–1860	23,763	39,962	35,523	25,789	1,695	126,732
–1880	33,155	41,957	26,609	11,821	8,873	122,415
–1920	13,996	23,412	35,454	28,669	4,643	106,174
Total	120,358	158,276	129,194	88,631	17,470	513,929

finding that seemingly unmotivated *do*, in positions where we would not expect it based on our knowledge of the present-day spoken dialects, occurs with some regularity in the corpus, including its latest sub-periods, as in the Examples (7a–d):

(7) a. I do ever feel gratefull to yous for your very kind care

(CowanRo2, 1886)

   b. Dear Son Rob, this Dos leave us all well

(SinclTo3, 1889)

   c. if Mary Lenighan <u>does</u> wright Home will you remember me to her

(Burke_02, 1882)

   d. My Kind Brother Done his best to find him out for me but to no a vail and Did search so much for him

(SinclJo2, 1894)

As is well known, free periphrastic *do* in non-emphatic affirmative positions was a widespread feature of seventeenth-century written English, but became obsolete in the educated standard soon after. The development of this type of usage has been discussed extensively in the context of tracing the initial rise of *do* as an auxiliary and its subsequent functional specialisation to non-affirmative or emphatic functions in Modern English, beginning with the classic study of Ellegård (1953) (see also Denison 1985; Kroch 1989). Its stylistic and social implications are analysed in Nurmi (1999), Nevalainen (1991) and others. By the nineteenth century, such usage had become thoroughly obsolete in educated standard English. While examples like the ones in (7) do look somewhat similar to earlier ones from the seventeenth-century type in emergent standard English, their preservation in the late nineteenth century is thus something of a surprise.

However, a second possible source must be considered at this point, namely that of authentic vernacular Irish English, because here too, free periphrastic *do* plays an important role. Yet, as we will soon see, this explanation cannot cover all of the usage observed in the letters, because the attested forms do not appear to match semantic patterns characteristic of dialectal Irish English.

According to the dialectological literature on Irish English (for a survey, see Hickey 2007: 213–33), periphrastic *do* is primarily a marker of habitual aspect. In this function, the simple form *do* + infinitive (8a) competes with the combined form *do be* + V-*ing* (8b):

(8)   a. He does play hurling

(Hickey 2007: 216)

      b. He does/do be buying and selling old cars

The literature on the topic (Harris 1986; Filppula 1999: 141; Hickey 2007: 218 and others) is in agreement that the simple *do* + V forms represent an older layer of vernacular speech, historically connected to dialectal input mainly from south-west England (see Ihalainen 1976, 1991; Klemola 1996) during the English colonisation of Ireland. The complex *do* + *be* forms (8b) are a more recent innovation arising out of the earlier simple *do* forms in a kind of structural reinforcement, possibly in partial structural imitation of similar habitual + progressive combinations in Irish (see Hickey 2007: 222–4). Its emergence can be dated no earlier than the early nineteenth century. In the present-day vernaculars, the plain type *do* + V is found only as a residual form 'in the south of Ireland in vernacular rural varieties', whereas the complex *do be* type is the most commonly used form in present-day vernacular Irish English elsewhere (*ibid.*).

In our corpus, the data for the *do be* construction appear to confirm this established picture. It is best attested in the south-east, with only a few attestations also in central Ulster and in the south-west, and missing completely in the 'Core Ulster Scots' areas of the north-east. All attestations in the corpus clearly have habitual meaning. The earliest examples are from the 1840s and 1850s. Most of them display *be* as a copula verb (9); the earliest token of *do be* V-*ing*, with *be* in auxiliary function, is from 1860 (10):

(9)   *do be* (copula)
      a. I do be at work hard sometimes loading Teams for up the Country

(Normil04, 1855)

      b. What happens in Ireland to day <u>does be</u> on the papers tomorrow

(EliotA05, 1900)

(10)   *do be* V-*ing*
      a. you need not be troubleing yourself mentioning so many neighbours as you <u>don'</u> <u>be</u> losing your time or wasting paper

(CurtiH01, 1845)

      b. the skin comes off and it <u>dose be</u> long healing.

(CarroJ09, 1860)

However, with simple *do* + lexical verb, a comparison of the attestations in the *HCIE* with the present-day Irish English vernacular, on the one hand, and the historically related south-west England dialects, on the other, reveals that the situation may be more complex. In south-west England, non-emphatic affirmative periphrastic *do* is attested both in the present and past tense. In both tenses, it has a strong tendency to correlate with the expression of habitual aspect, although it is not firmly restricted to this use (Klemola 1998: 45; Kortmann 2004: 255–6). In the present tense, the auxiliary is typically realised as an uninflected, invariant form *do*, typically in a phonologically weakened form [də]. Examples are provided following Klemola (1998: 41) (Example (11); from fieldworker notebook data of the *Survey of English Dialects*) and Wagner (2008: 435) (Example (12); from the *Freiburg Corpus of English Dialects*):

(11)   a. I do ([də]) know a bit about them
       b. He do ([də]) want to hide it

(12)   a. As I do say to my niece, I say, you know, you're far better off
       b. William, my son, do live down there
       c. . . . and then I <u>did</u> cut 'em off as they did grow

In contrast, those (conservative) modern Irish dialects that still have simple *do* + V are reported to use it only as a habitual, and only in the present tense (Bliss 1972: 80; Kallen 1989). The option of uninflected *do* is preserved partly in some Irish varieties (Hickey 2007: 175, 218), but today it alternates with inflected *do(es)*.

Based on these points of comparison, we would now expect the following situation in the data: simple periphrastic *do* should occur mainly in the south, especially the south-east, where the dialectal input from south-west England was most direct, but not in the Scots-influenced north. It should display a tendency to occur in the non-inflected *do* form. Its use should display a tendency towards becoming semantically specialised for the present-tense habitual meaning, although it may be expected that this specialisation might not yet be complete. Habitual simple periphrastic *do* should occur in the data earlier than the complex *do be* forms.

However, several of these expectations are not borne out. While free periphrastic *do* is relatively frequent across the whole corpus, with 214 examples in a corpus of just over 500,000 words, only a fairly small number of these (31 examples of simple *do*, plus 13 of the specific combination *do be*) appear to mark habituality. Whereas attestations in non-habitual environments are abundant from the earliest sub-periods of the corpus (Table 12.2), unambiguously habitual-iterative examples appear only from the middle of the nineteenth century onwards (13), at around the same time as the complex *do be* forms:

(13)   a. bees do thrive and multiply in this country far better than with youes

                                                        (CarroNo1, 1839, Co. Fermanagh)

Table 12.2 *Periphrastic* do *constructions in the* HCIE, *by sub-period*

| | | do | | | | do be | | Total | |
| | | non-habitual | | habitual | | | | | |
	words	No.	freq.	No.	freq.	No.	freq.	No.	freq.
–1830	130,583	24	1.8	2	0.1	–	0.0	26	1.9
–1870	231,291	37	1.6	5	0.2	4	0.2	46	1.1
–1940	147,278	49	3.3	24	1.6	9	0.6	82	5.6
Total	509,370	110	2.9	31	0.6	13	0.3	154	3

Table 12.3 *Periphrastic* do *constructions in the* HCIE, *by region*

| | | Non-habitual do + V | | Habitual do + V | | do be | |
	words	No.	freq.	No.	freq.	No.	freq.
NE Ulster	115,581	19	1.6	–	–	–	–
Central Ulster	158,276	42	2.7	10	0.6	2	0.1
South-east	129,194	33	2.6	10	0.8	9	0.7
South-west	88,631	12	1.4	9	1.0	2	0.2

b. all other things that <u>dos become</u> on small farm

(FoardMo1, 1847, Co. Sligo)

c. I do scend you & Mr. Shannon a paper every month.

(Normil13, 1863, Co. Clare)

Table 12.2 shows that there is no sign of the non-habitual attestations becoming less frequent towards the later parts of the corpus – if anything, the later texts show periphrastic *do* more frequently in all use types, habitual and non-habitual alike.

Geographically, attestations of habitual *do* + V appear relatively evenly distributed across the whole island except for the Scots-speaking areas of north-east Ulster. The *do be* construction is more strongly concentrated in the south, particularly the south-east. Non-habitual *do* + V, in contrast, appears everywhere in Ireland, including those north-eastern areas where the habitual constructions are missing (Table 12.3).

As for the morphological variants, uninflected *do* in third person singular environments appears only quite rarely in the corpus, in the texts of a single writer, Annie Carrol from Co. Louth, writing in the 1890s (Example (14)):

(14) a. she do all ways ask when I here from you

(CarroA15, 1895)

    b. she is well <u>she do</u> all way^s ask for you

(CarroA07, 1899)

In all other cases of periphrastic *do*, third person singular clauses display the regular inflected form *does* (nineteen tokens); moreover, inflected *does* is also found in eight out of fifteen tokens of third person plural clauses, showing that the periphrastic *do* constructions (both habitual and non-habitual) tend to partake of the general dialectal agreement pattern that licenses such plural verbal *-s*, the so-called Northern Subject Rule (see McCafferty 2004; Pietsch 2005).

5. Non-vernacular periphrastic *do*

We are thus left with the question of how to account for the high frequency and long persistence of the non-habitual *do* + V forms, which appear not to match the expected dialectal picture of modern Irish English. Could they be simply a leftover of the original vernacular forms of south-west English extraction? A first argument militating against such an account is that they fail to match expected dialectological properties. This applies to their structural form, i.e. their failure to co-occur with the non-inflected form of *do* inherited from south-west England. It also applies to their geographical distribution, i.e. the failure to show significant clustering in those dialect areas most strongly associated with south-west English settler input. Moreover, many instances of this kind of periphrastic *do*, especially in the earlier sub-periods of the corpus, occur in writers of relatively high levels of literacy, who display little vernacular interference in their writing otherwise.

On the other hand, these occurrences of *do* can easily be linked with those in formal written registers of emergent standard English of a much earlier time. But how long did such forms survive? While most historical-sociolinguistic studies of the development of standard English do not go much further than the seventeenth century, implying that free periphrastic *do* ceases to play a significant role after that time, Tieken-Boon van Ostade (1987) provides an analysis of its final demise. According to her analysis of sixteen representative writers of educated eighteenth-century prose from Daniel Defoe to Fanny Burney, free periphrastic *do* still occurs marginally around 1700 but is virtually absent in writings after *c.* 1710, except in certain favourable environments, where it continues to be found at a low rate throughout the eighteenth century. But even according to her account, a survival into the mid or even late nineteenth century would be unexpected.

Among the favouring environments are collocations with verbs like *assure, request, confess*. Tieken-Boon van Ostade's findings echo earlier remarks by authors such as Ellegård (1953: 172), who enumerates 'verbs of strong emotional content, such as *believe, beseech, assure, confess*' among the favouring environments, and Sweet (1898: 89–90), who speaks of 'verbs of requesting – *I do entreat you* – and asserting – *I do assure you*'. Most of the verbs in question are thus typical performative verbs. The *do* periphrasis appears to be used as a conventionalised rhetorical means of highlighting the communicative act performed through them.

Speech-act verbs such as *assure, entreat* or *request* are naturally frequent in the letters of the present corpus, and indeed, many of the attested tokens of non-habitual *do* occur in just these kinds of collocations with speech-act verbs (Example (15)):

(15) a. for *I do assure* you I did not mis writing to you in this world

(SteelJ02, 1806)

   b. Agness *does Request* me to warn you to look to yourself

(McCanc01, 1856)

   c. In Concluson *I do ask* you to Write to me and Gratify Me Before I do leave this uncertain World and when you do write pleas to Direct to the Care of Mr. James Ohanlin

(Hammon07, 1857)

Other sentences of a performative nature are also favoured, e.g. in (16):

(16) a. therefore *we Do Joyn* in requesting y.ᵉ favour

(ArmitJ01, 1724)

   b. *I doe Expect* to heere from you by next Crismas

(Wansbr02, 1728)

   c. and all your inqiring friends *do Send* their Love also

(ArmstJ01, 1825)

Another favourable context pointed out by Tieken-Boon van Ostade is found where certain adverbs intervene between the auxiliary *do* and the lexical infinitive. These contexts, too, are frequently found in the non-habitual instances in the *HCIE*, e.g. in (17):

(17) The good Bargains of your lands in that Country *Doe* greatly encourage me to pluck up my spirits

(Lindse01, 1758)

The hypothesis that the use of *do* in those non-habitual contexts where it cannot be motivated by the semantic patterns of the modern vernacular is directly related to the older use types in the emergent standard English of the seventeenth and eighteenth centuries is also supported by the observation that this form of *do* appears to co-occur in the output of the same writers with other features that are also apparently part of a conservative, intentionally formal written style. The corpus contains writings from authors of different degrees of exposure to standard English and different degrees of education, and some of them clearly are more strongly influenced by conservative models of perceived formal standard English than others. While it is not possible at present to quantitatively test hypotheses about co-occurrence between such features with statistical accuracy, owing to small numbers and skewed distribution of tokens in the corpus, it is nevertheless useful to include some qualitative discussion of relevant examples.

Among the features suitable for such a study are the introduction and salutation formulae mentioned earlier. As was pointed out at the beginning in Section 2, these were stylistic elements inherited from older forms of formal standard English. Detached from the stylistic development of standard written English proper as used by educated writers, they had been preserved and had assumed a life of their own in the letter-writing culture of less-educated writers, but were clearly regarded and intended by their users as an element of proper, formal style.

A good example of the kind of letter that contains non-habitual *do* together with these formulae is that of John Armstrong, a farmer from Antrim, writing in 1825. He has the classic introduction formula, in Example (18a), with a typical grammatical inconsistency – the anaphoric phrase *in the Same* is missing its conventional antecedent *in good health* – that clearly points to its character as a formulaic memorised element. He also uses the *no more but remains* formula, e.g. in (18b). Non-habitual *do* occurs in the context of another highly conventionalised element of letter writing, the transmitting of mutual greetings from and to *all your inqiring friends*, e.g. Example (18c):

(18)   a.   Dear Son and daughter we take this operunity Fo letting you know that
             we are All well Thank god for it hoping those fue Linds Will find you in
             the Same.

                                                                          (ArmstJo1, 1825)

       b.   no more remains at Present but Remains your loving Father and mother
             to Death

                                                                          (ArmstJo1, 1825)

       c.   and all your inqiring friends do Send their Love also

                                                                          (ArmstJo1, 1825)

The example from Mary Devlin, County Armagh (Fitzpatrick 1994: 384–5) is similar. She, too, uses a variant of the conventional introductory formula – albeit a somewhat shortened one, Example (19a) – as well as the typical final salutation formula, Example (19b). Non-habitual *do* occurs several times throughout the letter, once already in the initial formula itself and several times in contexts of performative speech acts related to the act of letter writing (*I do address, I do ask, I do acknowledge*, Examples (19c–d)):

(19) a. To you I do address this few lines and do hope the shall find you and
          Family possessing good helth and happiness.

                                                               (Hammon07, 1857)

      b. No more at present but Remains Your Affactionate Mother to death:

                                                               (Hammon07, 1857)

      c. In Concluson I do ask you to Write to me and Gratify Me Before I do
          leave this uncertain World and when you do write pleas to Direct to the
          Care of Mr. James Ohanlin.

                                                               (Hammon07, 1857)

      d. But to you My Son & Daughter With you all My Dear Grand Children
          to I do Most Greatfully Acknowledge the Kindness you dun to me.

                                                               (Hammon07, 1857)

Another stylistic indicator of an intended formal register of standard written
English is the use of complex subordinating sentence constructions, in particular
the use of sentence-level *which* relatives. Letter writers make frequent use of this
feature, often in the context of the opening formula. Many of the less-schooled
writers do so in a variety of non-standard ways, where the relativiser *which* lacks
either a clear referent in the preceding sentence, or a syntactic role in the following
clause, e.g. (20a–b):

(20) a. Mr Gamble has been often teling me that he saw you diff^nt times before
          he left that Country, and that you Could give him a very Good
          description of this part of the Country, <u>which</u> I was very Glad to Learn
          you was so well acqainted with the history of this new Country

                                                               (McArtho1, 1802)

      b. I got Your letter about 10 days ago which I often wandered were You
          dead or what became of You.

                                                               (Burke_03, 1884)

This type of unbound *which*, again, often co-occurs with non-habitual periphrastic
do in the same texts. Thus, for instance, David Lindsey, a farmer from Ulster
writing in 1758, has both (21a) and (21b). A similar observation holds for Robert
Cowan, a tenant farmer from County Down writing a hundred years later (22a–b),
and for Biddy Burke, an emigrant from Connacht in Australia writing in the 1880s
(23a–b; Fitzpatrick 1994: 185–8):

(21) a. I had upertunity of reading your letter that was sent to your fatherinlaw,
          which gave me great satisfaction to here you were all in good health

                                                               (Lindse01, 1758)

      b. The good Bargains of your lands in that Country Doe greatly encourage
          me to pluck up my spirits

                                                               (Lindse01, 1758)

(22) a. I add no more at prasant which remains your affectionate ancle until
      death Robert Cowan

(CowanR01, 1868)

      b. I do ever feel gratefull to yous for your very kind care

(CowanR02, 1886)

(23) a. Not forgetting my sister Winnifred & my One Dear Mary An & Delia
      which I am Longing for the day that I will be gone down the Bay to meet
      them

(Burke_02, 1882)

      b. I did feel the heat so much boath night & day we could not sleep.

(Burke_03, 1884)

A final question remains: if the use of non-habitual *do* is a register-specific feature of intended formal written English, and as such at least partly unrelated to the genuine vernacular use of *do* as a habitual marker in the spoken dialect, do these two types of use ever occur together in the same texts? Is there any indication that the two types of periphrastic *do* interacted with each other in the idiolectal performance of individual writers, for instance, in such a way that the availability of one form also increased the likelihood of use of the other? The answer, though not definite, appears to be largely negative. The letters tend to have either the vernacular habitual *do*, or the archaic formal *do*, but not both together. While there are a few writers who show both vernacular habitual *do* and some occasional use of past-tense *do* of seemingly unspecific semantic value, there is none that combines vernacular habitual *do* with the use types most characteristic of the archaic tradition illustrated above, in particular the use of present-tense *do* in performative speech acts.

6. Conclusions

We have found evidence that the use of non-habitual *do* in the corpus is a register-specific feature of intended formal written English and largely unrelated to the genuine vernacular use of *do* as a habitual marker in spoken Irish English. The question we are then left with is: through what channels were these use types preserved in this sub-literary written register and text type for such a long time, when the mainstream development of educated standard English had long disposed of them?

It appears that the conventional wisdom that regards letters as one of the historical text types most closely approximating spoken language needs to be treated with some reservations. In certain social and historical situations, letter writing can preserve stylistic and even grammatical features that reflect older forms originally associated with a high formal register of much earlier periods, and may thus take on the appearance of a linguistically conservative, even archaising medium. The explanation for this conservatism is without doubt related to the writers' lack of familiarity with the living mainstream of the written standard language of their time, but also to the degree of formality inherent in the situation of letter writing. For many writers of limited schooling and limited everyday contact with the written medium, letter writing was no light task to take up. Especially in the case of the emigrant families whose writings form the bulk of our corpus, it was often only extreme situations in a person's biography that caused them to 'take up their pen'. Writing letters in situations like this, negotiating the fates of entire families, or attempting to uphold family ties across the huge geographic and biographic distances of emigration meant that a family letter was automatically an occasion of much higher formality than we would otherwise associate with this text type.

Letter writers were thus undoubtedly under a strong expectation of attempting the best approximation of what they considered 'good' English grammar and a 'good' style. At the same time, writing standard English must have felt like an alien medium to many of them. What kinds of linguistic models would such writers then turn to? For many of them, exposure to genuine contemporary standard English in their everyday lives would have been fairly limited, except for the English they heard and read at church or through religious literature, occasional contact with the authorities and perhaps occasional reading of a newspaper. In this situation, letter writers were prone to resort to close imitation of the most direct kind of linguistic model they had available: other letters they had received or seen written in their immediate social environment. Letter writing could thus become a relatively self-contained domain of linguistic conventionalisation, with relatively little correcting input from the written standard English used in more educated sectors of society.

The availability of models for such imitation can be explained through the fact that correspondence through letters was in many instances not a merely private but a shared, social event, which ensured that its linguistic conventions could be transmitted across a local community of practice. Letters received from relatives abroad were preserved, cherished and frequently shared with friends or family members or read out in a family gathering – the letters themselves are full of references to such practices (see Elspaß 2005: 100 for a comparable observation regarding German writers). The memory of letters that were orally shared in this way no doubt provided many subsequent writers with the material for just that stylistic and formulaic imitation whose effects we have observed. In the absence of much other exposure to written English, the experience of listening to letters from others would, for some, constitute a substantial portion of an individual's overall intake of written English, crucially shaping their perception of what the norms of standard written English were. Another factor that certainly also contributed to an effect of conventionalisation, and thus, stylistic conservatism, was of course the widespread practice – extremely common among persons near the lower end of the literacy scale – of having letters written for them on dictation, by friends or acquaintances thought to possess a better command of standard English.

Taking these conditions into account, we can begin to understand how grammatical features that were originally part of an outdated and alien variety could become salient to speakers-writers in these local communities. People would perceive and appropriate them as markers of an intended linguistic register, of 'proper' written language, thus constructing their own social meaning for them, in an act of what Eckert (2008) and Agha (2004) have called 'enregisterment'. This register of 'intended' Standard English was defined through the shared linguistic practice of letter-writing communities held together by local family and friendship ties. While it essentially embodied the writers' stereotyped construction of the linguistic styles of other, higher social classes, it could to some extent maintain a life of its own away from the mainstream of the written Standard English those classes would have used themselves.[2] Thus, the shared practice of letter writing could result in the creation of a relatively stable linguistic tradition constituting its own, sub-literary, and possibly regionally confined, linguistic quasi-standard. This then was able to preserve outdated stylistic models and, with them, grammatical structures that were long obsolete in the mainstream of the development of Standard English.

[2] I am indebted to Richard Watts (p.c.) for stimulating feedback regarding the social significance of linguistic self-construction in this matter.

CHAPTER 13

Assessing heterogeneity

Lucia Siebers

1. Introduction

The study of letters as a source for the origin of African American English (hence-forth AAE) has become an established approach in the field of American dialectol-ogy. This approach goes back to a study in the early 1990s (Montgomery *et al.* 1993), in which the authors compare a set of letters written by African Americans during the Civil War with letters written by members of a Scotch-Irish immigrant family. While letters have been used for the purpose of studying dialectal characteristics since the 1950s (for Southern American Vernacular English, see Stephenson 1956), this source for AAE was only discovered for linguistic study two decades ago, since for a long time it was assumed that no such letters by African Americans existed due to the high rate of illiteracy among this ethnic group. Publications of such letters by social historians in the late 1970s and early 1980s (e.g. Starobin 1974; Miller 1978; Wiley 1980; Berlin *et al.* 1982) have shown that such letters indeed exist and have been preserved in some archives, although these letters arguably represent only a small fraction of literate and in most cases semi-literate writers of the African American population. As Montgomery *et al.* (1993) have convincingly shown, due to the fact that these letters are unedited and the writers were unschooled, they can be fruitfully used for dialectological purposes, as they potentially open up a win-dow on putative speech patterns of African Americans in the nineteenth century. Although they are written sources and therefore considered as indirect evidence, it is reasonable to assume that the lack of any standardising influences resulted in the survival of spoken-language forms (non-standard forms that normally would not have passed through the standard filter in writing) or at least speech-like patterns. One should add here that it is of course difficult to distinguish real spoken-language forms from those that merely appear as such (structures that the writers included because they assumed them to be 'standard'). While these letters are of particular interest in the controversy over the origin of AAE, they also contribute to recent approaches of a language history 'from below' (see Elspaß *et al.* 2007).

This chapter will analyse parts of a corpus of letters written by semi-literate African Americans from the 1760s to the 1910s. While this corpus comprises many different regions and time periods and thus potentially offers insights into earlier stages of the variety, it also poses a number of problems. With such a variety of periods and different sociohistorical conditions, and, what is more, different degrees of literacy, we should expect a high degree of heterogeneity. The main aim of this chapter is to approach and assess the heterogeneity of earlier AAE in this corpus. I will do so by subjecting the letters to an analysis of two selected non-standard features, *was/were* variation and present *be* and *have*. The sociohistorical contexts of the different collections contained in the corpus are so different that to group all the letters together in such an analysis would be to compare apples and pears. I have therefore selected two collections from under-researched regions to investigate the amount of regional heterogeneity and to test how the results compare to earlier studies, especially those on the so-called Deep South (Louisiana, Mississippi, Alabama, Georgia and South Carolina). Before I proceed with the analysis, the following sections will present an overview on literacy in nineteenth-century America and introduce the data.

2. The study of African American English and the notion of heterogeneity

Twentieth-century (urban) AAE is remarkably homogeneous, a characteristic of this variety that seems to have emerged throughout the southern colonies (Winford 1997: 308). Such homogeneity might have led many researchers to believe that this has always been the case in the development of this variety, ignoring the many differences that obtained with regard to the demographics and sociohistorical conditions in the different contact settings across the states.

Research into the origin and development of AAE has proved controversial and has led to a longstanding dispute, basically between two opposing camps, the creolist and the dialectologist position. Early views espoused by proponents of the two fields are no longer shared, since dialectologists as well as creolists based their explanations on the assumption that earlier AAE was a fairly homogeneous variety; the label 'monolithic' is often used in this context. As Winford has argued, the focus on a 'single-origin' explanation in both camps has actually fuelled the debate:

> Quite often, it seems to me, disagreements about the structure and continuing development of AAVE arise from failure to take account of the fact that AAVE has never been a single monolithic variety, but differs across regions and classes and urban and rural settings. (Winford 1997: 313)

More recent approaches are characterised by a much more differentiated account of earlier stages of the variety and one increasingly finds references to earlier forms of AAE where it is seen 'as a collection of varieties' (Montgomery *et al.* 1993: 353). Schneider (1997: 50) even argues that these are reasons 'to posit Black (or African American) English*es*' (emphasis in the original), acknowledging the complex social history and the very diverse contact scenarios. Exactly these very different contact scenarios, from which very different varieties emerged, have led various scholars (e.g. Winford 1997, 1998; Schneider 1997; Kautzsch and Schneider 2000) to espouse compromise positions:

> It is likely that the second language varieties of settler English spoken by Africans varied to some extent from area to area and from period to period, depending on the nature of the contact, the mix of languages and the model presented to them. (Winford 1997: 307–8)

These very different settings have resulted in very different outcomes, i.e. more creole-like as well as more dialect-like varieties, so proponents of both camps have had ample evidence to claim either a dialect or creole origin. The aim of this chapter is to have a closer look at the notion of the heterogeneity of earlier AAE and how this can be studied with a corpus of letters.

3. Letters as a source for earlier AAE

As already mentioned in the introduction, there are a number of advantages regarding the use of letters for the study of earlier AAE. The greatest advantage certainly lies in the fact that letters allow us to study AAE in periods for which no direct evidence (i.e. recordings) exists. Other valuable sources that have been used so far, e.g. the ex-slave narratives of the Federal Writers Project for the Works Project Administration (WPA) (Schneider 1989), are limited in terms of their time scope in that they usually do not allow us to make any claims about the development well before the Civil War. Thus, through the study of letters we can go further back in time. Furthermore, most letters are datable and localisable, i.e. they give us the time and region in which they were written.

Despite these advantages, there are also a number of problems that we encounter when using such letters. In an important article, Montgomery (1999: 22–6) has raised four issues concerning the linguistic validity of semi-literate letters that need to be considered when working with such documents. I will briefly discuss them at this point. The first deals with authorship. The greatest challenge is to try to make sure that the letters actually were written by African Americans. Since the illiteracy rate was so high among this group (see Section 4), it was not uncommon to use an amanuensis. Therefore, letters need to be critically evaluated as to whether they really stem from African Americans. It is impossible in many cases to make reliable judgements about authorship, but we have to make use of the available information. Wolfram (2000: 45) points out the necessity of this and recommends assessing the authenticity of these documents and 'imposing strict conditions that take into account the general historical situations, the specific sociolinguistic circumstances of the author, the nature of the text and the purposes for writing' (see also Section 5). Occasionally, we find explicit references to the amanuensis when he or she gives the reason for writing on behalf of someone else. In other cases, this is much more difficult, and only through a comparison of the handwriting in the originals can the letters be identified as dictations.

The next issue concerns the use of models. How exactly the semi-literate writers acquired their smattering of literacy we generally do not know. We therefore need to draw on literacy studies as much as possible to learn more about the acquisitional context. As Cornelius (1983: 173) has pointed out, the fact that 'neither slaves nor those slaveowners and other whites who taught them could proclaim their activities safely' makes it impossible in most cases to assess the degree of schooling they may have had. The use of formulae by the writers suggests that they were aware of certain letter conventions. Whether they were taught how to write a letter by somebody, used other letters as models or even used letter-writing manuals is difficult to ascertain, although some form of letter-writing instruction is not unlikely. However, the fact that even these formulae are written in non-standard orthography seems to indicate that these were not copied down from any of these sources. Montgomery (1999: 24) sees this as evidence that the semi-literate writers were oriented towards oral rather than written models.

The third point concerns the manipulation of the written code. The question here is whether the samples merely illustrate the struggles of the writers to come to terms with (standard) orthography or rather an approximation of it, or whether these attempts at literacy reveal 'orderly variation' (Montgomery 1999: 24). The many phonetic spellings seem to indicate that the writers did not produce unsystematic forms that are just not standard but rather wrote the way they spoke and thus possibly rendered local pronunciation or dialectal forms.

The last point is the question of representativeness. To what extent is the language studied in the letters representative of the community in question? With a high rate of illiteracy, it is likely that the writings mainly represent those of the literate elite. However, as Montgomery argues, this does not necessarily imply that the literate minority represented an elitist group. As will be discussed in the next section, literacy was often the result of fortunate circumstances.

4. Literacy in nineteenth-century America

In order to evaluate the letters and their linguistic significance, it is important to know more about African American literacy. While the letters themselves can be taken as direct evidence of African Americans' (partial) literacy, they usually tell us little about how reading and writing were learned. So we have to look for indirect evidence, which is likewise hard to come by. As Cornelius points out, the very fact that it is difficult to gain further insights into how well African Americans could read and/or write is not surprising, since neither those who taught nor those who were taught 'could proclaim their activity safely' (1983: 173). In addition to the fact that most slaveholders did not have an interest in teaching their slaves how to read and write, the situation was further complicated and the acquisition further hindered by a number of so-called anti-literacy statutes that were stipulated in many states; South Carolina was the first as early as 1740, which has to be seen as a direct consequence of the Stono rebellion in 1739 (Williams 2005: 13). Such rebellious attempts prompted the prohibition of writing because whites assumed that written communication was used by slaves in order to organise such rebellions. A century later, in 1831, Nat Turner's rebellion was the reason or the occasion for many other states, e.g. Georgia, North Carolina, Louisiana and Virginia, to implement similar laws.

Such attempts to prohibit the instruction of reading and writing did not have the desired effects, and literacy became more and more a symbol of resistance and power. In response, African Americans established clandestine schools and other forms of underground teaching and developed some form of 'eavesdropping intelligence network and grape-vine telegraph' (Williams 2005: 9). These were some of the strategies developed by African Americans in an environment where they were actively discouraged – to say the least – from learning to read and write, and this was usually the norm. However, there were a few exceptions when African Americans were taught to read mainly for religious purposes, for example by masters' (evangelical) wives. In even fewer cases, masters actively encouraged their slaves to read and write; one such master was the Virginian plantation owner John Hartwell Cocke. He participated in the repatriation scheme of the American Colonisation Society and considered the instruction of his slaves an important prerequisite for their emigration to Liberia (Miller 1990: 34).

Despite all efforts and laws to deny African Americans access to literacy, a minority succeeded in their 'covert mission' to become literate, and the letters that have survived (and even more so the motives and content of writing) suggest that letter writing formed part of this covert mission. In the following quotation, Monaghan and Troutman summarise some of the opportunities African Americans seized to learn to read and write:

> They learned occasionally from devout white masters and more often from devout white mistresses; they learned from white children, either openly or by trickery; they learned from free blacks; and they learned from other literate slaves, who passed on the precious knowledge in clandestine schools. (Monaghan 1999: 338–9)

> Literacy involved stealth, an evangelical mistress, a tolerant master, or all three. Among this tiny literate minority, few found much time to write. Fewer still succeeded in getting their letters past white censors. When slaves managed to write under such circumstances, they clearly had something important to say. (Troutman 2006: 216–17)

Reliable figures on the percentage of this minority are hard to come by. In estimating the numbers of literate African Americans, it is important to distinguish between the ability to read and to write. Naturally, the percentage of those who could read was much higher, usually rated at about 25% (Monaghan 1999: 339). As for writing, the estimates range between 5 and 10% (*ibid.*; Cornelius 1991: 8–9). While most of these figures are rough estimates, Cornelius (1983) has based her numbers on a quantitative investigation of reports on literacy matters in the ex-slave narratives. Out of the 3,428 interviews, 5% (179) reported having learned to read and write during slavery.

5. The data

The data that will serve as the basis for the subsequent analysis are all taken from the *Corpus of Older African American Letters* (henceforth *COAAL*), a project that was initiated at the University of Regensburg in 2007.[1] The corpus is the largest and most diverse repository of earlier AAE and consists of over 1,500 letters by several hundred writers, stretching from the 1760s to the 1910s, covering more than ten states (Louisiana, South Carolina, North Carolina, DC, Maryland, Missouri, Alabama, Kansas, Massachusetts, Connecticut, Tennessee, Georgia and Indian Territory).

First, the corpus draws together many letters by African Americans that were published in historical collections. These are general collections of letters by slaves and former slaves (Starobin 1974), letters by African Americans from Nova Scotia who emigrated to Sierra Leone (Fyfe 1991), letters written by emancipated slaves to the Federal Bureau of Refugees, Freedmen and Abandoned Lands, commonly referred to as Freedmen's Bureau (see also Berlin *et al.* 1982) and letters by immigrants to Liberia to their former masters or American Colonisation Society officials (American Colonisation Society Papers, Wiley 1980 and Miller 1978). Some of these letters have been used for linguistic analyses (e.g. Montgomery *et al.* 1993; Kautzsch 2002; Montgomery 1999; van Herk and Walker 2005). Secondly, the corpus contains new unpublished archival material that has not been considered for linguistic purposes as yet. As for the archival material, there are two collections on which this chapter is based: the Benecke Family Papers and the letters from the Chickasaws and Choctaw freedmen.

With regard to letter typology, a common distinction is that between private and official letters.[2] Due to the many obstacles African Americans had to overcome, writers usually had a good reason or, more precisely, a strong motivation to go to the trouble of writing a letter. In his 'typology of colloquial letter writers', Montgomery distinguishes between basically three types of semi-literate writers: 'desperadoes', 'lonelyhearts' and 'functionaries' (1999: 26). Good examples of 'lonelyhearts' are, for example, soldiers writing letters to their families during the Civil War. While loneliness no doubt must have been a strong motive to write to members of the family, most letters are concerned with matters that were vital for survival. A state of desperation provided motivation for the writers to compose such letters to authorities from whom they sought assistance. Therefore, a typical letter genre and a good example of the 'desperado' type is the official letter that is addressed to authorities. With regard to the motives and possibly the composition of the letters,

---

[1] Support from the German National Research Foundation (DFG) for the compilation of the corpus and the archival research is gratefully acknowledged (2007–11, Project director Edgar W. Schneider, DFG SCHN/388/12-1).

[2] A more fine-grained distinction, e.g. Bergs' socio-pragmatic approach (2007a), distinguishes between five sub-types: reports, requests, orders, counsel and phatic letters. However, such a typology in all its variety does not necessarily apply to those who could barely write. Almost all of the letters fall into the category of requests.

parallels can be drawn with the pauper letters discussed in this volume (see, e.g., Laitinen, Fairman, Allen). One such institution that was specifically created for providing assistance to African Americans after the Civil War was the Freedmen's Bureau mentioned above.

Other authorities or persons who provided help were the pension claim agents. They acted as a kind of intermediary between the pension applicants and the pension attorneys and forwarded the claims on behalf of the veterans (Shaffer 2004: 125). One such pension claim agent was Louis Benecke from Brunswick in Missouri, whose papers form part of the corpus and will be introduced below.

As I have argued above, in order to pay due attention to the heterogeneity involved in African American letters, it makes sense to look at some letter collections separately and say more about the context in which they were written. The Benecke Papers comprise 103 letters to pension claims agent Louis Benecke, spanning the years 1890–1910. The letters were written either by the veterans themselves or, in case of their decease, by their widows.[3] Benecke was one of the founders and later the commander of the Brunswick post of the Grand Army of the Republic (GAR), an organisation and network for war veterans (not least to advocate their pension claims) that was founded after the Civil War and revived in the 1880s (Benecke Family Papers, n.p.).

The second collection of letters also provides good examples of the desperado type. The institution addressed here is the government of the United States, i.e. the Commissioner of Indian Affairs or the Secretary of the Department of the Interior. This collection comprises sixty-two letters written between 1885 and 1905 by freedmen in Indian Territory in present-day Oklahoma.[4] These African Americans were former slaves of the Choctaws and Chickasaws, two Native American ethnic groups belonging to the Five Civilized Tribes in the south-east. The sociohistorical context of these two collections will be discussed in more detail in Section 7.

Notwithstanding the differences with regard to the writers' motivation, they can all be considered semi-literate writers, i.e. they lack formal education and were therefore largely unaffected by the standardising influence of formal writing. If the only familiar mode is the spoken mode, the usual differences found between spoken and written registers are not necessarily entirely absent, but the writing at least resembles speech. Some of the characteristics of semi-literate writing are discussed in the next section.

---

[3] With the Dependent Pension Act in 1890, the pension legislation was improved so that widows and children of African American veterans could also apply for a pension (Shaffer 2004: 122; Regosin 2002: 37). This resulted in the increase of the number of pension files. Many of the letters from the Benecke collection (see below) were written after the new pension act was passed, which also explains the large number of female writers. For further details regarding the pension application procedure, see Shaffer (2004) and Regosin (2002).

[4] I am greatly indebted to Claudio Saunt for bringing this collection to my attention and providing detailed references for the National Archives.

6. Heterogeneity in writing: individual literacies

The most obvious form of heterogeneity in (letter) writing is the mode of representation. Due to the absence of a standard in non-standard writing, every writer has his or her own interpretation of the written mode. First and foremost, this is borne out by phonetic spelling, which is a clear indicator that the writer is not familiar with standard orthography but largely writes as he or she speaks, which results in either very individual interpretations of unusual or infrequent words, or in actually quite similar non-standard variants which highlight the lack of correspondence between phonemes and graphemes in English orthography. Other characteristics are the lack of punctuation, random capitalisation, etc. While unconventional spellings support the idea that the writer is not highly educated, the spellings are not generally of interest unless they are phonologically significant. The same applies to grammar: while we often find a number of non-standard features in semi-literate writing, these do not necessarily tell us anything about the writer's vernacular. While non-standard writing is easily identified 'just by being not standard' (Fairman 2007c: 271), it is more difficult to evaluate the type of non-standardness that we typically find. This question has been addressed in a number of recent papers by Fairman (2006, 2007a, see below).

To illustrate the range of non-standardness that we find among the letters in the corpus, two examples are presented which can be seen as two opposite ends on the scale of non-standardness. The first is the letter from someone who obviously struggles to compose a letter for a number of reasons. It has been chosen to represent the pole furthest away from the standard, probably best captured by Fairman's notion of 'nowhere-near-Standard' scripts (Fairman 2007b: 172). First of all, the letter is remarkable in that it is the earliest extant direct record of an African-American in the colonial period, written in 1723, and the 'earliest known plea in the history of American slavery for liberation of a group of slaves' (Ingersoll 1994: 777–8). The dramatic nature of the letter can be seen by the addressee. Being aware that it could have had the most drastic consequences, the author(s?) preferred to remain anonymous. Ingersoll points out that the letter was written following a few rebellious plots in Virginia:

(1)   Anonymous letter by a Virginia slave to the Archbishop of London, 1723

      August the forth 1723
      [. . .] wee ~~humbly~~ your humbell
      and ~~pou~~ poore partishinners doo begg Sir your
      aid and assissttencce in this one thing which Lise
   5 as I doo understand of in your Lordships brest
      which is that ~~yr honour~~ your honour will
      by the help of our Suf~~fer~~vering Lord King George
      and the Rest of the Rullers will Releese us out of
      this Cruell Bondegg [. . .]

10   my riting is vary bad I whope yr honour
      will take the will for the deede
      I am butt a poore Slave ~~th~~ that
      writt itt and has no other ~~tinme~~ time
      butt Sunday and hardly that att Sumtimes
15   September the 8th 1723 [. . .]

(*Fulham Papers*, Lambeth Palace Library, London, cited in Ingersoll 1994: 781–2)

The letter is addressed to none less than the Archbishop of London, Edward Gibson, to whose see the colony of Virginia belonged. Although we can generally assume that letter composition must have been an enormous effort for an inexperienced semi-literate writer, we know very little about the circumstances under which the letters were written. Therefore it is particularly interesting that the letter itself gives us further insights into at least some parts of the writing process. First of all, we do not just have one date but two (4 August and 8 September), indicating that the letter-writing process was stretched over a period of more than four weeks, which seems to suggest that the author was straining to finish the letter. The hard conditions of the slaves and the lack of time are explicitly mentioned in the letter too: 'has no other ~~tinme~~ time butt Sunday and hardly that att Sumtimes', a fact that might also have prevented the author from finishing the letter. Furthermore, the many strike-throughs and self-corrections suggest that the author was very insecure about 'standard' orthography and the correct spelling of many words, and even if he knew the correct spelling, the mere mechanical act of writing the words correctly must have been an additional challenge. The 'text shows all the hallmarks of inexperience': there is no punctuation and the capitalisation is unsystematic (Monaghan 1999: 324). Given these 'hallmarks of inexperience', it is remarkable that the author nevertheless shows an awareness of the use of formulae in letters (e.g. the first two lines and lines 9 and 10).

The other letter to be looked at is one dated 17 August 1868 and written by Henry B. Stewart to the American Colonization Society (Wiley 1980: 306):

(2)   My Dear Sir:

       Your Kind Letter Dated Savannah, Ga., My 2d,
       Came to hand yesterday. I was more than glad to hear from you and Es-
       pecially the Cause of the Emigrants not Coming to this County. Many
       Reasons hast been Set up by others. Some thought it was the agent at
       Monrovia. Be this as it may, there is Some truth as Regards the Em-
       igrants that Came over in '66. Every thing was not as it Should of been.
       Much of the blame is with the Emigrants. They Came over unfortunately
       at a time of high political Excitement. Went into it by party persuassion,
       from January to May and no Entreaties from older Citizens were of any
       avail. Not one of them from that time would Leave the Beach. The fever

took them. Many of them Died from night Exposure. Their Rashions gave out, and not the best of medical attention. They became Dissatisfied and Knew not how to Remedy their Lost Condtion and with no inclination to work, Several of them Left for Grand Bassa Co [. . .]

While still being non-standard, we can see a clear difference from the first letter. Generally, the author uses punctuation, but capitalisation seems random. Although words like 'Emigrants', for example, are always capitalised and some verbs occasionally, we also find capitalised adjectives and adverbs. On the lexical level, the use of Latinate words such as 'excitement', 'persuassion', 'exposure', 'rashion' is remarkable and quite unusual for a semi-literate writer. This is an example of a fairly advanced writer approximating standard writing conventions, and it is therefore questionable whether such advanced writers can still be considered as semi-literate. This raises the question of who counts as a semi-literate and how his or her writing can be characterised.

The above examples were presented to illustrate the range of literacies of the authors in the corpus. While the two letters here are clearly to be found at the opposite ends of a continuum, there may be letters in which differences between the authors' extent of literacy are much more subtle, particularly with regard to the more advanced writers who master letter-writing conventions to a certain extent but who nevertheless exhibit, for example, inconsistencies in spelling or punctuation or non-standard grammatical features, etc. A first categorisation has been provided by Fairman, who distinguishes between minimally, partly, extensively and fully schooled[5] as different levels on a continuum of letteracy (2006: 56).[6] Of interest in the present context are, of course, mainly the letters of minimally schooled writers, whose writing is characterised by Fairman as 'comprehensible but largely unconventional' (2006: 57). In order to describe in more detail what exactly minimally schooled writings entail, a careful analysis of what Fairman calls the five 'literacy skills/subskills', orthography, lexis, grammar, syntax and handwriting (2007c: 268), is required. This analysis would at least have to comprise the detailed description of all five skills in a range of letters in trying to find characteristic traits of each skill for minimally schooled letters, similar to what Fairman has carried out for the lexical level recently (Fairman 2007b). Only such a comprehensive analysis of all five literacy skills, which is beyond the scope of this chapter, could shed more light on the question of who should count as semi-literate.

---

[5] Fairman points out that the term 'schooled' merely refers to some form of instruction and does not imply the attendance of a school.

[6] To avoid the ambiguity of the term literacy, Fairman has alternatively coined the term 'letteracy' when referring to the writers' competence in composing a letter.

7. Structural heterogeneity: non-standard features in earlier AAE

As highlighted above, the greatest challenge, of course, is to describe accurately the degree of non-standardness (e.g. Fairman, Allen this volume). Which types of non-standardness can be attributed purely to 'unconventional orthography' (see many of the examples in the two letters in the previous section) and which types are dialect features and therefore of interest in the reconstruction of a variety? Contrary to some of the other letters discussed in this volume (Fairman, Allen), the letters written by African Americans fortunately do show dialect structures, which is again evidence of the suitability of this type of source. While the letters in this corpus are remarkably similar in their non-standardness to other letters discussed in this volume, there is one remarkable difference that is phonologically significant: contrary to other frequently found uses of *as* and *is* for *has* and *his*, which most likely indicate that the writer did not pronounce the *h*, there are no such instances in the African American letters (or other American letters for that matter). While conclusions about negative evidence are usually problematic, this seems to be rather uncontroversial, as *h*-dropping has never been a feature of American English.[7]

As Wolfram (2000: 47) points out, a pivotal concern for any investigation of earlier AAE is the selection of so-called 'diagnostic structures'. In order to provide a more accurate picture of this variety, he advocates the selection of 'a wide array of dialect structures'. When testing the structural heterogeneity in a particular genre such as letters, the question is what can be expected in terms of non-standard features. Which features do occur in the letters of semi-literate writers that are of interest to the historical study of this variety? In a comparative analysis, Wolfram distinguishes the following four types of written data: letters, amanuenses' accounts, literary dialects and court records. He compares their dialect features and lists the following examples that are attested in African American letters (2000: 42):

- third person singular -*s* absence (e.g., *she go*)
- third person plural -*s* concord (e.g., *the dogs goes*)
- unmarked past (e.g., *yesterday she go*)
- regularised past (e.g., *they knowed*)
- levelling to *was* (e.g., *the dogs was there*)

Compared to other types of written data, letters show the lowest number of non-standard features. The other text types, especially amanuensis accounts and literary dialects, show far more vernacular features. Wolfram (2000: 45) points out that the authors of literary dialects might have been influenced by certain conventions (even the use of creole features) and the similarity between these two text types suggests that conventions in turn have influenced amanuenses when taking notes, for example, of conversations, and cautions us not to take such sources at face value.

---

[7] The first generations of new immigrants were an exception. As Garcia-Bermejo Giner and Montgomery (1997) have shown, British immigrants in the eighteenth century produce *h*-less examples in their writing but seem to have lost it in the next generation.

According to Wolfram's list, other well-known features such as multiple negation and copula absence are only attested for amanuenses' accounts and literary dialects in his analysis. However, further comparative studies (e.g. Kautzsch 2002) have shown that we also have to add multiple negation and copula absence to the list of features attested in letters.

The differences between written and spoken genres is not only a matter of absence and presence, but also of frequency. While we obviously find such examples even in writing, Kautzsch (2002: 227) has shown that these occur far less frequently compared to his speech corpus (in the case of negative concord, it is only 26% compared to 80% in the spoken sources). He attributes this to the impact of literacy (see Allen, this volume) and concludes that '[s]emi-literates can be aware of the stigmatisation of certain non-standard features in writing' (2002: 253). However, the fact that such features do surface in writing at all despite the stigmatisation, also seems to suggest that they have been stable features of this variety for a long time (2002: 227). Thus, literacy can have an impact on the absence or frequency of stigmatised features or produce hypercorrect forms (Montgomery 1999: 6). Thus, the actual mental process of putting pen to paper and the transition from a predominantly oral into a written code deserves more attention in future research on letters 'from below'.

All of the five features listed by Wolfram also occur in the letter corpus. This list is not exhaustive, but, for the present analysis, levelling to *was* and third person plural *-s* concord have been selected. The main questions addressed in this section are: how heterogeneous are the letters from the two different regions, and how does heterogeneity manifest itself in the letters by the occurrence of the two selected features? Do we find orderly heterogeneity (Weinreich, Labov and Herzog 1968: 100)? The next section will look at regional heterogeneity in more detail.

The assumption that community homogeneity correlates with linguistic homogeneity is a central tenet in the quantitative paradigm of sociolinguistics, also known as the homogeneity assumption (Wolfram and Thomas 2002: 164). If we take this as a valid assumption for the present context, it would be of interest to test whether the opposite holds true, i.e. the more heterogeneous a community is – which we take for granted since we have so many different contact settings – the more heterogeneous it is linguistically. To test whether this is the case is the central aim of the next section.

7.1 Regional variation

The extent of regional variation in earlier AAE is closely linked with the origin and development of this variety. It has always been assumed that if there are no dramatic differences across regions, the origin and development must have been quite similar despite regional differences in the sociohistorical conditions and demographics.

So far, regional variation has received relatively little attention. The only systematic analysis is Schneider (1989), who also subjected the selected morphosyntactic variables to regional analysis. Schneider shows that there are no discrete but quantitative differences between southern states and concludes that the Deep South can be considered as a fairly homogeneous area (Schneider 1989: 250). More recently, van Herk and Walker (2005) came to similar results. While the frequencies of verbal -*s* differ, the linguistic constraints are similar, which, as they argue, suggests a shared origin. The analysis in the present section will focus on the regional differences with regard to the two selected features. Such a heterogeneous letter corpus as *COAAL* lends itself nicely to a comparative analysis across regions. If we want to find out more about the extent of heterogeneity, it would be reasonable not to look at neighbouring (and therefore in all probability similar) states, but at states that are geographically apart and that have a different settlement history and demographics. Two such non-Deep Southern states are introduced in a short historical overview below.

7.2 Sociohistorical context: Missouri and Indian Territory

Since the settlement patterns and the demographic ecology are of particular importance in the reconstruction of earlier AAE (Wolfram 2000: 47–8), the sociohistorical local context of the letters will be looked at in more detail here. In contrast to the south-eastern colonies, Missouri was settled relatively late. Following the French and Spanish period, inner-American migration into Missouri began at the end of the eighteenth century with the movement of the western frontier (Gerlach 1986: 13). Most of the settlers hailed from Kentucky and Tennessee. They were native-born but had European ancestry, the largest and most dominant group among them being the Scotch-Irish. Many of the Ulster Scots were among the group of southern slaveholders 'who transplanted their slave-based plantation economy along the Mississippi well north of St. Louis and across the Missouri valley' (Gerlach 1986: 19). Many towns were founded along the Missouri River, and the area around the counties of Pike, Ralls, Audrain, Randolph, Callaway, Boone, Howard and Monroe was known as 'Little Dixie', 'reflecting the Southern character of the region' (1986: 19). This is where we also find the highest numbers of African American settlements. In these areas, the African American as well as the white population grew, and in 1830, Missouri had 26,000 slaves (18.6% of the population (Gerlach 1986: 19)). New slaves were imported and new slave owners from Kentucky, Tennessee and Virginia settled in 'Little Dixie' so that in the decades between 1830 and 1860 the population in this area increased rapidly (1986: 20). The overall slave population in Missouri was 114,931 in 1860, about 10% of the population (Berlin 2003: 274). After the beginning of the Civil War, the African American population declined to about 60,000, since thousands of African Americans served in the Union army or moved (or were removed by their owners) into neighbouring regions. After the Civil War, the population slowly increased again, and by 1870 it was back to the pre-Civil War level (Gerlach 1986: 30).

In the 1830s and 1840s, a major group of European immigrants in Missouri were the Germans, and pension claim agent Louis Benecke was one of them (Gerlach 1986: 26–7). He was based in Brunswick, a German settlement area in Chariton County. Not surprisingly, most of the letters written to Benecke were from the area around Brunswick or from the neighbouring counties such as Carroll, Randolph and Howard. Although Chariton was not directly situated on the Missouri River where the African American population in the respective counties exceeded 25%, the population of African Americans in Chariton at 22% in 1860 was nevertheless considerable (Gerlach 1986: 56).

With regard to the second letter collection of the Chickasaw and Choctaw freedmen, little is known about this group of former slaves, and since this form of bondage has largely been neglected in southern historiography until recently (Saunt 2004: 63), a few words are in order about the historical context. I will focus here on the Chickasaws and Choctaws because the letters discussed stem from the freedmen of these two ethnic groups. The Choctaws and Chickasaws are ethnically and linguistically closely related and share a similar history. Before the forced removal in the 1830s – also referred to as the 'Trail of Tears' – the Choctaws and Chickasaws resided in northern Mississippi, eastern Alabama and western Tennessee (Brightman and Wallace 2004: 478). By about 1750, Indians became slaveholders; not all Indians adopted this practice, but a minority of about 12% did, mostly wealthy and influential 'mixed bloods' with white ancestry (Brightman and Wallace 2004: 491). Plantations were established, but it was only at the beginning of the nineteenth century that slaveholding among Indians became more widespread (Miles and Naylor-Ojurongbe 2004: 755). With the Indian Removal Act in 1830, the Choctaws (and the Chickasaws in 1835) were forcibly removed to Indian Territory and took their slaves with them (Kidwell 2004: 524).

After the Civil War, negotiations between US Commissioners and representatives of the Five Civilized Tribes commenced in Arkansas, at Fort Smith (Saunt 2004: 71).[8] The aim was to reach an agreement between the United States and the Five Civilized Tribes with regard to the emancipation of the slaves and their incorporation into Indian Territory, as well as the establishment of a single territorial government (2004: 74). While the emancipation issue alone proved difficult, since many Indian planters feared a labour problem and were therefore reluctant to set their slaves free, the incorporation into the territory – which implied the granting of full rights to the ex-slaves – was opposed even more vehemently.

Since the negotiations proved extremely difficult, only a modest treaty was reached at Fort Smith in 1865, leaving many pertinent issues unsettled. As Saunt concludes, '[t]he negotiations at Fort Smith left slaves of Indians between bondage

---

[8] For a detailed account of the complex Reconstruction history in Indian Territory, see Saunt (2004).

and freedom, both legally and in practice' (2004: 77). The strongest opposition
not only to equal rights but even to emancipation came from the Choctaws and
Chickasaws. In 1866, many slaves were still in bondage, and the situation was
characterised by hostility towards and violence against the ex-slaves (2004: 79).
In 1866, the United States settled treaties separately with individual tribes. The
treaty with the Choctaws and Chickasaws was complicated and contained the
provision of a payment of $300,000 on the condition that by an incorporation
the freedmen were granted citizenship. If the adoption of the freedmen was not
completed within the following two years, the sum would be used for the relocation of the freedmen (Saunt 2004: 86). Despite this provision, the rights and the
exact political status of the freedmen remained unsettled and became the subject
of many negotiations in the years to follow. In the case of the Chickasaws, the
adoption was never implemented. The Choctaws, however, adopted their former
slaves in 1883, which resulted in a protest on the part of the freedmen regarding the conditions of their adoption (2004: 86). The letters give ample evidence
of this complex situation, as they contain many complaints by the freedmen about
their treatment and the neglect of their rights. The following quotation exemplifies
this:

> The Indian aurthoity say that they
> Will Put us out of the Nation If
> We Doe not Pay A Permit
> (1041, G. W. Hall, 1885)

All of this suggests that the linguistic situation must have been as complex as
the sociohistorical one. Since some African Americans were bilingual, they acted
as interpreters for enslavers whose command of English was restricted and thus
fulfilled the important role of cultural mediators in contact with other groups
not only before the removal, but also in antebellum Indian Territory (Naylor
2008: 97).

7.3 Was/were *variation*

While many of the structural features that were listed at the beginning of this
section do occur in many letters, this is not necessarily the case with all features;
therefore it is essential for an initial study to select a feature that occurs in sufficient
quantity. The main aim of this section is to test whether *was/were* has a diagnostic
value in earlier AAE.

Was/were has been studied in a number of varieties worldwide and lends itself
well to a cross-variety comparison (e.g. Tagliamonte and Smith 2000; Hay and
Schreier 2004). In the present study, it has been selected for two reasons: first of
all, it is suitable for the study of written registers as it occurs even in shorter letters,
and with a type of source in which the main purpose is to recount past events

Table 13.1 Was *by number, person and subject type*

was		Missouri		*was*		Indian Territory
	was	No.	%	*was*	No.	%
1st p sg	52	52	100	21	21	100
2nd p sg	5	8	62.5	0	1	0
3rd p sg	100	100	100	36	39	92.3
1st p pl	3	4	75.0	4	7	57.1
3rd p pl	7	12	58.3	8	18	44.4
NP	5	8	62.5	5	14	34.7
Pro	2	4	50.0	3	4	75.0

one is very likely to obtain a higher number of past than present forms of *be*. The second reason is that *was/were* variation has been studied well, and its external as well internal constraints are well known, so that it is possible to investigate to what extent the variation follows these constraints.

One such constraint is the so-called subject-type-constraint (STC), i.e. the levelling to *was* is more likely to occur with a full NP subject than with a pronoun. This phenomenon, in combination with the non-proximity-to subject constraint, is often referred to as the Northern Subject Rule (NSR) and has a Scots origin (Montgomery 1994).[9] The first systematic analysis of this pattern in earlier AAE was carried out by Montgomery *et al.* (1993). Since the pattern was very similar to that found in the letters of Scotch-Irish immigrants, they concluded that African Americans must have had extended contact with this group of immigrants.

All occurrences of past tense *be* in the two selected collections were extracted from the letters and coded according to number, grammatical person and subject type. This yielded the overall number of 292 for both collections. The results are quantified in Table 13.1.

Since there are reports for the occurrence of *was* across the verbal paradigm, it has been listed for all grammatical persons here. As might be expected, first and third person singular show 100% *was*, except for third person singular in the freedmen data, which is due to a few cases of singular *were*. It is mostly used in combination with third person singular pronouns or singular existentials as exemplified below:[10]

---

[9] The non-proximity-to-subject constraint is another condition that is connected to the NSR. Due to limited space, this constraint is not analysed in this chapter.

[10] The examples from Indian Territory are taken from Records of the Office of the Secretary of the Interior 1885–1888, Record Group 48, National Archives [IDs 1033–1094]) and the examples from Missouri are cited from the Benecke Family Papers 1816–1989, Western Historical Manuscript Collection [IDs 0001–0108]). I am most grateful to Michael Montgomery for making the letters from the Benecke Papers available.

(1)   the were nothening said about the corlore

(1065, John McDonald, 1887)

(2)   I think fram What I seen on the out sid of the letter that it were recorded on
       your Book

(1080, John McDonald, 1888)

(3)   this Blake More he were a Cherokee half Brede

(1058, Frank Robinson, 1887)

This rather unexpected result requires some explanation. Singular *were* is not
unknown; it also occurs in nineteenth-century Southern American Vernacular
English (SAVE) (Trüb 2006: 260), early South African English writing (Siebers
2010: 286) and Northern Irish English (though mainly with singular existentials,
Pietsch 2005: 124–5). There is considerable individual variation in earlier AAE and
SAVE, and the exact nature and origin of singular *were* (Pietsch suggests a Scots
origin) remain to be seen in a wider nineteenth-century southern context.

   Levelling to *was* is known for second person singular and first person plural
(Tagliamonte and Smith 2000; Schneider and Montgomery 2001; Montgomery
2004; Trüb 2006), and the results show that this is also the case here, apart from the
second person singular in the freedmen letters; there is just a single possible context,
and therefore it is not possible to judge whether the same kind of levelling to *was*
is in operation. Otherwise the extent of *was* levelling exceeds 50%; however, the
total number of occurrences is fairly low. Examples (4) and (5) show the levelling
for second person singular and first person plural:

(4)   i could see By the papers you was a way lots from Home

(0049, Sarah Fults, 1888)

(5)   Your Letter come to hand the 1 and we all was Glad to here from you indeed

(1059, W. N. Jackson, 1887)

   The most interesting grammatical person is the third person plural, as it can
be tested for the STC. The overall levelling rate is 58.3% and 44.4% in the two
collections. The following instances are examples of *was* in combination with full
NP subjects and pronominal *they*:

(6)   ther Children was going to school but they have turned them all out

(1069, Lee Kemp, 1887)

(7)   I was Then Sick in orleans when They was mustard out

(0016, Solomon North, 1904)

While the levelling rates are similar to the 54% in Montgomery *et al.*'s data (1993: 347), the differences become evident when looking at the STC. In the Missouri letters, there is only weak support for the STC, as the percentages for each type are almost on a par (compared to 78% for full NP and zero for *they* in Montgomery *et al.*'s data), and in the Indian Territory data the STC even seems to be reversed, i.e. *they* rather than full NPs as subjects seem to favour *was*. However, since there are so few instances with *they*, this is certainly the most tentative of the results. Moreover, as the following example shows, the more general levelling to *was* with both *they* and full NPs with some speakers might account for this unexpected finding:

(8)   at th close of the war I did not know where my Parents was and could Naht find out where their was untill afew years agoe when I found where they was

(1078, Edmund Brashears, 1888)

So the results show that *was* occurs in the third person plural much in the same way as elsewhere but that its usage is only weakly constrained (if at all in the case of the freedmen letters) by the subject type. Furthermore, we see clear tendencies of levelling to *was* in the second person singular and the first person plural. If we compare this again to the strong effect of the STC in the letters of Montgomery *et al.* (1993), the question arises as to whether it had never been so strong in Missouri and Indian Territory or whether this constraint weakened over time. Since the authors only analysed about forty letters and the overall occurrences are as low as thirteen contexts, it may be worthwhile to look at further letters from the same collection to find out whether the effect of the STC is indeed strong or whether the differences between the first two collections and these letters are due to differences in region and time (the freedmen letters were written between 1861 and 1867 by African Americans from across the eastern and southern United States). Following this, a further 140 letters written to the Freedmen's Bureau were analysed for *was/were*.[11] The results are given in Table 13.2.

As can be gleaned from Table 13.2, the results here clearly confirm the levelling to *was* in the second person singular and the first person plural that we also see in the other two collections. With regard to the third person plural, the strong effect of the STC is not borne out with this larger set of letters from the same collection. The frequency of 84.6% with full NPs is very high, but this subject type does not strongly favour *was*, as the frequency for *they* is also very high due to the high overall levelling rate of 79.6%. Thus, the strong effect of the subject type as found in Montgomery *et al.* for the smaller selection of letters cannot be confirmed here.

To sum up, concerning the questions raised above, a weakening of the STC over time can be discarded, as the STC is not very strong in all three collections.

---

[11] All the letters analysed here stem from the Record Group 105, National Archive, see references. Some of the letters are published in Berlin *et al.* (1982).

Table 13.2 Was *by number, person and*
subject type in the freedmen letters

	was	No.	%
1st p sg	144	149	96.6
2nd p sg	5	6	83.3
3rd p sg	177	182	97.3
1st p pl	11	15	73.3
3rd p pl	39	49	79.6
NP	33	39	84.6
Pro	6	10	60.0

Thus, the lower frequencies of levelling in the third person plural in the Missouri and Indian Territory letters can either be explained by regional variation, i.e. the frequencies were generally lower in Missouri and Indian Territory than in the Deep South states, or the frequencies decreased more generally between the 1860s and 1890s, but without the study of further letters this is difficult to answer.

How can all the results presented so far be interpreted? According to Montgomery (2004), there are three different patterns with regard to *was/were* variation in early nineteenth-century southern American English. The first pattern is the occurrence of a fairly standard verbal paradigm except for the third person plural, where the subject type has a very strong effect: the use of *were* with *they* and the use of *was* with NP subjects is near-categorical (2004: 10). The second pattern is the use of both *was* and *were* in both numbers (see singular *were* above), the origin of which is difficult to trace. The third pattern which Montgomery identified is the levelling of *was* to all persons and subject types across the paradigm. While the first pattern is attested for the eighteenth century – from Scotch-Irish immigrants in South Carolina in Montgomery's data – the third pattern is dominant and widespread in the nineteenth century, and it probably emerged from the first. The results from all three collections of letters presented here clearly provide support for a development towards this third pattern. Although we do not find full paradigmatic levelling here, it seems to be change in progress with a weakening of the STC (and the resultant generalisation to *they* as observed by Montgomery *et al.* 1993: 349) and incipient levelling to *was* in non-third person plural contexts, mainly second person singular and first person plural. The fact that this is true for regionally and historically diverse settings supports Montgomery's hypothesis that this pattern was fairly widespread in the nineteenth century. This is further corroborated for SAVE, as analyses of the letters from the *Southern Plantation Overseers Corpus* show (Schneider and Montgomery 2001; Trüb 2006). Trüb even suggests that 'analogical levelling of the paradigm has increased for all persons and superseded the subject type constraint in the past 150 years of SAVE' (2006: 262).

Table 13.3 *Third person plural verbal -s on auxiliary* be *and* have *by subject type*

	Missouri			Indian Territory		
	is	No.	%	*is*	No.	%
3rd p pl	5	17	29.4	15	49	30.6
NP	5	13	38.5	15	39	38.5
Pro	0	4	0	0	10	0
	has	No.	%	*has*	No.	%
3rd p pl	3	3	100	15	40	37.5
NP	3	3	100	15	30	50.0
Pro	0	0	0	0	10	0

7.4 Verbal -s on the auxiliaries be *and* have

In order to shed further light on the development of levelling and the STC, it is instructive at this point to look at other features more closely to check whether the constraints are similar across the verbal paradigm and what this tells us about the contact patterns. As Wolfram cautions us, any study on earlier AAE should ideally be based on more than one diagnostic feature (Wolfram 2000: 47, see also the fourth point of Montgomery's analytical standards 1997b: 127).[12] Therefore present *be* and *have* will be included in the discussion here, especially with regard to the strength of the STC. Other studies have shown that there are differences between the non-standard usage in the present and past *be* paradigm (Montgomery 1994; Trüb 2006). Trüb (2006: 259) has shown for earlier SAVE that the frequency of levelling to *was* is much higher than to *is* (63.3% compared to 35.4%) and that the lower frequency with present *be* is concomitant with a strengthening of the STC. Table 13.3 lists the results for auxiliary *be* and *have* in both collections (the results are restricted to third person plural).

The results show that the overall levelling rate is indeed lower compared to *was*: it is in both cases only around 30%, but there is a stronger effect of the STC: the levelling to *is* is in both cases 38.5%, and there is not a single use of *is* in connection with plural *they* as a subject type. The following examples illustrate this pattern:

(9) The three months is up and I would like to have my money

(0010, Martha Holland, 1874)

(10) my self is here yet having no vice with the choctaws and my children is out of school

(1073, J. Umphers, 1887)

---

[12] While this is generally desirable, such a comparison is even more important when the same constraints potentially occur in other features, too.

The pattern is similar for auxiliary *have*. With both auxiliaries the effect of the subject type is strong: there is not a single occurrence of *has* or *is* with *they* as subject. The levelling is even stronger with the auxiliary *have*, as Table 13.3 indicates. However, since there are only three occurrences in the Missouri data, the 100% of course has to be taken with a pinch of salt. The results for the auxiliaries compare nicely with the frequencies in Montgomery *et al.* (1993). The overall levelling rate for *is* and *has* in their data is 33.7% and 40.4% respectively, which is in line with the frequencies here. The STC is equally strong and *is* in combination with *they* occurs only twice and once in the case of *has* (Montgomery *et al.* 1993: 347). The auxiliary constraint, i.e. the prediction of higher frequencies of verbal -*s* with the auxiliaries *be* and *have* compared to lexical verbs, as attested for SAVE by Schneider and Montgomery (2001) and Trüb (2006) does not seem to hold for AAE. Neither do Montgomery *et al.*'s data indicate such a tendency (the levelling rate at 40% is as high as for *have*), nor do the Indian Territory letters here give evidence of this.[13]

If we compare the results of this section to the previous section, we can clearly see that the weak effect of the STC is typical of past *be* only. With present *be* and *have* the levelling rate is lower, but the STC is fairly strong.[14] Thus, an analysis of past *be* would only have presented a biased view of the STC. The levelling rate with past *be* is fairly high and the STC is weak, and vice versa with present *be* and *have*. Whether these two developments are connected or whether they are independent is difficult to say, and the analysis of further letters is necessary to answer this. From this comparison we can conclude that the patterning is not random but systematic (orderly heterogeneity) and discernible even with low frequencies. The two collections of letters were chosen to test to what extent writers from the non-Deep South conform to the patterns of variation with regard to non-standard features. As the results show, the features as found in the two collections here are remarkably similar, despite the very different settlement histories (contrary to expectation).

Finally, the question arises as to where the levelling to *was* and *is/has* and the NSR originated. Montgomery *et al.* (1993) have shown that the patterns of verbal concord marking in the third person plural in a set of letters written by African Americans are very similar compared to letters by Scotch-Irish immigrants from the same region. Since the NSR is a well-known feature of northern English dialects, particularly Scots, the results imply, they argue, that African Americans must have had extended contact with Scotch-Irish. A further analysis by region provided evidence for this pattern beyond the south Atlantic states. Therefore Montgomery *et al.* concluded that this feature was spread across all regions (1993: 350). This finding is supported by van Herk and Walker's (2005) regional study, too. When we find such patterns

[13] Lexical verbs were only analysed for the Indian Territory data. For this set of letters, there is no difference in usage between lexical verbs and auxiliaries. However, there are slight differences between the auxiliaries just as in Montgomery *et al.*'s letters. At 30.6% the rate for *be* is somewhat lower than the 35.5% for lexical verbs and the 37.5% for *have*.

[14] A further analysis of the Indian Territory letters shows that this pattern is not restricted to the auxiliaries, but also holds for verbal -*s* in lexical verbs. However, this has only been tested for the Indian Territory letters.

across all regions, we have to look for explanations. Since the NSR is such a distinct pattern of verbal concord marking, other explanations than a contact phenomenon seem unlikely. The occurrence of some form of NSR here, even in a weakened form, suggests some sort of Scotch-Irish influence. The most obvious form of influence is naturally direct contact. For the south-eastern settlements, especially the Carolinas, direct contact is most likely as shown above. The origin of the NSR in regions such as Missouri and Indian Territory require more extended explanation. Contrary to the south-eastern settlements, these regions were settled relatively late. As was shown in the section on historical context, settlers of Scotch-Irish origin were a major group during the settlement of Missouri; however, they were not recent immigrants but native-born descendants of immigrants to other states, especially Kentucky and Tennessee, who moved westwards with the frontier. Contact between these second-generation Scotch-Irish and African Americans seems plausible, but in contrast to the contact patterns outlined above, we have to assume a different type of influence, more indirect in this case, since original characteristic patterns of the Scotch-Irish might have undergone changes first within the time of a generation or two and second through the inner-American migration and thus mixing with other settler groups. It remains subject to some speculation in which way settlers from the south-eastern territories brought their own patterns and thus influenced the development in Missouri. With regard to Indian Territory, such indirect influence is in fact the only explanation. No Scotch-Irish settlements are known for this region, and the groups of Native Americans and African Americans forcibly removed were originally from Mississippi and parts of Tennessee. The extent to which both groups were in contact with white groups in their original states is difficult to trace. Since the African Americans were enslaved by the Choctaws and Chickasaws and were taken with them during the removal, it is reasonable to assume that the Native Americans were their main point of contact, even before the removal. However, there is evidence that African Americans (or African Indians as they are sometimes referred to) were a fairly heterogeneous group. On the one hand, there were those who had been enslaved by the Native Americans for a long time, spoke their language and to some degree adopted their customs and culture, and on the other hand, there were crossland slaves who had been formerly enslaved by a white master in another region and had only been enslaved by the Native Americans more recently (Naylor 2008: 99). The following characterisation of the former group by Naylor (2008: 101) hints at some of the cultural and linguistic complexities of this contact scenario:

> It is possible that some enslaved African Creeks in the Creek Nation, as well as enslaved people of the Cherokees, Seminoles, Choctaws, and Chickasaws, developed not only a facility for these Indian languages but also particular dialects that integrated, but did not entirely reproduce, aspects of southeastern Indian languages. Whether enslaved people of African descent became proficient in Indian languages or created a patois or creole infused with Indian words, they used the spoken word as another means of expressing their cultural connection to Indians and their inclusion within Indian nations.

Given the knowledge of Indian languages and the process of acculturation, it is not surprising that we find references to a possibly 'distinct' Indian African American English variety. Naylor (2008: 97) quotes a freedwoman who worked for whites in Kansas during the war and who had problems understanding them, as she 'didn't know white folks language'. This implies that the English spoken in Kansas must have been remarkably different from her own variety. In the light of these circumstances, it is reasonable to assume that the English of these African Americans in Indian Territory most likely differs from the variety that we find elsewhere. Similar comments from other freedmen quoted in (Naylor 2008: 101) such as 'them Creek negroes was so funny to talk to' further support this assumption.

It is striking, though, that the results show great similarities with the Missouri letters and do not suggest a 'distinct' variety. A possible explanation is that the authors of the letters were less acculturated and belonged to the second group outlined above. As this clearly shows, language contact between African Americans and Indians certainly awaits further research.

One last point to be considered in the discussion of contact settings is the relocation of 250,000 slaves between 1820 and 1850. This, as Winford reminds us, resulted among other things in 'a melting pot of cultural and linguistic influences from various parts of the Atlantic and upper south states, particularly the former' (Winford 1997: 316). In order to better understand the development of AAE, we need to pay more attention to the 'mix and flow of linguistic influences both within and across the colonies' (Winford 1997: 329). Such a flow facilitated the spread of certain features, e.g. the NSR, possibly not originally known for a region, and might be an explanation why we find similar patterns in geographically remote regions. As Pederson *et al.* (1986: 51) have pointed out, 'historically distinctive cultural forms from Virginia and South Carolina appear everywhere across the Gulf states where the plantation system took hold' (Little Dixie in Missouri is a good case in point). The above-mentioned mixing of different settler groups, for example through inner-American migration, also facilitated the levelling of certain features in American varieties (Winford 1997: 336). This is perfectly in line with the results here and with the widespread use of the NSR with *was/were* as postulated by Montgomery (2004).

8. Conclusion

The present study has shown that, despite the heterogeneity of the sources and contexts, the letters are surprisingly similar with regard to the features analysed, and we can detect orderly heterogeneity in the sense of Weinreich, Labov and Herzog (1968). So what can we conclude from that? With regard to regional variation, the extent is limited, at least for this period studied, the last two decades of the nineteenth century. With two regions that were fairly remote from the classical Deep South, the expectation was that we do not necessarily find the same amount of orderly heterogeneity, so this is fairly surprising. The conclusions are limited, since we get a picture for a limited period, but we do not know whether the similarities are the results of a process of homogenisation of different origins or whether similar origin varieties developed along the same developmental path.

The NSR seems to be fairly robust in the two collections here, with the exception of the reversal with past *be* in the Indian Territory letters. However, the low frequencies are an important caveat here. The results for *was/were* seem to support Montgomery's hypotheses regarding the development of *was/were*. The results are in line with his third pattern, an existent but weakened STC accompanied by levelling to *was* in other grammatical persons, a more recent pattern in the nineteenth century that superseded the first – most likely the older and original – pattern of exclusive and almost categorical use of *was* in the third person plural. With regard to the auxiliaries *have* and *be* in the present, the amount of levelling to *is* and *has* in the third person plural is lower than *was*, but the STC is much stronger. These results confirm most of Trüb's findings on a letter corpus of earlier SAVE from Louisiana, North and South Carolina dating from the first half of the nineteenth century. Although time and region are different, it shows that the analyses are comparable, and a more detailed analysis of this corpus and *COAAL* merits further attention.

To conclude, this chapter has shown that letters can be fruitfully studied in the context of earlier AAE and its origin and development. The study of further letters from the corpus and further features is necessary to provide a fuller picture of this variety in the nineteenth century.

CHAPTER 14

Hypercorrection and the persistence of local dialect features in writing

Daniel Schreier

1. Introduction

Historical sociolinguists and current models of language variation and change share a deep-seated methodological concern of how to generally assess data validity. In modern sociolinguistic theory, appropriate methodological tools for the study of spoken records include sociolinguistic interviews in the form of permanent recordings; these can be stored and reanalysed to meet the demands of Labov's well-known 'principle of accountability' (1972: 72). However, as soon as researchers stretch back in time, the study of spoken records is no longer available as an option, and 'variation and change has to be studied on the basis of written documents only' (Schneider 2002: 67). Whether or not spoken and written data can be compared *strictu sensu*, indeed even whether the former leave a 'vernacular' footprint in a different medium, is subject to debate (Bauer 1994; see also Fanego 2004). As Schneider (2002: 67–8) states, written records differ widely in this context: such documents may represent a more or less genuine historical speech act produced for a certain purpose in a specific time and place; others, in contrast, though rather fictional and attributed, are at least to some extent characteristic, for instance, the widespread, often stereotyped usage of features attributed to 'creole' varieties (discussion in Schreier 2008; Schreier and Wright 2010). Written records to some extent function as a 'filter' (Bauer 1994) between a speech event and the linguistic researcher; they represent a speech act, indirect and imperfect, that in some way is affected by the nature of the recording process. In consequence, one of the crucial questions in historical methodology concerns the effects of the filter or, to be more precise, how accurately original speech acts are represented by writers, and also to what level of accuracy these may vary along a 'continuum of faithfulness' (Schneider 2002). Schneider goes on to postulate that one of the primary tasks of the historical linguist is to 'remove this filter' (2002: 68), namely to reconstruct the speech event as accurately as possible while assessing the possible impact of the recording process.

Crucially, the availability of data is imperfectly balanced throughout the wider speech community (which is partly what Labov 1994: 10–11 referred to as the 'bad data problem'). As a consequence of a lack of general schooling and education for a privileged minority, written evidence is not available for the vast majority of the population. Yet even here the material available is scarce:

> In an ideal case we have in front of us a carefully edited collection based on letters that were actually delivered from one person to another. It is also important that these letters were written personally by people whose social backgrounds are fully identifiable. Collections like this exist, but unfortunately their number is not very large. (Nevalainen and Raumolin-Brunberg 1994: 137)

Moreover, as a result of standardisation from the seventeenth century onwards, writing became more and more homogeneous due to the imposition and vigilance of normative features. A writing period rich in regionally and socially diagnostic variation gradually became subject to one characterised by a lack of diagnostic variation, yielding less and less sociolinguistic information as codification progressed and schooling became available to the general populace. Moreover, vernacular (non-standard) forms were more likely to emerge in documents written by lower population strata whose speech intruded more directly into their writing; yet these were the groups who wrote infrequently and were least likely to have their writing preserved (see Montgomery 1999). In addition, issues related to authenticity and authorship loom large; very often illiterate members of the working class dictated their letters, which meant that their speech was rendered via an additional filter (resembling the rendering of court cases, where verbatim statements were transcribed by an official scribe; see Schreier and Wright's 2010 analysis of the significance of court evidence on the early history of St Helenian English; cf. Bergs, this volume).

The central issue for the analysis of writing is the validity of data in general, namely the conclusions one can draw on spoken vernaculars or the general authenticity of written documents. This 'elephant in the room' has been recognised as truly problematic. Following Schneider (2002), the nature of texts in general refers to the surface appearance of a text, i.e. to the presence/frequency of dialectal forms that manifest themselves in patterns of variation and create an overall impression of 'authenticity' (i.e. when there is a high frequency of features that have been demonstrated to feature prominently in the vernacular, though some speech patterns cannot be rendered in writing, particularly phonological ones, as Montgomery 1999 points out). The immediacy of the writing process and the recording conditions matter as well. The more the conditions are temporally, locally and personally removed from the original utterance or, put differently, the 'thicker' the filter, the less valid the rendering of a text is expected to be (Schneider 2002). Internal consistency, finally, refers to whether or not (variable) features are consistently portrayed in a similar fashion (if not, this might give insights into the conditioning of variation (see Allen, this volume)), whereas the general external fit is whether the results of a particular study concur with results of other studies and familiar linguistic distributions (if they do, then results are more trustworthy; Schneider 2002). It is the combination of all these factors that accounts for the complexity of assessing authenticity in historical sociolinguistics, the ultimate challenge being to make the best usage of so-called 'bad data'. Still, the analysis of letters contributes to our understanding of how local vernacular features emerge in a more formal writing code, which in turn may help us to speculate on why these features are maintained and what writing may signify for variation and change. In what follows, I wish to address these questions by analysing letters written by native speakers of Tristan da Cunha English, a variety of southern hemisphere English that has only recently opened up to the outside world.

2. Tristan da Cunha: a brief social history, with focus on education

Tristan da Cunha is one of the most isolated inhabited islands in the world. Located about halfway between Cape Town, South Africa, and Uruguay, the local variety (Tristan da Cunha English, henceforth TdCE) is one of the youngest varieties of postcolonial English. The island has a history of permanent settlement only since 1816, being previously uninhabited; there were no contacts between newly arriving and indigenous populations. Tabula rasa conditions of this kind are rather unusual in the canon of World Englishes. There is a lot of historical information on the community (in the form of logbooks, letters, travelogues, missionary reports, etc.) so that the social history of the island is well documented. The setting was a socio-linguistic melting pot par excellence (there has been only one village at all times): the founders of TdCE arrived from England and Scotland (Kelso, East London, Hull and Hastings), the USA (New London, Massachusetts), South Africa, the Netherlands and the island of St Helena. Crucially, there was restricted contact with the 'outside world' from the 1850s onwards due to technological innovations that revolutionised oceanic shipping (discussion in Schreier 2003a). The community's unusual social history has been discussed in detail elsewhere (Schreier 2002, 2003a, 2003b), so in this chapter, I will concentrate on the history of writing and education (Evans 1994), which is of great importance for the analysis to follow.

The Tristanians' isolation had far-reaching consequences for schooling. The founder of the community, Corporal William Glass, was born in Kelso in the Scottish Lowlands in 1787. As a Scottish Presbyterian, he had strong Christian beliefs; he read the Bible daily, and schooling was a great concern to him. He and his wife, Cape-born Maria Magdalena Leenders, had sixteen children altogether. As content a man as he seems to have been all his life, he was worried that his children did not have the opportunity to go to school. It is reported that early on, he agreed to send two of his children to Cape Town for education and paid a visiting captain for the transport. When Augustus Earle was stranded on the island in 1824 (Earle 1966 [1832]), Glass appointed him chaplain of the island. Together they held church services (in Glass' living room) and organised a rudimentary Sunday school for the children, teaching them basic reading and writing skills. His hopes received a boost when Benjamin Pankhurst stayed on the island in 1830–2, being in fact the first teacher on Tristan da Cunha. Pankhurst, however, was by no means the ideal person for the job, since, suffering from alcoholism, he was sent by his family to the most desolate place they could think of, where they assumed alcohol was not available (his departure in 1832 did not give rise to much lament in the population). Still,

Reverend John Applegate, who visited the island in 1831 and christened most of the children, noted that quite a few of them had basic writing skills (Evans 1994).

On 17 January 1834, the following advertisement appeared in a Cape Town newspaper:

> We the undersigned, being three of the senior principal inhabitants on the Island of Tristan d'Acunha [*sic*] do hereby agree to furnish any respectable middle-aged people (as man and wife) who are willing and capable to undertake the office as schoolmaster and mistress.

This is remarkable; not only does it attest to the determination to have official schooling on the island, but the Tristanians also managed to get a document with this text sent to South Africa, where a captain handed it over to a journalist (this endeavour alone would have deserved to meet with success; sadly, there were no applicants; Evans 1994).

Regular education finally came again in the form of Sunday school. The Society for the Propagation of Christian Knowledge sent out missionaries on a regular basis. The first was Revd William F. Taylor, who served on the island from 1851 to 1857, just after Corporal Glass, the founder of the community, had passed away. In his six years, he trained Tristanians, such as Frances Cotton, so that basic schooling was continued throughout the nineteenth century; at times, they received additional help from shipwrecked sailors (Cartwright 1895).

The situation improved in the twentieth century, particularly after the First World War. Revd J. G. Barrow (who served on the island from 1906 to 1909) wrote most insightful accounts of the community at the time, and his work was continued by Revd Martyn Rogers (1922–5), Revd R. A. C. Pooley (1927–9; with Philip Lindsay), Revd A. G. Partridge (1929–33) and Revd H. Wilde (1934–40; Evans 1994). All the influential members of the community lobbied in order to have official schooling (Peter Green, Glass' successor as spokesman of the island, Andrea Repetto, and also Frances Repetto (in 1940)). The results were quite remarkable; Dr Erling Christophersen, the leader of the Norwegian expedition that carried out research on the island in 1937/8, reported the following:

> Regarding illiteracy, it is impossible to give any definite figures as the knowledge of reading and writing varies greatly. However it is fairly correct to state that approximately 35% of the grown-up men, and 50% of the grown-up women can read and write, while most of the bigger children know letters, and many of them can read and write fairly well. (Christophersen 1940)

The Second World War brought many changes to the community (Schreier 2003a). A permanent military base was installed on the island, and for the first time great numbers of outsiders came to join the islanders. They were in need of a local infrastructure (dormitories, facilities, storage halls, a shop, etc.) and the local population was hired for the construction works. Revd C. P. Lawrence (1943–6) accompanied the garrison and was in charge of schooling, aided by army personnel. The status of the island as a colonial territory was recognised and, starting in 1946, there was a permanent administrator on the island (governing the island politically). All the departments were led by expatriates, and for the first time ever there was regular schooling (expatriates and locals trained on the job).

Derrick M. Booy, who wrote his experiences of life on the island in *Rock of Exile* (1957), stated that '[m]ost of the children learnt fairly quickly once they overcame the natural shyness imposed by the strange classroom. They studied elementary arithmetic and how to read and write. The biggest obstacle was that the English they were being taught to read and write was so different from the language they spoke.' Many teachers commented on the great discrepancy between the local variety and the one spoken by expatriate teachers and adapted as the medium of instruction ('The children simply spoke two languages – School English and Island English'; James Flint, head teacher 1963–5, as quoted in Evans 1994: 274).

To conclude this short and basic summary of Tristan's education history, we can say that, due to the isolation of the community, schooling was difficult to obtain until the Second World War. It was only thanks to the efforts of missionaries and locals that children learnt how to read and write. However, the local dialect differed considerably from the varieties spoken by the teachers from elsewhere, as many expatriates note in the twentieth century (Schreier 2003a). This latter point is central for the issue addressed here, since it provides us with an ideal opportunity to compare and contrast writing with speaking, i.e. to study whether or not local dialect features also make an appearance in writing.

3. A case in point: present *be* levelling in TdCE

The morphosyntax of TdCE has been fairly well studied (Schreier 2002, 2003a, 2003b, 2010), and we know that the variety emerged under conditions of extensive dialect contact (British and American inputs) with strong influence from a creolised variety of St Helenian English (StHE), perhaps intensified by second-language varieties of English spoken by settlers who originally came from Denmark, the Netherlands and Italy. The interaction of all these varieties gave rise to considerable restructuring in the tense, mood and aspect systems (completive *done*, remote *been* and *yuustu*, etc.) and to simplification in past tense formation (via extensive bare root extension).

The variable I would like to focus on here is present *be* levelling. This is a particularly diagnostic feature; the vast majority of English verbs display comparatively regular tense paradigms in that the bare root stems are inflected only for third person singular, past tense and progressive aspect. *Be* is unusual, however; with five allomorphs, three in present (*am, is, are*) and two in past tense (*was, were*), it is the only verb to maintain at least some of the paradigmatic complexity that was characteristic of verbal morphology in the Old and Middle English periods ('the irregular status of *be* is without parallel in the current configuration of subject–verb concord', Wolfram, Hazen and Schilling-Estes 1999: 75).

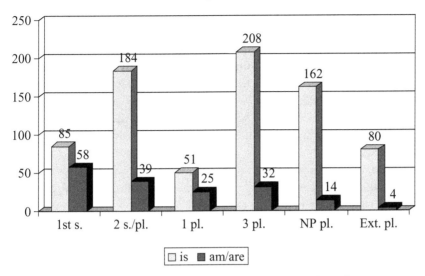

Figure 14.1 Present *be* concord with pivot form *is* in spoken TdCE

Present *be* levelling is not common in English around the world. If it does occur, then it is with the pivot form *is* (though *am* has been reported in earlier forms of African American Vernacular English). This levelling process is reported in the English North (see, for instance, the *Linguistic Atlas of England*, Map M1) though is fairly rare elsewhere. If it does occur, then it is mostly limited to existential constructions 'there's PL', for instance in New Zealand English (Hay and Schreier 2004). Schreier (2003a) reports levelling to *is* as widespread in TdCE. It is found with all grammatical persons, plural NPs and also with existentials (examples from Schreier 2003a):

- first person singular: *I's a bloke for gettin' aroun', you know* (3/11, 64m)
- second person singular: *if you ain't got the interes' you's not gonna do it* (23/17, 47m)
- first person plural: *We's planning a trip to Inaccessible next week* (4/14, 18m)
- second person plural: *Y'all is watchin' too much out the window* (28/3, 73f)
- third person plural: *usually the first trip they's quite small* (27/4, 11m)
- NP plurals: *you know what Tristan rumours is like* (40/15, 23f)
- Existentials: *oh yeah, it's hammerheads around Tristan* (35/14, 18m)

Based on the analysis of a subsample of twenty-nine speakers (942 tokens), born between 1906 and 1978, Schreier reported that *is* levelling in TdCE was 83.3% of all possible occurrences. Individual levelling rates were found to vary between 58.7% (first person singular) and 95.2% (second person plural). Figure 14.1 (adapted from Schreier 2003a: 130) shows that this feature is extraordinarily widespread and in fact a majority form in all six environments (second person singular and plural are collapsed into one category, simply because there were so few tokens for second person plural).

This extremely high percentage was attributed to contact dynamics under conditions of koïneisation and the eventual result of categorical levelling (Schreier 2003a) and as such is without parallel in the English-speaking world (with regard to past *be*, for instance, TdCE speakers born before the Second World War invariably had *was* with all persons; 'we was', 'the fishermen was', etc.). Though not categorical (at least not for all speakers), present *be* levelling is extremely common as well.

It is unclear to what extent the feature was present in the speech of the founder varieties, but historical records indicate that it was regularly used with outsiders in the 1920s and 1930s.

Crawford (1945) reports samples of 'Island Speech', where 'I is' is extremely common, and I quote the passage in which he recounts his first contact and interaction with the Tristanians in 1937:

> Encouraged by a few friendly smiles, I broke the silence by explaining that I was an Englishman and the rest of the party were Norwegians. But not a soul spoke, and I wondered if they understood me. After a long time someone eventually did speak, and it was the man at stroke.
>
> 'How's the king and queen?' he said.
>
> 'They are very well, thank you', I replied, making myself personally responsible for Their Majesties' well-being.
>
> 'Was they crowned?' I was asked almost before I had replied to the first question.
>
> 'Yes', I returned lamely, being quite overcome by the unexpectedness of the topic . . . The next question showed a grasp, even in this Utopia, of the untamable instincts of man.
>
> 'What wars is on?'

This exchange, remarkably the first encounter with strangers, thus by any means a formal setting, displays levelled forms to *is* and *was* (used with grammatical persons and plural NPs: 'How's the king and queen?', 'Was they crowned?', 'What wars is on?'). Of course, one must not generalise, since this is an impressionistic rendering and it is thus open to debate how much the 'recording conditions' (see above) may have influenced the authenticity of the exchange.

The question addressed here now is whether and how often these forms make an appearance in writing; in other words, having established the frequency of present *be* levelling in *spoken* TdCE, we can go on and ask whether or not it is found in writing as well. It is with this purpose that I turn to an analysis of a small corpus of letters, written by two women from Tristan da Cunha in 2001 and 2002.

4. Spoken TdCE features in letters: present tense concord as a case in point

The corpus is not extensive, consisting of ten letters with a total length of 3,619 words. Both authors are Tristanians, born in 1928 and 1946, both are female; both

were educated on Tristan and did not leave the island until 1961, when the island
was evacuated following the volcanic eruption. The letters are informal in tone,
recounting local life, some gossip and general news from the island. Of course,
given what was said above about the general validity of texts, representativeness is a
crucial issue when dealing with small sample sizes: data have to be interpreted with
great care, and representativeness has to be critically assessed whenever possible.
Moreover, one has to watch and keep a critical eye on the recording conditions.
Still, this represents an interesting case study; given that both women have high rates
of levelling to *is* in their speech, even a small corpus yields insights as to whether
there is a match with its usage in letter writing. What is the ultimate outcome
of competition between standard norms (imposed by school teachers) and local
vernacular features?

Starting with speaker A, born in 1946, we find all three allomorphs *am*, *is* and *are*
in her letters. Generally speaking, the usage of *am* and *are* in writing is standard,
forms such as <we is> or <I is> are not found. This differs somewhat in the two
second persons, the third person plural and NP plurals (where we have three out of
seven tokens). There are thus cases where *is* features instead of *are*, as in <Both of
me & Dad *is* keeping well> or <Hope both *is* well>, which would be in line with
spoken norms. Of course, the low token occurrence (45) calls for caution, but we
still do find that levelled *is* makes an appearance in letters as well, as the following
excerpt shows:

(1)

(for. Hope all is well with youll and enjoying you self. Hope that XXXX had
a nice time in amercia, glad to hear that you Germany course are coming on
nicely, an than you might be able to get a job. Me and XXXX are both well
working very hard also with planting and fishing we can miss XXXX and
XXX and XXXX, things is not the same at the factory, because it no fun like
it use to be.)

This excerpt illustrates both *are* in a standard context (<Me and XXXX are both well>) while the local form *is* appears also (<things is not the same at the factory>), evidence that both co-occur in the same document (in fact, in the same sentence). One also notes other non-standard features, such as the personal pronoun <youll> 'y'all' or copula absence (<it no fun like it use to be>), which indicates that vernacular features do indeed make an appearance in letters – so they provide valuable information.

Figure 14.2 sums up the findings: by and large, standards are maintained (across the board in first and third singular and first plural) though we also find *is* with second persons, third plural and plural NPs. However, and I must emphasise this again, the small number of letters only admits a general qualitative assessment.

Author B (TdC female, b. 1928) also uses local features in her writing, as we see in the following excerpt:

(2)

(I hope that you are both well and happy. uncle XXXX are a Bit Better to day But he as lost a lot of weight. he got no belly at all. his sugar were hight and the Doctor had to treat him for that then he had all the in side of his mouth sore he couldn't eat nor drink. the doctor gave him tablets for that, now it is Better his sugar are going down slowly. he cant have nothing sweet. all he can have his diabetes food. now he is weak granny have to take him to the toilet and Bring him out in the front room now I have to dress him in the morning and undress him at night).

This short passage has several vernacular forms:
- /h/-dropping (<But he as lost>)
- /h/-insertion (<all he can have his Diabetes food>)
- copula absence (<he got no Belly at all>)
- multiple negation (<he cant have nothing sweet>)
- third person singular present tense zero (<granny have to take him to the toilet>)

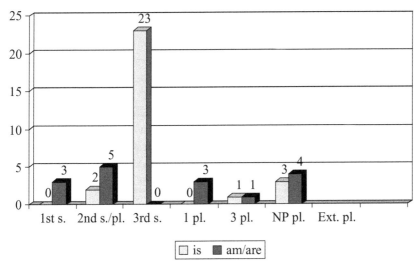

Figure 14.2 Present *be* levelling in letters of author A (TdC female, b. 1946)

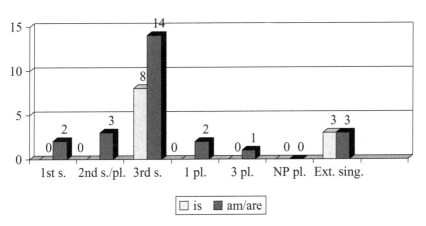

Figure 14.3 Present *be* levelling in letters of author B (TdC female, b. 1928)

All these features are attested in the literature (Schreier 2003b, 2010; Schreier and Trudgill 2006), so one might interpret this by saying that letters represent a valuable source for historical sociolinguists. As for *be* levelling (both present and past), however, a different picture emerges. Author B uses both *is* and *are* in her letters, yet she is much more standard since *is* for first singular and the plural persons makes no appearance at all; there we find <I hope that you are both well and happy>. If we look at the overall results, though, we see that the author could not differ more in terms of how she uses *are* in her letters (Figure 14.3).

The only two environments subject to variation are third singular and existentials. The latter, as we have already seen, attracts singular concord, and 'there's PL' is quite common. As for third person singular, we find a most unexpected pattern. This is an environment where a standard variety has no variation whatsoever, *is* being used canonically. Author B, however, has *are* as a majority form here, as in <uncle XXXX are a Bit Better to day>, <his sugar are going down slowly>. This is not an isolated phenomenon; in fact, *are* occurs in 63.6% (14/22) of all possible cases (put differently, where *is* would categorically occur in the standard).

With respect to this variable, authors A and B differ in that A uses more vernacular *is* forms in her writing (though only occasionally and by no means quasi-categorically, as in her speech; Schreier 2003a), whereas B is much more standard, writing *am* and *are* with all environments, including third person singular, where it would not occur in standard writing nor in her own speech.

5. Discussion and conclusion

Though this is a small corpus of letters (ten letters by two authors), which calls for caution, one can state that these documents do offer perspectives, indeed challenges, for text analysis in the context of language variation and change, and English historical linguistics. The locally spoken variety is quite well researched (Schreier 2002, 2003b, 2010; Schreier and Trudgill 2006) as a result of which it is known that present *be* levelling is unusually advanced in TdCE, so advanced, in fact, that *is* by some speakers is used quasi-categorically with all grammatical persons. Though *are* and *am* also occur (strictly in standard environments), they are minority variants.

Both authors studied here have extensive levelling to *is* in their speech (Schreier 2003a: 130–5). When it comes to analysing their writing in the form of letters, however, we do find an increase in the usage of standard forms in both authors. A and B have evidence of *is* levelling (even though it is restricted to plural NPs in B). This finding is by and large expected, and it is coherent with results from other studies (see Elspass, this volume, and Hundt, this volume). What is counterintuitive, however, is that the two writers have two techniques. Whereas we can describe A as an author who approaches the written standard while still showing a local vernacular undercurrent, speaker B generalises her writing to the extent that she uses non-local features in contexts where they would not feature in the written standard, such as *are* with third person singular present persons. It is truly remarkable that this is not found in her speech at all (in more than two hours of tape-recorded conversations!), and this is also not what she would have learnt at school during and after the Second World War. This seems to be an individual or, better, idiosyncratic writing strategy.

The most convincing explanation here is that we are looking at a classical hypercorrection process. Speaker B, when attending school that had become compulsory in the 1940s, must have been alerted to the 'incorrect' usage of local features. The local teachers were remarkably tolerant towards the local dialect and in fact showed much respect for it, as becomes clear from Evans' (1994) study of the history of education in the South Atlantic. Jim Flint, who served as local education officer from

1963 to 1965, is reported as saying, 'The children simply spoke two languages ... An attempt to change something I believed worth preserving played no part in our English course' (in Evans 1994: 274–5). All the evidence available suggests that the teachers in this period (Revd Lawrence 1943–6, Ms Handley 1946–9 and 1950–2, Ms Harvey 1949–50 and Mr Harding 1952–7) made no attempt to eradicate the local dialect in their pupils' speech, but rather tried to raise awareness about the different nature of TdCE vis-à-vis outside norms.

Still, the discrepancy between speech and writing in author B is most likely the result of awareness raising and comments from outsiders to the local usage of *is* (see above). Since she is aware of the fact that *is* abounds with all grammatical persons in the local dialect, she corrects to *are*, even in cases where this is against standard agreement, and this is probably a subconscious process. Since B is not familiar with the irregular patterning of the present *be* paradigm, she writes *are* when she would say *is*. This is a classical case of *hypercorrection*: 'Speakers of a lower prestige variety, in attempting to adopt features of a higher prestige variety, incorrectly analyse differences between the two varieties and overgeneralise on the basis of observed correspondences' (Trudgill 2003: 59–60).

Of course, we are dealing with an individual case here, and one must be careful with generalised interpretations. However, the relevance of this case study becomes obvious when we are trying to approach the findings from a historical perspective. What if, to illustrate, we did not have any recordings of the two speakers and our analysis was limited to the small collection of letters only? What conclusion would we draw on spoken TdCE? We would certainly notice the few instances of vernacular *is* but would be more impressed by author B's usage of *are* for *is* in third person singular contexts. Based on written material alone (i.e. Figures 14.2 and 14.3), one would speculate that present tense *be* was subject to variation and that *are* featured very generally in TdCE, which is historically unusual and utterly diagnostic. After checking the relevant dialect atlases and diachronic grammars and descriptions, it is not unlikely that researchers would have assumed this to be a local innovation (that would be very hard to answer, such as, for instance, why this change should operate in one environment only). Fortunately though, we do have spoken material and are in the privileged situation to be able to compare (Figure 14.1). Such an analysis renders the most likely interpretation that levelled *is* forms are hypercorrected to *are*, at least by some speakers. As a consequence, the difference between the two interpretations is highly relevant for the analysis of letters and (English) historical sociolinguistics in general.

So to conclude, the comparison of sociolinguistic variables in writing and speech in the two TdCE speakers at hand indicates that authors display some sensitivity to standard forms learnt via education, and that they are more standard in formal writing processes. The process of hypercorrection, which may accompany and be a consequence of such sensitivity, may yield a distorted picture and lead the linguist to false assumptions. Though small in length and not representative of the entire population, the Tristan letters looked into here pose a serious challenge to historical research; what happened in the case at hand may certainly have happened elsewhere as well. This emphasises the influence of scribal authorities, instructors or teachers. Any attempt to reconstruct the spoken variety may be rather challenging under these circumstances, with methodological and theoretical consequences, on Tristan and elsewhere.

CHAPTER 15

Epilogue: Where next?

Anita Auer, Daniel Schreier and Richard J. Watts

1. 'Orderly differentiation'

The day's fishing is now over, the angling historical sociolinguists – including two of the editorial team – have shown their catches to one another (and to the readers of this book) and have discussed the worms they chose to fish with. It is now the job of the three editors to metamorphose themselves fully into historical sociolinguists once more and to move from the angling metaphor back to the field onto which it was projected, i.e. historical linguists plotting the history of a language, in fact, any language.

One conclusion to be drawn from the contributions to this volume is that there is never just one history to be told, the 'real' history, the 'true' history, the 'correct' history of English, or any other language. Ultimately, it is simply not possible to say exactly what we mean when we talk of 'English' or 'German' – although, of course, to some researchers (and to many outside academia) the terms still mean 'standard English' or 'standard German'. When the multiple developments of 'a language' are considered from different *socio*linguistic perspectives, there will always be other histories to tell, histories which represent alternatives to what Mattheier warns us against, i.e. the belief that 'the "standard" language is the genuine teleological goal of any historical language development' (2010: 353).

Just as the number of approaches is likely to show heterogeneity, so too will a collection of this kind appear to offer a heterogeneity which motivates against any unity of theoretical principles. This, however, is an illusion, since the very nature of the sociolinguistic study of human language – particularly when it is focused on the fundamental issues of language change – is what Weinreich, Labov and Herzog (1968: 101) call 'orderly differentiation'. It was for this reason that we chose to look at letters and diaries as a truly fascinating source of language data that can be used precisely to reveal the orderly heterogeneity of language in use by writers from different points on the social hierarchy and at different points in time. As a sober antidote to the overwhelming use of print data, many of the contributors to this volume have decided to use databases of handwritten letters (and in Allen's case also diaries), particularly from a section of the population who are generally felt to have been 'illiterate' until well into the nineteenth century. The result has been a remarkably rich vein of language data that could and should be broadened and deepened, given that we have access to more handwritten materials.[1] But it also presents us with the following conundrum: what is the nature of the 'orderliness' in the heterogeneity? Is it simply the case that 'anything goes'? If not, what are the constraints, sociolinguistic and sociocultural, on what we consider to constitute 'anything' in the previous question? In Section 3 of this final chapter we wish to make a few suggestions about how this conundrum might be tackled.

2. A heterogeneity of sociolinguistic approaches

In his opening chapter, Watts discusses the applications of sociolinguistic approaches to historical language data and some of the major shifts in focus within mainstream sociolinguistics in the study of language variation, and the implications of those shifts for language change. Under the influence of interactional sociolinguistics, the more quantitatively oriented focus on variation within a speech community in variationist sociolinguistics has undergone a change from the speech community itself to the individual speaker within that community, and this has provided a new impetus in assessing how individuals introduce, adopt and help to diffuse innovative structures through the social networks, communities of practice and discourse communities in which they use language. In tackling these problems, a whole range of theoretical and methodological approaches has emerged in the study of how individuals deal with the cut-and-thrust of emergent social practice, how they position themselves and others in doing so, how they construct identities for themselves and others, and how they negotiate pragmatic and social meanings with others. Many of these approaches are used in this volume, and we will summarise these briefly in what follows.

Finding the balance between studying variation in a speech community and variation in individual speakers, i.e. in reconciling First Wave Variation Studies with Third Wave Variation Studies, lies at the very heart of two chapters. Fernandez-Campoy and Conde-Silvestre in Chapter 2 and Bergs in Chapter 7 tackle this sensitive problem head on in reconsidering their own work and the work of others on the Paston letters. What emerges from both discussions is a range of fascinating new insights involving the social nature of letter writing in which the focus shifts from the speech community to communities of practice. In both cases, it is crucial to note that this valuable family corpus of letters appears before the first explicit moves towards formulating 'standard English' in the sixteenth century, which helps to explain the intriguing amount of heterogeneity in the letters in which the direction of change towards more 'modern' constructions in English can be traced. At the same time, the absence of a standard also frees the researcher from having to focus on a teleological development in this direction and allows the application of more Third Wave approaches to the kinds of social meanings and identities constructed

---

[1] This is a point which we will deal with in Section 3 of this final chapter.

by the authors of the letters or, as Bergs points out, the scribes who were charged with writing them out.

An the other end of this spectrum lies Dollinger's Chapter 6 in which a focus on an emerging Canadian standard English in prescriptive grammars can be contrasted with what letter writers actually produce. An interesting point in Dollinger's chapter is that he chooses the alternation between the modal verbs *will* and *shall* in expressing futurity in English to illustrate the heterogeneity in the late eighteenth-century and nineteenth-century letters to the Surveyor-General or the Commissioner of Crown Lands written by settlers in Ontario (or what was then Upper Canada) in the *Corpus of Early Ontario English*. Variation between *will* and *shall* (and other constructions encoding states and events in future time) has also caused an unusual amount of insecurity in the writings of authors who might be said to have been fully competent in standard language usage in the early eighteenth century. One of the seven case studies investigated by Arnovick (1999) deals with the apparent insecurity concerning the appropriate structures to encode future time use evident in the corrections made by Swift in his handwritten manuscript drafts (see also Tieken-Boon van Ostade 2011: 246–8 on Robert Lowth's usage of *will* and *shall*).

Other chapters focusing more explicitly on Third Wave Variation Studies to explain the structural heterogeneity evident in the letter corpora looked at are Chapters 8 (Auer), 12 (Pietsch) and 9 (Fitzmaurice). Fitzmaurice's chapter is particularly interesting in this respect as she deals with letters written by aristocratic members of the early eighteenth-century Kit-Cat Club, who had acquired a thorough classical education and ought to have been very proficient in what was soon to become standard English.[2] Depending on the social frame in which the letters were written (age, degree of formality, type of letter, etc.), letter writers vary in their usage of constructions to express personal identities, degree of social distance and familiarity, i.e. to construct social relationships of different kinds with their addressees. They, too, display heterogeneity.

Chapter 13 (Siebers) is motivated by one of the classic disputes between two major strands of sociolinguistics (dialectology and creolistics) as to whether African American English developed as a creole or through protracted language contact with dialectal varieties of English imported from Britain to the American colonies and with those who later emigrated to the USA after the American Revolution. She provides evidence to show that with or without contact between African Americans and speakers of Scotch-Irish, certain significant constructions in this variety are present in the letter-writing data, and that this could be an incidence of Weinreich *et al.*'s 'orderly differentiation' or what she refers to as 'ordered heterogeneity'. The issues of mobility and migration are thus focused on in this chapter and are dealt

---

[2] We should make it clear at this point, however, that other expressions throughout the eighteenth century were used to refer to what was to become known as 'Standard English' in the nineteenth century, e.g. 'polite English' and 'educated English'.

with again in more detail in Pietsch's Chapter 12, in which he discusses the 'archaic' use of structures in emigrant letters that Irish settlers in America sent home to their friends and families in Ireland. Many of these structures are remnants of the 'standard' formulae that were required in letter writing, and may have been assumed by the writers to be part of the necessary formulaic nature of letter writing (and thus of what they may have imagined to be 'standard English'). It is quite possible here that a 'letter writer' persona was being constructed. Laitinen (Chapter 10) also deals with issues of internal geographical mobility (horizontal space) and social distance (vertical space) in the letters contained in Sokoll's corpus of Essex pauper letters. Once again, writers needed to evaluate their own changed social status and the social status of their addressees in constructing what Laitinen calls 'local' and 'translocal' meanings. They needed, in other words, to stylise themselves and their addressees in specific ways in order to achieve their aims.

Two other chapters by Elspaß (Chapter 3) and Hundt (Chapter 5) deal with emigrants' letters, but from two rather different standpoints, although, once again, heterogeneity connects them both and creates points of connection with all the other chapters in this volume. Elspaß's chapter is the only one in this collection which does not deal with English, but it is nevertheless interesting and significant from a number of points of view. First of all, it contains the same kinds of 'archaic' letter-writing formulae and linguistic constructions as those in Pietsch's chapter, and like Pietsch, Elspaß attributes the heterogeneity that is evident in the letters to an 'imagined' standard language and a set of assumed formulaic standards that must be adhered to in letter writing. We thus have two sets of emigrants to America, Irish and German, writing in two different languages, and yet displaying the same kinds of strategy. This cannot be pure chance; on the contrary, it gives rise to the hypothesis that letter writers from the lower ends of the social scale, writing to family and friends back 'home', key into the same kinds of expectations of what it means to 'write' rather than 'speak', and what it means to establish contact through letters regardless of the language they use.[3] Elspaß's chapter is also central to the whole collection in that it is a strong argument, by one of the founders of the Historical Sociolinguistics Network (HiSoN), that manuscripts from members of the lower end of the social scale should be studied within their sociohistorical and sociocultural contexts. Such study yields alternative histories 'from below' challenging language histories whose teleological driving force is uniquely towards the emergence of the standard language. This is one of the major themes of the

---

[3] One of the three editors (RJW) has had the privilege to look at facsimile copies of letters handwritten in Italian to friends and family members in the valleys of the Ticino by nineteenth-century emigrants to California from the canton of Ticino, Switzerland. As far as he is able to judge, the same kinds of strategies emerge in these letters. The writers do not write in dialect, but in an approximation to what they consider to be 'standard Italian'; they also use formulaic language in the salutation section, asking after their addressees' health, and leave-taking, which, like the material in Chapters 3 and 12, are taken to be standard expressions; and they show similar degrees of variation, i.e. heterogeneity. We believe that this phenomenon merits a large-scale study of handwritten manuscripts from emigrants to the Americas, to South Africa, Australia and New Zealand from a variety of linguistic regions in Europe.

volume, and it is explicitly addressed in a large majority of the chapters. In addition, Elspaß stresses the need to search out more handwritten textual material produced by members of the lower strata of the social hierarchy by invoking and applying Koch and Oesterreicher's model of conceptual orality along the continuum between the language of immediacy and the language of distance. Within this model, there is a wide variation of textual genres in the written medium in manuscript form that are still waiting to be discovered, and we shall return to this point in Section 3.[4]

Hundt's chapter looks at a set of letters that exist only in printed form. They were published in London in 1843 under the title *Letters from Settlers & Labouring Emigrants, in the New Zealand Company's Settlements of Wellington, Nelson, & New Plymouth. From February, 1842, to January, 1843*, presumably under the auspices of the New Zealand Company with the aim of attracting new settlers from Britain to New Zealand. The collection is not therefore a corpus of letters but rather a collection consisting of letters to the editor, official letters and a majority of private letters from new settlers. We can therefore assume that they had been heavily edited before publication, and we might also assume that all traces of the linguistic varieties spoken by the settlers had been obliterated. But when we read the first letter in the collection from a Mr Francis Bradey, which is a veritable eulogy to the excellence of New Zealand as a goal of emigration, we note that, although spellings might have been corrected, punctuation adjusted and all traces of London dialect erased, the letter still shows the undeniable signs of 'conceptual orality'.[5] Hundt reveals that, despite the editing process, there are still plenty of traces of non-standard varieties of English to be found in the letters and, as we have just indicated in footnote 5, it is practically impossible to eradicate the signs of conceptual orality without completely rewriting the letter. The letter would become, in other words, no longer a private letter, a letter from a successful emigrant trying to encourage others to take the same step, but some other type of letter or perhaps even a pamphlet.

Methodological issues also present difficulties in the present volume, and the greatest difficulty with which historical sociolinguists are confronted is the complete lack of any objective record of how interactants communicated with one another in social practice before the advent of sound recordings around the beginning of the twentieth century. A further methodological stumbling block concerns the amount

[4] Watts (2011: ch. 3) has adapted Koch and Oesterreicher's model to explain the breakdown in an important discourse archive represented by the Anglo-Saxon Chronicles caused by the scribe's personal introduction of an oral narrative style of great emotional force (language of immediacy) into what was originally designed as a quasi-official reporting of events (language of distance). The term he uses for 'conceptual orality' is 'inscribed orality'.

[5] Here, for the record, is the final paragraph: 'I may add that I was carrying on the business of a master boot-maker for 20 years, in the Old Kent-road, and a rate-payer of the parish of St. George's, Southwark, and a freeholder of the county of Surrey; and I transferred the whole of my property to New Zealand, and it was the most fortunate speculation I ever made.' Note the effect of the concatenation of clauses connected with *and*. The facts of his carrying out the profession as bootmaker, being a rate-payer, being a freeholder, of having transferred his property to New Zealand and of this final fact having been 'the most fortunate speculation I ever made', are listed one after another, as if they were part of an oral narration.

of data that is at our disposal, particularly when our major aim is the attempted reconstruction of speech 'from below'. Again and again contributors express caution in assessing their analysis of letter materials on the grounds that the overall scarcity of the data will not support the kinds of statistically reliable statements that we wish to make. In Chapter 14, Schreier discusses these issues, in particular the nature of the filter of the handwritten text through which we are forced to attempt such a reconstruction. However, his analysis deals with a contemporary collection of letters in his possession from people whose everyday oral language usage is known to him intimately from his fieldwork on Tristan da Cunha and from his close connections with the community. It is precisely the kind of valuable material which may allow us to go back through time and make relatively confident statements about what is going on when ordinary people decide to put pen to paper to communicate through the written medium with friends and relations separated from one another by large geographical distances. Comparing in detail what they say with what they write is an invaluable aid to discovering the principles at work when anyone, from above or below, makes the transition from speech to writing.

We now come to the chapters by Allen and Fairman (Chapters 11 and 4), since it is within these chapters that we are given, implicitly in the case of Allen and very explicitly in the case of Fairman, two sets of theoretical tools that we need to consider in any further sociolinguistic work on letters. Both Allen and Fairman, as indeed all the other contributors to this volume, see the world of the written medium as representing very different kinds of communication through the use of language (cf. also Elspaß in Chapter 3). Allen uses the creolist distinction between basilect, mesolect and acrolect forms of language to assess the degrees of standardness or non-standardness of a letter writer, thus allowing us to assess very roughly how close to the standard language a letter writer gets. But we still need to ask two things. Firstly, could a letter writer not fluctuate between different points along this continuum depending on the social and sociocultural contexts of the relationship between writer and addressee that is being established through the letter, and could this not happen either within the same letter or from one letter to the next? The evidence in all the chapters in this volume would suggest that this is the case. Secondly, what are we to do when, as in the case of the Paston letters, there is no explicitly accepted standard variety of the language that can be compared with the language in which the letter is written? Surely it would not then be possible to say whether a writer displays more basilectal, mesolectal or acrolectal structures.

In Chapter 4, Fairman argues that the different forms of language within hand-written texts, i.e. not just letters, cannot be assessed as closer to or further away from a 'standard' since he 'argues for a sociolinguistic model of pools of handwritten and printed literacies and writers'. Language committed to the medium of writing can only be learnt, it is not acquired face-to-face in socio-communicative interaction with others, and this means, in his eyes, that what we read is a form, or forms, of literacy, not language. This is an extreme position, but if we assume that when we write, we transform language into writing and when we read, we use the writing that we see to reconstruct language, it is certainly an acceptable position, extreme or not. After all, what we as historical sociolinguists are constantly doing is moving from written manuscripts – and this should be the case rather than only moving from print, in Fairman's eyes – to derive the language of the speaker, i.e. what s/he may have said in oral interaction.

3. What next and where next?

3.1 What next?

A number of contributors to the present volume, who are perhaps happier working with quantitative methods involving sophisticated statistical analyses, have expressed their misgivings concerning the small size of their databases and the concomitant lack of sufficient tokens of the linguistic constructions they wished to analyse, which prevented them from making reliable predictive statements about what to expect in new data sets. This is a perfectly understandable concern, and one with which we are continually confronted when dealing with historical data. Nevertheless, we feel that there are four possible responses to these misgivings.

The first response is related to the focus shift that has taken place between First and Third Wave Variation Studies in sociolinguistics, and it argues for the need to focus on both types of study. In evaluating language change, we naturally consider changes that affect whole speech communities, but the jury is still debating the question as to what actually constitutes a 'speech community' (Patrick 2001). If we take a speech community as being composed of a large number of subgroups, among and within many of which individuals may move, the logical consequence is that a speech community can never be pinned down to an exact number or type of speaker. And if we let go of the teleological direction of language change in the direction of an ultimate standard, we must conclude that standards, like any other varieties of a language, are always subject to language change.

The second response is that innovative new structures are more frequently introduced 'from below', i.e. from individuals involved in ongoing socio-communicative verbal interaction, than from above, i.e. through conscious manipulation by those in power and the social institutions that they have set up (e.g. government, education, business, the media, and so on). Although it is perfectly legitimate to investigate how certain new structures are distributed socially, socioeconomically and socioculturally through other and/or larger groups (e.g. speech communities), they first occur – unfortunately almost without exception unbeknown to historical sociolinguists – in communities of practice. It is at this point that Third Wave Variation Studies becomes important, since it is through individuals adapting their own use of language to position themselves and others, aligning themselves through ongoing identity construction with others in emergent communities of practice that social meanings are constructed which may be diffused to other groups. We find it difficult to see how these individual instances of language usage can be analysed quantitatively, but it is still interesting to carry out quantitative analyses of language change in large populations and to correlate the results with the more qualitative judgements of how individuals construct social meanings in social practice.

The third response concerns a fundamental misunderstanding about what quantitative and qualitative research methods can achieve. The results of quantitative analyses present facts with respect to statistically representative sections of a population, and they make reliable predictions about what a researcher is likely to find in a further statistically representative section of the same or another population, but they can never guarantee that those facts *will* reoccur. Qualitative analyses are interpretative models of what might be found to hold beyond the level of small group analysis at the level of a statistically representative section of a population, and they may be considered to constitute the first step in filtering out candidate structures that may be involved in language change. On the other hand, the heterogeneity evident in the letter data reveal a high level of idiosyncratic language use which may sometimes be explained through appeals to dialect influence or non-standard usage, but which should in no way be interpreted as representing 'wrong' or 'ungrammatical' language.

This leads us to our fourth response. In searching out handwritten manuscript material[6] from those in the lower echelons of the social hierarchy, we do not have a large range of text genres to choose from. As Fairman points out, learning to read and write requires a conscious effort by individuals across the whole range of the social strata, and without schooling of some kind or other, however minimal, it is hardly possible to acquire those skills. Acquiring forms of literacy is therefore language-plus-schooling, i.e. it is more than language, which is of course not to say that it has nothing to do with language. But in the little time available to labouring people beyond working for a living and struggling to survive, the number of written text genres on offer to read must have far exceeded those that they were compelled to use for writing. However, we have hardly scratched the surface of collecting and collating in the form of corpora all the extant handwritten manuscripts that must have survived the ravages of time. Fairman also maintains that linguists have made easy lives for themselves by focusing on printed materials, since the problems of deciphering manuscripts at the graphemic level demand large amounts of time and patience. He may be right, but we can at least confidently assert that the study of early forms of language that only exist in handwritten manuscripts and have later been transcribed to suit the print medium has undoubtedly allowed scholars to disregard important aspects of the manuscripts themselves. In some cases it has even led to constructions of language history which lack any objective evidence and have been handed down to generation after generation of students as if they were

---

[6] And the reader should recall at this point that there is no other linguistic evidence available to the historical linguist prior to recording techniques introduced at the beginning of the twentieth century, apart from printed material.

'true' (like the presentation of a monolithic standard as the 'one and only' variety).[7] We need to search out every scrap of paper or parchment that may contain the writings of members of the lower classes, and create from them a carefully tagged corpus. Nor should we then forget to do the same for writers at all the other levels of the social hierarchy (see Fitzmaurice, Chapter 9). We need to revise our arsenal of theoretical concepts to account for the fact that those who speak dialect rarely if ever write in dialect, but instead aim to meet certain imagined standards, linguistic, social and genre-specific, that they have acquired at some point in their lives as being required by the text genre in which they want to frame their writing. We have seen time and again in this volume that letter writers are aware of constraints on forms of address, layout, formulaic textual content (such as asking after the addressee's health), Latinate forms of expression, ways of finishing a letter, the need to write in an aesthetically pleasing script, etc., and that these imagined constraints determine the language they use. In the final subsection of this chapter, we wish to suggest a further approach to letter writing that might yield interesting and possibly surprising results.

3.2 Where next?

Having reached the end of this collection of chapters on sociolinguistic approaches to historical letters as a source of data to set up alternative histories of a language (in this case English, but also German in Chapter 3), it is incumbent on us to suggest how we might proceed to broaden our knowledge of letter and diary writing in the future and so to deepen the significance of this source of data for constructing 'language histories from below'. In the opening chapter Watts mentioned the concept of 'performance', and this was picked up during the second chapter, on the Paston letters, but only figured very marginally throughout the volume. The concept of 'performance' has recently taken on a new lease of life through the special issue of the *Journal of Sociolinguistics* guest-edited by Allan Bell and Andy Gibson, published in 2011, and it is also currently the subject of Watts and Morrissey's present research into the language of British folk song. However, before we mention that research more explicitly, consider Pietsch's statement that 'letter writers were prone to resort to close imitation of the most direct kind of linguistic model they had available: other letters they had received or seen written in their immediate social environment' (p. 238). He goes on to say that '[l]etter writing could thus become a relatively self-contained domain of linguistic conventionalisation, with relatively

---

7 One of the most spectacular results of this form of scholarly neglect has led to speculative reconstructions of the early history of English that have been discursively constructed from the early nineteenth century on as 'true'. We are referring here to the assumed history of the *Beowulf* manuscript, which, when one spends a long laborious period of time examining the only extant, damaged manuscript of the poem, begins to reveal fascinating alternative interpretations to the assumed antiquity of the text itself (see Kiernan 1997 and Watts 2011: ch. 2).

little correcting input from the written standard English used in more educated sectors of society' (*ibid.*).

He then provides us with the following perfect scenario for looking at letters as performances:

> The availability of models for such imitation can be explained through the fact that *correspondence through letters was in many instances not a merely private but a shared, social event,* which ensured that its linguistic conventions could be transmitted across a local community of practice. *Letters received from relatives abroad were preserved, cherished and frequently shared with friends or family members or read out in a family gathering – the letters themselves are full of references to such practices* (cf. Elspaß 2005: 100 for a comparable observation regarding German writers). The memory of letters that were orally shared in this way no doubt provided many subsequent writers with the material for just that stylistic and formulaic imitation whose effects we have observed. (p. 238; our italics)

The letters were not written in dialect precisely because the writers were following 'a relatively self-contained domain of linguistic conventionalisation', but they would have been talked about and discussed at such gatherings in dialect.

An analogous situation occurred in the performances of folk song throughout Britain and Ireland in the 1930s to the 1970s by traditional lower- and working-class singers born some time between 1890 and 1920.[8] Material recorded by the BBC (now available in the form of CDs) immediately before the Second World War and then again soon after the war in the late 1940s during live Saturday night singing sessions at a pub called 'The Eel's Foot' in Suffolk reveals that conversation and banter between the songs by the locals present was carried out in dialect, but that the songs display a similar range of linguistic variation as we have seen in lower-class letter writing in this volume, i.e. in pauper letters, in letters from emigrants and letters from African Americans, whether enslaved or not, seeking help from persons in authority.[9] In other words we appear to have a second 'domain of linguistic conventionalisation', this time, however, one which applies to oral production rather than written production. Watts and Morrissey have checked these data against other CDs made from recordings during the 1950s, 1960s and 1970s of traditional singers, and the same phenomenon occurs. Singers do not use their dialects to perform the songs, although they may introduce elements from them to a greater or lesser extent. Singers who appear to be using dialect, i.e. those from industrial areas of northern England and from Scotland, can be shown to have modified those dialects notably when singing. Significantly, Irish singers use 'linguistic conventionalisation' more than Scottish or urban northern English singers.

---

[8] We are talking here of older traditional singers (rural- and urban-based) and not of folk-song revivalists.

[9] Obviously, the standard formulaic expressions that lower-class letter writers imagined to be part of the genre of letter writing are not used in the songs, but other kinds of formulaic language that serve similar kinds of function and were taken to be 'standard' in traditional folk singing most definitely *are* present.

We would like to leave the reader of this book with a strong hypothesis that will need sociolinguistic verification in further research on letters:

> *Hypothesis*: When speakers, at whatever social level, move from oral language use to language + (in these two cases *language + literacy/'letteracy'* and *language + song*), they do so consciously, and when they do so, they key into the performance mode, which involves them in various kinds of 'linguistic conventionalisation'.

The performance mode may draw from standard language, imagined standard language, non-standard linguistic features, dialect constructions, 'expected' forms of formulaic language and other possible modes of expression that remain to be looked at closely in future research. Writers and singers, whatever their social standing, are not using 'standard' or 'dialect', but a mixture of forms which are calculated by the former to have some effect on the 'audience', i.e. the reader or the listener. During the performance, forms of stylisation are bound to occur and will strengthen the effect on the audience. Judging letter writing (and folk singing) solely on the basis of the standard language obscures the significance of performance as a valid concept within sociolinguistics. We suggest that this alternative way of looking at letters, whether 'from above' or 'from below', may open up new opportunities for productive research in the future.

References

PRIMARY SOURCES

American Colonization Society Records. 1792–1964. 331 microfilm reels. Washington, DC: Library of Congress.

ARCHER: A Representative Corpus of Historical English Registers. 2006. First constructed by Douglas Biber and Edward Finegan. Website: www.alc.manchester.ac.uk/subjects/lel/ research/projects/archer/

Bank of Canadian English. 2006–. Ed. by Stefan Dollinger, Laurel Brinton and Margery Fee. Vancouver, BC: University of British Columbia.

Benecke Family Papers. 1816–1989. Military Papers, Subseries 2455–2676, Black Claims, Western St Louis, MO, Historical Manuscript Collection.

Corpus of Early English Correspondence (CEEC). 1998. Led by Terttu Nevalainen, co-founded by Helena Raumolin-Brunberg, University of Helsinki. Website: www.helsinki.fi/ varieng/CoRD/corpora/CEEC/ceece.html

Corpus of Early English Correspondence Extension (CEECE). 2006. Led by Terttu Nevalainen, University of Helsinki. Website: www.helsinki.fi/varieng/CoRD/corpora/ CEEC/ceece.html

Corpus of Early English Correspondence Sampler (CEECS). 1998. Led by Terttu Nevalainen, co-founded by Helena Raumolin-Brunberg, University of Helsinki.

Corpus of Early English Correspondence Supplement (CEECSU). 2006. Led by Terttu Nevalainen, University of Helsinki. Website: www.helsinki.fi/varieng/CoRD/corpora/ CEEC/ceecsu.html

Corpus of Early Ontario English, pre-Confederation Section (CONTE-pC). 2006. *Version 0.9*. Ed. Stefan Dollinger, University of Vienna.

Corpus of English Dialogues 1560–1760. Compiled by Jonathan Culpeper and Merja Kytö. Website: www.engelska.uu.se/Research/English_Language/Research_ Areas/Electronic_Resource_Projects/A_Corpus_of_English_Dialogues/

Corpus of Late 18c Prose. 1994. Compiled and coded by David Denison, University of Manchester. Website: http://personalpages.manchester.ac.uk/staff/david.denison/ late18c.html

Corpus of Nineteenth-Century Business Correspondence, see *Corpus of Nineteenth-century Scottish Correspondence*.

Corpus of Nineteenth-century Scottish Correspondence (19CSC). Under construction. Led by Marina Dossena and Richard Dury, University of Bergamo. Website: www.unibg.it/ dati/persone/246/5194–19CSC_site.pdf

Corpus of Older African American Letters (COAAL). Led by Edgar W. Schneider, University of Regensburg, and Lucia Siebers (PI), University of Regensburg.

See under: www.uni-regensburg.de/language-literature-culture/english-linguistics/world-englishes/current-projects/index.html

Corpus of Scottish Correspondence (CSC). 2007. Led by Anneli Meurman-Solin, University of Helsinki.

Early English Books Online, 1475–1700. 1999. Cambridge: Chadwyck Healey literature collections. Website: http://eebo.chadwyck.com/home

Eighteenth Century Collections Online (ECCO). n.d. Gale Group. Website: http://gale.cengage.co.uk/product-highlights/history/eighteenth-century-collections-online.aspx

Essex Pauper letters, 1731–183. 2001. Ed. Thomas Sokoll. Oxford: Oxford University Press.

Federal Writers Project for the Works Project Administration (WPA). 1936–1940, Washington, DC: Library of Congress.

Freiburg Corpus of English Dialects (FRED). Supervised by Bernd Kortmann, University of Freiburg i. Br., Website: www2.anglistik.uni-freiburg.de/institut/lskortmann/FRED/

Fulham Papers (Papers of the Bishops of London). Records of the diocese of London, 18th–19th centuries. London: Lambeth Palace Library. http://gale.cengage.co.uk/product-highlights/history/eighteenth-century-collections-online.aspx

Letters of Artisans and the Labouring Poor, c. 1750–1834 (LALP). Under construction. Compiled by Tony Fairman, Maidstone, and converted into a corpus by Anita Auer and Moragh Gordon, Utrecht University, and Mikko Laitinen, Linnaeus University. http://lalpcorpus.wordpress.com

Old Bailey Proceedings Online, 1674–1913. 2003. Tim Hitchcock, Robert Shoemaker, Clive Emsley, Sharon Howard and Jamie McLaughlin, *et al.*, University of Sheffield. Website: www.oldbaileyonline.org/index.jsp

Parsed Corpus of Early English Correspondence (PCEEC). Tagging by Arja Nurmi, University of Helsinki, syntactic annotation by Ann Taylor, University of York. Distributed by the University of Oxford Text Archive at www.ota.ox.ac.uk

Records of the Bureau of Refugees, Freedmen and Abandoned Land (Record Group 105), series 42–39, Letters Received, National Archives II, College Park, MD.

Records of the Department of the Interior (Record Group 48), Records of the Indian Territory Division, Special Files 1898–1907, Choctaw and Chickasaw Freedmen, Entry 713, Box No. 48, National Archives II, College Park, MD.

The Hamburg Corpus of Irish English (HCIE). 2003. Led by Peter Siemund, University of Hamburg. Website: www.uni-hamburg.de/sfb538/projekth5_e.html Website: www.uni-hamburg.de/sfb538/projekth5_e.html

SECONDARY SOURCES

Adamson, Sylvia. 1998. Literary language. *The Cambridge History of the English Language.* Vol. IV: *1776–1997*, ed. Suzanne Romaine, 589–692. Cambridge: Cambridge University Press.

Adelung, Johann Christoph. 1781. *Deutsche Sprachlehre: Zum Gebrauche der Schulen in den Königl. Preuß. Landen.* Berlin: Voß.

Admoni, Wladimir. 1990. *Historische Syntax des Deutschen.* Tübingen: Niemeyer.

Ágel, Vilmos and Mathilde Hennig (eds.). 2006. *Grammatik aus Nähe und Distanz: Theorie und Praxis am Beispiel von Nähetexten 1650–2000.* Tübingen: Niemeyer.

Agha, Asif. 2004. Registers of language. *A Companion to Linguistic Anthropology*, ed. Alessandro Duranti, 23–45. Oxford: Blackwell.

Allen, Barbara. 2006. The acquisition and practice of working-class literacy in the nineteenth-century Sussex Weald. Unpublished PhD thesis, University of Sussex.

2007. Looking at writing to learn about reading. *Journal of Reading, Writing and Literacy* 2(2): 31–48.

forthcoming. Introduction to *The Journals of Joseph Denner Blake*. Hampshire Record Series, Hampshire Record Office.

Alston, R. C. 1965. *A Bibliography of the English Language from the Invention of Printing to the Year 1800*. Vol. I: *English Grammars Written in English*. Leeds: E. J. Arnold and Son.

Anderwald, Lieselotte. 2007. 'He rung the bell' and 'she drunk the ale' – non-standard past tense forms in traditional British dialects and on the Internet. *Corpus Linguistics and the Web*, ed. Marianne Hundt, Carolin Biewer and Nadja Nesselhauf, 271–85. Amsterdam: Rodopi.

2009. *The Morphology of English Dialects: Verb-Formation in Non-standard English*. Cambridge: Cambridge University Press.

2011. Norm vs. variation in British English irregular verbs: The case of past tense *sang* vs. *sung*. *English Language and Linguistics* 15(1): 85–112.

Anonymous. 1762. *The Art of Letter-Writing, Divided into Two Parts: The First, Containing Rules and Directions for Writing Letters on all Sorts of Subjects: . . . The Second, a Collection of Letters on the Most Interesting Occasions in Life*. London. [Retrieved from *Eighteenth Century Collections Online*. Gale. University Library Utrecht. 29 September 2011.]

Anonymous. 1763. *The Ladies Complete Letter Writer*. London. [Retrieved from *Eighteenth Century Collections Online*. Gale. University Library Utrecht. 29 September 2011.]

Anonymous. 1798. A little learning is a dangerous thing. *The Gentleman's Magazine*. October 1797: 820.

Archbold, W. A. J. 2004. 'Lumley, Henry (c.1658–1722)', rev. Timothy Harrison Place, *Oxford Dictionary of National Biography*, Oxford University Press; online edn, May 2006. www.oxforddnb.com/view/article/17177, accessed 9 August 2011.

Arnovick, Leslie. 1999. *Diachronic Pragmatics: Seven Case Studies in English Illocutionary Development*. Amsterdam: Benjamins.

Auer, Anita. 2006. Precept and practice: The influence of prescriptivism on the English subjunctive. *Syntax, Style and Grammatical Norms: English from 1500–2000*, ed. Christiane Dalton-Puffer, Dieter Kastovsky, Nikolaus Ritt and Herbert Schendl, 33–53. Bern: Peter Lang.

in prep. *Writing across the Social Spectrum: Letter Writing Practices in Nineteenth-Century Northern England*. Berlin and New York: Mouton de Gruyter.

Auer, Peter (ed.). 2007. *Style and Social Identities: Alternative Approaches to Linguistic Heterogeneity*. Berlin: Walter de Gruyter.

Austen, Jane. 1813 [1985]. *Pride and Prejudice*. London: Penguin Classics.

1814 [1996]. *Mansfield Park*. London: Penguin Classics.

Austin, Frances 1973. Epistolary conventions in the Clift family correspondence. *English Studies* 54: 129–40.

2000. Letter writing in a Cornish community in the 1790s. *Letter Writing as a Social Practice*, ed. David Barton and Nigel Hall, 43–62. Amsterdam: Benjamins.

2004. 'Having this importunity': The survival of opening formulas in letters in the eighteenth and nineteenth centuries. *Historical Sociolinguistics and Sociohistorical Linguistics* 4. Accessed at www.let.leidenuniv.nl/hsl_shl/heaving_this_importunity.htm

Austin-Jones, Frances. 2007. A thousand years of model letter-writers. *Linguistica e filologia* 25: 7–20.

Avis, Walter S. 1973. The English language in Canada. *Current Trends in Linguistics*, Vol. X/1, ed. Thomas Sebeok, 40–74. The Hague: Mouton.

Avis, Walter S., Charles Crate, Patrick Drysdale, Douglas Leechman, Matthew H. Scharill and Charles L. Lovell (eds.). 1967. *A Dictionary of Canadianisms on Historical Principles*. Toronto: Gage.

Bailey, Richard. 1982. The English language in Canada. *English as a World Language*, ed. Richard W. Bailey and Manfred Görlach, 134–76. Ann Arbor: University of Michigan Press.

Bailey, Richard W. 1996. *Nineteenth-Century English*. Ann Arbor: University of Michigan Press.

Baker, Frank (ed.). 1980. *The Works of John Wesley*. Oxford: Clarendon Press.

Bannet, Eve Tavor. 2007. Printed epistolary manuals and the transatlantic rescripting of manuscript culture. *Studies in Eighteenth Century Culture* 36: 13–32.

Barber, Richard. 1986. *The Pastons: A Family in the Wars of the Roses*. Woodbridge: The Boydell Press.

Barry, Michael V. 1981. The southern boundaries of Northern Hiberno-English speech. *Aspects of the English Dialects in Ireland*, ed. Michael V. Barry, 52–95. Belfast: Queen's University, Institute of Irish Studies.

Barton, David. 1994. *Literacy: An Introduction to the Ecology of Written Language*. Oxford: Blackwell.

Barton, David and Nigel Hall. 2001. Introduction. *Letter Writing as a Social Practice*, ed. David Barton and Nigel Hall, 1–15. Amsterdam: John Benjamins.

Bauer, Laurie. 1994. *Watching Language Change: An Introduction to the Study of Linguistic Change in Standard Englishes in the Twentieth Century*. London and New York: Longman.

Baugh, Alfred and Thomas Cable. 1993. *A History of the English language*. 4th edn. London: Routledge.

2002. *A History of the English language*. 5th edn. London: Routledge.

Beal, Joan. 2004. *English in Modern Times 1700–1945*. London, New York: Arnold.

Behaghel, Otto. 1900. Geschriebenes Deutsch und gesprochenes Deutsch. Festvortrag, gehalten auf der Hauptversammlung des Allgemeinen Deutschen Sprachvereins zu Zittau am 1. April 1899. *Wissenschaftliche Beihefte zur Zeitschrift des Allgemeinen Deutschen Sprachvereins* H.17/18: 213–32.

Bell, Allan. 1984. Language style as audience design. *Language in Society* 12: 145–204.

2007. Style in dialogue: Bakhtin and sociolinguistic theory. *Sociolinguistic Variation: Theories, Methods, and Applications*, ed. R. Bayley, 90–109. Cambridge: Cambridge University Press.

Bennet, Henry S. 1990/1995. *The Pastons and their England: Studies in an Age of Transition*. Cambridge: Cambridge University Press.

Benskin, Michael. 1977. Local archives and Middle English dialects. *Journal of the Society of Archivists* 5(8): 500–14.

1982. The letters <þ> and <y> in Later Middle English, and some related matters. *Journal of the Society of Archivists* 7: 13–30.

1992. Some new perspectives on the origins of Standard Written English. *Dialect and Standard Language: Dialekt und Standardsprache in the English, Dutch, German and Norwegian Language Areas*, ed. J. van Leuvenstejn and J. Berns, 71–105. Amsterdam: North Holland.

Benson, Larry. (ed.). 1987. *The Riverside Chaucer*. Oxford: Oxford University Press.

Bergs, Alexander. 2004. What if one man's lexicon were another man's syntax? A new approach to the history of relative *who*. *Folia Linguistica Historica* 21(1/2): 93–109.

2005. *Social Networks and Historical Sociolinguistics: Studies in Morphosyntactic Variation in the Paston Letters (1421–1503)*. Berlin and New York: Mouton de Gruyter.

2007a. Letters: A new approach to text typology. *Letter Writing*, ed. Terttu Nevalainen and Sanna-Kaisa Tanskanen, 27–46. Amsterdam: Benjamins.

2007b. Spoilt for choice? <The> problem <þe> in <Ðe> *Peterborough Chronicle*. *The Language of the Peterborough Chronicle*, ed. Alexander Bergs and Janne Skaffari, 45–56. Bern: Peter Lang.

2012. The uniformitarian principle and the risk of anachronism in language and social history. *The Handbook of Historical Sociolinguistics*, ed. Juan Manuel Hernández-Campoy and Juan Camilo Conde-Silvestre, 80–98. Malden, MA: Wiley-Blackwell.

Bergs, Alexander and Dieter Stein. 2001. The role of markedness in the actuation and actualization of linguistic change. *Actualization: Linguistic Change in Progress*, ed. Henning Andersen, 79–93. Amsterdam and Philadelphia: John Benjamins.

Berlin, Ira. 2003. *Generations of Captivity: A History of African-American Slaves*. Cambridge, MA: The Belknap Press of Harvard University Press.

Berlin, Ira, Joseph P. Reidy and Leslie S. Rowland (eds.). 1982. *Freedom: A Documentary History of Emancipation, 1861–1867. Series 2: The Black Military Experience*. Cambridge: Cambridge University Press.

Best, Geoffrey. 1979. *Mid-Victorian Britain 1851–75*. London: Fontana.

Bex, Tony and Richard Watts (eds.). 1999. *Standard English: The Widening Debate*. London: Routledge.

Biber, Douglas, Susan Conrad and Randi Reppen. 1998. *Corpus Linguistics: Investigating Language Structure and Use*. Cambridge: Cambridge University Press.

Biber, Douglas and Edward Finegan. 1989. Styles of stance in English: Lexical and grammatical marking of evidentiality and affect. *Text* 9: 93–124.

Biber, Douglas, Stig Johannson, Geoffrey Leech, Susan Conrad and Edward Finegan. 1999. *Longman Grammar of Spoken and Written English*. London: Longman.

Blake, Norman. 1992. Introduction. *The Cambridge History of the English Language*. Vol. II: *1066–1476*, ed. Norman Blake, 1–22. Cambridge: Cambridge University Press.

1996. *A History of the English Language*. Basingstoke: Macmillan.

Bliss, Alan J. 1972. Languages in contact: Some problems of Hiberno-English. *Proceedings of the Royal Irish Academy*, Section C 72: 63–82.

Blommaert, Jan. 2008. *Grassroots Literacy: Writing, Identity and Voice in Central Africa*. London: Routledge.

2010. *The Sociolinguistics of Globalization*. Cambridge: Cambridge University Press.

Blommaert, Jan and Ben Rampton. 2011. Language and superdiversity. *Diversities* 13(2). Available at www.unesco.org/shs/diversities/vol13/issue2/art1. Accessed 21 May 2012.

Blume, Richard. 1882. Die Sprache der Paston Letters. *Beitrag zur historischen Grammatik des Englischen*. Programm der Realschule beim Doventhor zu Bremen.

Board of Registration and Statistics. 1853. *Census of the Canadas 1851–2*. First Report of the Secretary of the Board of Registration and Statistics. Quebec: J. Lovell.

Boberg, Charles. 2008. Regional phonetic differentiation in Standard Canadian English. *Journal of English Linguistics* 36(2): 129–54.

Booy, Derrick M. 1957. *Rock of Exile: A Narrative of Tristan da Cunha*. London: J. M. Dent and Sons Ltd.

Boulton, Jeremy. 2000. 'It is extreme necessity that makes me do this': Some 'survival strategies' of pauper households in London's West End during the early eighteenth century. *International Review of Social History* 45: 47–69.

Bowers, Fredson. 1976. Transcription of manuscripts: The record of variants. *Studies in Bibliography* 29: 212–64.

Boyd, Julian and Zelda Boyd. 1980. *Shall* and *will*. The State of Language, ed. Christopher Ricks and Leonard Michaels, 43–53. Berkeley: University of California Press.

Brant, Clare. 2006. *Eighteenth-Century Letters and British Culture*. Basingstoke: Palgrave Macmillan.

Brewer, John. 1997. *The Pleasures of the Imagination: English Culture in the Eighteenth Century*. New York: Farrar Straus Giroux.

Brightman, Robert A. and Pamela S. Wallace. 2004. Chickasaw. *Handbook of North American Indians*. Vol. 14: *The Southeast*, ed. Raymond Fogelson and William Sturtevant, 520–30. Washington, DC: Smithsonian Institution.

Burnett, John. 1982. *Destiny Obscure: Autobiographies of Childhood, Education and Family from the 1820s to the 1920s*. London: Allen Lane.

  1974. *Useful Toil: Autobiographies of Working People from the 1820s to the 1920s*. London: Allen Lane.

Burnett, John, David Vincent and David Mayall. 1984. *The Autobiography of the Working Class: An Annotated, Critical Bibliography*. Vol. I: *1790–1900*. Vol. III: *Supplement 1790–1945*. Brighton: Harvester Press.

Burton, Mary E. (ed.). 1958. *The Letters of Mary Wordsworth, 1800–1855*. Oxford: Clarendon Press.

Caffyn, John. 1998. *Sussex Schools in the 18th Century: Schooling, Provision, Schoolteachers and Scholars*. Totton: Hobbs, for the Sussex Record Society.

Cameron, W., S. Haines and M. McDougall Maude. 2000. *English Immigrant Voices: Labourers' Letters from Upper Canada in the 1830s*. Ithaca, NY: McGill-Queen's University Press.

Cannadine, David. 1998. *Class in Britain*. London: Penguin.

Carter, Philip. 2005. Kit-Cat Club (*act*. 1696–1720). *Oxford Dictionary of National Biography*, online edn, Oxford University Press, October 2005; online edn, October 2009 [www.oxforddnb.com/view/theme/73609, accessed 15 October 2009].

Cartwright, George Herbert. *c.* 1895. *Journal of Captain George Herbert Cartwright*. Unpublished manuscript.

Castor, Helen. 2004. *Blood and Roses: The Paston Family in the Fifteenth Century*. London: Faber and Faber.

Chambers, J. K. 1986. Three kinds of standard in Canadian English. *In Search of the Standard in Canadian English*, ed. William C. Lougheed, 1–19. Kingston, Ont.: Queen's University.

1991. Canada. *English around the World: Social Perspectives*, ed. Jenny Cheshire, 89–107. Cambridge: Cambridge University Press.

2004. 'Canadian Dainty': The rise and decline of Briticisms in Canada. *Legacies of Colonial English: Studies in Transported Dialects*, ed. Raymond Hickey, 224–41. Cambridge: Cambridge University Press.

Cheshire, Jenny. 1998. Double negatives are illogical. *Language Myths*, ed. Laurie Bauer and Peter Trudgill, 113–22. Harmondsworth: Penguin.

Christophersen, Erling. 1940. *Tristan da Cunha: The Lonely Isle*. London: Cassell and Co.

Coates, Richard (ed.). 1992. *De A.B.C. Psalms. Put into de Sussex Dialect and in due A.B.C. Feshion by Jim Cladpole*. April 1938. Brighton: Younsmere Press.

Coates, Richard. 2010. *The Traditional Dialect of Sussex*. Lewes: Pomegranate Press.

Cobbett, William and John Wright. 1808. *The Parliamentary History of England, from the Earliest Period to the Year 1803*. Vol. IV: *A.D. 1660–1668*. London: Longman.

Colquhoun, Patrick. 1806. *A Treatise on Indigence*. London.

Comrie, Bernard. 1976. *Aspect*. Cambridge: Cambridge University Press.

Conde Silvestre, J. Camilo. 2007. *Sociolingüística histórica*. Madrid: Gredos.

Conde-Silvestre, J. Camilo and Juan Manuel Hernández-Campoy. 2004. A sociolinguistic approach to the diffusion of Chancery written practices in late fifteenth-century private correspondence. *Neuphilologische Mitteilungen* 105(2): 133–52.

Cooke, Thomas. 1775. *The Universal Letter-Writer; Or, New Art of Polite Correspondence*. London.

Cook-Gumperz, Jenny (ed.). 1986. *The Social Construction of Literacy*. Cambridge: Cambridge University Press.

Cornelius, Janet. 1983. We slipped and learned to read: Slaves and the literacy process, 1830–1865. *Phylon* 44: 338–59.

Cornelius, Janet Duitsman. 1991. *When I Can Read my Title Clear: Literacy, Slavery, and Religion in the Antebellum South*. Columbia: University of South Carolina Press.

1999. *Slave Missions and the Black Church in the Antebellum South*. Columbia: University of South Carolina Press.

Coupland, Nikolas. 1985. 'Hark, hark the lark': Social motivations for phonological style-shifting. *Language and Communication* 5(3): 153–72.

2001. Language, situation and the relational self: Theorising dialect-style in sociolinguistics. *Style and Sociolinguistic Variation*, ed. Penelope Eckert and John R. Rickford, 185–210. Cambridge: Cambridge University Press.

Crawford, Allan. 1945. *I Went to Tristan*. London: Allen and Unwin.

Cressy, David. 1980. *Literacy and the Social Order: Reading and Writing in Tudor and Stuart England*. Cambridge: Cambridge University Press.

Crowley, Tony. 2003. *Standard English and the Politics of Language*. 2nd edn. Basingstoke: Palgrave Macmillan.

Culpeper, Jonathan and Merja Kytö. 2010. *Early Modern English Dialogues: Spoken Interaction as Writing*. Cambridge: Cambridge University Press.

Curme, George. 1912. A history of the English relative constructions. *Journal of English and Germanic Philology* 11: 10–29, 180–204, 355–80.

Curtis, Bruce. 1985. The speller expelled: Disciplining the common reader in Canada West. *Canadian Review of Sociology and Anthropology* 22(3): 346–68.

Davidson, Alexander. 1845 [1840]. *The Canada Spelling Book. Intended as an Introduction to the English Language*. Niagara: George Hodgkinson.

Davies, Winifred V. and Nils Langer. 2006. *The Making of Bad Language: Lay Linguistic Stigmatisations in German Past and Present*. Frankfurt am Main: Peter Lang.

Davis, Norman O. 1954. The language of the Pastons. *Middle English Literature: British Academy Gollanz Lectures*, ed. James A. Burrow, 45–70. Oxford: Oxford University Press.

Davis, Norman O. (ed.). 1971. *Paston Letters and Papers of the Fifteenth Century*. 2 vols. Oxford: Clarendon Press.

   1983. The language of two brothers in the fifteenth century. *Five Hundred Years of Words and Sounds: A Festschrift for Eric Dobson*, ed. E. G. Stanley and D. Gray, 22–8. Cambridge: D. S. Brewer.

Denison, David. 1985. The origins of periphrastic 'do': Ellegård and Visser reconsidered. *Papers from the 4th International Conference of English Historical Linguistics*, ed. Roger Eaton, 44–60. Amsterdam: Benjamins.

   1998. Syntax. *The Cambridge History of the English Language*. Vol. IV: *1776–1997*, ed. Suzanne Romaine, 92–329. Cambridge: Cambridge University Press.

   2007. Syntactic surprises in some English letters: The underlying progress of the language. *Germanic Language Histories from below (1700–2000)*, ed. Stephan Elspaß, Nils Langer, Joachim Scharloth and Wim Vandenbussche, 115–27. Berlin: de Gruyter.

Dennett, Maurice (ed.). 1991. *Cherry Valley Chronicles: Letters from Thomas Buckley of Massachusetts to Ralph Buckley of Saddleworth 1845–1875*. Saddleworth: Saddleworth Historical Society.

Deumert, Ana and Wim Vandenbussche (eds.). 2003. *Germanic Standardization: Past to Present*. Amsterdam and Philadelphia: John Benjamins.

Digby, Anne and Peter Searby. 1981. *Children, School and Society in Nineteenth-Century England*. Basingstoke: Macmillan.

Dodsley, Robert. 1754. *The Preceptor*. London: Dodsley.

Dollinger, Stefan. 2008a. *New-Dialect Formation in Canada: Evidence from the English Modal Auxiliaries*. Amsterdam: Benjamins.

   2008b. Colonial variation in the Late Modern English business letter: 'Periphery and core' or 'random variation'? *Studies in Late Modern English Correspondence: Methodology and Data*, ed. Marina Dossena and Ingrid Tieken-Boon van Ostade, 257–87. Bern: Peter Lang.

   2008c. A canary in a coalmine? *DSNA Newsletter* 32(2): 1, 3. http://mac10.typepad.com/DSNA_FALL08.pdf (31 January 2013).

   2012. Canadian English in real-time perspective. *English Historical Linguistics: An International Handbook*. Vol. II. (HSK 34.2), ed. Alexander Bergs and Laurel Brinton, 1858–1880. Berlin and New York: Mouton de Gruyter.

Dollinger, Stefan, Laurel Brinton and Margery Fee. 2006–. *The Bank of Canadian English. Online Database*. Vancouver, BC: University of British Columbia.

Dollinger, Stefan and Sandra Clarke. 2012a. On the autonomy and homogeneity of Canadian English. *World Englishes* 31(4): 449–66.

Dollinger, Stefan and Sandra Clarke (eds.). 2012b. Symposium Issue 'On the autonomy and homogeneity of Canadian English'. *World Englishes* 31(4): 449–548.

Dollinger, Stefan and Luanne von Schneidemesser. 2011. Canadianism, Americanism, North Americanism? A Comparison of DARE and DCHP. *American Speech* 86(2): 115–51.

Dossena, Marina. 2007. 'As this leaves me at present': Formulaic usage, politeness and social proximity in nineteenth-century Scottish emigrants' letters. *Germanic Language Histories 'from below', 1700–2000*, ed. Stephan Elspaß, Nils Langer, Joachim Scharloth and Wim Vandenbussche, 13–30. Berlin: de Gruyter.

Dossena, Marina and Susan M. Fitzmaurice (eds.). 2006. *Business and Official Correspondence: Historical Investigations*. Bern: Peter Lang.

Dossena, Marina and Gabriella Del Lungo Camiciotti (eds.). 2012. *Letter Writing in Late Modern Europe*. Amsterdam: John Benjamins.

Dossena, Marina and Ingrid Tieken-Boon van Ostade (eds.). 2008. *Studies in Late Modern English Correspondence: Methodology and Data*. Bern: Peter Lang.

Duden. 2007. *Richtiges und Gutes Deutsch: Wörterbuch der sprachlichen Zweifelsfälle*. 6th rev. edn. Mannheim: Dudenverlag.

Dunthorne, Hugh and David Onnekink. 2004. Bentinck, Hans Willem, first earl of Portland (1649–1709). *Oxford Dictionary of National Biography*. Oxford University Press, September 2004; online edn, October 2007 [www.oxforddnb.com/view/article/2160, accessed 9 November 2009].

Durrell, Martin. 2000. Standard language and the creation of national myths in nineteenth-century Germany. *Das schwierige neunzehnte Jahrhundert. Germanistische Tagung zum 65. Geburtstag von Eda Sagarra im August 1998*, ed. Jürgen Barkhoff, Gilbert Carr and Roger Paulin, 15–26. Tübingen: Niemeyer.

Earle, Augustus. 1966. *Narrative of a Residence on the Island of Tristan D'Acunha in the South Atlantic Ocean.* (1st edn 1832) Oxford: Clarendon Press.

Eckert, Penelope. 1989. *Jocks and Burnouts: Social Categories and Identity in the High School.* New York: Teachers College Press.

1997. Age as a sociolinguistic variable. *The Handbook of Sociolinguistics*, ed. Florian Coulmas, 151–67. Oxford: Basil Blackwell.

2000. *Linguistic Variation as Social Practice*. Malden, MA and Oxford: Blackwell.

2005. Variation, convention and social meaning. Paper presented at the Annual Meeting of the Linguistic Society of America, 6–9 January, Oakland, California.

2008. Variation and the indexical field. *Journal of Sociolinguistics* 12(4): 453–76.

2012. Three waves of variation study: The emergence of meaning in the study of sociolinguistic variation. *Annual Review of Anthropology* 41: 87–100.

Eckert, Penelope and Sally McConnell-Ginet. 2003. *Language and Gender*. New York: Cambridge University Press.

Eckert, Penelope and John R. Rickford (eds). 2001. *Style and Sociolinguistic Variation*. Cambridge: Cambridge University Press.

Eichhoff, Jürgen. 2000. *Wortatlas der deutschen Umgangssprachen*, Vol. IV. Bern and Munich: Saur.

Edgeworth, Maria and Richard Lovell Edgeworth. 1815. *Essays on Practical Education*, Vol. II. London.

Einenkel, Eugen. 1887. *Streifzüge durch die mittelenglische Syntax unter besonderer Berücksichtigung der Sprache Chaucers*. Münster: Schöninigh.

Eisenberg, Peter. 2004. *Grundriß der deutschen Grammatik*. Vol. II: *Der Satz*. 2nd rev. edn. Stuttgart and Weimar: Metzler.

Eliot, George. 1860 [1993]. *The Mill on the Floss*. Ware: Wordsworth Editions.

Ellegård, Alvar. 1953. *The Auxiliary 'do': The Establishment and Regulation of its Use in English*. Stockholm: Almqvist and Wiksell.

Elspaß, Stephan. 2005. *Sprachgeschichte von unten: Untersuchungen zum geschriebenen Alltagsdeutsch im 19. Jahrhundert*. Tübingen: Niemeyer.

   2007. A twofold view 'from below': New perspectives on language histories and historical grammar. *Germanic language histories 'from below' (1700–2000)*, 3–9. Berlin and New York: de Gruyter.

   2008. Vom Mittelneuhochdeutschen (bis ca. 1950) zum Gegenwartsdeutsch. *Zeitschrift für Dialektologie und Linguistik* 75: 1–20.

   2012a. The use of private letters and diaries in sociolinguistic investigation. *The Handbook of Historical Sociolinguistics*, ed. Juan Manuel Hernández-Campoy and Juan Camilo Conde-Silvestre, 156–69. Oxford: Wiley-Blackwell.

   2012b. Between linguistic creativity and formulaic restriction. Cross-linguistic perspectives on nineteenth-century lower class writers' private letters. *Letter Writing in Late Modern Europe*, ed. Marina Dossena and Gabriella Del Lungo Camiciotti, 45–64. Amsterdam and Philadelphia: Benjamins.

Elspaß, Stephan, Nils Langer, Joachim Scharloth and Wim Vandenbussche (eds.). 2007. *Germanic Language Histories 'from below' (1700–2000)*. Berlin and New York: de Gruyter.

Englebretson, Robert (ed.). 2007. *Stancetaking in Discourse: Subjectivity, Evaluation, Interaction*. Amsterdam and Philadelphia: John Benjamins.

Escribano, José Luis G. 1982. Word-order and stylistic distortion in the letters of William Paston I, 1425–1442: A transformational approach. *Anglo American Studies* 2: 85–112.

   1985. Retórica epistolar en la Inglaterra del siglo XV: el caso de William Paston, 1378–1444. *Estudios literarios ingleses: Edad Media*, ed. J. F. Galván Reula, 253–84. Madrid: Cátedra.

Evans, Dorothy. 1994. *Schooling in the South Atlantic Islands 1661–1992*. Oswestry: Anthony Nelson.

   2004. On reanalysis and actualization in syntactic change: The rise and development of English verbal gerunds. *Diachronica* 21(1): 5–55.

Eves, K. 1939. *Matthew Prior: Poet and Diplomatist*. New York: Columbia University Press.

Facchinetti, Roberta. 2000. The modal verb *shall* between grammar and usage in the nineteenth century. *The History of English in a Social Context*, ed. Dieter Kastovsky and Arthur Mettinger, 115–33. Berlin: Mouton de Gruyter.

Fairman, Tony. 1989. Let grammarians return to describing the language. *English Today* 5(1): 3–5.

   2000. English pauper letters 1800–34 and the English language. *Letter Writing as a Social Practice*, ed. David Barton and Nigel Hall, 63–82. Amsterdam: John Benjamins.

   2002. 'Riting these fu lines': English Overseers' correspondence, 1800–1835. *Koninklijke Academie voor Nederlandse Taal- en Letterkunde* 3: 557–73.

   2003. Letters of the English labouring classes and the English language, 1800–34. *Insights into Late Modern English*, ed. Marina Dossena and Charles Jones, 265–82. Bern: Peter Lang.

2005. Schooling the poor in Horsmonden 1797–1816. *The Local Historian* 55(2): 120–31.

2006. Words in English Record Office documents in the early 1800s. *Nineteenth Century English: Stability and Change*, ed. Merja Kytö, Mats Rydén and Erik Smitterberg, 56–88. Cambridge: Cambridge University Press.

2007a. 'Lower-order' letters, schooling and the English language, 1795 to 1834. *Germanic Language Histories from below (1700–2000)*, ed. Stephan Elspaß, Nils Langer, Joachim Scharloth and Wim Vandenbussche, 31–43. Berlin: de Gruyter.

2007b. Writing and the 'Standard' 1795–1834. *Multilingua* 26: 167–201.

2007c. Letters of the English labouring class and the English language, 1800–1834 *Insights into Late Modern English*, ed. Marina Dossena and Charles Jones, 265–82. Bern: Peter Lang.

2008a. Strike-throughs: What textual alterations can tell us about writers and their scripts, 1795–1835. *Studies in Late Modern English Correspondence: Methodology and Data*, ed. Marina Dossena and Ingrid Tieken-Boon van Ostade, 193–212. Bern: Peter Lang.

2008b. The study of writing in sociolinguistics. *Socially-Conditioned Language Change: Diachronic and Synchronic Insights*, ed. Susan Kermas and Maurizio Gotti, 53–75. Lecce: Edizioni del Grifo.

2012. Letters in mechanically-schooled language: Theories and ideologies. *Letter Writing in Late Modern Europe*, ed. Marina Dossena and Gabriella del Lungo Camiciotti, 205–28. Amsterdam: John Benjamins.

Fanego, Teresa. 2004. On reanalysis and actualization in syntactic change: The rise and development of English verbal gerunds. *Diachronica* 21: 5–55.

Fauconnier, Gilles and Mark Turner. 2002. *The Way we Think: Conceptual Blending and the Mind's Hidden Complexities*. New York: Basic Books.

Fee, Margery and Janice McAlpine. 2007 [1997]. *Guide to Canadian English Usage*. 2nd edn. Toronto: Oxford University Press.

Fens-de Zeeuw, Lyda. 2008. The letter-writing manual in the eighteenth and nineteenth centuries: From polite to practical. *Studies in Late Modern English Correspondence: Methodology and Data*, ed. Marina Dossena and Ingrid Tieken-Boon van Ostade, 163–92. Bern: Peter Lang.

Filppula, Markku. 1999. *The Grammar of Irish English: Language in Hibernian Style*. London: Routledge.

Finegan, Edward. 1998a. English grammar and usage. *The Cambridge History of the English Language*. Vol. IV: *1776–1997*, ed. Suzanne Romaine, 536–88. Cambridge: Cambridge University Press.

1998b. Usage. *The Cambridge History of the English Language*. Vol. VI: *English in North America*, ed. John Algeo, 358–421. Cambridge: Cambridge University Press.

Fischer, Olga. 1992. Syntax. *The Cambridge History of the English Language*. Vol. II: *1066–1476*, ed. Norman Blake, 207–408. Cambridge: Cambridge University Press.

Fischer, Olga, Ans van Kemenade, Willem Koopman and Wim van der Wurff. 2000. *The Syntax of Early English*. Cambridge: Cambridge University Press.

Fitzmaurice, Susan. 2000. *The Spectator*, the politics of social networks, and language standardization in eighteenth century England. *The Development of Standard English 1300–1800*, ed. Laura Wright, 195–218. Cambridge: Cambridge University Press.

2002a. Politeness and modal meaning in the construction of humiliative discourse in an early eighteenth-century network of patron–client relationships. *English Language and Linguistics* 6(2): 239–66.

2002b. *The Familiar Letter in Early Modern English: A Pragmatic Approach*. Amsterdam and Philadelphia: John Benjamins.

2003. The grammar of stance in early eighteenth-century English epistolary language. *Corpus Analysis: Language Structure and Language Use*, ed. Charles Meyer and Pepi Leistyna, 107–31. Amsterdam: Rodopi.

2004. Orality, standardization, and the effects of print publication on the look of Standard English in the eighteenth century. *Methods and Data in English Historical Dialectology*, ed. Marina Dossena and Roger Lass, 351–83. Bern: Peter Lang.

2006. Diplomatic business: Information, power, and persuasion in Late Modern English diplomatic correspondence. *Business and Official Correspondence: Historical Investigations*, ed. Marina Dossena and Susan Fitzmaurice, 77–106. Bern: Peter Lang.

2008. Epistolary identity: Convention and idiosyncrasy in Late Modern Letters. *Studies in Late Modern English Correspondence: Methodology and Data*, ed. Marina Dossena and Ingrid Tieken-Boon van Ostade, 77–112. Bern: Peter Lang.

2010. Mr. Spectator, identity and social roles in an early eighteenth-century community of practice and the periodical discourse community. *Social Roles and Language Practices in Late Modern English*, ed. Päivi Pahta, Minna Nevala, Arja Nurmi and Minna Palander-Collin, 29–53. Amsterdam: John Benjamins.

2011. Poetic collaboration and competition in the late seventeenth century: George Stepney's letters to Jacob Tonson and Matthew Prior. *Communicating Early English Manuscripts*, ed. Päivi Pahta and Andreas Jucker, 118–32. Cambridge: Cambridge University Press.

Fitzpatrick, David. 1994. *Oceans of Consolation: Personal Accounts of Irish Migration to Australia*. Cork: Cork University Press.

Forgacs, David (ed.). 1988. *A Gramsci Reader*. London: Lawrence & Wishart.

Fries, Charles C. 1925. The periphrastic future with *shall* and *will* in Modern English. *PMLA* 40: 963–1024.

Fulwood, William. 1568. *The Enemie of Idlenesse*. London: Henry Bynneman. [Retrieved from *Early English Books Online*. University Library Utrecht. 29 September 2011.]

1571. *The Enemie of Idlenesse*. 2nd edn. London: By T. East and H. Middelton. [Retrieved from *Early English Books Online*. University Library Utrecht. 29 September 2011.]

Fyfe, Christopher (ed.). 1991. *Our Children Free and Happy: Letters from Black Settlers in Africa in the 1790s*. Edinburgh: Edinburgh University Press.

Garcia, Erica. 1985. Shifting variation. *Lingua* 67: 189–224.

Garcia-Bermejo Giner, Maria F. and Michael Montgomery. 1997. British regional English in the nineteenth century: The evidence from emigrant letters. *Issues and Methods in Dialectology*, ed. Alan Thomas, 167–83. Bangor: University of North Wales Press.

2001. Yorkshire English two hundred years ago. *Journal of English Linguistics* 29(4): 346–62.

Garfinkel, Harold. 1967. *Studies in Ethnomethodology*. Englewood Cliffs, NJ: Prentice-Hall.

Gerlach, Russel L. 1986. *Settlement Patterns in Missouri: A Study of Population Origins (with a Wall Map)*. Columbia: University of Missouri Press.

Giddens, Anthony. 1991. *Modernity and Self-Identity*. Cambridge: Polity.

Gies, Frances and Joseph Gies. 1998. *A Medieval Family: The Pastons of Fifteenth-Century England*. New York: Harper Collins.

 1999. *A Medieval Family*. London: Harper Collins.

Giles, Howard. 1973. Accent mobility: A model and some data. *Anthropological Linguistics* 15: 87–105.

Giles, Howard and Peter F. Powesland. 1975. *Speech Style and Social Evaluation*. London: Academic Press.

Gisborne, Nikolas. 2000. The complementation of verbs of appearance by adverbs. *Generative Theory and Corpus Studies: A Dialogue from 10 ICEHL*, ed. Ricardo Bermúdez-Otero, David Denison, Richard M. Hogg and C. B. McCully, 53–75. Berlin and New York: Mouton de Gruyter.

Goffman, Erving. 1959. *The Presentation of Self in Everday Life*. New York: Anchor Books.

Gómez-Soliño, José. 1997. Pastons, Celys and the standard language in the late fifteenth century. *Proceedings of the IXth International Conference of the Spanish Society for Medieval English Language and Literature*, ed. M. Giménez Bon and V. Olsen, 117–39. Vitoria-Gasteiz: Universidad del País Vasco.

Gordon, Elizabeth, Lyle Campbell, Jennifer Hay, Margaret Maclagan, Andrea Sudbury and Peter Trudgill. 2004. *New Zealand English: Its Origins and Evolution*. Cambridge: Cambridge University Press.

Görlach, Manfred. 1998. *An Annotated Bibliography of Nineteenth-Century Grammars of English*. Amsterdam: John Benjamins.

 1999. *English in Nineteenth-Century England: An Introduction*. Cambridge: Cambridge University Press.

Gramsci, Antonio. 1971. *Selections from the Prison Notebooks*. Trans. and ed. Quintin Hoare and Geoffrey Nowell Smith. New York: International Books.

Greenbaum, Sidney. 1988. *Good English and the Grammarian*. London, New York: Longman.

 1996. *The Oxford English Grammar*. Oxford: Oxford University Press.

Gregg, Robert J. 1972. The Scotch-Irish dialect boundaries in Ulster. *Patterns in the Folk Speech of the British Isles*, ed. Martyn F. Wakelin, 109–39. London: Athlone Press.

 1993. Canadian English lexicography. *Focus on Canada*, ed. Sandra Clarke, 27–44. Amsterdam: Benjamins.

Greul, Walter. 1934. Das Personalpronomen der 3. Person Pluralis im Frühmittelenglischen. *Das Personalpronomen der 3. Person in spätangs. und frühmittelenglischen Texten: Ein Beitrag zur altenglischen Dialektgeographie*, ed. Bernard Gericke and Walter Greul. Leipzig: Mayer and Müller.

Grillo, Ralph. 1989. *Dominant Languages*. Cambridge: Cambridge University Press.

Grimm, Jacob and Wilhelm Grimm. 1854. *Deutsches Wörterbuch*, Vol. I. Leipzig: Hirzel.

Gumperz, John. 1982. *Discourse Strategies*. Cambridge: Cambridge University Press.

Gumperz, John and Dell Hymes (eds.). 1964. The ethnography of communication. Special issue of *American Anthropologist* 66(6).

 1972. *Directions in Sociolinguistics: The Ethnography of Communication*. New York and London: Holt, Rinehart and Winston.

Gustafsson, Larisa Oldireva. 2002. *Preterite and Past Participle Forms in English 1680–1790: Standardisation Processes in Public and Private Writing*. Uppsala: Uppsala University.

Habermann, Mechthild. 1997. Das sogenannte 'Lutherische e'. Zum Streit um einen armen Buchstaben. *Sprachwissenschaft* 22: 435–72.

Hackert, Stephanie. 2012. *The Emergence of the English Native Speaker: A Chapter in Nineteenth Century Linguistic Thought*. Berlin and New York: Mouton de Gruyter.

Hall, Helena. 1967. *Dictionary of the Sussex Dialect and a Collection of Provincialisms in Use in the County of Sussex*, by the Rev. W. D. Parish. Bexhill: Gardner's.

Hall, Nigel J. 1987. *The Emergence of Literacy*. Sevenoaks: Hodder and Stoughton.

    2000. The materiality of letter writing: A nineteenth-century perspective. *Letter Writing as a Social Practice*, ed. David Barton and Nigel Hall, 83–108. Amsterdam and Philadelphia: John Benjamins.

Han, Chung-hye and Anthony Kroch. 2000. The rise of *do*-support in English: Implications for clause structure. *Proceedings NELS University of Pennsylvania* 30(1): 311–26.

Handley, Stuart. 2004a. Montagu, Charles, Earl of Halifax (1661–1715). *Oxford Dictionary of National Biography*. Oxford University Press, September 2004; online edn, October 2005 [www.oxforddnb.com/view/article/19004, accessed 9 November 2009].

    2004b. Talbot, Charles, Duke of Shrewsbury (1660–1718). *Oxford Dictionary of National Biography*. Oxford University Press, September 2004; online edn, January 2008 [http://www.oxforddnb. com/view/article/26922, accessed 5 November 2009].

    2004c. Whig Junto (*act. c.*1694–c.1716). *Oxford Dictionary of National Biography*. Oxford University Press. [http://www.oxforddnb.com/view/theme/92792, accessed 17 February 2011]

Hansard. *Parliamentary Debates*. London.

Hansard. 1816. *Report from Select Committee of the House of Commons Appointed to Enquire into the Education of the Lower Orders in the Metropolis*. London.

Härd, John Evert. 1981. *Studien zur Struktur mehrgliedriger deutscher Nebensatzprädikate: Diachronie und Synchronie*. Gothenburg: Acta Univerversitatis Gothoburgensis.

Harris, James. 1751. *HERMES: OR, A Philosophical Inquiry Concerning LANGUAGE AND UNIVERSAL GRAMMAR*. London: H. Woodfall.

Harris, John. 1986. Expanding the superstrate: Habitual aspect markers in Atlantic Englishes. *English World-Wide* 7: 171–99.

Hawkins, John A. 2004. *Efficiency and Complexity in Grammars*. Oxford: Oxford University Press.

Hay, Jennifer and Daniel Schreier. 2004. Reversing the trajectory of language change: Subject–verb agreement with *be* in New Zealand English. *Language Variation and Change* 16: 209–35.

Heath, Shirley Brice. 1983. *Ways with Words: Language, Life, and Work in Communities and Classrooms*. Cambridge: Cambridge University Press.

Heffernan, Kevin, Alison J. Borden, Alexandra C. Erath and Julie-Lynn Yang. 2010. Preserving Canada's 'honour': Ideology and diachronic change in Canadian spelling variants. *Written Language and Literacy* 13(1): 1–23.

Helbich, Wolfgang, Walter D. Kamphoefner and Ulrike Sommer (eds.). 1988. *Briefe aus Amerika: Deutsche Auswanderer schreiben aus der Neuen Welt, 1830–1890*. Munich: C. W. Beck.

Henderson, Edmund H. 1980. Developmental concepts of word. *Developmental and Cognitive Aspects of Learning to Spell: A Reflection of Word Knowledge*, ed. E. H. Henderson and J. W. Beers, 1–14. Newark, DE: International Reading Association.

Henry, Maura A. 2002. The making of elite culture. *A Companion to Eighteenth-Century Britain*, ed. H. T. Dickinson, 311–28. Malden, MA and Oxford: Blackwell Publishing.

Hernández-Campoy, Juan Manuel. 2008. Overt and covert prestige in late Middle English: A case study in East Anglia. *Folia Linguistica Historica* 29: 1–26.

2012. Mood distinction in late Middle English: The end of the inflectional subjunctive. *Language and History, Linguistics and Historiography: Interdisciplinary Approaches*, ed. N. Langer, S. Davies and W. Vandenbussche, 389–406. Bern: Peter Lang.

Hernández-Campoy, Juan Manuel and J. Camilo Conde-Silvestre. 1999. The social diffusion of linguistic innovations in 15th-century England: Chancery spellings in private correspondence. *Cuadernos de Filología Inglesa* 8: 251–74.

Hernández-Campoy, Juan Manuel and J. Camilo Conde-Silvestre (eds.). 2012. *The Handbook of Historical Sociolinguistics*. Malden: Wiley-Blackwell.

Hernández-Campoy, Juan Manuel and Juan Antonio Cutillas-Espinosa. 2012. Introduction: Style-shifting revisited. *Style-Shifting in Public: New Perspectives on Stylistic Variation*, ed. J. M. Hernández-Campoy and J. A. Cutillas-Espinosa, 1–18. Amsterdam and Philadelphia: John Benjamins.

Hickey, Raymond. 2007. *Irish English: History and Present-Day Forms*. Cambridge: Cambridge University Press.

Hilton, Boyd. 2006. *A Mad, Bad and Dangerous People? England: 1783–1846*. Oxford: Clarendon Press.

Hitchcock, Tim, Peter King and Pamela Sharpe. 1997. Introduction: Chronicling poverty – the voices and strategies of the English poor, 1640–1840. *Chronicling Poverty: The Voices and Strategies of the English Poor, 1640–1840*, ed. Tim Hitchcock, Peter King and Pamela Sharpe, 1–18. London: Macmillan.

Hobsbawm, Eric. 1962. *The Age of Revolution: Europe 1789–1848*. New York: World Publishing Company.

Hodge, Robert and Gunther Kress. 1993. *Language as Ideology*. 2nd edn. London: Routledge.

Hodson, Jane. 2007. *Language and Revolution in Burke, Wollstonecraft, Paine, and Godwin*. Aldershot: Ashgate.

Hoffman, Michol F. and James A. Walker. 2010. Ethnolects and the city: ethnic orientation and linguistic variation in Toronto English. *Language Variation and Change* 22: 37–67.

Hoffmann, Walter. 1988. Vom variablen Usus zur Kodifizierung der Norm: Die Geschichte der 'unorganischen participia mit *ge-*' im Frühneuhochdeutschen. *Studien zum Frühneuhochdeutschen. Festschrift für Emil Skála*, ed. Peter Wiesinger, 167–84. Göppingen: Kümmerle.

Hogg, Richard. 1992. Phonology and morphology. *The Cambridge History of the English Language*. Vol. 1: *The Beginnings to 1066*, ed. Richard Hogg, 67–167. Cambridge: Cambridge University Press.

2006. English in Britain. *A History of the English Language*, ed. Richard Hogg and David Denison, 352–83. Cambridge: Cambridge University Press.

Holmes, Geoffrey. 1993. *The Making of a Great Power: Late Stuart and Early Georgian Britain 1660–1722*. London: Longman.

Horgan, A. D. 1994. *Johnson on Language*. Basingstoke: Macmillan.

Houston, Cecil and William J. Smyth. 1991. *Irish Emigration and Canadian Settlements: Patterns, Links and Letters*. Toronto: University of Toronto Press.

Houston, R. A. 1982. The development of literacy: Northern England, 1640–1750. *The Economic History Review* 35(2): 199–216.

Hua, Zhu and Annabelle David. 2008. Study design: Cross-sectional, longitudinal, case, and group. *The Blackwell Guide to Research Methods in Bilingualism and Multilingualism*, ed. Li Wei and Melissa G. Moyer, 88–107. Oxford: Blackwell.

Huber, Magnus. 2007. The Old Bailey Proceedings, 1674–1834: Evaluating and annotating a corpus of 18th- and 19th-century spoken English. *Annotating Variation and Change*, ed. Anneli Meurman-Solin and Arja Nurmi. *Varieng* 1. Available at: www.helsinki.fi/varieng/journal/volumes/01/huber/. Accessed 7 June 2011.

Hundt, Marianne. 1998. *New Zealand English Grammar: Fact or Fiction?* Amsterdam and Philadelphia: John Benjamins.

   2004. The passival and the progressive passive. *Corpus Approaches to Grammaticalization in English*, ed. Hans Lindquist and Christian Mair, 79–120. Amsterdam and Philadelphia: John Benjamins.

Hundt, Marianne, Jennifer Hay and Elizabeth Gordon. 2004. New Zealand English: Morphosyntax. *A Handbook of Varieties of English*. Vol. 2: *Morphology and Syntax*, ed. Bernd Kortmann, Kate Burridge, Rajend Mesthrie and Edgar Schneider, 17–49. Berlin and New York: de Gruyter.

Hutcheon, Linda. 2004. Circling the downspout of empire: Post-colonialism and postmodernism. *Unhomely States: Theorizing English–Canadian Postcolonialism*, ed. Cynthia C. Sugars, 71–93. Peterborough, Ont.: Broadview Press.

Hymes, Dell (ed.). 1964. *Language in Culture and Society: A Reader in Linguistics and Anthropology*. New York: Harper and Row.

Hymes, Dell. 1974. *Foundations in Sociolinguistics: An Ethnographic Approach*. Philadelphia: University of Pennsylvania Press.

Ihalainen, Ossi. 1976. Periphrastic *do* in affirmative sentences in the dialect of East Somerset. *Neuphilologische Mitteilungen* 77: 608–22.

   1991. Periphrastic *do* in affirmative sentences in the dialect of East Somerset. *Dialects of English: Studies in Grammatical Variation*, ed. Peter Trudgill and Jack Chambers, 148–60. London: Longman.

   1995. The dialects of England since 1776. *Cambridge History of the English Language*. Vol. V: *English in Britain and Overseas: Origins and Development*, ed. Richard Burchfield, 197–274. Cambridge: Cambridge University Press.

Ingersoll, Thomas N. 1994. 'Releese us out of this cruell bondegg': An appeal from Virginia in 1723. *The William and Mary Quarterly* 51(4): 777–82.

Ireland, R. J. 1979. Canadian spelling: An empirical and historical survey of selected words. PhD Thesis: York University, Ont.

Irvine, Valerie. 2005. *The King's Wife: George IV and Mrs Fitzherbert*. London and New York: Hambledon.

Jaffe, Alexandra. (ed.). 2009. *Stance: Sociolinguistic Perspectives*. Oxford: Oxford University Press.

Jenkins, Carol. 1997. The major silence: Autobiographies of working women in the nineteenth century. *Writing and Victorianism*, ed. Jane Bullen, 38–53. Harlow: Addison Wesley Longman.

Johnson, Samuel. 1775. *The Dictionary of the English Language*. London: Dodsley.

Johnstone, Barbara. 2000. The individual voice in language. *Annual Review of Anthropology* 29: 405–25.

Joseph, John. 1987. *Eloquence and Power: The Rise of Language Standards and Standard Languages*. London: Francis Pinter.

Jucker, Andreas H. 1992. *Social Stylistics: Syntactic Variation in British Newspapers*. Berlin and New York: Mouton de Gruyter.

Jucker, Andreas H. (ed.). 1995. *Historical Pragmatics: Pragmatic Developments in the History of English*. Amsterdam: John Benjamins.

Kachru, Braj. 1985. Standards, codification and sociolinguistic realism: The English language in the Outer Circle. *English in the World: Teaching and Learning of Language and Literature*, ed. Randolph Quirk and Henry G. Widdowson, 11–36. Cambridge: Cambridge University Press.

Kallen, Jeffrey. 1989. Tense and aspect categories in Irish English. *English World-Wide* 10: 1–39.

Kamm, Josephine. 1965. *Hope Deferred: Girls' Education in English History*. London: Methuen.

Kautzsch, Alexander. 2002. *The Historical Evolution of African American English: An Empirical Comparison of Early Sources*. Berlin and New York: Mouton de Gruyter.

Kautzsch, Alexander and Edgar W. Schneider. 2000. Differential creolization: Some evidence from earlier African American Vernacular English in South Carolina. *Degrees of Restructuring in Creole Languages*, ed. Ingrid Neumann-Holzschuh and Edgar W. Schneider, 247–74. Amsterdam: Benjamins.

Keller, Rudi. 1995. The epistemic *weil*. *Subjectivity and Subjectivisation: Linguistic Perspectives*, ed. Dieter Stein and Susan Wright, 16–31. Cambridge: Cambridge University Press.

Kenyon, Olga. 1992. *800 Years of Women's Letters*. Stroud: Sutton.

Kidwell, Clara Sue. 2004. Choctaw in the West. *Handbook of North American Indians*. Vol. XIV: *The Southeast*, ed. Raymond Fogelson and William Sturtevant, 520–30. Washington, DC: Smithsonian Institution.

Kiernan, Kevin S. 1997. *Beowulf and the Beowulf Manuscript*. Ann Arbor: University of Michigan Press.

Kirkham, Samuel. 1831. *English Grammar in Familiar Lectures.... Designed for the Use of Schools and Private Learners*. 24th edn enlarged and improved. Rochester, NY: Marshall, Dean & Co. http://www.gutenberg.org/etext/14070 (31 January 2013).

Kiviima, Kersti. 1966. 'The' and 'that' as clause connectives in Early Middle English with especial consideration of pleonastic 'that'. *Commentationes Humanarum Litterarum* 39: 1–271.

Klemola, Juhani. 1996. Non-standard periphrastic DO: A study in variation and change. PhD thesis, University of Essex, Colchester.

    1998. Semantics of *do* in southwestern dialects of English English. Do *in English, Dutch and German: History and Present-Day Variation*, ed. Ingrid Tieken-Boon van Ostade, 25–51. Amsterdam: Stichting Neerlandistiek.

Koch, Peter and Wulf Oesterreicher. 1985. Sprache der Nähe – Sprache der Distanz: Mündlichkeit und Schriftlichkeit im Spannungsfeld von Sprachtheorie und Sprachgeschichte. *Romanistisches Jahrbuch* 36: 15–43.

1994. Schriftlichkeit und Sprache. *Writing and its Use: An Interdisciplinary Handbook of International Research*, Vol. I, ed. Hartmut Günther and Otto Ludwig, 587–604. Berlin and New York: de Gruyter.

Kortmann, Bernd. 2004. *Do* as a tense and aspect marker in varieties of English. *Dialectology Meets Typology*, ed. Bernd Kortmann, 245–76. Berlin: Mouton.

Kristiansen, Gitte. 2008. Style-shifting and shifting styles: A socio-cognitive approach to lectal variation. *Cognitive Sociolinguistics*, ed. Gitte Kristiansen and René Dirven, 45–88. Berlin and New York: Mouton de Gruyter.

Kroch, Anthony. 1989. Function and grammar in the history of English: periphrastic 'do'. *Language Change and Variation*, ed. Ralph Fasold and Deborah Schiffrin, 133–72. Amsterdam: Benjamins.

Kuhn, Thomas S. 1970. *The Structure of Scientific Revolutions*. 2nd edn. Chicago: University of Chicago Press.

Kytö, Merja. 1991. *Variation and Diachrony, with Early American English in Focus*. Frankfurt: Peter Lang.

1997. *Be/have* + past participle: The choice of the auxiliary with intransitives from Late Middle to Modern English. *English in Transition: Corpus-Based Studies in Linguistic Variation and Genre Styles*, ed. Matti Rissanen, Merja Kytö and Kirsi Heikkonen, 17–85. Berlin: Mouton de Gruyter.

Kytö, Merja, Mats Rydén and Erik Smitterberg. 2006. *Nineteenth-Century English: Stability and Change*. Cambridge: Cambridge University Press.

Labov, William. 1966. *The Social Stratification of English in New York City*. Washington, DC: Center for Applied Linguistics.

1972. *Sociolinguistic Patterns*. Philadelphia: University of Philadelphia Press.

1994. *Principles of Linguistic Change. Part I: Internal Factors*. Oxford and Cambridge, MA: Blackwell.

2001. *Principles of Linguistic Change. Part II: Social Factors*. Malden, MA: Wiley-Blackwell.

2007. Transmission and diffusion. *Language* 83(2): 344–87.

2010. Where should I begin? *Telling Stories: Language, Narrative and Social Life*, ed. D. Schiffrin, A. De Fina and A. Nylund, 7–22. Washington, DC: Georgetown University Press.

Langer, Nils. 2001. *Linguistic Purism in Action: How Auxiliary* tun *was Stigmatized in Early New High German*. Berlin and New York: de Gruyter.

Langford, Paul. 1991. *Public Life and the Propertied Englishman 1689–1798*. Oxford: Clarendon Press.

Laqueur, Thomas. 1976a. The cultural origins of popular literacy in England 1500–1850. *Oxford Review of Education* 2: 255–75.

1976b. Working-class demand and the growth of English elementary education 1750–1850. *Schooling and Society*, ed. Lawrence Stone, 192–205. Baltimore, MD: Johns Hopkins University Press.

Laslett, Peter. 1971. *The World we Have Lost – Further Explored*. London: Methuen & Co.

Lass, Roger. 1980. *On Explaining Language Change*. Cambridge: Cambridge University Press.

1987. *The Shape of English: Structure and History*. London: Dent.

1992. Phonology and morphology. *The Cambridge History of the English Language*. Vol. 2: *1066–1476*, ed. Norman Blake, 23–156. Cambridge: Cambridge University Press.

Lawson, John and Harold Silver. 1973. *A Social History of Education in England*. London: Methuen & Co.

Layton, Irving. 1992. *Fornalutx: Selected Poems*. Montreal: McGill-Queen's University Press.

Legg, Leopold George Wickham (ed.). 1939. *Tusmore Papers: A Collection Of Papers Relating to the Fermor Family*. Oxfordshire Record Series, Vol. 20. Oxford: Issued for the Society.

Leitner, Gerhard. 2004. *Australia's Many Voices: Australian English – the National Language*. Berlin: Mouton de Gruyter.

Lerer, Seth. 1997. *Courtly Letters in the Age of Henry VIII*. Cambridge: Cambridge University Press.

Levene, Alysa, Steven King, Alannah Tomkins, Thomas Nutt, Peter King, Deborah A. Symonds and Lisa Zunshine (eds.). 2006. *Narratives of the Poor in Eighteenth Century Britian [sic]*, 5 vols. London: Pickering and Chatto.

Levine, Kenneth. 1986. *The Social Context of Literacy*. London, Boston and Healey: Routledge and Kegan Paul.

Lindert, Peter H. 1997. Unequal living standards. *The Economic History of Britain since 1700*, ed. Roderick Floud and Deirdre McCloskey, 357–86. Cambridge: Cambridge University Press.

Linn, Andrew R. and Nicola McLelland (eds.). 2002. *Standardization: Studies from the Germanic Languages*. Amsterdam and Philadelphia: John Benjamins.

Love, Harold. 1993. *Scribal Publication in Seventeenth-Century England*. Oxford: Clarendon Press.

Lowth, Robert. 1762. *A Short Introduction to English Grammar*. London: A. Millar and R. and J. Dodsley.

Ludwig, Otto. 1998. Alphabetisierung und Volksschulunterricht im 19. Jahrhundert: Der Beitrag der Schreib- und Stilübungen. *Sprache und bürgerliche Nation. Beiträge zur deutschen und europäischen Sprachgeschichte des 19. Jahrhunderts*, ed. Dieter Cherubim, Siegfried Grosse and Klaus J. Mattheier, 148–66. Berlin and New York: Walter de Gruyter.

Lyons, John. 1968. *Introduction to Theoretical Linguistics*. Cambridge: Cambridge University Press.

MacMahon, Michael K. C. 1998. Phonology. *The Cambridge History of the English Language*. Vol. IV: *1776–1997*, ed. Suzanne Romaine, 373–535. Cambridge: Cambridge University Press.

Magnusson, Lynne. 1999. *Shakespeare and Social Dialogue: Dramatic Language and Elizabethan Letters*. Cambridge: Cambridge University Press.

Mandler, Peter. 1990. *The Uses of Charity: The Poor on Relief in the Nineteenth-Century Metropolis*. Philadelphia: Pennsylvania University Press.

Marlborough, Sarah (Duchess of). 1838. *Private Correspondence of Sarah, Duchess of Marlborough*. London: Henry Colburn.

Marshall, Alan. 2004. Yard, Robert (*c.*1651–1705). *Oxford Dictionary of National Biography*, Oxford University Press; online edn, January 2008 [http://www.oxforddnb.com/view/article/65809, accessed 9 Aug 2011].

Maryns, Katrijn and Jan Blommaert. 2001. Stylistic and thematic shifting as a narrative resource: Assessing asylum seekers' repertoires. *Multilingua* 20(1): 61–82.

Mattheier, Klaus. 2010. Is there a European language history? *Multilingua* 29(3/4): 353–60.

McCafferty, Kevin. 2003. 'I'll bee after telling dee de raison . . .': *Be after V-ing* as a future gram in Irish English, 1601–1750. *The Celtic Englishes,* Vol. III, ed. Hildegard Tristram, 298–317. Heidelberg: Winter.

2004. '[T]hunder storms is verry dangese in this countrey they come in less than a minnits notice . . .': The Northern Subject Rule in Southern Irish English. *English World-Wide* 25: 51–79.

McCafferty, Kevin and Carolina P. Amador-Moreno. 2014. '[The Irish] find much difficulty in these auxiliaries . . . putting *will* for *shall* with the first person': the decline of first-person *shall* in Ireland, 1760–1890. *English Language and Linguistics* 18(3): 407–29.

McCarthy, William. 2009. *Anna Letitia Barbauld: Voice of the Enlightenment.* Baltimore, MD: Johns Hopkins University Press.

Mendoza-Denton, Norma. 1997. Chicana/Mexicana identity and linguistic variation: An ethnographic and sociolinguistic study of gang affiliation in an urban high school. PhD dissertation, Stanford University.

Mesthrie, Rajend and Rakesh M. Bhatt. 2008. *World Englishes: The Study of New Linguistic Varieties.* Cambridge: Cambridge University Press.

Michael, Ian. 1991. More than enough English grammars. *English Traditional Grammars,* ed. G. Leitner, 11–26. Amsterdam: Benjamins.

Miles, Tiya and Celia E. Naylor-Ojurongbe. 2004. African Americans in Indian societies. *Handbook of North American Indians.* Vol. 14: *The Southeast,* ed. Raymond Fogelson and William Sturtevant, 753–9. Washington, DC: Smithsonian Institution.

Millar, Robert McColl. 2012a. The problem of reading dialect in semi-literate letters. *Letter Writing in Late Modern Europe,* ed. Marina Dossena and Gabriella Del Lungo Camiciotti, 164–7. Amsterdam: John Benjamins.

2012b. *English Historical Sociolinguistics.* Edinburgh: Edinburgh University Press.

Miller, Kerby, Arnold Schrier, Bruce Boling and David Doyle. 2003. *Irish Immigrants in the Land of Canaan: Letters and Memoirs from Colonial and Revolutionary America, 1675–1815.* Oxford: Oxford University Press.

Miller, Randall (ed.). 1990. *Dear Master: Letters of a Slave Family.* Athens: University of Georgia Press.

Milroy, James. 1992. *Linguistic Variation and Change: On the Historical Sociolinguistics of English.* Oxford and Malden, MA: Blackwell.

2001. Language ideologies and the consequences of standardization. *Journal of Sociolinguistics* 5(4): 530–55.

2005. Some effects of purist ideologies on historical descriptions of English. *Linguistic Purism in the Germanic Languages,* ed. Nils Langer and Winifred V. Davies, 324–42. Berlin and New York: de Gruyter.

Milroy, James and Lesley Milroy. 1999. *Authority in Language: Investigating Standard English.* London: Routledge.

2012. *Authority in Language: Investigating Standard English.* 4th edn. London: Routledge.

Milroy, Lesley. 1980. *Language and Social Networks.* Oxford: Basil Blackwell.

Milroy, Lesley and Matthew Gordon. 2003. *Sociolinguistics: Method and Interpretation.* Oxford: Blackwell.

Mitch, David F. 1992. *The Rise of Popular Literacy in Victorian England: The Influence of Private Choice and Public Policy.* Philadelphia: University of Pennsylvania Press.

Monaghan, E. Jennifer. 1999. Reading for the enslaved, writing for the free. *Proceedings of the American Antiquarian Society* 108(2): 309–41.

Montgomery, Michael. 1989. Exploring the roots of Appalachian English. *English World-Wide* 10: 227–78.

1991. The Anglicization of Scots in early seventeenth century Ulster. *The Language and Literature of Early Scotland*, ed. Gary Ross, Patrick Scott and Lucie Roy, 50–63. Columbia: University of South Carolina.

1994. The evolution of verb concord in Scots. Studies in Scots and Gaelic: *Proceedings of the Third International Conference on the Languages of Scotland*, ed. Alexander Fenton and Donald A. MacDonald, 81–95. Edinburgh: Cannongate Academic.

1995. The linguistic value of Ulster emigrant letters. *Ulster Folklife* 41: 26–41.

1997a. A tale of two Georges: Regional variation in 18th century Hiberno-English. *Focus on Ireland*, ed. Jeffrey Kallen, 227–54. Amsterdam: Benjamins.

1997b. Making transatlantic connections between varieties of English: The case of plural verbal -s. *Journal of English Linguistics* 25: 122–41.

1999. Eighteenth-century Sierra Leone English: Another exported variety of African American English. *English World-Wide* 20(1): 1–34.

2004. The crucial century for English in the American South. Keynote lecture delivered at the Language Variety in the South III conference.

Montgomery, Michael and Janet M. Fuller. 1996. What was verbal -s in 19th-century African American English? *Focus on the USA*, ed. Edgar W. Schneider, 211–30. Amsterdam: Benjamins.

Montgomery, Michael, Janet M. Fuller and Sharon DeMarse. 1993. 'The Black Men has wives and Sweet harts [and third person plural –s] Jest like the white men': Evidence for verbal -s from written documents on 19th-century African American speech. *Language Variation and Change* 5: 335–57.

More, Charles. 2000. *Understanding the Industrial Revolution*. London and New York: Routledge.

Morris, Richard. 1882. *Historical Outlines of English Accidence*. London: Macmillan.

Morse-Gagné, Elise. 1992. Borrowing hierarchies in the Middle English acquisition of Scandinavian pronouns. Unpublished MS of a talk presented on 16 October 1991 at NWAV XXI, Ann Arbor.

Mugglestone, Lynda. 1995. *'Talking proper': The Rise of Accent as Social Symbol*. Oxford: Clarendon Press.

Mühlhäusler, Peter. 1996. *Linguistic Ecology: Language Change and Linguistic Imperialism in the Pacific Region*. London: Routledge.

Munson, James. 2001. *Maria Fitzherbert: The Secret Wife of George IV*. New York: Carroll and Graf Publishers.

Murray, John R. 2012. *A Tour of the English Lakes with Thomas Gray & Joseph Farington RA*. London: Frances Lincoln.

Murray, Lindley. 1795. *English Grammar, Adapted to the Different Classes of Learners*. York: Wilson, Spence, and Mawman.

Mustanoja, Tauno F. 1960. *A Middle English Syntax*. Helsinki: Société Néophilologique.

Myers, Victoria. 2003. Model letters, moral living: Letter-writing manuals by Daniel Defoe and Samuel Richardson. *The Huntington Library Quarterly* 66(3/4), Studies in the cultural history of letter writing: 373–91.

Naylor, Celia E. 2008. *African Cherokees in Indian Territory: From Chattel to Citizen*. Chapel Hill: University of North Carolina Press.

Nelson, James. 1753. *An Essay on the Government of Children*. London.

Nevalainen, Terttu. 1991. Motivated archaism: The use of affirmative periphrastic *do* in Early Modern English liturgical prose. *Historical English Syntax*, ed. Dieter Kastovsky, 303–20. Berlin: Mouton de Gruyter.

1996. Gender difference. *Sociolinguistics and Language History: Studies Based on the Corpus of Early English Correspondence*, ed. Terttu Nevalainen and Helena Raumolin-Brunberg, 77–92. Amsterdam and Atlanta: Rodopi.

1997. The process of adverb derivation in Late Middle and Early Modern English. *Grammaticalization at Work*, ed. Matti Rissanen, Merja Kytö and Kirsi Heikkonen, 145–89. Berlin and New York: Mouton de Gruyter.

1999. Making the best use of bad data: Evidence for sociolinguistic variation in Early Middle English. *Neophilologische Mitteilungen* 100(4): 499–533.

2001. Continental conventions in Early English correspondence. *Towards a History of English as a History of Genres*, ed. Hans-Jürgen Diller and Manfred Görlach, 203–24. Heidelberg: C. Winter.

2007. Introduction. *Letter Writing*, ed. Terttu Nevalainen and Sanna-Kaisa Tanskanen, 1–11. Amsterdam and Philadelphia: John Benjamins.

2012. Historical sociolinguistics. *English Historical Linguistics: An International Handbook. (HSK 34.2)*, ed. Alexander Bergs and Laurel Brinton, 1438–56. Berlin and New York: Mouton de Gruyter.

Nevalainen, Terttu and Helena Raumolin-Brunberg. 1994. Sociolinguistics and language history: The Helsinki Corpus of Early English Correspondence. *Hermes, Journal of Linguistics* 13: 135–43.

Nevalainen, Terttu and Helena Raumolin-Brunberg (eds.). 1996. *Sociolinguistics and Language History: Studies Based on the Corpus of Early English Correspondence*. Amsterdam: Rodopi.

Nevalainen, Terttu and Helena Raumolin-Brunberg. 1998. Reconstructing the social dimension of diachronic language change. *Historical Linguistics 1995. Vol II: Germanic Linguistics*, ed. R. M. Hogg and L. van Berger, 189–209. Amsterdam and Philadelphia: John Benjamins.

2003. *Historical Sociolinguistics: Language Change in Tudor and Stuart England*. London: Longman/Pearson.

Nevalainen, Terttu and Sanna-Kaisa Tanskanen (eds.). 2007. *Letter Writing*. Amsterdam and Philadelphia: Benjamins.

Nordlund, Taru. 2007. Double diglossia: Lower class writing in 19th-century Finland. *Multilingua* 26(2/3): 229–46.

Nurmi, Arja, 1999. *A Social History of Periphrastic 'do'*. Helsinki: Societé Néophilologique.

Nurmi, Arja and Minna Palander-Collin. 2008. Letters as text type: Interaction in writing. *Studies in Late Modern English Correspondence: Methodology and Data*, ed. Marina Dossena and Ingrid Tieken-Boon van Ostade, 21–49. Bern: Peter Lang.

Nurmi, Arja, Minna Nevala and Minna Palander-Collin. 2009. The language of daily life in the history of English: Studying how macro meets micro. *The Language of Daily Life in England (1400–1800)*, ed. Arja Nurmi, Minna Nevala and Minna Palander-Collin, 1–26. Amsterdam and Philadelphia: John Benjamins.

O'Connell, Lucille. 1980. Kealing Hurly's script book: An Irish immigrant in America, *Eire-Ireland* 15: 105–12.

ODNB = Oxford Dictionary of National Biography, Oxford University Press, 2004 [www.oxforddnb.com/themes/theme.jsp?articleid=92738] [www.oxforddnb.com/view/article/17177, accessed 9 August 2011] [www.oxforddnb.com/view/article/2160, accessed 9 November 2009] [www.oxforddnb.com/view/theme/73609, accessed 15 October 2009] [www.oxforddnb.com/view/article/19004, accessed 9 November 2009] [www.oxforddnb.com/view/article/26922, accessed 5 November 2009] [www.oxforddnb.com/view/theme/92792, accessed 17 February 2011] [www.oxforddnb.com/view/article/65809, accessed 9 August 2011] [www.oxforddnb.com/view/article/12344, accessed 10 August 2011]

Oesterreicher, Wulf. 1997. Types of orality in text. *Written Voices, Spoken Signs*, ed. Egbert Bakker and Ahuvia Kahane, 190–214. Cambridge, MA: Harvard University Press.

O'Farrell, Patrick. 1984. *Letters from Irish Australia, 1825–1929*. Belfast: Ulster Historical Foundation.

O'Rourke, Kevin and Jeffrey Williamson. 2000. When did globalization begin? *NBER Working Paper 7632*. Available at www.nber.org/papers/w7632. Accessed 15 August 2012.

Orton, Harold and Eugen Dieth (eds.). 1967. *Survey of English Dialects*. Leeds: Arnold.

Orton, Harold, Stewart Sanderson and John Widdowson (eds.). 1978. *The Linguistic Atlas of England*. London: Croom Helm.

Orton, Harold and Martyn F. Wakelin (eds.). 1967. *Survey of English Dialects (B) The Basic Material*. Vol. IV: *The Southern Counties*. Leeds: Arnold.

Oxford English Dictionary Online. 2nd edn, with additions. Oxford: Oxford University Press.

Pahta, Päivi, Minna Nevala, Arja Nurmi and Minna Palander-Collin (eds.). 2010. *Social Roles and Language Practices in Late Modern English*. Amsterdam: John Benjamins.

Palander-Collin, Minna, Minna Nevala and Arja Nurmi. 2009. The language of daily life in the history of English: Studying how macro meets micro. *The Language of Daily Life in England (1400–1800)*, ed. Arja Nurmi, Minna Nevala and Minna Pallander-Collin, 1–23. Amsterdam and Philadelphia: John Benjamins.

Parish, The Rev, William D. 1875. *A Dictionary of the Sussex Dialect and Collection of Provincialisms*. Lewes: Farncombe & Co. (ed. Dick Richardson. Bakewell: Country Books, 2001.)

Parr, Samuel. 1786. *A Discourse on Education and on the Plans Pursued in Charity-Schools*. London.

Parry, Adam (ed.). 1935/1971. *The Making of Homeric Verse: The Collected Papers of Milman Parry*. Oxford: Oxford University Press.

Parsons, Talcott. 1951. *The Social System*. London: Routledge and Kegan Paul.

Patrick, Peter. (2001). The speech community. *Handbook of Language Variation and Change*, ed. J. K. Chambers, P. Trudgill and N. Schilling-Estes, 573–97. Malden, MA: Wiley-Blackwell.

Paul, Hermann. 1917. *Deutsche Grammatik*. Vol. II, part III: *Flexionslehre*. Halle: Niemeyer.

  1920. *Deutsche Grammatik*. Vol. IV, part IV: *Syntax, Zweite Hälfte*. Halle: Niemeyer.

Pederson, Lee A., Raven I. McDavid, Jr, Charles W. Foster and Charles E. Billiard (eds.). 1986. *Linguistic Atlas of the Gulf States*. Vol. I: *Handbook for the Linguistic Atlas for the Gulf States*. Athens: University of Georgia Press.

Pennycook, Alastair. 2010. *Critical Applied Linguistics: A Critical Introduction*. New York and Abingdon: Routledge.

Pietsch, Lukas. 2005. *Variable Grammars: Verbal Agreement in Northern Dialects of English*. Tübingen: Niemeyer.

2009a. English in Ireland: Grammar in language contact. Post-doctoral thesis, University of Hamburg.

2009b. *Hamburg Corpus of Irish English*. Hamburg: Collaborative Research Centre on Multilingualism.

Podesva, Robert Jay. 2006. Phonetic detail in sociolinguistic variation: Its linguistic significance and role in the construction of social meaning. PhD thesis, Stanford University.

Polenz, Peter von. 1994. *Deutsche Sprachgeschichte vom Spätmittelalter bis zur Gegenwart*. Vol. II: *17. und 18. Jahrhundert*. Berlin and New York: De Gruyter.

1999. *Deutsche Sprachgeschichte vom Spätmittelalter bis zur Gegenwart*. Vol. III: *19. und 20. Jahrhundert*. Berlin and New York: De Gruyter.

Porter, Roy. 1990. *English Society in the Eighteenth Century*, 2nd rev. edn. London: Penguin.

Pratt, Terrence K. 1993. The hobglobin of Canadian English spelling. *Focus on Canada*, ed. Sandra Clarke, 45–64. Amsterdam: Benjamins.

Preston, Jean F. and Laetitia Yeandle. 1992. *English Handwriting 1400–1650: An Introductory Manual*. Binghamton: Pegasus.

Priestley, Joseph. 1761. *The Rudiments of English Grammar, Adapted to the Use of Schools: With Observations on Style*. London: Griffiths.

Quintilianus, Marcus Fabius. 1963. *Institutio orationis*, 4 vols. Ed. H. E. Butler, 35–110, Loeb Classical Library. Cambridge, MA: Harvard University Press.

Ramsbottom, John D. 2002. Women and the family. *A Companion to Eighteenth-Century Britain*, ed. H. T. Dickinson, 209–22. Malden, MA and Oxford: Blackwell Publishing.

Raumolin-Brunberg, Helena. 2000. 'Which' and 'the which' in Late Middle English: Free variants. *Placing Middle English in Context*, ed. Irma Taavitsainen, Terttu Nevalainen, Päivi Pahta and Matti Rissanen, 209–25. Berlin and New York: Mouton de Gruyter.

2003. Review of Thomas Sokoll, *Essex pauper letters 1731–1837*. *Historical Sociolinguistics – Sociohistorical Linguistics*. Available at www.let.leidenuniv. nl/ hsl_shl/. Accessed 31 October 2009.

2005. Language change in adulthood: Historical letters as evidence. *European Journal of English Studies* 9(1): 37–51.

2009. Lifespan changes in the language of three early modern gentlemen. *The Language of Daily Life in England (1400–1800)*, ed. Arja Nurmi, Minna Nevala and Minna Pallander-Collin, 165–96. Amsterdam and Philadelphia: John Benjamins.

Raumolin-Brunberg, Helena and Terttu Nevalainen. 2007. Historical sociolinguistics: The Corpus of Early English Correspondence. *Creating and Digitizing Language Corpora*. Vol. II: *Diachronic Databases*, ed. Joan Beal, Karen Corrigan and Hermann Moisl, 148–71. Houndsmills: Palgrave Macmillan.

Regosin, Elizabeth. 2002. *Freedom's Promise: Ex-Slave Families and Citizenship in the Age of Emancipation*. Charlottesville and London: University Press of Virginia.

Richmond, Colin. 1990/2002. *The Paston Family in the Fifteenth Century*. Vol. I: *The First Phase*. Cambridge: Cambridge University Press.

1996. *The Paston Family in the Fifteenth Century* Vol. II: *Fastolf's Will*. Cambridge: Cambridge University Press.

Rickford, John R. 1997. Prior creolization of African-American Vernacular English? Sociohistorical and textual evidence from the 17th and 18th centuries. *Journal of Sociolinguistics* 1: 315–36.

Rickford, John R. and Russell J. Rickford. 2000. *Spoken Soul: The Story of Black English*. New York: John Wiley.

Rissanen, Matti. 1999. Syntax. *The Cambridge History of the English Language*. Vol. III: *1476–1776*, ed. Roger Lass, 187–331. Cambridge: Cambridge University Press.

Robinson, Eric and David Powell. 1984. *John Clare*. Oxford: Oxford University Press.

Rogers, Nicholas. 2002. The middling orders. *A Companion to Eighteenth-Century Britain*, ed. H. T. Dickinson, 172–82. Malden, MA and Oxford: Blackwell Publishing.

Rohdenburg, Günter. 2003. Cognitive complexity and *horror aequi* as factors determining the use of interrogative clause linkers in English. *Determinants of Grammatical Variation in English*, ed. Günter Rohdenburg and Britta Mondorf, 205–51. Berlin and New York: Mouton de Gruyter.

Romaine, Suzanne. 1982. *Socio-Historical Linguistics: Its Status and Methodology*. Cambridge: Cambridge University Press.

1988. Historical sociolinguistics: Problems and methodology. *Sociolinguistics: An International Handbook of the Science of Language and Society*, Vol. II: , ed. U. Ammon, N. Dittmar, and K. J. Mattheier, 1452–69. Berlin and New York: Walter de Gruyter.

1998. Introduction. *The Cambridge History of the English Language*. Vol. IV: *1776–1997*, ed. Suzanne Romaine, 1–56. Cambridge: Cambridge University Press.

Romaine, Suzanne (ed.). 1998. *The Cambridge History of the English Language*. Vol. IV: *1776–1997*. Cambridge: Cambridge University Press.

Rose, Jonathan. 2010. *The Intellectual Life of the British Working Classes*. New Haven and London: Yale University Press.

Rose, Michael E. 2002. Review of *Essex Pauper Letters*, ed. Thomas Sokoll. Oxford University Press. *The English Historical Review* 117, 473: 997–8.

Rule, J. 1991. Land of lost content? The eighteenth-century Poor Law. *Revue Française de Civilisation Britannique* 6, 104–8.

Rydén, Mats. 1979. *An Introduction to the Historical Study of English Syntax*. Stockholm: Almqvist and Wiksell International.

1983. The emergence of *who* as relativiser. *Studia Linguistica* 37: 126–34.

Salmon, Vivian. 1999. Orthography and punctuation. *The Cambridge History of the English Language*. Vol. III: *1476–1776*, ed. Roger Lass, 13–55. Cambridge: Cambridge University Press.

Sanderson, Michael. 1995. *Education, Economic Change and Society in England 1780–1870*. 2nd edn. Cambridge: Cambridge University Press.

Sankoff, Gillian. 2005. Cross-sectional and longitudinal studies. *Sociolinguistics: An International Handbook of the Science of Language and Society*, Vol. II, ed. Ulrich Ammon, Norbert Dittmar Klaus J. Mattheier and Peter Trudgill, 1003–13. Berlin and New York: Walter de Gruyter.

Saunt, Claudio. 2004. The paradox of freedom: Tribal sovereignty and emancipation during the reconstruction of Indian Territory. *The Journal of Southern History* 70: 63–94.

Schäfer, Ursula. 1996. The Late Middle English Paston letters: A grammatical case in point for reconsidering philological methodologies. *Anglistentag 1995 Greifswald*, ed. Jürgen Klein and Dirk Vanderbeke, 313–23. Tübingen: Niemeyer.

Schilling-Estes, Natalie. 2002. Investigating stylistic variation. *The Handbook of Language Variation and Change*, ed. J. K. Chambers, P. Trudgill and N. Schilling-Estes, 375–401. Malden, MA: Wiley-Blackwell.

Schneider, Edgar W. 1989. *American Earlier English: Morphological and Syntactic Variables*. Tuscaloosa: University of Alabama Press.

    1997. Earlier Black English revisited. *Language Variety in the South Revisited*, ed. Cynthia Bernstein, Thomas Nunnally and Robin Sabino, 35–50. Tuscaloosa and London: The University of Alabama Press.

    2001. Investigating variation and change in written documents. *The Handbook of Language Variation and Change*, ed. J. K. Chambers, Peter Trudgill and Natalie Schilling-Estes, 67–96. Malden, MA: Blackwell.

    2002. Investigating variation and change in written documents. *The Handbook of Language Variation and Change*, ed. J. K. Chambers, Peter Trudgill and Natalie Schilling-Estes, 67–96. Malden, MA: Blackwell.

    2007. *Postcolonial English: Varieties around the World*. Cambridge: Cambridge University Press.

Schneider, Edgar and Michael B. Montgomery. 2001. On the trail of early non-standard grammar: An electronic corpus of Southern U.S. antebellum overseers' letters. *American Speech* 76(4): 388–410.

Schofield, Roger S. 1981. Dimensions of illiteracy in England 1750–1850. *Literacy and Social Development in the West: A Reader*, ed. Harvey J. Graff, 201–13. Cambridge: Cambridge University Press.

Schötensack, Heinrich August. 1856. *Grammatik der neuhochdeutschen Sprache: Mit besonderer Berücksichtigung ihrer historischen Entwickelung*. Erlangen: Enke.

Schreier, Daniel. 2002. Terra incognita in the Anglophone world: Tristan da Cunha, South Atlantic Ocean. *English World-Wide* 23: 1–29.

    2003a. *Isolation and Language Change: Contemporary and Sociohistorical Evidence from Tristan da Cunha English*. Houndmills/Basingstoke and New York: Palgrave Macmillan.

    2003b. Tracing the history of dialect transplantation in post-colonial English: The case of 3rd person singular zero on Tristan da Cunha. *Folia Linguistica Historica* 23(1/2): 115–31.

    2008. *St Helenian English: Origins, Evolution and Variation*. Amsterdam and Philadelphia: John Benjamins.

    2010. Tristan da Cunha. *The Lesser-Known Varieties of English*, ed. Daniel Schreier, Peter Trudgill, Edgar Schneider and Jeffrey P. Williams, 245–60. Cambridge: Cambridge University Press.

Schreier, Daniel and Peter Trudgill. 2006. The segmental phonology of 19th century Tristan da Cunha English: Convergence and local innovation. *English Language and Linguistics* 10: 119–41.

Schreier, Daniel and Laura Wright. 2010. Earliest St Helenian English in writing: Evidence from the St Helena Consultations (1682–1723). *Varieties in Writing: The Written Word as Linguistic Evidence*, ed. Raymond Hickey, 245–62. Amsterdam and Philadelphia: Benjamins.

Schwitalla, Johannes. 2006. Kommunikative Funktionen von *tun* als Hilfsverb. *Konstruktionen in der Interaktion*, ed. Susanne Günthner and Wolfgang Imo, 127–51. Berlin and New York: de Gruyter.

Scragg, Donald G. 1974. *A History of English Spelling*. Manchester: Manchester University Press.

Scribner, Sylvia and Michael Cole. 1981. *The Psychology of Literacy*. Cambridge, MA: Harvard University Press.

Seton, George. 1870. *Gossip about Letters and Letter-Writers*. Edinburgh: Edmonston and Douglas.

Shaffer, Donald R. 2004. *After the Glory: The Struggles of Black Civil War Veterans*. Lawrence: University Press of Kansas.

Sharpe, Pamela. 1997. The bowels of compation. *Chronicling Poverty: The Voices and Strategies of the English Poor, 1640–1840*, ed. Tim Hitchcock *et al.*, 87–108. London: Macmillan.

Sheridan, Thomas. 1769. *A Plan of Education for the Young Nobility and Gentry of Great Britain*. London.

Siebers, Lucia. 2010. 'An abundant harvest to the philologer'? Jeremiah Goldswain, Thomas Shore and nineteenth-century South African English. *Varieties of English in Writing: The Written Word as Linguistic Evidence*, ed. Raymond Hickey, 263–294. Amsterdam: Benjamins.

Sinclair, John. 1994. Trust the text. *Advances in Written Text Analysis*, ed. Malcolm Coulthard, 12–25. London: Routledge.

Skedd, Susan. 1997. Women teachers and the expansion of girls' schooling in England, c. 1760–1820. *Gender in Eighteenth-Century England: Roles, Representations and Responsibilities*, ed. Hannah Barker and Elaine Chalus, 101–25. London: Longman.

Smith, Adam. [1776] 1976. *An Inquiry into the Nature and Causes of the Wealth of Nations*. Ed. R. H. Campbell and Andrew S. Skinner. Oxford: Clarendon Press.

Sokoll, Thomas. (ed.). 2001. *Essex Pauper Letters, 1731–1837*. Oxford: Oxford University Press.

Southey, Robert. 1832. *Essays, Moral and Political*. London: John Murray.

Speck, W. A. 2007. Harley, Robert, First Earl of Oxford and Mortimer (1661–1724). *Oxford Dictionary of National Biography*. Oxford University Press, 2004; online edn, October 2007 [www.oxforddnb.com/view/article/12344, accessed 10 August 2011].

Spitzer, Leo. 1921. *Italienische Kriegsgefangenenbriefe: Materialien zu einer Charakteristik der volkstümlichen italienischen Korrespondenz*. Bonn: Hanstein.

Spufford, Margaret. 1982. *Small Books and Pleasant Histories: Popular Fiction and its Readership in Seventeenth-Century England*. London: Methuen.

Stanhope, Eugenia (ed.). 1774. *Letters of the Earl of Chesterfield to his Son*. London: James Dodsley. Reprinted, R. K. Root (ed.). 1929. *Lord Chesterfield's Letters to his Son and Others*. London: Dent.

Starobin, Robert (ed.). 1974. *Blacks in Bondage: Letters of American Slaves*. New York: New Viewpoints.

Stenroos, Merja. 2006. A Middle English mess of fricative spellings: Reflections on thorn, yogh and their rivals. *To Make his English Sweete upon his Tonge*, ed. M. Krygier and L. Sikorska, 9–35. Frankfurt am Main: Peter Lang.

Stephenson, Edward A. 1956. Linguistic resources of the Southern Historical Collection. *American Speech* 31: 271–7.

Storey, Mark. (ed.). 1985. *The Letters of John Clare*. Oxford: Clarendon Press.

Street, Brian V. 1995. *Social Literacies: Critical Approaches to Literacy in Development, Ethnography and Education*. Harlow: Pearson Education Limited.

Stubbs, Michael. 1996. *Text and Corpus Analysis*. Oxford: Blackwell.

Sullivan, James. 1921–57. *Papers of Sir William Johnson*. 12 vols. Albany: New York State.

Sundby, Bertil, Anne Kari Bjørge and Kari E. Haugland. 1991. *A Dictionary of English Normative Grammar 1700–1800*. Amsterdam: Benjamins.

Sutherland, Gillian. 1971. *Elementary Schooling in the Nineteenth Century*. London: The Historical Association.

Sweet, Henry. 1898. *A New English Grammar Logical and Historical. Part II: Syntax*. Oxford: Clarendon.

Taavitsainen, Irma. 2001. Changing conventions of writing: The dynamics of genres, text types, and text traditions. *European Journal of English Studies* 5(2): 139–50.

2010. Discourse and genre dynamics in Early Modern English medical writing. *Early Modern English Medical Texts: Corpus Description and Studies*, ed. Irma Taavitsainen and Päivi Pahta, 29–54. Amsterdam: John Benjamins.

Tagliamonte, Sali and Jennifer Smith. 2000. Old was; new ecology: Viewing English through the sociolinguistic filter. *The History of African American English*, ed. Shana Poplack, 141–71. Oxford: Blackwell.

Tanabe, Harumi. 1999. Composite predicates and phrasal verbs in the Paston letters. *Collocational and Idiomatic Aspects Of Composite Predicates in the History of English*, ed. Laurel J. Brinton and M. Akimoto, 97–132. Amsterdam and Philadelphia: John Benjamins.

Tett, Gillian. 2009. *Fool's Gold: How Unconstrained Greed Corrupted a Dream and Unleashed a Catastrophe*. London: Little Brown.

Thomason, Sarah G. and Terrence Kaufman. 1988. *Language Contact, Creolization, and Genetic Linguistics*. Berkeley: University of California Press.

Thrale, Mary (ed.). 1972. *The Autobiography of Francis Place*. Cambridge: Cambridge University Press.

Thurmair, Maria. 2001. *Vergleiche und Vergleichen: Eine Studie zu Form und Funktion der Vergleichsstrukturen im Deutschen*. Tübingen: Niemeyer.

Tieken-Boon van Ostade, Ingrid. 1985. 'I will be drowned and no man shall save me': The conventional rules for *shall* and *will* in eighteenth-century English grammars. *English Studies* 66(2): 123–42.

1987. *The Auxiliary 'do' in Eighteenth-Century English: A Sociohistorical-Linguistic Approach*. Dordrecht: Foris.

2009. *An Introduction to Late Modern English*. Edinburgh: Edinburgh University Press.

2011. *The Bishop's Grammar: Robert Lowth and the Rise of Prescriptivism in English*. Oxford: Oxford University Press.

Timm, Erika. 1986. Das Jiddische als Kontrastsprache bei der Erforschung des Frühneuhochdeutschen. *Zeitschrift für Germanistische Linguistik* 14: 1–22.

Toolan, Michael. 2007. Trust and text, text as trust. *International Journal of Corpus Linguistics* 12(2): 269–88.

Toynbee, Paget and Leonard Whibley (eds.). 1971. *Correspondence of Thomas Gray*. 2nd edn. Oxford: Clarendon Press.

Traugott, Elizabeth. 1972. *A History of English Syntax: A Transformational Approach to the History of English Sentence Structure*. New York: Holt, Rinehart, Winston.

Traugott, Elizabeth Closs and Suzanne Romaine. 1985. Some questions for the definition of 'style' in socio-historical linguistics. *Folia Linguistica Historica* 6(1): 7–39.

Troutman, Phillip. 2006. Correspondences in black and white: Sentiment and the slave market revolution. *New Studies in the History of American Slavery*, ed. Edward E. Baptist and Stephanie M. H. Camp, 211–42. Athens and London: The University of Georgia Press.

Trudgill, Peter. 1999. Standard English: What it isn't? *Standard English: The Widening Debate*, ed. Tony Bex and Richard Watts, 117–28. London: Routledge.

    2003. *A Glossary of Sociolinguistics*. Edinburgh: Edinburgh University Press.

Trudgill, Peter and Richard Watts. 2002. Introduction: In the year 2525. *Alternative Histories of English*, ed. Richard Watts and Peter Trudgill, 1–3. London: Routledge.

Trüb, Regina. 2006. Non-standard verbal paradigms in earlier white Southern American English. *American Speech* 81(3): 250–65.

Van Bergen, Linda and David Denison. 2003. *Corpus of Late 18th Century Prose*. Oxford Text Archive. Oxford: University of Manchester.

    2007. A corpus of late eighteenth-century prose. *Creating and Digitizing Language Corpora*. Vol. II: *Diachronic Databases*, ed. Joan C. Beal, Karen P. Corrigan and Hermann Moisl, 228–46. Basingstoke: Palgrave.

Vandenbussche, Wim. 2006. A rough guide to German research on 'Arbeitersprache' during the 19th century. *Germanistik genießen: Gedenkschrift für Doc. Dr. phil. Hildegard Boková*, ed. Hana Andrášová, Peter Ernst and Libuše Spáčilová, 439–58. Vienna: Praesens Verlag.

Vandenbussche, Wim and Stephan Elspaß. 2007. Introduction: Lower-class language use in the 19th century. *Multilingua* 26: 145–8.

Vandenbussche, Wim and Stephan Elspaß (eds.). 2007. Lower class language in the 19th century. Special issue of *Multilingua* 26(2/3).

van der Wal, Marijke. 2006. *Onvoltooid verleden tijd: Witte vlekken in de taalgeschiedenis*. Amsterdam: Koninklijke Nederlandse Akademie van Wetenschappen.

van der Wal, Marijke, Gijsbert Rutten and Tanja Simons. 2012. Letters as loot: Confiscated letters filling major gaps in the history of Dutch. *Letter Writing in Late Modern Europe*, ed. Marina Dossena and Gabriella Del Lungo Camiciotti, 139–61. Amsterdam: John Benjamins.

Van Herk, Gerard and James A. Walker. 2005. S marks the spot? Regional variation and early African American correspondence. *Language Variation and Change* 17: 113–31.

Vertovec, Steven. 2007. Super-diversity and its implications. *Ethnic and Racial Studies* 29(6): 1024–54

Vicinus, Martha. 1974. *The Industrial Muse: A Study of Nineteenth-Century British Working-Class Literature*. New York: Croom Helm.

Vincent, David. 1981. *Bread, Knowledge and Freedom: A Study of Nineteenth-Century Working-Class Autobiography*. London: Methuen & Co.

1989. *Literacy and Popular Culture: England 1750–1914*. Cambridge: Cambridge University Press.

Wagner, Susanne. 2008. English dialects in the Southwest: Morphology and syntax. *Varieties of English 1: The British Isles*, ed. Bernd Kortmann and Clive Upton, 417–39. Berlin: Mouton de Gruyter.

Wales, Katie. 2002. North of Watford Gap: A cultural history of Northern English (from 1700). *Alternative Histories of English*, ed. R. Watts and P. Trudgill, 45–66. London: Routledge.

Wales, Tony. 2000. *Sussex as she wus spoke: A Guide to the Sussex Dialect*. Seaford: SB Publications.

Warner, Anthony. 1990. Reworking the history of English auxiliaries. *Papers from the Fifth International Conference on English Historical Linguistics*, ed. Sylvia Adamson, Vivien A. Law, Nigel Vincent and Susan Wright, 537–58. Amsterdam and Philadelphia: John Benjamins.

Watts, Richard. 2011. *Language Myths and the History of English*. New York: Oxford University Press.

2012a. The actuation problem revisited. English historical linguistics. *English Historical Linguistics: An International Handbook. (HSK 34.2)*, ed. Alexander Bergs and Laurel Brinton, 1490–508. Berlin and New York: Mouton de Gruyter.

2012b. Myths of the English language; or, alternative histories of 'English'. *English Historical Linguistics: An International Handbook (HSK 34.2)*, ed. Alexander Bergs and Laurel Brinton, 1256–73. Berlin and New York: Mouton de Gruyter.

2012c. Language myths. *Handbook of Historical Sociolinguistics*, ed. Juan Manuel Hernández-Campoy and Juan Camilo Conde-Silvestre, 585–606. Malden, MA: Wiley-Blackwell.

Watts, Richard and Peter Trudgill (eds.). 2002. *Alternative Histories of English*. London and New York: Routledge.

Wegera, Klaus-Peter. 2000. 'Gen, oder wie Herr Gottsched will, chen.' Zur Geschichte eines Diminutivsuffixes. *Wortschatz und Orthographie in Geschichte und Gegenwart: Festschrift für Horst Haider Munske zum 65. Geburtstag*, ed. Mechthild Habermann, Peter O. Müller and Bernd Naumann, 43–58. Tübingen: Niemeyer.

Weinreich, Uriel, William Labov and Marvin Herzog. 1968. Empirical foundations for a theory of language change. *Directions for Historical Linguistics*, ed. W. Lehmann and Y. Malkiel, 95–195. Austin: University of Texas Press.

Werner, Otmar. 1991. The incorporation of Old Norse pronouns into Middle English: Suppletion by loan. *Language Contact in the British Isles: Proceedings of the Eighth International Symposium on Language Contact in Europe, Douglas, Isle of Man*, ed. Peer Sture Ureland and George Broderick, 369–401. Tübingen: Niemeyer.

Whyman, Susan. 2009. *The Pen and the People: English Letter Writers 1660–1800*. Oxford: Oxford University Press.

Wiley, Bell Irvin. 1980. *Slaves no more: Letters from Liberia, 1833–1869*. Lexington: The University of Kentucky Press.

Willan, Thomas S. 1970. *The Eighteenth-Century Shopkeeper ABRAHAM DENT OF KIRKBY STEPHEN*. Manchester: Manchester University Press.

Williams, Heather Andrea. 2005. *Self-Taught: African American Education in Slavery and Freedom*. Chapel Hill, NC and London: The University of North Carolina Press.

Wilson, Ben. 2005. *The Triumph of Laughter: William Hone and the Fight for the Free Press*. London: Faber & Faber.

Wilson, J. Donald. 2000. Davidson, Alexander. *Dictionary of Canadian Biography Online*, ed. John English and Réal Bélanger. www.biographi.ca/index-e.html (31 January 2013).

Winford, Donald. 1997. On the origins of African American Vernacular English – A creolist perspective. Part I: The sociohistorical background. *Diachronica* 14(2): 305–44.

1998. On the origins of African American Vernacular English – A creolist perspective. Part II: Linguistic features. *Diachronica* 15(1): 99–154.

Witt, Ronald. 1982. Medieval 'Ars Dictaminis' and the beginnings of humanism: A new construction of the problem. *Renaissance Quarterly* 35(1): 1–35.

Wolfram, Walt. 2000. Issues in reconstructing earlier African-American English. *World Englishes* 19(1): 39–58.

Wolfram, Walt, Kirk Hazen and Natalie Schilling-Estes. 1999. *Dialect Change and Maintenance on the Outer Banks*. Tuscaloosa: University of Alabama Press.

Wolfram, Walt and Erik Thomas. 2002. *The Development of African American English*. Malden, MA: Blackwell.

Wood, Johanna L. 2007. Text in context: A Critical Discourse Analysis approach to Margaret Paston. *Letter Writing*, ed. Terttu Nevalainen and Sanna-Kaisa Tanskanen, 47–71. Amsterdam and Philadelphia: John Benjamins.

Wordsworth, William. 1835. *A Guide through the District of the Lakes in the North of England, with a Description of the Scenery, &c. for the Use of Tourists and Residents*. Kendal: Hudson & Nicholson.

Wordsworth, William and Samuel Taylor Coleridge. 1798. *Lyrical Ballads with a Few Other Poems*. Bristol: Biggs and Cottle.

Wyld, Henry Cecil. 1920. *A History of Modern Colloquial English*. London: T. Fisher Unwin.

Yokoyama, Olga T. 2008. *Russian Peasant Letters*. Wiesbaden: Harrassowitz.

Person index

Adelung, Johann Christoph 42, 43, 44, 47, 48
Admoni, Wladimir 45
Ágel, Vilmos 40n.2
Agha, Asif 239
Allen, Barbara 204, 204n.1, 208n.8
Alston, R. C. 202
Anderwald, Lieselotte 86
Arnovick, Leslie 279
Auer, Anita 78n.7, 84, 138n.9
Auer, Peter 15, 133
Austin(-Jones), Frances 139, 143, 224
Avis, Walter 101, 104

Bailey, Richard 101, 214
Baker, Frank 56
Baker, Robert 208
Barber, Richard 21n.5, 24
Barry, Michael V. 228
Barton, David 54, 59, 60, 61, 193, 212n.11
Bauer, Laurie 216, 264
Baugh, Alfred 208, 211, 214
Beal, Joan 84, 85, 85n.14, 101, 103, 106, 107, 214
Behaghel, Otto 52
Bell, Allan 15, 133, 134, 285
Bennet, Henry 21n.5
Benskin, Michael 18n.2, 25, 26
Benson, Larry 121
Bergs, Alexander 21, 23n.6, 24, 25, 26n.7, 31, 114, 122, 125, 126, 127, 129, 131, 245n.1
Berlin, Ira 240, 245, 252, 257n.11
Best, Geoffrey 205
Bex, Tony 3
Bhatt, Rakesh 101
Biber, Douglas 59, 60, 127
Blake, Joseph 208
Blake, Norman 26, 213
Bliss, Alan J. 231
Blommaert, Jan 11, 65, 186, 187, 189, 197
Blume, Richard 21

Boberg, Charles 101
Booy, Derek M. 268
Boulton, Jeremy 192
Bowers, Fredson 60
Boyd, Julian 106
Boyd, Zelda 106
Brant, Clare 140n.12
Brewer, John 156, 157
Brightman, Robert A. 253
Brinton, Laurel 103
Burnett, John 203
Burton, Mary E. 149

Cable, Thomas 208, 211, 214
Caffyn, John 61, 62, 63, 67
Cameron, W. 203
Cannadine, David 68
Carter, Philip 158
Cartwright, George Herbert 267
Castor, Helen 21n.5, 25, 33
Chambers, Jack 101, 104, 112
Cheshire, Jennifer 45
Christophersen, Erling 267
Clarke, Sandra 101
Coates, Richard 213, 220
Cole, Michael 61
Colquhoun, Patrick 63, 66, 67
Conde-Silvestre, Juan Camilo 16, 18n.2, 23, 40
Cook-Gumperz, Jennifer 61
Cornelius, Janet 243, 244
Coupland, Nikolas 134
Crawford, Allan 270
Cressy, David 115, 118
Crowley, Tony 3, 4, 201
Culpeper, Jonathan 185, 185n.1
Curme, George 122
Curtis, Bruce 106
Cutillas-Espinosa, Juan Antonio 14

319

Subject index

abbreviations 56, 148, 152, 157n.1, 166, 167
accent 15, 72, 104, 109, 110, 221
   standard 101, 112
accommodation, speech 72, 124, 133, 134
accountability, principle of 264
acrolect 204, 205, 206, 207, 208, 282
act
   communicative 234
   conventional 168
   epistolary 168
activity, social 30
actuation 7, 26, 26n.7, 122
address, opening 169
affiliations, social 134
agency 15, 16
amanuensis/scribe 9, 10, 12, 17, 23n.6, 25, 26,
      141, 160, 161, 162n.9, 163, 167, 242, 247,
      250, 265, 279
anthologies/collections, manuscript 162
anthropology, social 60
apostrophe 167, 216, 219
archaisms 202, 223–39
archives, public 40, 118
aristocracy 5, 156, 157–60
art, epistolary 178
attitudes
   ideological 202
   social 202
authenticity 16, 30, 73, 242, 265, 270
   social 15
authors
   educated 205, 206, 207, 216, 221
   schooled 205, 206, 207, 209, 219
   vs. scribes 114–32
authorship 17n.1, 23n.6, 189, 242, 265

background
   educational 224
   regional 74
   social 17n.1, 74, 75, 76, 265

basilect 204, 205–6, 207, 208, 209, 217, 222, 282
behaviour
   linguistic 18, 20, 21, 28, 31, 33, 103
   sociolinguistic 14, 26n.7
blend, syntactic 86

Canadian Dainty 104, 108, 109, 110
capitalisation 143, 203, 209, 215–17, 248, 249
   random 247
change 117
   communal 18, 18n.3, 19, 20, 21, 28, 31, 33, 34
   from above vs. change from below 8, 18, 18n.2,
      21, 26, 29, 31, 33, 34, 35, 40, 283
   generational 18, 19, 20, 21, 28, 31, 33, 34
   grammatical 41
   life span 18n.3, 19n.3, 20, 31
   linguistic/language 16, 18, 18n.2, 29, 33, 38, 51,
      55, 131, 133, 155, 277, 278, 283, 284
   social 201
   sociocultural 187
   stylistic 154
   variation and 19n.3, 18–21, 39, 73, 156, 264,
      266, 274
children
   higher-rank 64, 65
   lower-rank 63
   middle-rank 64, 65
   working-class 205
choice 190
   decontextualised 190
   lexical 177
   stylistic 20, 33, 133, 134, 190, 191, 196, 197
circumstances, sociolinguistic 242
class(es)
   higher/upper 62, 63, 64, 67, 69, 82, 135, 136,
      138, 185, 203, 239
   lower/lowest 5, 8, 11, 18n.2, 30, 37, 40, 46, 53,
      60, 62, 63, 64, 65, 67, 68, 80, 135, 138,
      143, 155, 161, 177, 186, 228, 265, 281, 285,
      286

CPSIA information can be obtained
at www.ICGtesting.com
Printed in the USA
LVHW102037140519
617810LV00007B/153/P